REES VC

the first of the original 'Few'

W Alister Williams

W Alister Williams

bridge
books

The core of this book was first published by Bridge Books in 1989 under the title
Against the Odds, the Life of Group Captain Lionel Rees, VC.

This expanded new publication
Rees VC, the first of the original 'Few'
was published in Wales in 2017
by
BRIDGE BOOKS
Orchard House
20 Bryn Estyn Road, Wrexham
LL13 0BF

Reprinted 2023

Cover illustrations:
Front cover: *DH2 in combat* (extract) by James Morton
[W Alister Williams]
Caernarvon 1875 (extract)
by John Brett
Back cover: *Lt-Col L W Brabazon Rees, VC, OBE, MC, AFC,*
Royal Artillery, RFC and RAF by Cowan Dobson, ARBA [Imperial War Museum]
The decorations and medals of
Group Captain LWB Rees, VC, OBE, MC, AFC
[Eastbourne College]

ISBN 978-1-84494-110-0

Printed and bound by
Book Empire
Leeds

CONTENTS

Introduction and acknowledgements   5

I   A Caernarfon Background (1884–1912)   9
II   Into the Air (1914–15)   25
III   11 Squadron, RFC (1915)   43
IV   32 Squadron, RFC (1916)   78
V   Washington DC (1917)   127
VI   Aerial Combat Schools (1918–19)   141
VII   RAF College, Cranwell (1920–25)   167
VIII   Palestine and Transjordan (1926–29)   192
IX   Archaeology (1926–29)   216
X   Retirement (1929–31)   239
XI   The *May* (1932–33)   245
XII   Cruising (1933–5)   259
XIII   War (1936–42)   274
XIV   Andros (1942–66)   290

Appendices
I   Royal Flying Corps, School of Aerial Fighting, War
         Establishment (Provisional)   303
II   Roll of Honour, RAF Turnberry, 1917–18   307
III   Gordon-Shephard Memorial Prize, Second Prize, 1929   309

Bibliography   330

Index   333

Maps

RFC airfields in north-east France   48

11 Squadron area of operations, 1915   52

Villers-Bretonneaux aerodrome   58

Area over which Rees fought his VC action, 1 July 1916   113

Palestine and Transjordan, 1920s   194

Rees' Caribbean cruise, 1933–4   262

Introduction

On 1 July 2016 a small crowd gathered in Castle Street, Caernarfon, outside the offices of Gwynedd County Council, for the unveiling of a memorial plaque to Lionel Rees, the town's only recipient of the Victoria Cross. The date was exactly one hundred years since he had fought a heroic action above the trenches of the Western Front, some two hours before the opening of the Battle of the Somme, on what proved to be the most disastrous day in British military history. After the short ceremony, those assembled looked skywards to witness a fly-past by Hawk jet trainers from RAF Valley on Anglesey, arranged in tribute to the man who has come to be regarded as the world's first official fighter pilot, and one of the founders of flying training in the Royal Air Force.

Close by, on the outer wall of Porth-yr-Aur, the medieval gateway into the old walled-town of Caernarfon, is a second plaque which commemorates Rees' outstanding achievements as a solo trans-Atlantic yachtsman during the 1930s. Very little has ever been written or recorded about the life of this remarkable man who deserves to be placed, not only among the pioneers of military aviation, but also in any list of notable solo yachtsmen, aerial archaeologists and navigators. He was a man who squarely faced up to any and all challenges which life threw at him whilst remaining a self-effacing and thoroughly decent human being. Even in his birthplace, he is virtually unknown and in the RAF he is usually overshadowed by those who followed in his footsteps — aces such as Albert Ball, James McCudden and Mick Mannock.

Some thirty years ago I wrote the first version of this book* in an attempt to rectify this oversight. Since then, many new facts have emerged and in this much expanded book, I have endeavoured to not only clarify a number of issues in the narrative, but also to include significantly more photographs, maps and illustrations that will hopefully facilitate our understanding of a man who deserves to be remembered as a quite remarkable individual.

Since the publication of the first version of this book, a great deal of water has flowed under the bridge. New contacts have been made and good friends have been lost. It was through my research into the story of Lionel Rees that I came into contact with Wing

---

* W Alister Williams, *Against the Odds the life of Group Captain Lionel Rees, VC*, Bridge Books (Wrexham, 1989).

Commander Gwilym H Lewis, DFC (another Welshman with strong links to the town of Caernarfon), almost the last surviving British fighter ace of the Great War. Gwilym, whom I had the great honour to regard as a friend, passed away in 1997 just short of his 100th birthday. He played an important role in the writing of *Against the Odds* (not least by allowing me access to his own letters, diaries, photographs and memories of that now distant conflict, but also by facilitating my visit to the Bahamas to meet Rees' family and friends), and I hope he would have been pleased with this new version of the life of the man he knew and described as 'The bravest man in the world.' He said back in 1985 that he owed Rees an enormous debt in that, had he not been so thoroughly well trained by him in early 1916, he would not have survived that first great conflict in the air.

Also gone is the great aviation historian, Chaz Bowyer who played such a significant part in encouraging me to complete the original book. His knowledge and archives were great sources to which he generously allowed me access.

Rees' family, Alan, Eileen and particularly Olvin, very kindly assisted me with the original research and I hope this pen portrait of their father goes some way towards thanking them for their generosity and creates a clearer image of the man whom they had so little time to get to know.

As the Great War slips further into history, and our memories of the men who actually fought in it have begun to fade, we would do well to remember that they were all ordinary young men who achieved remarkable things in extraordinary circumstances. Far too many paid the ultimate price, others, like Lionel Rees, survived and went on to contribute much more to a world at peace than they had done during their time in combat. They should all have a special place in our memory. Another good friend of mine, the late Brigadier Guy F Gough, DSO, MC (himself a survivor of two world wars) once told me how annoyed he always was to see the incribed words 'They gave their lives' on war memorials – they did not *give* their lives, their lives were taken from them.

In researching this story over very many years, I always had the feeling that there was a great deal more information to be uncovered, particularly relating to Rees' later service life, and was very fortunate in being able to conduct one-to-one research with a number of individuals who knew him personally. From the information which they supplied, I have tried to build up an image of the of man he was. Most of this research was, however, completed over thirty years ago and consequently nearly all of these eye witnesses are no longer with us; even some of the institutions that I contacted then have by now ceased to exist.

In addition to those individuals already mentioned above, I would like to express my most sincere thanks to the very many organisations and individuals who have given me information, materials and, perhaps most importantly, their time and advice. If I have omitted to mention anyone, I trust that they will accept my apologies and an assurance that such an oversight was unintentional. What use I have made of their information is my own responsibility and any errors which may have crept in are mine alone.

Institutions: RAF Air Historical Branch (particularly Air Commodore HA Probert, MBE, MA); RAF Museum Library, Hendon; RAF College, Cranwell (particularly Miss Jean Buckberry); RAF Personnel Records; RAF Regiment Museum; Nᵒ 11 Squadron, RAF (particularly Air Commodore SN Bostock); RMA, Sandhurst; Royal Artillery Institution; Imperial War Museum; Commonwealth War Graves Commission; Royal Archives, Windsor Castle; National Archives, Kew; National Library of Wales; British Library; Wrexham Public Library; Gwynedd Archives Service (Caernarfon Area Office); Bahamas Record Office, Nassau; British High Commission, Nassau (particularly Michael Holmes and Alan Greenwood); Royal Welsh Yacht Club, Caernarfon; Eastbourne College (particularly Michael Harral and Michael Partridge), British Museum; Lloyd's Register of Shipping; Law Society; Probate Registry; National Library of Congress, Washington, DC; United States Air Force; United States Coastguard; Institute of Archaeology, Hebrew University, Jerusalem; Royal Geographic Society; Institute of Archaeology, London University; the Field Museum Chicago (particularly Gretchen Rings and Nina Cummings).

Individuals: Air historians AE Ferko of Salem, Ohio, G Stuart Leslie, J Bruce, Michael Schmeelke and Alex Revell; Rev M Hutcheson (Nassau); Mrs Mallie Lightbourne (formerly of Nassau); JA McKinney (Nassau); Stanley and Mary Toogood (formerly of Nassau), Prof Cyrus Sharer; Willie de MP Davids (of Sao Paulo); Mrs Margery O Erikson; R Beach; Wing Commander William Fry, MC; Lady Joan Portal; Lester Brown, DFC; Air Chief Marshal Sir Walter Dawson, KCB, CBE, DSO; Marshal of the RAF Sir Dermot Boyle, GCB, KCVO, KBE, AFC; Air Vice-Marshal Hugh Brooks, CB, CBE, DFC; Air Marshal Sir Edward Chilton, KBE, CB; Air Vice-Marshal Sir Geoffrey Worthington, KBE, CB; Air Vice-Marshal Wilfred Alan Gilmore, CB, CBE; Air Vice-Marshal Wilfred Freebody, CB, CBE, AFC; Wing Commander HE Rossiter; Air Marshal Sir Richard Jordan, KCB, DFC; Air Vice-Marshal George Chamberlain, CB, OBE; Air Vice-Marshal John Franks, CB, CBE, AFRAeS; Air Commodore TB Prickman, CB, CBE; Squadron Leader Dudley Apthorpe; Air Commodore ELS Ward, CB, DFC; Air Chief Marshal Sir Theodore McEvoy, KCB, CBE, AFRAes; Michael Brindle-Selle; Dr Dov Gavish; Mrs Aline McLaughlen; Dr FG Walton-Smith, PhD, DSc, DS; Miss Denise Dane; HE Jones; Philip Farrington; John Winton; Dr David Kennedy; Barrington Gray; MCA MacDonald; Dr Alison Betts; Miss Jayne Mason and Mike Insall

My good friend Mrs Anne Pedley kindly consented to check this work and comment upon its accuracy with regard to the military details of the period.

Finally, I must thank my wife Susan who has acted as a sounding board for many of my ideas and theories and diligently read through and checked my many draft typescripts. As I noted in the original book *Against the Odds*, I cannot begin to praise her enough for her ability to have Lionel Rees to breakfast, lunch, tea and supper every day for more years than I care to remember, without a penny extra on the housekeeping. Now, thirty years later, that gratitude is even more heartfelt.

W Alister Williams
2017

The plaque unveiled outside Plas Llanwnda,
Caernarfon on 1 July 2016.
[Author]

I

A CAERNARFON BACKGROUND
(1884–1912)

THE ANCIENT FORTRESS TOWN OF CAERNARFON STANDS ON A SMALL PENINSULA between the river Seiont and the Menai Strait, against the backdrop of the Snowdonia mountain range. Founded by the Romans as Segontium, an outpost fortress of the XX Legion based in Chester, the site was also selected by Hugh d'Avranches, the first Norman earl of Chester, as the location for a motte and bailey castle, possibly on the top of Twt Hill, but more likely on the site of the present day castle. It was, however, the English king, Edward I, who finally established a permanent settlement there when he ordered the construction of the key fortress of Caernarfon under the direction of his master builder, the Savoyard, James of St George, at the end of the thirteenth century; legend has it that the design was based on the walls of the Byzantine-Roman fortress at Constantinople. As well as the castle which was intended to overawe and subjugate the native *Cymru*, Edward built a town in the form of a grid of straight streets enclosed by a curtain wall and defensive ditch. The castle and town were to be the administrative capital of the colonial English control of north Wales. Although the town walls were finished by 1292, the castle was incomplete two years later when Madoc ap Llywelyn led a rebellion against the English, overran the town and seriously damaged the castle. Settlers were then brought to Caernarfon from England to establish it as a mercantile and administrative centre and the local population was forbidden to live inside the walls until 1507. Edward's mighty fortress came under attack several times during its history, but it was as a market town that Caernarfon developed, serving a rather impoverished area where the population scratched a living from the poor soil of small upland farms. By the turn of the nineteenth century, the district underwent dramatic changes as the effects of the industrial revolution reached this remote corner of north Wales, and the town became increasingly important as a seaport for the rapidly expanding slate industry. The final restoration of peace in Europe after the defeat of Republican France allowed the pace of this expansion in the town's trade to increase. Although many industries suffered a devastating slump after 1815, this was not the case with slate, as the lack of building caused by the war resulted

Caernarfon Castle, the estuary of the river Seiont and the Slate Quay, c 1890. [Author]

in an upsurge in demand once peace had been restored. By 1825, the quarries of Caernarfonshire were commencing a period of unprecedented expansion. This change in the local economy brought with it an influx of outsiders from other parts of Wales and indeed from every corner of the British Isles, men who brought with them not only their industrial and entrepreneurial skills, but also an alien culture and traditions which were quickly assimilated by the local population so that this corner of the principality developed its own unique social composition.

Some of the immigrants came to add their sweat to that of the former dispossessed agricultural labourers in the slate quarries and copper mines, whilst others came to seek employment and fortune in the rapidly expanding businesses that were established to service this new-found prosperity. As well as being the economic centre of the region, Caernarfon developed into the cultural and political capital of north Wales and it was in this atmosphere that the great Welsh romantic and nationalistic revival took root and flowered.

Amongst the outsiders who made their way to Caernarfon was James Rees, born in Carmarthen on 31 January 1803 and already a man experienced in the ways of the wider world having left his native west Wales for London where he had been apprenticed to a printer and risen to become a master of his trade. His arrival in Caernarfon in 1831 was the result of being appointed foreman printer with the firm of RM Preece & Co, of Turf Square, publishers of a new newspaper, the *Carnarvon Herald*.[1] With James came his young wife Anne, the daughter of Walter and Hannah Wilmot of Bristol, an outsider in a predominantly monoglot Welsh region. In the tradition of the time, the Rees family grew substantially in numbers. James and Anne's first child, Walter John, was born in 1834 and at regular intervals a further four sons and four daughters arrived to fill the family home, first at Bron Gwylfa, then Plas Gwilym in Pool Street, then in the High Street.[2] In September 1849, they moved into Plas Llanwnda, a substantial stone-built Georgian house in Castle Street, one of the main thoroughfares inside the walled town.

When James and Anne Rees arrived in Caernarfon there was little to indicate that they were any different to the hundreds of others who had moved into the area, but James soon found the town suited his temperament and began to create his own niche in its social and business life. When the *Herald* changed hands in 1832 and became the property of William Potter & Company,[3] Rees was retained by the new management, having become an indispensable part of the business. The economic and social forces in Caernarfon were perfect for the newspaper, and it soon became the focus of radical views throughout north Wales. The economic success which followed was due in no small measure to the talent and enterprise of the intelligent, ambitious and very capable Mr Rees. By 1835, his opinion was being sought by the leading Liberal figures in the county and he played an important role in the election of Major-General Sir Love Jones Parry of Castell Madryn as the Member of Parliament for the Caernarfon Boroughs constituency. The election was a close-run thing and paved the way for the radical tradition of Caernarfon's future parliamentary representation.

In 1840, William Potter retired and James Rees succeeded him as the owner, editor and publisher of the *Herald* and, from his office at the family home in High Street, the paper

Castle Street, Caernarfon, looking up towards the main entrance to the castle, c 1850. Plas Llanwnda, was accessed through the gateway at bottom left. [Author]

James Rees, the grandfather of Lionel Rees,
in his robes as Mayor of Caernarfon.
[Rees Family Archive]

went from strength to strength. Aware of the increasing political conscience of his compat-riots, and realising that an English-language newspaper was failing to reach a large pro-portion of the local population, Rees established a second publication in 1855, *Y Herald Cymraeg*,[4] which proved to be an immediate success and became the focus of Welsh Liberal opinion for nearly a century. As well as politics, *Y Herald Cymreig* also covered all aspects of Welsh culture, employing some of the leading Welsh writers of the era, such as the journalist, novelist and bard Lewis William Lewis (Llew Llwyfo) and short-story writer Richard Hughes Williams. The atmosphere in the Rees home must have been very dynamic with the family members becoming involved, almost by osmosis, in not only the business but also the political and cultural life of the town.

James Rees' status in the community and his commitment to the future of the town was clearly reflected by his election to the Borough Council, his eventual elevation to the honoured position of alderman and his service as mayor in 1856–7 and November 1872–4 (during which time the new Town Hall was built). In his maturity, in the only known photograph of him when he was serving as mayor, he appears a typical Victorian patriarch, a man proud of his humble beginnings and of the success which he had made of his chosen path through life.

Life at Plas Llanwnda was not all plain sailing, and the Rees family suffered a series of tragedies as four of their sons and one daughter died young, leaving the youngest, Charles, to carry on the family business with his father. James Rees retired in 1868 and Charles took over as the proprietor of the newspapers, taking John Evans as a partner. James then devoted his remaining years to serving the community; as well as his work on the Council he was also on the management committee of the Bangor Normal College, was a highly regarded and diligent member of the Carnarvon Harbour Trust, Chief Magistrate in the Borough Court and High Bailiff of the County Courts of Caernarfon, Porthmadog and Pwllheli.

James Rees lost his wife in 1878 and two years later, he died at his home in Castle Street, aged 77. He was given a civic funeral in Llanbeblig during which all business in the town was suspended. A rival local newspaper described him at the time as:

A kind hearted and charitable gentleman, that in many instances where committals in default of payments of debts followed as a necessity upon the procedure of the court, he in almost innumerable instances, prevent the breaking up of homes, and spared many a man the disgrace of a debtors' prison, by taking upon himself all responsibilities … it was by his anxiety for the welfare of the town and its inhabitants that he gained for himself that esteem in which he was generally held … As an employer … Mr Rees's conduct at all times tended to lessen the gap which too often exists between master and workman. Mr Rees was a member of the Established church, but had a wide and kindly sympathy with every branch of the Christian Church. His private life was as exemplary as his public conduct, and it can truely be said of him that he was a fond husband and kind father … [we cannot speak of him] but in terms of the greatest respect and commendation. Whether we look at the life of the deceased as a citizen, as a politician, as a journalist, or in its social and domestic relations, we find little of which we can speak in any but terms of the greatest respect and commendation, and sincerely we believe that his death will cause a gap not easily filled up.[5]

Enillodd iddo ei hun barch ac edmygodd pawb oedd yn ei adnabod. Rhyddfrydwr twymgalon oedd ef o ran golygiadau gwleidyddol.[6]

Charles continued to run the family newspapers until 1876 when he sold out to his partner, John Evans. His heart was clearly not in the world of journalism and he took up a new career in law, qualifying as a solicitor in June 1880, a few days after his father's death, and establishing his own legal practice at the family home in Castle Street. Like his father, Charles became involved in various aspects of community work and served as the presiding officer for elections in Caernarfon, was a member of the Harbour Trust and the Royal Welsh Yacht Club, secretary of the Segontium Permanent Building Society and the Carnarvon Horticultural Society, and treasurer of the Segontium Lodge of the Freemasons. His great passion, however, appears to have been the local military and in 1875 he was commissioned a sub-lieutenant in the 3 Carnarvonshire Volunteer Rifles, eventually rising to the rank of lieutenant-colonel of the 3 (Volunteer) Battalion, Royal Welsh Fusiliers.[7]

Charles Rees married Caernarfon-born Leonora Maria Davids, the daughter of Smith William and Anna Maria Davids of Twt Hill East, Caernarfon, on 18 October 1881. Her

Lieutenant-Colonel Charles Herbert Rees, the
father of Lionel Rees. [Rees Family Archive]

Leonora Maria Rees (née Davids), the mother of
Lionel Rees. [Rees Family Archive]

father, a slate quarry agent and managing partner of the Penybryn quarry in Nantlle, had
come to the town as a young man when his father, Thomas Davids, moved the family
there from Crayford in Kent. Her mother was Irish, the daughter of the Reverend George
Brabazon of Paynestown, County Meath, a very distant seventh cousin once removed to
the eleventh earl of Meath. Anna died in 1875 and Smith Davids remarried the following
year to Anglesey-born Annie Telford Elizabeth Clarges, daughter of Major-General Arthur
Gore (formerly of the Bengal Army), who lived at Plas Maesincla, Caernarfon. Leonora
was born in Church Street, Caernarfon in 1859 and her family had been known to the Rees
family since the 1840s.

    Charles and Leonora quickly settled into married life at Plas Llanwnda and their names
appear regularly in the local press when they attended a variety of social functions in the
county. Charles was a member of both the Royal Welsh Yacht Club (although there is no
evidence that he ever owned a yacht) and the Carnarvon Rowing Club (serving as stroke
in a five-man boat). Politically, he had shifted his allegiance away from the Liberal cause
so espoused by his late father, to that of the Conservatives, and he and his wife were strong
supporters of the Primrose League.[8] Resident with the newly-weds were Kate and Ethel
Rees, the widow and daughter of James Wilmot Rees, Charles' eldest brother.

    On 31 July 1884, the family in Castle Street celebrated the birth of Charles and
Leonora's first child, a son, who was christened Lionel Wilmot Brabazon, names which

brought together the maiden names of his two grandmothers. Two years later, the birth of a daughter, Muriel, completed the family. Charles' legal practice appears to have prospered and the two children lived in a secure middle-class environment, each devoted to the other, Lionel always there to protect his younger sister and Muriel hero worshipping her older brother.

Lionel grew into a strong, highly intelligent, good-looking, but somewhat shy boy who seems to have been happy in his own company. He appears to have found it difficult to make friends but, those he did relate to, remained friends for the rest of his life. He loved his home town which he regarded as fascinating, steeped as it was in history and culture, and with so many outlets for an active and adventurous boy. He always thought of himself as a Caernarfon boy, or *hogyn o'r Dre*, and, at the end of the nineteenth century, the town was a marvellous place for a small boy to grow up in, teeming with life, with small trains bringing in the slates from Dyffryn Nantlle to the Slate Quay (for which his grandfather had been a prominent advocate) where they were loaded aboard ships for export to other parts of Britain, Europe and North America. There can be little doubt that Lionel, along with countless other small boys, must have appreciated their predecessors' enterprise as they sat enthralled in the shadow of the great medieval castle, listening to the fanciful tales of the sea and distant ports told by tough sailors. Each day the small ships would pass out of the narrow estuary into the Menai Strait, carrying not only the rocks hewn from the nearby mountains, but also the dreams of the youths who watched them sail by. A small boy could run in less than a minute from the Rees home in Castle Street to the Promenade which flanked the Strait, and in two minutes from there to the Slate Quay. It was there, and in the Aber Woods across the river, that a child's imagination would create adventures in faraway places, and Lionel must surely have come closer to fulfilling those dreams than any of his contemporaries.

His natural intelligence, coupled with an enquiring mind and a fascination with all things mechanical, made him a respected but rather isolated member of his peer group. It was to him that other boys came when a dispute or a problem seemed unsolvable. His

Lionel Rees, aged about five. [Rees Family Archive]

Plas Llanwnda, the Rees family home in Castle Street, Caernarfon. The house is now part of the offices of Gwynedd County Council. The stone pillar in what was the front garden is a memorial to Llywelyn ap Gruffydd, Prince of Wales. The VC centenary plaque is located in the corner behind the stone pillar. [Author]

father's association with the Volunteers and the Royal Welsh Yacht Club no doubt had a profound effect on him and his future course in life was charted, not by ambitious parents but by his own experience and inclinations. One can even see the seeds of the future aviator being sown in the days before the development of powered flight. A life-long friend, Griffith Lloyd-Jones, later recalled:

In those far off days there were several large families living within the walls and their natural playground was the promenade where the flying of kites was very much in vogue. Lionel's box kite, made by himself, was always sailing so very much higher than any of the paper ones flown by the rest of us. I, as a very small boy flying a very small kite, hero-worshipped this much bigger boy, three years older than I, who also possessed the largest ever dog, an immense Newfoundland, of which I was rather frightened until Lionel told him to be friendly, after which he even allowed me to ride on his back.[9]

WG Thomas of Caernarfon recalled a ten-year-old Lionel Rees who, having been given a camera as a gift, used his kite to attempt to take an aerial photograph of the town – again a possible indicator of things to come?

Lionel's formal education began in 1891 when, aged only seven, he was enrolled as a boarder at the Elms Preparatory School in Colwall, Worcestershire. The school had been founded in 1614 by the Worshipful Company of Grocers, making it the oldest prep school in England. A small establishment, catering only for some fifty boys, the Elms was situated in the shadow of the Malvern Hills and placed great emphasis on physical as well as academic excellence, and it would have been here that Lionel first acquired a passion for formal competitive games which was to remain with him throughout his life. He left the school in 1895 and, three years later, in March 1898, became a pupil at Eastbourne College

in Sussex, where he was to spend some of the happiest years of his life. Founded in 1867, the school had struggled to attract sufficient numbers of pupils to remain open until the appointment of the Reverend Charles Crowden as headmaster who brought with him some ninety boys from Cranbrook School, thereby making Eastbourne economically viable.

As well as pursuing a successful academic school career, Lionel threw himself into every aspect of school activity. Placed in Blackwater House under the tutorage of classical scholar and ornithologist, Edward Carleton Arnold, he was among the first boys to be selected to represent his house and the school at rugby, and the 1901 school magazine recorded that he was 'One of the hardest workers in the team and a good player in other respects when once roused, but it takes an awful lot to rouse him.' The following year he was described as 'An honest, hard-working, but somewhat sleepy forward. A good tackler and rush stopper.' Both comments seem to fit his later personality exactly. As well as rugby, he also represented the school at both running and shooting. He became a prefect, head of Blackwater House and a sergeant in the Officer Training Corps which had been established in 1896, and by 1901 had a strength of 163 of all ranks. Although membership of the OTC was voluntary, the school records that eighty percent of the pupils joined and, having 'enlisted' had to attend all drills and pay for their uniforms. The boys paraded three times each week, drilled twice and had a uniform parade. Particular emphasis was placed upon physical training and rifle drill. Rees would appear to have taken to the latter and proficiency in 'skill at arms' became a passion of his throughout his future career.

Early in his school life, he had decided on a career in the army, perhaps influenced by his father's years of service in the Volunteers, and was subsequently placed in the school's army class in order that he might prepare for the entrance examination to one of the military academies. Some pupils undoubtedly used these classes as a means of escaping

Eastbourne College 1st XV, 1900–01. Lionel Rees is standing, third from the right. [Eastbourne College Archives]

from the rigours of the traditional public school classical education. This was certainly not the case with Lionel as there can be little doubt that the choice of a military career was anything other than a positive decision. He clearly had the aptitude to succeed in both the academic and practical aspects of school life, and a career as an army officer offered him perhaps the best possibility of making full use of his talents whilst also providing a continuation of the school atmosphere which he so obviously enjoyed. There is nothing to suggest that he ever considered any other career and he certainly never seemed to have expressed any desire to follow in his father's legal footsteps.[10] In the summer of 1901, he obtained first-class passes in arithmetic and additional mathematics in the Oxford & Cambridge Lower School Certificate examination, with further second-class passes in Latin, French, geography, mechanics and physics.

Eastbourne College OTC, 1901. Corporal Lionel Rees is in the centre row, eighth from the left. [Eastbourne College Archives]

Having settled on trying to achieve a military career, Lionel set himself the target of gaining admission to the Royal Military Academy (RMA) at Woolwich, a decision which is clearly indicative of how he saw his future. Entry to the Royal Military College, Sandhurst, would have resulted in a commission in either the cavalry or the infantry, neither of which held any appeal for him despite the fact that entry into either was considerably easier than entry into the Royal Artillery or Royal Engineers which were the two branches catered for at Woolwich. The RMA offered him the promise of adventure, physical challenges and a high degree of academic achievement. Traditionally, the two corps which drew their junior 'officers from The Shop' (as the RMA was affectionately called) were the choice of men of intelligence and a high standard of education, who intended making the service their life-long profession.

Entry into the RMA was by examination for which competition was high. Three sections, or classes, had to be sat, of which two were compulsory in all their elements. Class I (compulsory) covered mathematics (including arithmetic, algebra, Euclid and plane trigonometry), Latin, French or German and English history. Class II (candidates had to choose any two subjects for study) included higher mathematics, French or German, Greek, English composition, chemistry, physics, physical geography or geology. Class III (compulsory) dealt with freehand drawing and geometric drawing. As the examination was the same for both Woolwich and Sandhurst, selection for the former was made by picking those with the highest grades, while the residual candidates who had passed would be offered places at Sandhurst. Rees passed into the RMA an inconspicuous 62nd out of the 1901 entry of 80, and realised that he had a great deal of hard work ahead of him if he was to have any say regarding which corps, either RE or RA, he was to enter in two years' time.

Each day at Woolwich commenced with *reveille* at 06.15 hours and the cadets paraded at 07.15. Within an hour, they had to breakfast and be either at their desks for the first subject of the day (in the junior year this was invariably mathematics) or parading for outdoor instruction in such subjects as field fortification and military topography. At noon, cadets were given one hour of drill, riding or gymnastics, followed by lunch parade at 13.15 when they were carefully inspected by the corporals; a single speck of dust usually being rewarded by extra drill. By 14.15 hours the cadets were again outside where, for a further hour, they participated in drill, riding or artillery exercises after which they were allowed a two-hour break which they were expected to spend either in personal study, playing games or making use of the workshops. At 17.15 they began two hours of classroom instruction in French or German, drawing or, in the case of senior classes, chemistry, physics, tactics, military administration and law. After dinner, each cadet had to involve himself in private study, dance practice or additional voluntary subjects in the workshops. At 22.00 hours a final roll call was taken and the day ended. Life at Woolwich was certainly no sinecure.

In addition to his academic work, Rees exhibited his usual flair for competitive sports and, whilst at the RMA earned something of a reputation as an athlete. At the Royal Military Tournament held on Derby Day 1903, he represented the Academy in the Sabre versus Sabre competition, taking the first prize. During his two years at Woolwich he worked hard at his studies and, in the final examinations, passed out 16th out of 83 candidates. Such was his success that he was awarded the Tombs Memorial Prize which was given annually to the artillery cadet achieving the highest marks in the finals.[11] Although the prize was worth £56 (£3,000 at current rates), its greatest value to a newly-commissioned officer was the kudos which it might bring as the award entitled the recipient to have his name recorded on a panel in the dining room at Woolwich by way of inspiration to future generations of cadets – he would also hope that it would become 'engraved' in the memories of those senior to him in the service and thereby enhance his career. Rees also managed to win both the Field Survey and the Drill Prizes.

Whether Rees had failed to get sufficiently high marks for entry into the Royal Engineers, or whether the Royal Artillery had always been his first choice, was not recorded, and neither was the reason for his decision to take a commission in the Royal Garrison Artillery (RGA). Certainly, as the Tombs cadet of 1903, the choice of any branch of the artillery was open to him and traditionally the Royal Horse Artillery (RHA) and Royal Field Artillery (RFA) were regarded as the elite units of the corps; a career in either was however regarded as being best suited to a young man who had sufficient private resources to afford the social life which was synonymous with those two branches. The RGA on the other hand attracted those young men of limited means who wished to follow as inexpensive a career as possible while still serving in a highly professional unit. Although the Rees family was financially secure, Lionel's father was not a wealthy man and therefore monetary considerations may well have had a part to play in his choice. Another, possibly more decisive factor, may have been the belief that RGA gunners had far more opportunity for active service, being almost continuously engaged at the sharp end of Britain's minor imperial conflicts throughout the world, particularly on the north-west frontier of India. Finally, a third factor that may well have influenced his decision was the question of equestrian skills. Having an urban upbringing, Lionel Rees had little experience of horsemanship and the riding certificate issued to him at Woolwich stated that, after 111 lessons in military equitation, 'LWB Rees ... is a fair rider.' The RFA and RHA were the horse worshippers of the Gunners and anyone who was less than skilled as a rider would do well to avoid them. A few years later another Woolwich cadet made the same decision and, in his memoirs published over forty years later, he commented on his choice:

I ought to have realized the overwhelming importance of horse worship throughout the British Army of that day, and above all its importance to the 'Gunners' ... I was fond of horses and riding myself, but I foolishly never realized till too late how vital it was for an aspring gunner subaltern to affect an adoration bordering on the fanatical for that intelligent quadruped. To select deliberately the 'unhorsey' branch of the regiment was in those days to commit an unforgiveable sin. It was very doubtful whether any of us who started life in that unfashionable branch [Royal Garrison Artillery] ever lived this stigma down throughout our service, as can be seen by the low proportion of 'Gambardiers' as compared to Field and Horse Gunners who rose to really high command ... It seems unlikely that all the great commanders should have gone into the horsey branch and all the 'duds' into the other![12]

Second Lieutenant Lionel Rees, Royal Garrison Artillery, 1903. [Rees Family Archive]

Two final factors that may have influenced Lionel's decision to join the RGA may have been the location just outside the town walls of Caernarfon, at the end of the Promenade, of the so-called 'Silent Battery' of the Royal Naval Artillery Volunteers, and the presence in Caernarfon of 8 Company, 1 Cheshire & Carnarvon Artillery Volunteers which became part of the RGA Territorial Force in 1908.

Members of 9 Company, RGA, Gibraltar, 1906. Lieutenant Lionel Rees seated, third from left. [Rees Family Archive]

He was commissioned as a second lieutenant in the Royal Garrison Artillery on 23 December 1903. At that time the RGA was involved with the guns used in the forts and fortresses of the British Empire, including coastal artillery batteries and siege artillery and Rees spent six weeks at the Depot in Woolwich before being posted to 9 Company, RGA in Gibraltar where he spent four uneventful years learning the skills of his profession. In accordance with the 'time served' tradition of promotion, he became a lieutenant after two years, a rank in which he was to remain until the outbreak of war in 1914.

Unlike many others who served on the 'Rock,' Rees liked the station and was captivated by its lack of similarity to anywhere that he had previously known. Although of immense strategical importance, guarding as it did the entrance to the Mediterranean and the route to the East, life in Gibraltar was not too demanding and, after a time, became

Rees, seated at the table, acting as paymaster to 9 Company, RGA, Gibraltar, c. 1906. [Rees Family Archive]

Lieutenant Lionel Rees, Royal Garrison Artillery, Gibraltar, attached to the Native Local Artillery, West African Frontier Force. His gun crew are operating a 2.5-inch mountain gun which could be broken up into four parts, each of which could be carried by one soldier (usually on his head). [Rees Family Archive]

rather tedious for anyone with a taste for adventure. Realising that he enjoyed the heat and exotic nature of an overseas posting, Rees determined to make the most of the potential for travel which military service offered.

In 1908, he was serving with 50 Company RGA in Sierra Leone, West Africa, which provided coastal defences in the area of Freetown, but returned to Britain on six months' leave in July 1909 after which he joined 10 Company RGA on Spike Island in Cork, Ireland. Whilst there he attended the 1910 and 1911 gunnery courses at the School of Gunnery in Shoeburyness and obtained a 'Very Good' pass in the examinations in both years and was deemed sufficiently proficient in the use of quick-firing guns to pass as an instructor.[13] In July 1911, he went on a two-month pre-embarkation leave after which he was posted back to West Africa on secondment to the Native Local Artillery, Sierra Leone Company, a locally recruited unit that was trained and commanded by British officers and NCOs and equipped with six 2.5-inch quick-firing mountain guns.[14]

It would have been during this time in West Africa that Rees acquired two great passions. The first, a love of discipline and training, was probably inherent in him but only manifested itself at the time when idleness could easily have become lethargy leading in turn to incompetence. The second was a love of the tropics. The so-called 'White Man's Grave' that was West Africa seemed to awaken in Rees a certain romantic streak and, like others before him, he was enthralled by what he saw as he led troops on training exercises into the mountains and forests, and he found the challenge of surviving in the tropics invigorating. Although he was probably unaware of this attraction at the time, it was to draw him back time and again in the future. It was here that he first encountered and grew to admire and respect the native, black population. The men under his command, although very different from the British soldiers he had been accustomed to, had their own qualities and Rees, together with the other British officers in the colony, turned them into an efficient military force, probably a match for any comparable European unit serving in the tropics.

But, however rewarding it may have been to train men in the skills and standards of the Royal Artillery, and to see them carry out those duties efficiently on exercises and manoeuvres, it was an activity that lacked excitement and, when Rees returned to Britain at the end of 1912, his mind was receptive to the offer of a new challenge. It came in the form of a frail, under-powered flying machine.

Notes

1. Founded in 1831, the newspaper had been bought by Richard Mathias Preece later that year. The name was changed in 1836 to the *Carnarvon & Denbigh Herald*. Preece was the father of Caernarfon-born Sir William Henry Preece, KCB, FRS (1834–1913), of Penrhos, Caeathro, pioneer telegraphic engineer.
2. The Rees children were: (1) Walter John Rees, b.1832, later employed as a compositor and reporter. d.1853; (2) Sarah Sinclair Rees, b. 1834, married Dr Morris Davies, d.1864, mother of David James Davies (b.1861), Dr Walter Llewelyn Davies (b.1863) and Sarah Sinclair Davies (b.1864); (3) James Wilmot Rees, b.1837, served as a captain 2 (V) RWF, he married Mary Anne Hodges of Chester, two sons Ernest Wilmot (b.1867) and Percy Llywelyn (b.1868), d. 1869 at Weston Cottage, Twt Hill, ' a kind and genial young man'; (4) Anna Sinclair Rees, b. 1836, d. Aberdeen 1885; (5) Catherine (Kate) Mary Rees, b. 1841, d. 1927, Bromley; (6) Frances Ellen Rees, b. 1845, married John Cole; (7) Thomas Llewelyn Rees, b. 1842, later employed as a reporter, he married Kate Mary Garwood and d. 1876; (8) Arthur Edward Rees, b. 1846, d. 1853; Charles Herbert Rees, b. 1848, later the proprietor of the newspapers until he became a solicitor. He d. 1930, Bromley, Kent.
3. Of Caernarfon and Chester, his Caernarfon print works was located in Pen Deitsh.
4. By 1857 it was selling 9,000 copies each week and by 1869, 14,000, when its parent paper the *Herald* was selling only about 1,200–1,500 copies.
5. *North Wales Express*, 25 June 1880.
6. 'He earned for himself the respect and admiration of all who knew him. Politically his views were those of a warm-hearted Liberal,' *Y Goleuad*, 26 June 1880.
7. The Rifle Volunteers were established in 1859 as a means of augmenting the Local Defence Volunteers, established by the Volunteer Act of 1804. They was associated to their home county until consolidated into battalions of the local infantry regiment of the Regular Army after the Regulation of the Forces Act 1871. The 1907 Territorial and Reserve Forces Act merged the Volunteers, Militia and the Yeomanry to the Territorial Force. After 1892, any officer serving for twenty years with the Volunteers was awarded the Volunteer Decoration (VD) which, after the creation of the Territorial Force, became the Territorial Decoration (TD).
8. The Primrose League was founded in 1883 to further the cause of the Conservative Party throughout the United Kingdom. It grew from under 1,000 members in 1884 to over 1 million by 1891.
9. Letter from Griffith Lloyd Jones of Caernarfon, shown to the author by the late Ivor Wynn Jones.
10. Lionel's father retired from his legal practice in 1906.
11. The Tombs Memorial Prize was instituted in 1877 in memory of Major-General Sir Henry Tombs, VC, KCB, of the Bengal Artillery. It took the form of an annual award of about £56 which was made to the senior cadet of each intake.
12. Richard Hilton, *Nine Lives* (London, 1955), pp 13–14.
13. During this leave in 1911, Lionel's mother, who had travelled to Queensland in Australia to live with her brother, Smith William Davids and his family, died in Cairns on 6 August.
14. *History of the Royal West African Frontier Force*, AHW Haywood, FAS Clarke, London, 1964.

II

Into the Air
(1912–15)

When Louis Blériot made his somewhat unsteady landing in the grounds of Dover Castle in July 1909, he achieved more than the first crossing of the English Channel by a heavier-than-air machine, he also ended Britain's isolated position as an island off the coast of Europe. Despite the enormous advances which had taken place in the infant science of aeronautics, admirably illustrated by this achievement, the British government failed to recognise its importance and, when it discovered during the course of the same year, that the British taxpayer had already contributed £2,500 towards experiments with flying machines, it decided that enough was enough and cancelled any further expenditure. At the same time Germany was spending £40,000 per annum on military aviation.

Two years later, the situation had not improved and the Chief of the Imperial General Staff is on record as having declared that 'Aviation is a useless and expensive fad advocated by a few individuals whose ideas are unworthy of attention.'[1] Fortunately, not all those in authority agreed with this viewpoint and during the spring of 1911 the Army set up an Air Battalion of the Royal Engineers comprising 1 Company, equipped with airships and based at South Farnborough, and 2 Company, equipped with heavier-than-air machines, based at Lark Hill on Salisbury Plain. Fear of Germany's plans for the future and the ever-increasing sums of money which that country was expending on military aviation, led the British government to finally set up a committee to investigate the state of military flying in Britain which, after careful deliberation, published its findings in February 1912. The most important of its recommendations was that a 'Flying Corps' should be established by the amalgamation of those units of the Army and the Royal Navy which were already 'dabbling' in flying. The new corps was to have five sections – a military wing, a naval wing, a reserve, a central flying school (which should be established at Upavon in Wiltshire) and an aircraft factory (to be built at Farnborough), with the latter being responsible for the design, development and manufacture of machines for the entire corps. With a speed almost unprecedented in official circles the recommendations were accepted and within one month the corps was granted the Royal Warrant and came into being as the Royal Flying Corps (RFC) on 13 May 1912.

Initially, the RFC was to have a strength of seven squadrons, each of which would have twelve aeroplanes, with two pilots for each machine. The total establishment of the Corps was to be 364 pilots, of which half would be commissioned officers. In addition, the Central Flying School would have a further twelve officers and sixty-six non-commissioned officers and men who would be responsible for training a total of 180 pilots each year. After training, the pilots would serve in either the Military or Naval Wing. The first commanding officer of the new force was Captain (Temporary Major) Frederick Sykes of the 15 Hussars.[2]

Although the government had clearly stipulated that both naval and military flying was to be developed within the framework of the RFC, the Royal Navy very quickly began to assert its independence and, after only a few months, adopted the title Royal Naval Air Service (RNAS) for its own air corps which became a separate unit in the summer of 1914.

In September 1912, the Army held its first manoeuvres in which the RFC was invited to participate. Despite being under very close scrutiny, the aviators acquitted themselves well and the success of the winning side was due in no small measure to the invaluable information supplied to its staff officers by the novice reconnaissance pilots. A War Office memorandum issued afterwards stated that 'There can no longer be any doubt as to the value of airships and aeroplanes in locating an enemy on land and obtaining information which would otherwise only be obtained by force.'

At the end of the year, the War Office declared its support for the expansion of the RFC and actively encouraged officers already serving in other units to learn to fly and, if necessary, to transfer to the RFC. One such officer was Lieutenant Lionel Rees on home leave from Sierra Leone.

The governing body of British flying was the Royal Aero Club (RAeC) which had been founded in 1901 by Frank Hodge Butler, his daughter Vera and the Honorable Charles Rolls (of Rolls-Royce fame) to foster an interest in aviation and further its development in Britain. It established its first flying ground at Leysdown on the Isle of Sheppey in 1909[3] and began manufacturing aeroplanes under licence from the Wright Company of the USA, initially at Leysdown, then Eastchurch (also on the Isle of Sheppey). From 1905, it began to issue certificates for what were termed 'balloonists,' and in 1910 became responsible for issuing certificates for aeroplane pilots. The RAeC was given responsibility for supervising all initial flying training, not only for civilian aviators but also for military pilots. These flying courses cost the budding aviator approximately £75 (nearly £5,000 in current value) which, if passed and the individual was accepted for service with the RFC,

Rees and some of the Bristol School flying instructors and Royal Aero Club examiners who enabled him to gain his certificate in 1913. Clockwise from top right: Gordon England, Sydney Sippe, Vivian Wadham, Robert Brooke-Popham, Norman Percival, Eric Harrison, Collyns Pizey and Henri Jullerot. Centre, Lionel Rees, the photograph used for his RAeC certificate record. [Royal Aero Club via Ancestry.co.uk]

was fully refundable. If however the intrepid airman failed, the government had been put to no unnecessary expense, a procedure which continued until late into 1915/early 1916.

Lionel Rees commenced his flying training at the Bristol & Colonial Aeroplane Company school at Lark Hill aerodrome on Salisbury Plain in Wiltshire. The Bristol School had been established in February 1911 under the control of chief instructor, Frenchman Henri Jullerot.[4] Pupils were taught the rudiments of flying (such as was known to the instructors at the time) on either Henri Farman or Bristol 'Boxkite' machines (the latter being direct copies of the former, so much so that *Monsieur* Farman considered legal action against the Bristol Company for infringement of his patents). The company's advert stated that pupils of the Bristol Flying Schools would have 'good grounds, good machines and good instructors' and that 'pupils not only learn to fly, they also receive practice and instruction in assembling, adjusting and repairing machines and motors.' The skills which the novice airmen learned were very basic and, when they had acquired them to the instructor's satisfaction, they had to complete a fixed flying test under the scrutiny of the Royal Aero Club's observers before they could be issued with a certificate of competence. The flying course did not cover a fixed period of time, but depended upon the pupil's aptitude for flying and, most importantly, the weather conditions prevailing at the time. Pupils either travelled down to Salisbury Plain and lodged at a local hostelry until they had completed the course, came for one or two days each week or, if one of the many artillery officers who learned to fly at this time, probably lived at the nearby Bulford artillery camp. One student, Lieutenant Wilfred Parke, RN, completed the flying course on 25 April 1911, after only three sessions at the controls of an aeroplane,[5] others took considerably longer.

Rees was taken up on his first flight by instructor Eric Harrison[6] on 7 November 1912. He next ventured into the air two days later with instructor Collyns Pizey[7] who noted that his 'pupil is shaping very well.' Pizey also took Rees up with him on an aeroplane flight test that same day. The weather then intervened and the open expanse of Salisbury Plain was pounded by wind and rain, making flying impossible for several days and the pupils underwent instruction in the hangars on the mechanics of flying. On Friday, 15 November, Pizey took Rees up for a flight in a Bristol Boxkite, followed by one in a Bristol monoplane (in which they reached a height of 1,200 feet), and then two further flights with Pizey in the Boxkite. His comments afterwards were that 'Lieut Rees is making really excellent progress and although only at the school a few days will commence solos at the next opportunity.'[8] Perhaps by way of a control check, Rees was then taken for a flight by instructor Gordon England.[9] He had two flights on 27 November when he was taken up in a biplane by England and then by another instructor, Sydney Vincent Sippe,[10] for

Students and instructors at the
Bristol Flying School, Lark Hill,
January 1913. Lionel Rees
(wearing a white scarf) is seated
on the starboard wing
of the aircraft.
[via Timothy C Brown]

landing practice. Two further flights followed on 5 December, when England again took
him up despite the wet conditions, and in the afternoon the honours fell to Harrison.

By this stage Rees had been well and truly bitten by the flying bug and the following
morning ventured away from the training flights of the flying school and went across to
the RFC base at nearby Netheravon where Norman Percival[11] was demonstrating the
revolutionary Dunne D7 biplane.[12] Despite adverse weather conditions the previous week,
Percival had made a thirty-minute flight at a height of 1,000 feet and on the morning when
Rees arrived, had taken up Major Henry Brooke-Popham[13] for a trip and, after lunch, took
his fellow artilleryman up for a flight around Shrewton at a height of 800 feet. Rees was
evidently keen to take to the air whenever the opportunity presented itself.

The following week, England took him up for another trip and a 'trial' in a biplane.
There then appears to have been a gap until 3 December, when he was again taken up by
Pizey who 'put the pupil in the pilot's seat and [he] sitting behind.' England then gave
Rees two more tuition trips before deciding that the weather was 'unfavourable … for
pupils' solos.'[14]

The following Friday, Rees was taken up in the afternoon by the chief instructor
Jullerot, a clear indicator of his near readiness to go solo. The weather then took a decided
turn for the worse and there were several days when no flying could be carried out. On
the 10th, England took him up for a flight, followed by Harrison, but the weather was
deemed to be too bad for solo flying. The school then appears to have closed over the
Christmas period and it was not until 30 December that Rees is recorded as being 'on one
of the biplanes for three really fine solos.' Three days later, after another tuition session,

Bristol Biplane (commonly known as the 'Boxkite'). Designed by the Bristol & Colonial Aeroplane Company in 1910, was closely based upon the Henri Farman III biplane and utilising parts from a Zodiac machine. Powered by a 50 h.p. Gnome 'pusher' engine, it was capable of a maximum speed of 40 mph. A second seat could be fitted behind that of the pilot. This was the type that Rees learned to fly at the Bristol School and in which he gained his RAeC certificate in January 1913. This replica machine is located at the RAAF Museum.

The revolutionary Dunne biplane. Designed by Anglo-Irishman Lieutenant John William Dunne with wings swept back at 35 degrees. This was powered by a 70hp Green engine. This photograph shows the single-seater D8 (Rees flew in a two-seater D7 bis model).

A lesser known aeroplane, the Bristol Monoplane, was designed by Pierre Prier in 1911. Based upon the Bleriot monoplane, and powered by the 50 hp Gnome 'tractor' engine. Some were fitted with two seats for training purposes, and Rees flew in one of these whilst training at Lark Hill. [Flight magazine]

Rees set out to undergo the first half of the tests which he was required to complete for his RAeC Certificate. According to the school, these 'he accomplished in fine style' before the weather closed in again and the Saturday was spent in hangar tuition. Finally, on 7 January, Rees was able to complete the necessary tests and gained his certificate, number 392.[15] In addition to demonstrating his ability on control of Boxkite on the ground, take off and land successfully and carry out climbs, descents and turns, he had to execute five figure-of-eight circuits of the aerodrome. The observers for his tests were Major Brooke-Popham and Lieutenant Wadham.[16]

Although now qualified as a civilian pilot, Rees did not go on to complete his training at the Central Flying School and thereby gain entry into the RFC. Instead, he was posted to serve for two months in the Adjutant's Department at the School of Gunnery in Shoeburyness before, once again, being posted back to the tropics on secondment to the Nigeria Regiment, West African Frontier Force. This would suggest that his sojourn into the fledgling world of aviation was a personal choice and that he had completed his flying course during his leave period.

Rees remained in Nigeria until the summer of 1914 when he again returned to Britain, travelling on the SS *Burutu*, landing at Plymouth on 3 July. One month later, Great Britain declared war on Germany and, after eleven years of peacetime soldiering, Rees was ideally placed to be posted on active service. Had he remained in West Africa he would undoubtedly have become involved in the campaign in Cameroon which would have directed his life on a totally different course. As it was, Rees, who had found flying appealed to his sense of adventure, immediately volunteered for service with the RFC. If the Corps expanded, his opportunities for promotion would be greatly enhanced. His application was accepted, subject to the proviso that his flying abilities met the standards laid down by the RFC and so, on 10 August, he commenced the short five-week course at the Central Flying School which would qualify him to serve as a military pilot. He completed the course early and on 12 September was award RFC Certificate 221. On 28 September he became one of the original members of 7 Squadron[17] which was officially formed on that date equipped with a motley collection of machines – two Morane-Saulnier H monoplanes, two Blériot XI monoplanes, two Farman F20 biplanes, one Vickers FB5 biplane and three BE 8 (Bloater) biplanes.[18] He later recalled:

Everybody was most anxious to get to the front, as all our friends were there, and we did not
like being left in England. Looking back it is very funny to remember how we tried to get all
the flying we could and how we called people who had even a few more minutes flying than

ourselves 'Air Hogs.' After about four weeks we were all split up, some of us going to the front – lucky men – others remaining as instructors and others, amongst whom I found myself, being posted to reserve squadrons.

When we joined these squadrons we had done very little cross-country flying. On the first morning, I was sent to land on another aerodrome. Having done this fairly successfully I thought I had now really become an aviator. On the way back, I had trouble with my engine control and eventually my engine stopped at a height of 6,000 feet. Knowing nothing of the difficulty of judging a long, straight glide, I thought I could just reach my aerodrome and came in over the sheds with about a foot to spare. On landing, instead of being congratulated on my judgement as I had expected, my Flight Commander said 'Don't ever risk your machine again in that manner.'

This altered my outlook on aviation and in future I never risked my machine again.[19]

7 Squadron had originally been formed at Farnborough in May 1914 under the command of Major JM Salmond,[20] but had been broken up three months later in order that other, more senior units could be brought up to strength prior to their embarking with the BEF. The RFC was at this time undergoing a period of significant expansion as plans had already been drawn up to more than double the number of squadrons in existence. The British Expeditionary Force (BEF) had begun its embarkation for France on 9 August and, two days later, the Headquarters of the RFC left Farnborough en route for Amiens which it reached on the 13th. On the same day, N[os] 2 and 3 Squadrons, and two flights of 4 Squadron, had flown across the Channel from Dover to Boulogne and then on to Amiens where they were joined by 5 Squadron two days later, the whole force being under the command of Brigadier-General Sir David Henderson, KCB, DSO.[21]

The RFC's front line strength was sixty-three machines which were armed with neither bomb nor gun, all being intended for purely reconnaissance work. However, it was only a matter of days before individual pilots and observers began to carry rifles (which were stripped down to reduce weight) and pistols on patrol with a view to 'discouraging' any enemy machine which they might come across. Inexperienced though they were, the pioneers of British aerial power very quickly began to build up a reputation to be proud of and in his despatch dated 7 September the Commander-in-Chief of the BEF, Sir John French, stated:

I wish particularly to bring to your Lordship's [Field Marshal Lord Kitchener, Secretary of State for War] notice the admirable work done by the Royal Flying Corps … their skill, energy and perseverance has been beyond all praise. They have furnished me with the most complete and accurate information, which has been of incalculable value to the conduct of operations. Fired at constantly by both friend and foe, and not hesitating to fly in any kind of weather, they have remained undaunted throughout. Further, by actually fighting in the air, they have succeeded in destroying five enemy machines.

By early October, the hard-pressed units of the RFC already in France were desperately in need of reinforcement and 6 Squadron, equipped with six BE2s, two BE8s and four Farmans, was ordered at very short notice to Belgium where it was to assist in the attempt to relieve Antwerp.[22] Due to the haste with which the squadron went overseas and its remoteness from the remainder of the RFC, its commanding officer, Major John Becke,[23] soon found himself in difficulties regarding spares and supplies and wrote to the OC RFC Military Wing at Farnborough requesting materials. As a consequence of this, Rees received the following order dated 11 October 1914.

To Lieutenant Rees

You and N° 97 Sergeant H Austin[24] and N°s. 1346 2A/M J Hunnisett,[25] will entrain at North Camp,[26] South Eastern Station, at 7.13 a.m. on Monday, the 12th instant, en route for Folkestone and ——— [redacted for the purpose of secrecy]. On arrival at North Camp Station you will ensure that the truck containing the stores for N° 6 Squadron is put on the train. You will also see that when you change at Redhill and Tonbridge that the truck accompanies you. You will arrive at Folkestone Harbour at 11.9 a.m. where you will report to the Embarkation Staff Officer and hand in your permits and embark with the stores. On arrival at ——— [redacted] you will ascertain where N° 6 Squadron is, and deliver over to the Officer Commanding N° 6 RFC or an officer of N° 6 Squadron, the stores you have brought. You will find out from him what other stores he requires, and return with Sergeant Austin and with the list.

You will leave 2A/M Hunnisett with N° 6 Squadron. Before leaving you will endeavour to find a suitable place of an Aircraft Park. You will then return to England with all possible speed.[27]

The following message was sent to Belgium:

I propose to start a small Aircraft Park mainly with a view to supplying in the field. Lieutenant Rees and Sergeant Austin will probably form nucleus. It will consist of Motor Repair Lorry and Flight Repair Lorry with most of the stores to keep you a month in the field. This will form your A[ircraft] P[ark] Stores.[28]

Rees and his companions embarked as directed from Folkestone on the afternoon of

12 October bound for Ostend. It was not the glamorous entry into the war that he had hoped for, arriving at the front in command of a truck full of spares and one sergeant and one air mechanic, with orders to return to England 'with all possible speed.' It was, however, better than remaining at South Farnborough as who knew what might transpire once he was across the Channel.

No sooner had Rees arrived in Ostend Harbour at about midnight, than he was advised to re-embark for England as the Germans had broken through the front line and it would only be a matter of hours before they overran the port. 'I already knew the Huns were fairly close, but seeing a number of Tommies outside the station calmly smoking, I decided that there was not much the matter. So I got transport from a squadron which was billeted near, and spent a very comfortable night with them.'[29] He managed to reach 6 Squadron which was located on a cycle track close to the sea front at Ostend from where pilots had been flying some seventy miles to the north-east to obtain reports on the deteriorating situation in Antwerp. He immediately made arrangements for the stores to be delivered from the docks before settling down for the night, rolled in a blanket on the floor of the race track pavillion '… at least I was in France [sic] and the Germans were only a few inches away.'[30]

The following morning, reconnaissance patrols were sent up to locate the advancing enemy forces but, despite perfect visibility, no sightings were made, but in view of the increasing danger of the squadron being overrun, it was decided to move the airfield further down the coast the following day.

Next morning all the machines flew back to Dunkirk. One machine had engine trouble and we saw it disappearing down the main street at Ostend. We sent a light tender after it and found it had managed to reach the water and there it was with the tide rising round it. We took out the engine and instruments and then burnt the machine so the Huns could not use it.[31]

Shortly before the squadron started away from Ostend a funny old Taube appeared. Everybody started firing at it except ourselves, who were armed only with revolvers, although the machine was clearly out of range. It was at a great height! – we thought so then – it must have been 5,000 feet up.

Although I was in the Royal Flying Corps I had never seen the Corps on the move before and I was greatly taken by the way all vehicles were lined up, ready for the road. On a certain whistle sound all the men fell in and the sergeant major made certain that everything was left clean and that nothing had been left behind. At the next whistle sound, everybody got aboard his allotted vehicle and then we started.

The road was lined with troops going both ways, and with refugees from Ostend. We left

Some of the original officers of 6 Squadron, 1914. Clockwise from top right, Lieut GAK Lawrence, Lieut LS Metford, Lieut SW Smith, Capt GB Rickards, Lieut BF Moore, Lieut CY McDonald, Lieut FP Adams, Capt HCT Dowding. Centre: Capt HC McDonnell.
[Royal Aero Club via Ancestry.co.uk]

the race-course at noon, and the Germans came in at 4 p.m. … I was given a seat on a light
tender and travelled that way for the next few days.[32]

The Germans entered Ostend less than four hours after the squadron had left.

As he was supernumerary and therefore without his own aeroplane, Rees' activities
during the retreat from Belgium were officially confined to the ground, and he busied
himself by serving as quartermaster to the squadron. It was quite obvious that it was
impossible for him to establish an aircraft park until the situation stabilized and the
squadron found a more permanent home; he therefore interpreted his orders as being to
remain with 6 Squadron.

After one day at Dunkirk, they were again on the move and six machines and a large
number of personnel and vehicles left for Ypres and Poperinghe in Belgium. The rest of
the officers (Rees amongst them), NCOs and men, along with three machines and several
vehicles remained in Dunkirk until the following morning when they moved to Boulogne.
It was at this time that Rees made his first war patrol in the air.[33] Not having an allocated
aeroplane, he flew as an observer but, as it was not an officially sanctioned flight, no
documentation exists to pinpoint the date or the pilot's name. Indeed, the only reference
to it is in a note made by Rees himself:

> I was taken up as an observer over the lines and saw all the little villages burning as the Huns
> advanced and all the little bits of trenches here and there. The machines we flew were slow
> and bad climbers, and the pilots did not like anyone wearing a heavy coat.[34]

During the third week of October, the activity in 6 Squadron intensified as more and
more patrols were mounted to try and ascertain the exact location of the front line and
the logistical situation behind the German lines.

On 20 October, Rees arrived in Poperinghe in command of the squadron transport
which had been left in Boulogne. No sooner had he arrived than the squadron received
orders to hold itself in readiness to be relieved by 4 Squadron when it was to move to
RFC Headquarters at St Omer, an event which occurred the next day. For Rees, this was
the end of his sojourn at the front as there was no longer any need of a separate aircraft
park for 6 Squadron which had now joined the main RFC force and, on 22 October, he
embarked for England where he re-joined his unit. His ten days of active service had given
him a taste for war flying and an understanding of the fluidity of the situation in Belgium
as the BEF tried desperately to stem the German advance. It also meant that he was later

eligible for the award of the 1914 Star (with Clasp), the so-called 'Mons Star.' The weeks that followed, however, although filled with activity and fraught with danger, must have seemed very frustrating for Rees who had received a taster of what he could be involved in if he could only get back across the Channel on active service.

His days with 7 Squadron were limited as, on 30 October, after nearly eight years as a lieutenant, he was promoted to the rank of captain[35] which meant that he was eligible for the command of a flight and, as no such position was available in the squadron, he could expect a posting in the near future to one of the newly-forming squadrons.[36]

Fears of German air raids on Britain had prompted the authorities to station aircraft around London, more in an attempt to placate public opinion than as a serious attempt to either deter or destroy the enemy. The main effort in this defensive plan was the responsibility of the RNAS which had units of both land and sea aeroplanes based in the Thames estuary and Kent. The RFC was given a part to play in the scheme with units based at Hounslow[37] and Joyce Green.[38] In the event of an aerial attack on London the officers on duty at the two bases were to be informed and they could then take steps to attack the hostile aircraft. The OC South Farnborough would also be informed in order that he might despatch reinforcements from other squadrons.

Although 7 Squadron was officially based at Netheravon after 24 October, a detachment (which seems to have included Rees) remained at South Farnborough. The air defence plan for London laid out that each evening two machines would be flown to Hounslow and a further two to Joyce Green. They would remain at those stations until morning when they would return to South Farnborough. By mid November, with no attacks having materialised, the War Office rescinded this order.

At 13.00 hours on 21 December a German Friedrichshafen FF29 seaplane (203), piloted by *Oberleutnant-zur-see* Stephan Prondzynski (accompanied by *Fähnrich-zur-see* von Frankenburg as his observer), crossed the Kent coast and dropped two 20 lb bombs into the sea south west of Admiralty Pier in Dover. Three days later, at 10.45 hours, the same pilot dropped a bomb near Dover Castle. It landed in a private garden making a crater about four feet deep and shattering a few windows of the nearby rectory, but otherwise causing no real damage. In both instances the raiders were well on their way home before any defence aeroplanes could take off and attempt an interception.[39] Fearing further attacks, the RNAS set up standing patrols in the Dover area and the RFC resumed the stationing of machines at Hounslow and Joyce Green.

The first RNAS patrol took off at 08.00 hours on Christmas Day but saw nothing. A little over four hours later, at 12.20, just as the unwary population of south-east England

German Friedrichshafen FF29 seaplane. This may be the actual machine flown by Prondzynski on his bombing missions over south-east England in December 1914. [Author]

began to settle down to their first festive lunch of the war, a Friedrichshafen seaplane of *See Flieger Abteilung 1* based at Zeebrugge, and again piloted by *Oberleutnant-zur-see* Prondzynski, was seen crossing over Sheerness in the Thames estuary at a height of about 7,000 feet. Several anti-aircraft batteries opened fire but to no avail. From Eastchurch on the Isle of Sheppey and Grain on the north side of the Medway estuary, two RNAS machines took off but failed to catch the intruder which reduced its height to about 4,000 feet and continued on its westerly course over Gravesend, Tilbury and Dartford. Ahead of it went telephone messages and the War Office ordered machines up from Joyce Green, South Farnborough and Brooklands (in Surrey) in the hope that one of them might be able to intercept the German raider as he turned for home.[40]

The German pilot's intended target was one of the London docks, and he managed to reach the London suburb of Erith near Bexley when, no doubt feeling that he had chanced his arm far enough, he decided to reverse his course and begin the long journey home. By this time the air defences, such as they were, had been fully alerted and anti-aircraft batteries at Cliffe Fort opened fire and, either in an attempt to lighten his load and increase his height and speed, or out of sheer awkwardness, Prondzynski dropped two bombs on Cliffe Station, fortunately causing little significant damage.

At South Farnborough, Rees was one of the two pilots on stand-by and he was ordered to attempt an interception.

I was fog-bound at Farnborough [and] … had great difficulty in obtaining any alcohol on Christmas Day as none of the public houses would sell me any. Eventually, I managed to get a bottle of gin which I put in the water jacket of my gun to prevent the water freezing.

The pilot of one of our machines was adjusting the controls of his machine when suddenly the raider appeared over the aerodrome [Joyce Green]. The pilot and mechanic immediately jumped aboard, the gunner gave them a gun, somebody started the engine, and away they went. Both the raider and our machine were fired on by anti-aircraft guns all the way down the Thames. The machines exchanged shots, and chips were seen to fly off the raider. Unfortunately, the gunner's hands got frost bitten and he could no longer work the gun, so our machine had to return and allow the raider to escape. I believe the machine failed to reach Germany.[41]

Insult was later added to injury when an old Thames barger, on seeing the British aircraft approaching the airfield, dived into his cabin and re-appeared with a duck gun with which he promptly opened fire. Fortunately, he did no damage, other than to the pilot's ego, and the Vickers made a safe landing. Indeed, squadrons attempting to defend the capital were in greater danger of sustaining casualties from flying accidents than they were from enemy action, and Rees later recorded two such incidents which happened to members of 7 Squadron during the first winter of trial and error.

One machine went up over London and saw the lights [of the city] 4,000 feet down. The pilot ran into a rain cloud and very shortly afterwards the lights of London were above him – the aneroid showed forty feet only. Chimneys loomed up in front and the pilot turned sharply and crashed into a bank. he took his electric torch out of his pocket and looked at the observer's seat, only to find him gone. On searching round the machine he suddenly saw the observer sitting on the ground with an enormous Zep bomb [designed to be dropped on a raiding Zeppelin airship] under each arm.

A second machine went up, directly the pilot and observer were out of sight of the aerodrome, the engine failed. The machine made for the Thames, or rather for where they thought the river ought to be, and hit the marshes on the bank. The machine crashed in a ditch which had about one foot of water. Again the observer was missing from his seat, and was seen lying on his back in one foot of water apparently swimming.

'Is the water deep?' asked the pilot.

'Seven feet deep and no bottom,' replied the observer, who went on kicking hard.[42]

Like his fellow pilots, Rees had no success intercepting any German raiders, but he did manage to equal their record for accidents when he made his first crash landing as a result of his engine stopping 'with a bang' whilst flying in a Vickers over the Kent countryside early in 1915. Looking at the snow-covered ground below, he saw that he was over what appeared to be a heavily wooded area. Losing height he then spotted one large,

Vickers FB5 (1650) which Rees crashed on landing in a Kent field.
[Muriel Rees deposit, Imperial War Museum Box 69/8/2]

clear field. With difficulty he made his approach and touched down smoothly. As the aeroplane rolled over the surface, Rees spotted, directly in his path, what appeared to be an elderly lady who was watching his progress. As he was heading straight towards her, and his machine had no brakes, and the lady appeared not to be moving, he was compelled to take avoiding action by turning as quickly as he could which caused two tyres to come off the wheels of his undercarriage resulting in the machine tipping up and coming to a halt with its nose in the ground. Unhurt, Rees climbed out of the cockpit and went to apologise to the spectator. Before he could say anything, she called out 'How well you did that. I thought at first you were going to run into me,' to which Rees felt like adding, 'So did I.'[43] Despite the vision of impending doom hurtling towards her, the lady had made no attempt to move away, presumably believing implicitly in the skill of the unknown pilot at the controls. Such is the faith engendered by blissful ignorance.

In February 1915, Rees received his new posting. He was to take command of a flight in a new squadron that was being formed at Netheravon from a nucleus of men taken from 7 Squadron. Rumour had it that this new squadron was destined for service in France. At last, Rees was legitimately en route for the front, it was only a matter of time.

Notes

1. General (later Field Marshal) Sir William Gustavus Nicholson (1845–1918) who served as Chief of the General Staff from 1908–09 and Chief of the Imperial General Staff 1909–12.
2. Later Air Vice Marshal the Right Honorable Sir Frederick Hugh Sykes, GBE, GCSI, GCIE, KCB, CMG, PC (1877–1954). He served as Chief of Staff of the RFC 1911–15 and OC Royal Naval Air Service in Gallipoli 1915. After various postings in the War Office he was appointed Chief of the Air Staff in 1918 and did much to established the newly-founded Royal Air Force. He was Controller of Civil Aviation 1919–22 and Conservative MP for Sheffield Hallam 1923–28 and Nottingham Central 1940–5.
3. The first flight by a British pilot was carried out here by J.T.C. Moore-Brabazon, later Lord Brabazon of Tara (1884–1964) who was a distant relative of Lionel Rees through his maternal grandmother's family. Coincidentally, he served in the RFC during the Great War and played a major role in the development of aerial photography and transferred to the RAF with the rank of lieutenant-colonel in 1918. During the 1930s, he became involved in boat design and was probably the first person to sail a boat with an auto-gyro rig.
4. Henri Jullerot, qualified (France) 2 May 1910.
5. Lieutenant Wilfred Parke, RN (1889–1912) had qualified at Lark Hill on 25 April 1911. He was killed, with Arkell Hardwick (managing director of Handley-Page Ltd) in a flying accident at Wembley Park on 15 December 1912 which was caused by the high gusting winds on that day.
6. Eric Harrison (1886–1945) had qualified at Lark Hill on 12 September 1911. He had emigrated from Australia in 1911 (in the company of Harry Hawker), returning in 1912. Later Group Captain, known as the 'Father of the RAAF.'
7. Later Flight-Lieutenant Collyns Price Pizey (1883–1915), RNAS, he qualified on 14 February 1911. He died of dysentery in Athens on 11 June 1915.
8. *Flight* magazine,
9. Eric Cecil Gordon England (1891–1976), he qualified at Lark Hill on 25 April 1911. As well as an early aviator (RAeC certificate 68), he was also a racing car driver, engineer (pioneering the design of motor vehicles with lightweight bodies) and business consultant. During the Great War he was a test pilot and aeroplane designer.
10. Sydney Vincent Sippe (1889–1968), he qualified on 9 January 1912. He became the British pilot to take off from the sea (1914). Later Major Sippe, DSO, OBE, FRAeS, he carried out a raid on the Zeppelin sheds at Friedrichshafen in November 1914.
11. Norman Scott Percival (1881–1959), had qualified at Brooklands on 1 August 1911. He later served in the RFC. His brother, Lieutenant David Percival (1884–1954), was an exact contemporary of Lionel Rees in the Royal Garrison Artillery and had qualified to fly at Lark Hill on 4 June 1912.
12. *Flight* magazine, 21 December 1912, p1201. The Dunne D.8 was a tailless, swept-wing biplane designed by John William Dunne, an officer in the Wiltshire Regiment, which had taken part in the Lark Hill Military Trial in August 1912.
13. Later Air Chief Marshal Sir Robert Henry Robert Moore Brooke-Popham, GCVO, KCB, CMG, DSO, AFC (1878–1953). He had qualified on 18 July 1911.
14. *Flight* magazine
15. *Flight* magazine, various issues November 1912–January 1913.
16. Later Captain Vivian Hugh Nicholas Wadham (1891–1916), RFC, he qualified on 16 July 1912. He was killed in action, Flanders, 17 January 1916.
17. The original officers who formed the nucleus of 7 Squadron were: Captain AG Board (CO); Captains HC McDonnell (A/Flight Commander), GB Rickards, HCT Dowding (A/Flight Commander); Lieutenants LWB Rees, BF Moore, CY McDonald; Second Lieutenants GAK Lawrence, SW Smith, FP Adams, LS Metford. In addition, there were two flight sergeants, six sergeants, six corporals and fifty-one air mechanics.
18. Draft History of 7 Squadron, RFC, National Archives, AIR 1/687/21/20/7.
19. Article 'My Personal Experiences' by Lt-Col LWB Rees, VC, MC, RFC, published in *Air Travel*, September 1917.
20. Later Marshal of the Royal Air Force Sir John Maitland Salmond, GCB, CMG, CVO, DSO & Bar (1881–1968), educated Wellington College and Sandhurst. King's Own Loyal Lancaster Regiment. RAeC certificate 272, 12 August 1912. Seconded to RFC 1912. OC 7 and 3 Sqns, II V and VI Brigades RFC, GOC Training Division (1917), GOC RFC in the Field (1918). He became Chief of the Air Staff (1930) and Marshal of the RAF (1933).
21. Later Lieutenant-General Sir David Henderson, KCB, KCVO, DSO (1862–1921), a Scotsman who had served with the Argyll and Sutherland Highlanders in Egypt and South Africa and been appointed Director of Military Intelligence to Lord Kitchener in 1901. He had learned to fly in 1911, aged 49, and was appointed Director of Military Aeronautics in 1913 and GOC RFC in France in 1914.

22. 6 Squadron left Farnborough for active service on the Western Front on 5 October. The pilots who flew across the Channel were: Major JHW Becke (CO); Captains FH Cogan, ACE Marsh, CLN Newall, GH Cox, Ross-Hume and W Lawrence; Lieutenants K Rawson-Shaw, JBT Leighton, LG Hawker and CY McDonald; Sergeant C Gallie. Crossing by sea were: Captains HCT Dowding and E Hewlett; Lieutenants CH Marks, JE Tennant, JA Cunningham, JL Kinnear; Second Lieutenant RO Peterson and 113 Other Ranks. Captain WC Adamson also flew to France and joined the squadron on 10 October.

23. Later Brigadier-General John Harold Whitworth Becke, CMG, DSO, AFC (1879–1949), a Liverpudlian, he had served in South Africa with the Sherwood Foresters and had learned to fly in 1912 on being seconded to the RFC.

24. Sergeant Henry Austin who would appear to have been one of the earliest members of the RFC.

25. 2nd Class Air Mechanic John E Hunnisett of Walworth, London, who had previously crossed over to France with the initial deployment of the RFC on 12 August. His brother George was also an air mechanic in the RFC.

26. North Camp, Aldershot.

27. The source of this order was examined in the National Archives in 1987, but on re-examination in 2016, the author was unable to locate it. This is, however, an accurate transcription of the order.

28. Ibid.

29. LWB Rees, 'Some Flying Stunts in the first Two Years of the War', article published in the USA in the *Georgetown Gazette*, 3 July 1917.

30. Ibid.

31. Captain Alexander Ross Hume (Cameron Highlanders, attached RFC, later lieutenant colonel), the pilot of this machine was fortunate in being able to ditch into the sea without serious mishap as his observer was Captain Hugh Dowding, the future Commander-in-Chief of Fighter Command during the Battle of Britain in 1940.

32. 'My Personal Experiences', op cit.

33. This was almost certainly in a BE2, a two-seater, tractor engined aeroplane, designed by Geoffrey de Havilland.

34. 'My Personal Experiences' op cit.

35. *London Gazette*, 27 November 1914, p 9994.

36. The official dates of the formation of the pre-war squadrons of the RFC were: 1 – May 1912; 2 – May 1912; 3 – May 1912; 4 – August 1912; 5 – July 1913; 6 – January 1914; 7 – May 1914. The first phase of wartime squadron establishment commenced in December 1914: 8 – January 1915; 9 – December 1914; 10 – January 1915; 11 – November 914; 12 – February 1915; 13 – January 1915; 14 – February 1915; 15 – March 1915; 16 – February 1915; 17 – February 1915 and 18 – May 1915.

37. Hounslow (Hounslow Heath) had been used as an airfield since 1910. Located just to the east of the present-day London Heathrow Airport, it became the world's first international airport in 1919 and served as such only until 1920 when Croydon was developed for that purpose.

38. Joyce Green was located on the south bank of the river Thames, close to the present-day Dartford Crossing and Britannia Road Bridge.

39. *The War in the Air*, Sir Walter A Raleigh & Henry A Jones, v3, Oxford, 1922, p 89.

40. Article 'My Personal Experiences' op cit.

41. Ibid.

42. Ibid.

43. Ibid.

III

11 Squadron, RFC
(1915)

THE AGGRESSIVE STYLE OF AERIAL WARFARE which made its appearance over the Western Front during the latter days of 1914, for which the airmen of the RFC were probably more responsible than their German counterparts, demanded the creation of a new type of operational unit. When the RFC went to war its squadrons were equipped and trained for one purpose only – reconnaissance. As pilots began to attack each other as a matter of routine, it became evident that a new approach was required and that squadrons were required that were capable of aerial combat, that could take the fight to the enemy and, in doing so, prevent his machines from carrying out their all-important reconnaissance duties. The result of lengthy deliberations was the formation of 11 Squadron, the RFC's first designated fighter squadron, which had been officially formed on 28 November, but did not become an independent unit until 14 February 1915. Although ground staff, both officers and men, had been posted to it beforehand, Captain Lionel Rees was the first pilot to join. Arriving at Netheravon, a brick-built former cavalry camp on Salisbury Plain, he became the RFC's first official 'fighter' pilot, the forerunner of an elite group of combatants who were to carve a special niche in the public's affection in two world wars.

Left: Capt Patrick 'Pip' Playfair.
[Royal Aero Club via Ancestry.co.uk]

Right: Capt Charles Darley, RA
[Royal Aero Club via Ancestry.co.uk]

*Vickers FB5
'Gunbus'. [Author]*

Rees was given command of A Flight and was joined by Captain 'Pip' Playfair[1] (commanding B Flight) and Captain Charles Darley[2] (commanding C Flight). Command of the squadron was initially given to Major Andrew Board,[3] but passed to Major GWP Dawes[4] on 8 March.

Originally equipped with the Bristol Scout D and Vickers Bullet D, 11 Squadron was re-equipped with Geoffrey de Havilland's Vickers Fighting Biplane, designated the FB5 and commonly referred to as the 'Gunbus,' a strongly constructed two-seater biplane, powered by the 100 hp Gnome Monosoupape pusher engine. The positioning of the engine in the rear of the aeroplane gave the observer, who sat in the forward cockpit, a clear field of fire for his single, stripped .303 Lewis machine gun. In addition, the crew usually carried one stripped .303 Lee-Enfield rifle, two revolvers, up to four 20 lb Hale's bombs which could be dropped through an RL Tube and, often, a few hand grenades. The pilot sat in the rear cockpit in front of the engine. Despite its maximum speed in level flight of only 65–70 mph, the FB5 was seen as a formidable fighting machine. AJ Insall, who joined 11 Squadron as an observer recalled in his memoirs:

> The Vickers Fighter was a wonderful aeroplane. Immensely strong, with its framework and tail booms of mild steel, and its four-poster twin skid undercarriage, it could be thrown about with something approaching abandon … . The VFB had no vices, and it is doubtful whether anybody ever killed himself in one; if he did, it must have been extremely merited.[5]

Both pilot and observer were fully exposed to the elements but, if anything, the latter's position was the more uncomfortable.

It was bitterly cold there, huddled up and entirely passive, with scarcely more protection from the wind of our own making than that afforded to a ship's figurehead facing an Arctic gale, and my hands and feet … lost all sense of feeling, while my knees were just solid areas of bent leg. Elsewhere, circulation was normal and the mediocre amount of movement the confines of my cell allowed me was all I needed to make life bearable.[6]

In the back of their minds must have been the thought that, if they should be forced to land, the engine positioned behind them had an unpleasant habit of breaking loose and crushing the trapped crew.

The Vickers took sixteen minutes to climb to 5,000 feet and could, if the headwind was strong enough, find forward progress impossible. It was even known to fly backwards, an extremely uncomfortable sensation at any time, but particularly so when operating on the wrong side of the front line! A later arrival in the squadron, Major TO Hubbard, who was to be given command in December 1915, described the Vickers Fighters supplied to the squadron:

The twelve machines were French-built Vickers Fighting Biplanes, commonly known as 'Mossies', the legend being that they were so slow that they accumulated moss in the air. As a matter of fact, apart from being the coldest machine it has ever been my lot to fly, they were quite good machines, very strong and averaging anything under eighty miles per hour. The 100 HP Monosoupape Gnome engines gave very satisfactory results – due to excellent fitters – and had been known to get a ceiling of 15,000, though 10,000 to 12,000 was their usual limit.[7]

As the senior flight commander in 11 Squadron, Rees was sent on a short trip to the Western Front in mid April.

I went for a few days to a squadron of fighting machines in France near Ypres. This was after the first gas attack, and looking down one saw a great V of brown over which the gas had drifted.

At this time the anti-aircraft guns were beginning to make themselves objectionable. The first day out I asked about the guns, and was told: 'At 8,000 feet you are safe – they cannot reach you.'

Unfortunately I believed this and went as slowly as I could down the trenches on the German side, looking at what was happening and, incidentally, seeing no movement of any kind on the ground. I saw all the little white puffs below me and shouted with laughter, when suddenly there was a bang behind me and my engine started missing and vibrating. I looked behind and found the engine had been hit, and most of the bits of shell had gone through the top centre section of the wings. I came home frightfully angry because the Huns had spoiled a perfectly good engine, to say nothing of my nice machine.

We had a week of lovely weather, and game — the enemy machines — was scarce on our front. The German machines were faster than ours but they would never fight. This was just before the celebrated Fokker machine made its appearance.

One day we decided to draw a cover — namely an enemy aerodrome. We sent some machines to beat from the sea towards the enemy aerodrome, while others sat over the aerodrome at about 8,000 feet. Just before sunset the enemy machines started coming in, chased by our men. I was in one of the machines over the enemy aerodrome, and we dashed at every machine we saw. We exchanged shots with about four but could not get near enough to do any damage. As I said, the enemy machines were faster. Of course the AA guns shot at us the whole time but the shooting was not good in those days, and it was easy to avoid being hit.[8]

As they returned to their base they spotted two Zeppelin airships heading towards the North Sea, en route to carry out a bombing raid on Britain. The following morning, at dawn, Rees and the other airmen from his host squadron were up patrolling the coast, trying to catch the Zeppelins as they returned. They spotted the giant airships, but lost them in the early morning fog and had to return to base without making contact.

11 Squadron was brought up to a full complement of aircrew, ground staff and equipment, a total of 157 personnel, 32 motor vehicles and 6 motor cycles, and then commenced a period of intensive training which was to last until July. Newly qualified pilots trained first on the Henri Farman biplane before graduating to the Vickers FB5. When King George V visited the Central Flying School at nearby Upavon on 23 July 1915, the squadron was decreed to be in a state of sufficient readiness to participate in the proceedings and consequently six machines landed at the CFS where they were inspected by the King and, when he left by car to journey to Bulford, they took off to provide an aerial escort, probably the first in history. What transpired, however, was not quite in accordance with the plans that had been carefully drawn up. John Ditchfield, then a corporal in the squadron recalled:

I'm afraid it was a ragged escort as our engines had the habit of koncking out frequently or missing on half the cylinders which meant we could not keep together (I won't say in formation) and three of the six had to break off and go home.[9]

An inauspicious start to the squadron's public service, but the problems with the Monosoupape engine were legendary and they were certainly not solved before the pilots went on active service. Originally manufactured by the Seguin brothers in Paris and then under licence by WH Allen, Son & Co of Bedford, the single-valved rotary engine was ideal in theory in that the design had significantly reduced the number of moving parts used in other rotary engines. The designer Tommy Sopwith had described it as 'one of the greatest single advances in aviation' and, for its day, it was rated as a high performance engine. But, under the stress of regular use, it developed a tendency to fail at the most awkward moments. Part of the problem was the inexperience of the maintenance crews who had to service the engine under the most difficult and primitive conditions. Throughout its service career, the 'Mono' never lost its reputation for unreliability.

A few weeks after the embarrassment of the royal escort, the same six machines flew cross country to Oxford where they landed without incident; the greatest threat on that occasion coming from the civilian population who turned to greet them and threatened to destroy the machines in their desire for souvenirs. Gradually, however, the squadron's efficiency improved and the day drew ever closer when it would be sent to France.

Although officially on record as being present on the Western Front from 25 July 1915, the bulk of 11 Squadron did not actually leave Netheravon until two days later,[10] twelve aircraft taking off at 06.55 hours and flying at a height of 4,500 feet to Folkestone where, at about 09.00, only six landed — the jinxed engines having caused the others to make forced landings en route; one was fired upon by anti-aircraft guns having wandered over Southend-on-Sea in Essex and the pilot was forced to land at Felixstowe![11] Later that same day, the survivors left England for the British Army Headquarters at St Omer, France, but again the unpredictable engines took their toll and only two machines reached their destination as planned. Fortunately, this disastrous crossing of the Channel had not resulted in any injuries to either men or machines and it was felt that a delay of two days would enable the stragglers to catch up. Rees, with his brief experience of active service, was sent on ahead in Vickers FB5 (1649), accompanied by 1st Class Air Mechanic ER Batten (2233), to prepare for the squadron's arrival at Vert Galant,[12] twelve miles north of Amiens. He was not, however, exempted from the engine trouble which had plagued the remainder of the squadron and, as he and Batten flew south, was forced to make a landing near Fruges where hasty repairs were carried out. Taking off again, he was forced to make a second landing at Beauval where the aeroplane's skids became entangled in some corn which pitched it forward onto its nose. Although both skids were broken, neither Rees nor Batten sustained any injuries and were able to continue their journey after temporary

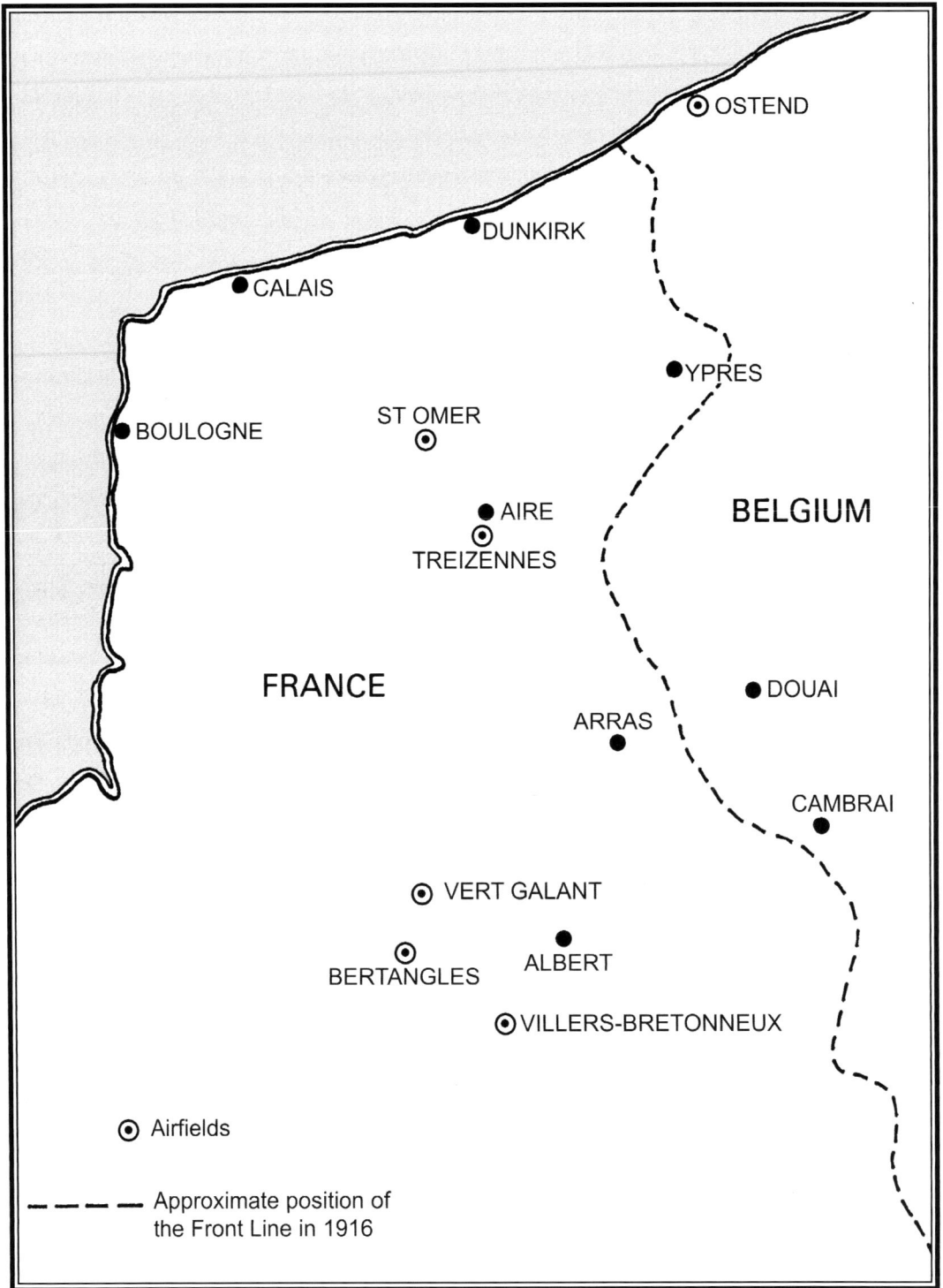

RFC Airfields north-east France as mentioned in the text.

repairs had been effected. Third time lucky, they reached Vert Galant without further incident. After making arrangements with the officer commanding 4 Squadron (which occupied the same airfield) for the allocation of quarters for 11 Squadron, Rees joined Batten and assisted in effecting repairs to the Vickers.

The following morning, as the ground crews and some of the observers arrived from St Omer by road, Rees, accompanied by Flight Sergeant James McKinley Hargreaves (1232) as his observer,[13] took off in FB5 (1649) and headed east; he had waited a long time to get within reach of the enemy.

It was a perfect day, and the visibility was good. I had enquired about 'Archie,' the anti-aircraft guns, and was told that he was not good at 6,000 feet. I climbed to this height, and proceeded just on the other side of the lines as slowly as I could, to see what there was to be seen. All the Archie shells were bursting well below. … The Observer had the only gun which fired to the front. I always carried a pistol, hoping that some day I would get close enough to a Hun to use it.[14]

Having climbed to his patrol height, he spotted a British reconnaissance machine returning from a mission, with a German Fokker *Eindecker*[15] climbing beneath its tail. Rees opened his throttle to close as fast as he could with the enemy machine, and positioned himself behind it from where, although still out of effective range, his observer opened fire in an attempt to warn the unsuspecting British pilot of the danger and in the hope that he might distract the German pilot. The tactic worked and the Fokker turned to confront the Vickers, whereupon Rees dived into the attack thinking he had an easy target. Suddenly, the German opened fire from a gun fixed to fire forwards, taking him completely by surprise, breaking one of the main spars and piercing another. Despite the

Fokker EI Eindecker. The 7.92mm Spandau machine gun can be seen on top of the nacelle. [Michael E Schmeelke]

Fokker EI Eindecker.
[Michael E Schmeelke]

fact that he fully expected the wing to collapse at any moment, Rees made no attempt to break away so as to enable his observer to open fire. When he did so, the German was hit and suddenly the monoplane dived almost vertically through the clouds. As he could not hope to follow and had succeeded in thwarting the attack on the reconnaissance machine, Rees turned for home and landed safely. Later that day a report arrived at the squadron office to the effect that a German monoplane had been seen to crash behind the enemy lines.[16]

When the other pilots of 11 Squadron landed at Vert Galant on the morning of 29 July, they found their '… senior flight commander [Rees] … covered in oil and happy as Larry, working like a navvy on his machine, which had already collected a sprinkling of scars from a scrap.'[17] He was in one of 4 Squadron's RE7 canvas sheds, changing the mainplane that had sustained damage to its main spar that morning. 'Practically the whole time we were at Vert Galand (sic), [Rees] lived in a Leyland office-lorry on the road-side, and went over to Bapaume every morning and sat there to greet the dawn and the Hun.'[18] Thus the tone of the squadron was established right from the outset, earning Rees the honour of being the first official fighter pilot to take part in an aerial combat and drive down an enemy machine, a fact that came as no surprise to the junior members of the squadron. His experience and age had already made him the focus of attention and this, coupled with his aggressive philosophy of 'When you see a Hun, go for him!' had enhanced his reputation long before their departure from Netheravon. Now he had shown that he was willing to practice what he preached. AJ Insall recalled many years later:

Lieut Algernon John 'Jack' Insall, who flew as an
observer in 11 Squadron. [© Michael Insall]

LWB Rees had a tremendous influence on the RFC in that way that in other squadrons Lanoe Hawker, VC,[19] Harvey-Kelly[20] and Lewis,[21] to name three only out of three score, had, and in our case Rees' mantle fell first on HA Cooper,[22] and from Cooper's shoulders on to those of Ball.[23] Had LWB Rees been a few years younger. Captain Rees was one of those rare men who were born leaders, who never flap, and who believe essentially in precept – and who never despise the novice. Rees it was, also, who taught us in N° 11 Squadron that our cardinal rule of behavior on the battlefront must always adhere to the Flying Corps' watchword: 'Go in to the attack! Whenever you see the Hun, no matter where he is, be he alone or accompanied, go for him, and shoot him down.' Of commanding appearance and stature, possessed, I should say, of the most captivating eye-twinkle of any officer whom I can recall, Rees was respected and liked by all those who came into contact with him. I was never in his flight, and yet I never passed him by without receiving some smiling acknowledgement of my existence.[24]

The squadron had arrived in France under the command of Major George Dawes who was '… a quite well known character and well versed in the art of keeping the Squadron's nose a little bit ahead of the next one's.' Undoubtedly a man of exceptional talents in command of a group of gifted

Major GWP Dawes,
OC 11 Squadron, RFC.

individuals, Dawes recognised that the untried role of a fighter squadron was different to anything experienced by any other unit which had served in France up to that time. He therefore permitted his officers a degree of flexibility as they struggled to establish a style of their own. Such a style of command suited Rees as he set about putting his training, experience and theories into practice. The men under Dawes' command were pioneers in aerial warfare who, if successful, would show the way for others to follow in the weeks and months to come. Errors would undoubtedly be made and some might have to pay a high price for the experience gained but, in making such mistakes, valuable lessons would be learned for the future.

The squadron had already lost members in fatal accidents whilst training at Netheravon, but such events were accepted as an occupational hazard of flying. Accidents were expected, as were losses in combat, but it was hard to accept those losses which could easily have been avoided, forced upon the individuals concerned by an apparently mindless hierarchy who had little knowledge or understanding of flying. Corporal Ditchfield recalled, nearly forty years later, one particularly unfortunate death:

GOMMECOURT

BUCQUOY

ACHIET-LE
-PETIT

ARRAS

CAMBRAI

PYS

BAPAUME

LE SARS

ALBERT

BRAY-SUR-SOMME

R SOMME

HERBÉCOURT

PERONNE

AMIENS

ESTRÉES

ST QUENTIN

Approx position of
the Front Line, 1915

1" = approx 3 miles

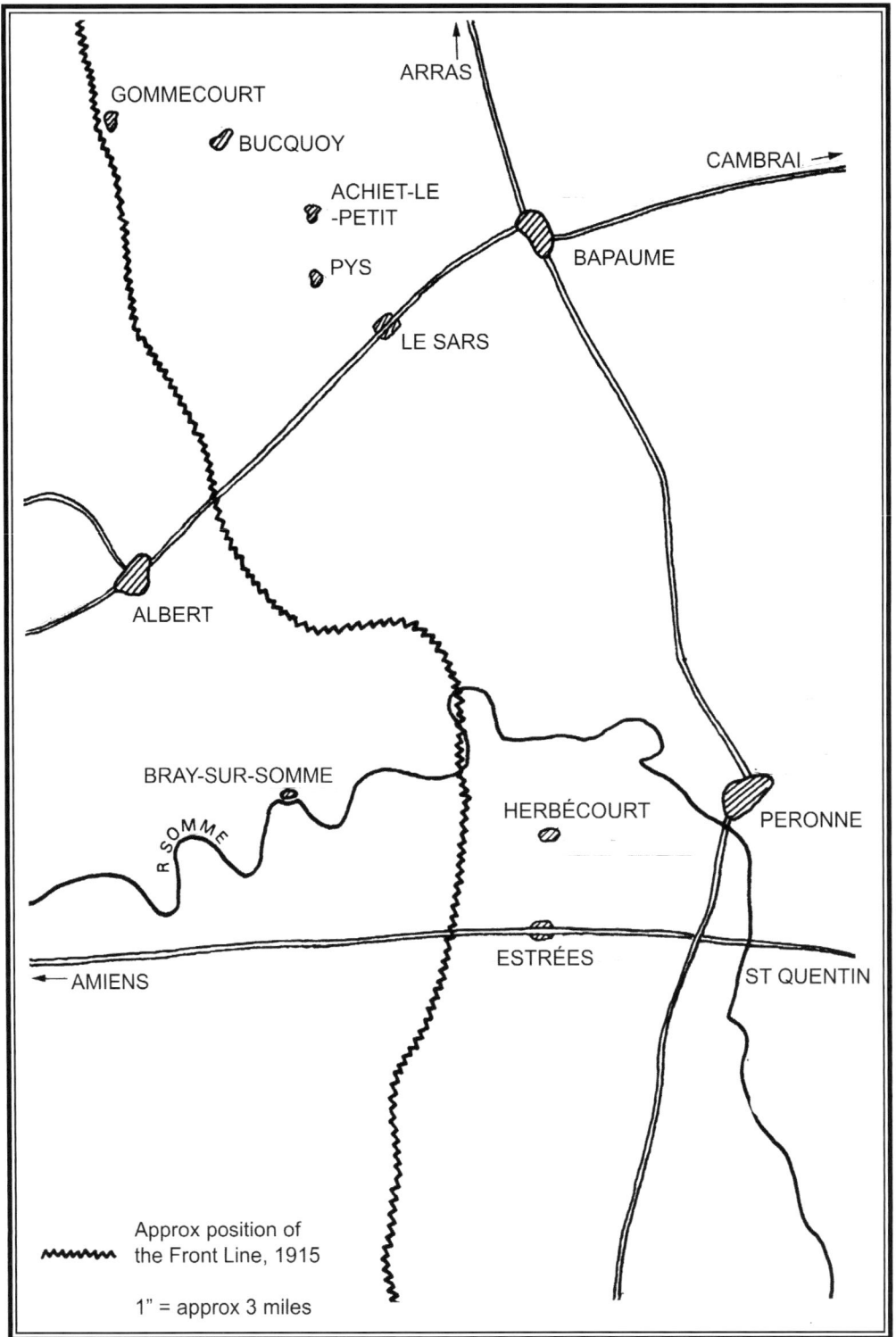

11 Squadron area of operations, 1915

One day … a dense fog settled over our drome at Vert Gallant [sic], visibility 20 yards. Major Dawes received a phone message from headquarters (where possibly the sun was shining) ordering him to despatch a plane at once over the line as Jerry machines had been reported. He explained to headquarters that flying was impossible in such conditions, only to have his head snapped off, telling him to damn well obey orders as one is taught to do, and the young second lieutenant that he chose did likewise, knowing that he was going to his death. 'We watched him rev up and start forward into the fog and we *heard* him die 200 yards away. What a waste.'[25]

Vert Galant was an established airfield, situated on the crossroads of the main Amiens to Doullens road (now the N25) and the D117, which cut through the centre of the aerodrome. Administration and quarters were centred around a number of farm buildings and, although some servicemen had a roof over their heads, most were accommodated in bell tents. By no stretch of the imagination could the airfield be regarded as luxurious for either men or machines. 4 Squadron (which departed for Baizieux shortly after the arrival of 11 Squadron) had not cut the grass and the canvas hangers left much to be desired. There was barely enough room to land safely and then only if the pilot made a good landing and the clover was wet enough to slow the machine down before it ran downhill, without brakes, towards the sheds.[26]

The squadron's role was to provide 'aggressively defensive patrols over the Third Army front, from Bray-sur-Somme to Gommecourt,' a distance of some twenty miles, and, towards the end of August, using hand-held wooden cameras, provide aerial photographs of the front and the area to the rear of the German lines. In addition, the airmen were to act as escorts for the BE2 squadrons, mount reconnaissance patrols behind enemy lines and serve as artillery observers.

They set to work almost immediately, and soon the sight of FB5s, with a Lewis gun protruding from their nacelles was sufficient cause for most enemy machines that ventured across the lines to dive eastwards for safety. Rees recalled:

The Huns hated the type of machine I was flying at this time. They hardly ever attacked us at odds of less than four to one. If there were two of our machines together, we scarcely ever got attacked at all.[27]

Consequently, drawing the German pilots into combat became a matter of cunning as each British pilot tried out different methods to ensnare his opponents. One particularly successful ploy was to turn away from any German machine which might have crossed the lines (the enemy pilots, particularly of the Fokker DR1 monoplane, were under instruction not to cross over the front line) and attempt to lure him westwards. If he took the bait, the FB5s would gradually turn until they were facing east when, at the last moment, they would reverse direction and attack, making the German machine the prey instead of the hunter. The enemy pilot could then either retreat (which meant flying further over the British lines) or accept combat in an attempt to return to his own side of the front lines. If the FB5 had the advantage of height, the chances of a successful outcome to the combat were greatly increased. On one occasion, the squadron decided to set a trap for the enemy deep behind the German front line,

> The machines found it so hard to catch the Huns that one day we arranged a Hun drive. Two of us went and sat over a Hun aerodrome while the rest of the squadron drove from the north and from the south. We did this towards evening, so that the Huns would be sure to go straight to the aerodrome and not try to escape. My machine exchanged shots with three Huns, but they were diving home so fast when they passed that we did not get them.[28]

'Dog fights', as the swirling aerial combats of the latter part of the war came to be known, were rare events in 1915 and indeed the name had yet to be coined. Most combats were short, sharp affairs, but 11 Squadron slowly began to build up its score of destroyed enemy machines and in doing so acquired a reputation as a highly aggressive unit.

Rees was constantly involved in the operations carried out by the squadron during the summer and early autumn of 1915, and his reputation continued to grow. These were not the days of the high-scoring aces who became household names in 1917 and 1918, and to achieve the destruction of an enemy machine was exceptional due to the limitations of the aeroplanes then in service and, in terms of performance, the FB5 was outclassed by many aircraft, including some of the two seaters which it was meant to protect. If, however, an enemy machine could be drawn into combat, a skilled pilot could achieve success.

On 1 August, Rees, accompanied by Lieutenant Lane as his observer, encountered a hostile machine about three miles on the British side of the front lines. As he had not seen any German aeroplanes for some days, he closed with it and followed at a distance of about 300 yards. He twice attempted to attack it, but Lane had problems with his gun. On both occasions, the German refused to be drawn into a fight and eventually dived for the ground with the apparent intention of leading Rees over an anti-aircraft battery. When the two machines were at a height of about 800 feet, the guns opened fire but all the shells

A captured German LVG C.II (displaying French markings).

burst well behind the Vickers and did not cause any damage. Rees, however, flew so close behind the German machines that the pilot found himself forced to skim over villages and wooded areas 'as though he were steeple-chasing.' Troops on the ground opened on the Vickers with small-arms fire but failed to gain any hits.[29]

This went on for some miles, and was quite one of the most amusing days I have had. We were low, and low flying was so new, that nobody shot at us for a long time. One could see all the sentries on the cross roads looking up and wondering who we were and what we were doing. By the time they had decided we were the enemy, we were out of range. One Archie[30] battery opened fire on us, but the shells were set at 3,000 feet, so we did not worry much. Eventually, this Hun got away.[31]

Rees re-crossed the front lines at about 1,000 feet, flying through another barrage of small-arms fire. When he landed back at Vert Galant, both he and Lane were surprised to find that their aeroplane had only been hit by one bullet which had gone horizontally through the rudder.

His next combat took place on 31 August when he was flying in FB5 (1649) at about 7,000 feet between Bucquoy and Bapaume. Accompanied again by Flight Sergeant Hargreaves, he came across a two-seater LVG, a much faster machine than the Vickers.[32] The German pilot decided to stay and fight and throttled back to allow Rees to catch him. When the Vickers had closed to about 200 yards, the German observer opened fire with an automatic rifle. Hargreaves returned the fire but, before he could achieve any hits on the enemy, the pilot increased his speed and pulled away out of range. This cat and mouse game continued for about forty-five minutes and the two observers opened fire on each other about five or six times before Hargreaves discovered that he had fired off all four drums and was out of ammunition.[33] He signalled this information to Rees who then broke away from the chase and headed back for Vert Galant. As he landed, despite the noise of his engine, Rees could be heard shouting for more ammunition. Without having switched off his engine he took off again and began the slow climb back towards his patrol area, desperately keen to see if the enemy machine was still there. Near the same location he found the LVG flying about 1,000 feet below him. Rees immediately dived and Hargreaves fired off one drum of forty-seven rounds. The German seemed to react quickly and dived for the clouds. The steep angle of Rees' dive caused the gravity-fed petrol in the Vickers to run to the top of the tank and his engine stopped. Unable to follow his adversary, Rees was forced to set a course for home, undoubtedly feeling highly frustrated at his apparent failure to achieve a second victory.[34]

This combat was witnessed by another machine from 11 Squadron, crewed by Second Lieutenants Cooper and AJ Insall, who were patrolling near Achiet-le-Petit. They saw the German machine break through the cloud and fall in what they described as spirals and irregular 'S' turns, apparently badly hit, before it disappeared from view. Reports from British troops on the ground later stated that an enemy machine had been seen to crash. Rees and Hargreaves were credited with having destroyed the LVG.[35]

Almost daily, weather permitting, the machines of 11 Squadron mounted regular patrols over the front. These were mostly tedious affairs and the pilots would seek distractions to liven up the day.

Patrolling is very dull work. Sometimes we are sent up for hours at a time and have to stay in the air over a certain place or area with nothing to do or see.

One A[nti] A[ircraft] battery used to annoy us tremendously. He was right out in the open near Peronne, and used to fire groups of four rounds with the regularity of clockwork. We always started the day by dropping two twenty-pound bombs on him. The best … we did was to get one bomb on either side of a gun, about twenty yards away. I do not think we ever did any real damage. We never dropped the bombs seriously as we were always on some other job and the bomb dropping was only by the way.

Opposite our front was a push balloon – a kite balloon – which was always annoying us by having itself pulled down just before we could drop bombs on it. One day we decided to settle the thing, so the first three patrols on their way dropped bombs and unfortunately missed. The fourth man was frightfully pleased because the balloon remained up. He went along chortling, and just as he was about to drop his bombs, was suddenly surrounded by AA shell bursts. The guns had been brought up and of course had the height of the balloon to the inch. He managed to crawl back just over the trenches, his planes [wings] riddled with bits of shell. The Germans all stood up to fire [at him]. Our infantry shot at the Germans. Their Minnies [*Minenwerfer* short-range trench mortars] joined in, and our men asked for retaliation from the guns, and the battle raged for two days. After that we were stopped from promiscuous balloon strafing.

The last patrol in the evening usually does the flash patrol work. That is, he tries to spot gun flashes which are very visible in the twilight, while the main features of the landscape are still visible. As one goes down the line a dark belt follows below one, as no gunners like to fire if they hear a machine above, and in the dark the marks on the machine cannot be seen.[36]

Sometime during the late summer or early autumn of 1915, Rees crashed his Vickers [probably FB5 1649) as he approached his airfield.

I was returning in the dark, and I had told the people on the aerodrome that I would not want landing lights, as I would try a new special flare which we had.

The flare did not work properly, but I thought it was sufficiently good to land by. The night was very dark, and when I was still a little way from my aerodrome I suddenly crashed. I had hit the wrong rise in the ground by mistake. The propellor burst and the engine raced, showing a ring of green flame. The engine control had come away in my hand and it took me a second after the crash to realize it was broken.

I turned off the petrol for the engine and then there was complete darkness. I turned on my electric light to find out the damage and saw that my machine, which had carried me 120 hours and … through all kinds of excitement, was, as we say, 'done in.'[37]

That summer, the British High Command began their preparations for a major assault on the enemy in an attempt to break the stalemate on the Western Front. The war was one year old and the casualty returns had long since assumed horrific proportions, but there seemed to be no alternative to the slogging match which had typified the conflict since the advent of trench warfare. Marshal Joffre, the French Commander-in-Chief, was convinced that a combined assault by his forces in the region of Lens–Arras and Champagne, and the British forces in the La Bassée–Loos area, could bring success because, once the front line had been broken, the Germans would be unable to halt the Allied advance.

On paper, the plan seemed highly feasible, but in practice it was doomed to fail primarily because of the lack of artillery in the British sector and also because of the open nature of the landscape around Loos. The attack was scheduled to commence with a 96-

hour bombardment of the German trenches and, in order to achieve the maximum effect with the limited resources available, the British preparations called for regular, detailed aerial photography of the German front and reserve lines to ensure that any changes to the defences were recorded and dealt with by the artillery. The battlefield covered an area of gentle chalk slopes which meant that any excavation, be it in the trenches or in constructing underground mines (of which there were a number in the area), was easily visible from the air as any exposed white chalk showed up clearly in a photograph. In addition to the main area of the battlefield, photographic missions were also mounted over other sectors of the front in an effort to confuse the enemy. These missions also ensured that there were no significant changes which might indicate that the Allied plans had been discovered and that no German forces were moved in anticipation of the assault.

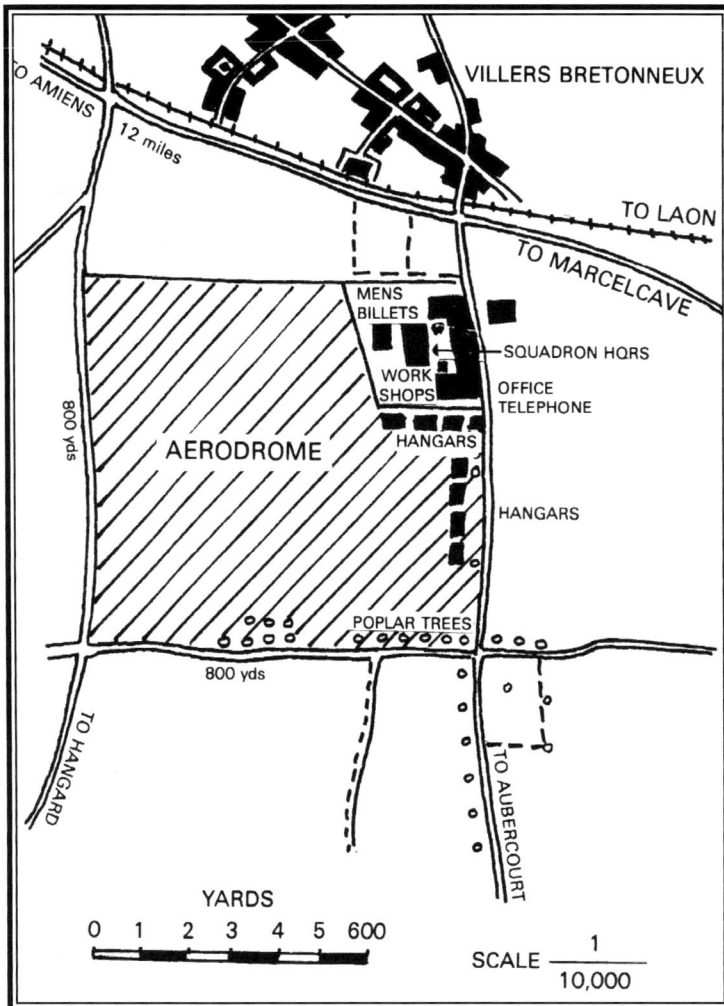

Villers Bretonneux Aerodrome as it was when occupied by 11 Squadron in September 1915. [Re-drawn from the original held in the National Archives. AIR1/2395/255/2]

The farmyard at Villers Bretonneux which was utilised as the squadron mess by 11 Squadron in 1915. Most of the buildings shown here, including the farmhouse, were destroyed during the heavy fighting of 1918. Originally built with a timber frame, the farmhouse was rebuilt after the war in a grand 'Chateau' style.

In preparation for the battle of Loos, two flights of 11 Squadron, A and C, left Vert Galant and flew to Villers Bretonneux, twelve miles south east of Amiens, on 20 September. The airfield being located on the west side of the Rue de Demuin (D23) on the land of La Couture Farm.

The following morning, four days before the commencement of the battle, Rees and Hargreaves were ordered to fly a mission to photograph the German front-line trenches between Peronne and Esterre.[38] The machine was fully prepared and Hargreaves carefully stowed away the camera and its eighteen glass plates. The FB5 took off and made its way without incident to the Peronne end of the target area. Hargreaves later recalled his memories of the mission:

I arranged with the pilot [Rees] that we should patrol the lines twice to enable me to work out the central objectives of each succeeding photograph. Naturally, for the first picture I was all ready and set, hanging over the front just waiting to reach the perpendicular line over the pre-arranged objective. This successfully accomplished, I quickly reloaded and just managed to get over in time to take the second objective.

By the time I had performed the changing of the plates etc, and got over the front again, I found that we had overshot our third objective. Without hesitation, I knelt up and swung my head round in a circular manner to indicate to my pilot that we had gone too far. To my geat satisfaction he immediately heeled over and retraced our path, so that I had ample time to pick up my third objective. This operation had to be repeated several times, but without any prearrangement my pilot grasped the situation perfectly.

Our third trip along the line brought us hundreds of greetings from our friends, the 'Archies.' Their efforts were persistent and fairly accurate. Much credit was due to the masterly art of piloting by Captain Rees, who performed all sorts of misleading evolutions to the watchful eyes of 'Archies' attendants.

Flt-Sgt James McKinley Hargreaves, DCM, 11 Squadron.

Without hitch or hindrance, we shot every plate successfully. Before commencing operations each plate was numbered and arranged so that numbers 1, 2, 3 etc, should correspond exactly to that particular section on the country below, but in spite of the careful survey of equipment before leaving the aerodrome, I found that after the first exposure, I had forgotten to hang up an empty bag to receive them when I had finished. Having no receptacle to receive them I was compelled to place them on the floor of the machine in front of me. This caused me considerable inconvenience when getting over the front again; I had to keep pushing them forward away from my knees. Just after completion, and before I had time to collect the scattered plates from the floor of the nascelle, Captain Rees drew my attention to a machine coming up from the German lines with the obvious intention of pushing us off, or at least shaking our morale. My pilot immediately switched his engine off and glided down towards the German machine. After dropping some 2,000 feet we were slightly above it and about 200 yards apart; we could clearly see that she was a new bus and vastly different from anything we had encountered before. The arrangement of the two fuselages with tractor screws and a nacelle with a propellor behind gave them an excellent distribution of gun power, of which I believe they had three – one forward and two aft.[39]

AGO C 'Two Tails'. In configuration, a machine very similar to the Vickers in concept, with a twin-boom fuselage and a pusher engine. The two booms protruded beyond the leading edge of the lower wing, giving the impression that it was a twin-engined machine. [Author]

Albatros C.I.

It is generally accepted that this machine was an AGO C, a two-seater, single-engined 'pusher' biplane which made its first appearance during the summer of 1915. It is, however, of interest to note that in his combat report Rees also declared that the machine which they encountered had at least two engines. From this date onwards, the type was regularly encountered by the machines of 11 Squadron and were always referred to as 'Two-Tails'; there is no record of the squadron identifying them as AGOs on that occasion or later.[40]

Hargreaves held his fire until the enemy machine was well within range. The German had the advantage of speed and, as the two began to circle each other, took the outer course. As Rees came alongside, the German observer fired bursts of about 50 rounds, reputedly from two guns, at a range of between 100 and 200 yards, but failed to hit the Vickers. At a height of about 7,000 feet, and with the range closing, Hargeaves fired off half a drum which seemed to have caused some vital damage as the enemy pilot immediately began to stall and spin before regaining control and putting his machine into a glide and heading back towards his base. He was later observed to crash whilst trying to make a forced landing near Herbécourt. Both the German aircrew appear to have survived.

Climbing again, Rees continued to patrol the area, challenging any other enemy pilot who might wish to try and drive him down. The sky remained empty and eventually he headed for home where Hargreaves safely delivered the photographic plates.

Later that same day, again accompanied by Hargreaves, Rees took off to patrol the area south east of Albert. At about 17.30 hours they spotted an Albatros two-seater flying at about 2,000 feet above Le Sars. Without hesitation, Rees made his attack. Bullets from

Hargreaves' gun were seen to strike the German machine which immediately dived away at a very steep angle with his engine sounding as if it was on full power. Rees estimated that the German was flying at about 150 mph and, as he was unable to follow, discontinued the action. As there were no reports received about the eventual fate of the Albatros, no claim was made. Again, there are no extant German reports of any losses on the Western Front that day.

When the photographic plates taken by Rees and Hargreaves that morning were processed their accuracy and clarity led to high praise from Third Army Headquarters staff who declared them to be '... the finest series of photographs ever taken in France to that date.' For the destruction of the AGO C Hargreaves was awarded the Distinguished Conduct Medal.[41] Rees received the Military Cross for his actions on 28 July, 31 August and 21 September.[42]

Rees encountered another AGO 'Two-Tails' a few days later.

Not even the Two-Tails liked the type of machine we were flying at this time [Vickers FB5]. They were faster and could climb faster than we could. One day we spent three-quarters of an hour two or three hundred feet below one of these machines. We were eight miles on the Hun side of the lines, and this machine refused to fight, although we did all we knew to entice him down. All he could do was to fire every now and then from a long range indeed, so far that we could hardly hear the bullets. Eventually we fired thirty rounds at him, and he went home.[43]

Nine days later, the partnership of Rees and Hargreaves attacked an Albatros C.I[44] near Gommecourt. In 1917, Rees briefly outlined the action:

One morning it was fearfully cold and we had been up about two and one-half hours with doing nothing, when suddenly we saw A[nti] A[ircraft] shells bursting in the distance. Off we went, and there we saw an enemy machine. I do not know what he was doing, as apparently he was making aimless circles above the clouds. As soon as he saw us he made for us. It was the first time we had met a machine which wanted to close and fight. When we were quite close he turned and fired six rounds. The sixth made a white line on my jacket and bent a valve on the engine. My gunner, I am pleased to say, put the enemy's gun out of action at that moment ... and [he] dived through the clouds.

We followed and my gunner then cut one of the enemy's wings right off. Much to my horror, I saw one of our machines directly below, and the German on his way down missed this machine only by a few feet.[45]

Hargreaves had in fact emptied a full drum of ammunition at the enemy machine before the German pilot dived towards a cloud and Rees followed. Hargreaves then fired off a second drum, and the enemy machine began to spiral and then nose-dived towards the ground. The official records of the time recorded that the anti-aircraft guns then again opened fire and the Albatros was thought to have received a hit to its starboard wing which was seen to break away at about 5,000 feet. The fate of the two German airmen was sealed and the wreckage was seen to hit the ground on the British side of the front line. Upon investigation of the bodies, it was discovered that the pilot had been hit in the head by a machine-gun bullet and was therefore dead before the artillery re-commenced firing on his machine. The credit for bringing the Albatros down was therefore given to Rees and Hargreaves. The pilot of the Albatros (of *Feldflieger Abteilung 23*) was twenty-four year old *Leutnant der Reserve* Fritz Kölpin of Barth, and his observer, who was also killed, was twenty-five year old *Oberleutnant* Ernst Leonhardi of Blasewitz (the latter being in command of the aeroplane).[46]

Not all combats were so clear cut in their outcome and the phrase 'fog of war' was probably more applicable to aerial fighting than any other form of warfare. Even at the comparatively slow speeds involved in 1915, the effects of an aerial combat were difficult to ascertain. On 22 October, during an early morning patrol, Rees, accompanied by Lieutenant Skeate[47] as his observer, spotted an Albatros some 2,000 feet below that seemed to be unaware of their presence. As the Vickers dived towards it, Skeate opened fire, emptying one drum before the German realised that he was under attack. The enemy machine then turned and commenced a dive for the relative safety of its own lines. Rees followed and his observer fired a second drum at the Albatros and both of them saw something break away from the enemy machine but neither could tell whether it was a piece of fabric or simply a map falling from the cockpit. They reported having seen the majority of the bullets entering the enemy's nacelle but, due to the superior speed of the Albatros, Rees was unable to keep up with it and the German machine was last seen, under control, heading eastwards.

At 10.00 hours the same day, Rees, this time accompanied by Lieutenant Slade,[48] took off in pursuit of an LVG which had audaciously flown over Villers Bretonneux aerodrome. Climbing to 5,500 feet and about eight miles behind the German lines, they lost their target, but a second German machine, a 'Two-Tails', was spotted flying about 2,000 feet below them. Unaware of their presence, the enemy pilot continued on his course until anti-aircraft fire drew his attention to the fact that he was not alone in the air and he began to circle and climb above them. Rees then turned to climb after him. When the Vickers was about 500 feet below the LVG which was still climbing, the German observer opened fire. Slade, however, did not return fire, preferring to wait until he was in a more favourable position. The German had no intention of becoming involved in close combat and headed off deeper into his side of the lines. En route back to the airfield at Villers Bretonneux, Rees spotted yet another German machine which, as soon as it saw the Vickers, escaped eastwards. Yet again, the lack of speed of the Vickers had prevented any decisive combats taking place and allowed the enemy machines to fight another day. The enemy had certainly learned not only to respect the Vickers FB5 as a combat machine, but also that discretion was the better part of valour and that if they decided to make a run for home there was little chance of their being caught.

On 27 October, 11 Squadron was again on the move, this time to Bertangles, about five miles north of Amiens. This was described as being 'very comfortable quarters. The aerodrome was a good one though inclined to get swampy in parts during the wet weather.'[49] Four days later, Rees and Flight Sergeant Raymond[50] were patrolling at 7,000 feet over Bapaume when they spotted an LVG approaching with the obvious intention of catching them unawares. As soon as Rees turned to meet the attack, the hostile machine began to turn away, and in desperation, at an extreme range of about 400 yards, Raymond opened fire and the LVG commenced a dive westwards in the direction of Pys with the Vickers in pursuit. For once Rees saw the gap between the two machines beginning to close and continued the chase until both machines were at a height of between 500 and 800 feet, when the enemy pilot levelled off his descent. Both Rees and Raymond reported having seen what appeared to be fabric falling from the German aircraft. The Vickers was now at a dangerously low height, immediately above a German anti-aircraft battery and became the target for every machine gun between Pys and Ivnes. In level flight, the enemy pilot began to widen the gap between himself and his pursuer and Rees was reluctantly compelled to abandon the chase. He landed back at Bertangles without further incident only to discover that his machine had been peppered with small arms fire from the ground.

This was to be Rees' last combat whilst serving with 11 Squadron as during November he received orders to return to England where he was to take up an appointment as an instructor at the Central Flying School. However, shortly before his departure, an event occurred which was to become famous in the history of the squadron and served to illustrate its aggressive and persevering nature.

On 7 November, the crews of 11 Squadron had a busy day patrolling the whole Third Army front to provide cover for 8 and 13 Squadrons which had been involved in bombing the Achiet-le-Petit area. At about 14.30 hours, Lieutenant Gilbert Insall[51] and 1/Air Mechanic TH Donald[52] (3022) were patrolling in FB5 (5074) at a height of 7,000–8,000 feet between Bois d'Adinfer and Bapaume when they spotted an enemy kite balloon. Diving into the attack, Insall decided to drop an incendiary bomb in an effort to destroy it, but misjudged his approach and was forced to break away amidst intensive anti-aircraft rocket fire. Noting the position of the enemy battery, he began to climb away when he saw an Aviatik two-seater approaching from the north, some 2,000 feet higher. Turning west, Insall got his machine into a position whereby Donald could open fire at long range with his Lee-Enfield rifle. This action caused the German pilot to change course and

Lieut Gilbert Insall, VC.

head east out of harm's way. Insall continued to head towards the British lines hoping to lull the German into believing that he was heading for home. The ruse worked and the Aviatik again changed course and resumed his patrol of the front line. Suddenly the Vickers changed direction and Donald opened fire with the Lewis gun and, for the second time the German pilot turned away in an effort to avoid combat or, perhaps to lure the Vickers back over the anti-aircraft battery. Undaunted, Insall gave chase and, as the Aviatik dived, so did he, determined to close the gap and bring the German within range. Again Donald opened fire and the enemy's engine was seen to stop just before both machines disappeared into a cloud. When the Vickers emerged from the other side, its prey was down at ground level about to make a forced landing in a ploughed field.

Both the German pilot and his observer were seen climbing out of their machine once it had come to a halt and the latter was carrying his machine gun. As Insall passed overhead, Donald fired again at the stationary machine and its retreating crew and, as they made a second pass, dropped an incendiary bomb that had originally been intended for the kite balloon. Whether by luck or good judgement, the bomb hit the Aviatik and set it ablaze.

By this time, the Vickers was coming under an increasing amount of small arms fire from the ground and Insall commenced as rapid a climb as the Monosoupape was capable of. As they approached the front line, he dropped towards the ground and Donald raked the German trenches as they passed. Hit in numerous places, the Vickers was on the verge of escaping when one bullet hit the fuel tank and, as the engine depended upon a pressure feed system for its fuel supply, it immediately stopped. There was very little time to think as they were so close to the ground and Insall just managed to clear a small wood near the village of Agny, about 500 yards inside the French lines. Despite heavy shelling from the Germans, the Vickers survived without further damage until darkness fell.

Back at Bertangles, Lieutenant Robin Hughes-Chamberlain was in the squadron office with the commanding officer.

> Dawes was cursing Insall up hill and down dale because he hadn't arrived back – 'What the hell was the fellow doing now?' … and then the telephone rang and he started to blaspheme until Insall got it into his head to tell him 'We've shot down a German aircraft.' Dawes was highly excited. He yelled for Rees (the senior flight commander of 11 Squadron, a good organiser and very efficient fellow), who came along and Dawes said, 'Take a tender, put in a new tank, all the appliances and petrol and everything else that you want, and some mechanics to run the show.' Rees was very good at anything of that kind; first class man in fact.[53]

Rees and his small band of men drove down to the landing site which was some distance away from the aerodrome, located the Vickers and, under masked lights, supervised the removal of the damaged fuel tank and the fitting of a replacement. They then made all the checks that were possible in the circumstances and, almost too late, realised that the new tank was also leaking, but managed to resolve the problem and declared the machine fit to fly. It was pointless risking two lives trying to bring back one aeroplane, so Donald returned with the mechanics and his place in the front cockpit was filled with sandbags which served as ballast. As the first light of dawn crept over the German trenches, Insall made a successful take off and, a few minutes later, landed safely at his base. One week later, both he and Donald were wounded and forced to land behind German lines where they were taken prisoner and it was in these circumstances that Insall received the news that he had been awarded the Victoria Cross for his action on 7 November and that Donald had received the Distinguished Conduct Medal.

There can be little doubt that the airmen of 11 Squadron helped to lay a foundation for the RFC of highly skilled, aggressive aerial combatants upon which the reputation of Britain's fighter pilots in two world wars was built. They were the worthy forerunners of men like Ball, McCudden, Mannock, Tuck, Malan and Johnson, and no-one deserves more credit for creating this reputation than Lionel Rees, the very first of the original 'Few.' They were men who braved the skies in fragile machines of wood, fabric and wire to prove that aerial combat was possible as long as airmen were well trained, well led and fired with the belief that they were better than the enemy. This was the message which Rees took back with him to England on 21 November and which, after a week's leave, he carried to the CFS at Upavon. Not only had he firmly established his own reputation as a combat pilot, but he had also (in conjunction with Flight Sergeant Hargreaves) proved himself to be the most successful pilot of the Vickers FB2, with a 'score' of six aerial victories.

No sooner was Rees back from his leave than he was commissioned by the RFC to put his and the Corps' philosophy on aerial combat into words and, early in 1916, he published a 32-page booklet entitled *Fighting in the Air*, which is of interest not only because it was the very first of its kind, paving the way for others in later years, but also for its comparative brevity, simplicity and rather naive approach to the deadly business of this aspect of aerial warfare. Based mainly upon his own experience, the booklet also drew upon the knowledge of others, and for that reason it can be said to be representative of the views of front-line pilots and observers at that time. His selection to write *Fighting in the Air* is an indicator of the regard in which he was held by those in high office and the fact that such a publication was commissioned at all showed clearly that there was a new attitude to military aviation by the end of 1915. On the outbreak of hostilities the previous year, supporters of military aviation had hoped that it would serve as the eyes of the army, but many senior officers thought that even that lowly ambition was too high an expectation of the new corps. Sir Douglas Haig had said in July 1914 'I hope none of you gentlemen is so foolish as to think that aeroplanes will be able to be usefully employed for reconnaissance in the air.' By the time of the battle of Loos, the effectiveness of aerial reconnaissance had been proved and had led to the extension of the combatant nature of the war to the third element as armed machines set out to deliberately destroy the enemy's reconnaissance machines in order to prevent observations being carried back to the military planners. Haig had declared then that if bad weather prevented aircraft from flying, they should call off the attack, and in his first despatch as C-in-C from GHQ on 19 May 1916 he wrote, 'In the air there is seldom a day, however bad the weather, when aircraft are not busy reconnoitering, photographing, and observing fire. All this taking place constantly at any hour of the day or night, and in any part of the line.' It has been argued that the efforts made by both sides during the four years of aerial warfare were to no avail as, if aeroplanes had not been used for military purposes, both sides would have been at an equal disadvantage or, if aeroplanes were to be used, there was little purpose in the great emphasis placed upon their mutual destruction as the intelligence which they carried was of little long-term value; it did not take numerous reports from airmen to confirm to either side that an attack was imminent, the scale of the preliminary artillery barrage served as a more than adequate warning.

Fighter units such as 11 Squadron were organised primarily for the purpose of attacking and bringing down the enemy's machines and carried offensive armament, whereas reconnaissance squadrons were equipped with machines that were, on the whole, heavier and less manoeuvreable and were intended to observe the enemy's movements, photograph his positions and, if necessary, bomb selected targets. These roles were, however, interchangeable and very often fighter pilots and observers carried out reconnaissance patrols while reconnaissance pilots often had to fight their way to and from a target. The heavier losses sustained by the RFC in 1915 required a new approach to military flying, leading to the obvious conclusion that the more highly trained and better informed the novice airman was *before* he went to the front, the better were his chances of surviving once he was posted to a service squadron.

One former RFC officer who served under Rees' command in 1916, recalled that he was a good pilot, but probably not a great one, and that in terms of tactics he held a very simplistic view, namely attack the enemy whenever he was encountered and that in comparison to the great 'aces' he was a very long way behind tactically. If this opinion is an accurate assessment of Rees' talents then one must question why it was that he was selected to produce the first manual of aerial combat? Today, with the benefit of hindsight it is possible to argue that Rees was perhaps a better pilot and tactician than might have been apparent in 1916.

The period of Rees' actual combat flying was very short and, at the end of 1915 amounted to only four months during a period when machines were underpowered and had very limited fighting capabilities. The relatively simple and lightly armed Vickers FB5 would have been no match for the later, much more powerful and sophisticated Sopwith Camel and SE5A which dominated aerial combats during the latter stages of the war. When the men who were recognised as great tacticians, Ball[54] and Mannock[55] in particular, made their names, aircraft design was very much more advanced. Ball began his flying career in the sluggish BE2c and later flew the Bristol Bullet, but met with no success against an enemy who was then armed with superior machines. It was not until he joined 11 Squadron in May 1916 and was given a Nieuport Scout that he was able to enter into combats of his own volition and, even then, it was some time before he was able to achieve any success in terms of enemy machines destroyed. Ball, however, was lucky and managed to survive this dangerous period of his career while evolving his own tactics, learning to stalk his opponent until he was in a position (ideally immediately below the German machine) to open fire with the Lewis gun which was fitted to his upper wing. The Nieuport, although a fine aeroplane for the time, had one major weakness, its wings tended to collapse if it was pushed too hard in a dive. Ball's *modus operandi* went a long way towards eliminating this danger in combat. When, in 1917, the squadron in which he was then serving was equipped with the SE5, he received special permission to carry on flying the Nieuport in which he continued to achieve success.

That other great RFC fighter pilot, Mick Mannock, deemed by many to have been the greatest of them all, was viewed with some suspicion by his colleagues for a considerable time during the early part of his flying career. For him, the Nieuport Scout was a jinxed machine in which he initially found it almost impossible to obtain a confirmed 'kill' (he was airborne for over forty hours during April 1917, a period of intense German activity in the air, before he managed to bring down an opponent). Careful study of the problem and plenty of practice, coupled with the good luck to stay alive long enough, eventually paid off. Once the skill had been mastered, Mannock analysed the methodology, believing there must be a formula for destroying an enemy machine, just as he believed there was for other problems. From this point, his successes began to mount and he became almost unbeatable when flying the SE5A; if Mannock entered a combat he was expected to win. If the problem facing him did not conform to his formula for success, he would avoid action until it did. His motto, which he always passed on to young and inexperienced pilots was very simple, 'Always above, seldom on the same level and never beneath.' It was easy to abide by this ruling in 1917–18 when machines like the SE5a could climb to 19,000 feet and reach 10,000 feet in a little under thirteen minutes. The Vickers which Rees flew had a ceiling of 9,000 feet and took sixteen minutes to reach 5,000 feet. If one adds the ever-increasing numbers of enemy machines which flew over Allied lines to the mechanical advantages enjoyed by pilots during the latter part of the war, then it is not surprising that personal scores were higher. Very few pilots who flew in the opening rounds of the air war were still flying by 1917–18, many of those that had survived held command positions, but of those who did fly it is noticeable that it was during the latter period that they achieved most of their success in terms of the destruction of enemy machines. Rees' compatriot, Ira 'Taffy' Jones,[56] had the highest score rate of any British pilot during the war, claiming his first success on 9 May 1918 and his thirty-seventh on 7 August, a period of only ninety days. Between his first victory on 28 July and his sixth (his last with 11 Squadron) on 31 October (95 days), Rees had encountered fewer than ten German machines in the air, but had claimed victory over six of them.

By the last year of the war, a number of squadrons were gaining reputations for the scores which their pilots were accumulating. This was a result of the introduction of formation flying; no longer were individual machines venturing out alone, or even in pairs. The usual patrol strength in 1918 was a flight, or even a full squadron, and this security in numbers paid dividends in the total of enemy machines destroyed. In 1915, such tactics were beyond the capabilities of the aircraft then in service as had clearly been shown by 11 Squadron during its attempt to escort the King on his visit to Netheravon. Given the advantages enjoyed by pilots in later years, there would seem to be little doubt that Rees, and probably many others, would have accumulated substantial scores and one cannot but pose the question what would the pilots of 1918 have managed to achieve had their combat service been restricted to the earlier part of the war and the aeroplanes then in use?

Rees was a member of that school of military gentlemen who had seen their world vanish in August 1914; a world where it was counted a blessing to have been born British, destined by divine authority to control half the world. Today, patriotism, empire, even loyalty are words which have become viewed as objects of derision, but to the generation that fought the Great War they were almost a religion, badges to be worn with pride. To serve King and Country was an obligation which they (and hundred of thousands of volunteers) felt honoured to fulfil and, in the days before mass communications enlightened even the most basically educated, there is little wonder that the propaganda stories of atrocities commonplace during the early days of the conflict were accepted so readily when the entire nation had been indoctrinated with such opinions. Rees' attitudes are clearly evident in *Fighting in the Air*.

> The British pilot always likes the idea of fighting and is self reliant. He is a quick thinker compared with the enemy, so that he has the advantage in manoeuver [sic]. He fights for the sport of the affair, if for no other reason. The Enemy Pilot on the other hand, is of a gregarious nature from long national training, and often seems bound by strict rules, which cramp his style to a great extent. The Enemy Pilots are often uneducated men, being looked upon simply as drivers of the machine, while the Gunner or Observer is considered a grade higher than the Pilot. This last gives a great advantage to us, as, whereas our Pilots act from a sense of *Noblesse Oblige*, the Enemy, when in a tight corner, often fails to seize and press an advantage.

Although this statement reads as naive propaganda, there is a great element of truth in it. Rees' opinion of Germans as combatants is supported by many other Allied airmen of the time who state that the enemy rarely flew missions over the British lines and, when they did, they were either in large numbers or very high up, which made interception very difficult. The British airmen on the other hand, were actively encouraged (some might argue foolishly so) to cross the front line in pursuit of the enemy. The Germans certainly, throughout the war, saw the observer as the senior member of the two-man crew of their aeroplanes and he was therefore the commissioned officer, whilst the pilot was often an NCO. This changed somewhat when the Germans introduced the concept of the single-seater fighter but, even then, they flew in large numbers as evidenced by the infamous Flying Circus of the renowned ace Manfred von Richthofen, the so-called 'Red Baron'. Many RFC pilots did not regard Richthofen as the great knight of the air that he was portrayed as by the media during and after the war. Gwilym Lewis,[57] who served with Rees in 32 Squadron and later with Mannock in 40 Squadron, and who finished his service with a score of twelve enemy machines destroyed, when asked by a television interviewer in 1987 what he thought of Richthofen replied, 'I never liked Richthofen. He was, eh, can you tell me the right word for bullshitter? He rather threw his weight about, had a chap looking after his tail most of the time. He was unattractive.'[58] At about the same time, in conversation with the present author, Lewis described Richtofen simply as, 'Bastard, he picked off the weakest in a combat.'

Rees saw the role of the fighter pilot as being very clear cut – to engage the enemy and destroy him. By the enemy he meant the machine and this would seem to hint at the chivalry which is believed to have existed during the early years of the war. For him the death of an enemy airman was the only means of ensuring the destruction of the enemy machine.

… it is not sufficient to make a machine land, as machines are comparatively easy to obtain. Every effort should be made to disable the Enemy Pilot as this nearly always ensures the destruction of the machine as well.[59]

When Gwilym Lewis was asked what he thought of this chivalry, he replied, 'Mostly I would say it's a lot of balls. I think in the early stages of the war, in 1914 and early part of 1915, they used to pop at each other with sporting rifles … they would miss and probably wave. But I never waved to a Hun if there was any chance of shooting him down and I never knew a Hun who would spare any effort to shoot me down if he could. I never, nor any of my colleagues, saw any acts of chivalry on our side or the German side.'[60] Freddy West, VC, recalled, 'I never saw, nor any of my colleagues, any act of chivalry either on the German side or on our side. What is war, you are going to war to kill your enemy?'[61] If the pilot was to be hit then he had to be the main target. He was a comparatively small area at which to aim, Rees estimated it to be no larger than 2 feet x 1 foot 6 inches x 1 foot 6 inches. He believed that it should be the prime ambition of every British pilot or observer to be able to hit such a target consistently and, in order to achieve this, the method of attack had to be carefully studied and practised. 'A pilot,' he said, 'must be constantly on the alert, always ready to make a surprise attack on the enemy by approaching the target unobserved and, at the same time, ensuring that he was not himself caught off guard by another enemy machine' – lines so reminiscent of the mantra of fighter pilots in the Second World War.

> If an unobserved machine opens fire it takes at least 2 seconds [for the attacked airman] to pick him up and come into action. By that time the enemy has fired twelve rounds, which are quite enough to do serious damage.[62]

There was little purpose in a fighting machine being in a position to destroy the enemy only to discover that he was out of ammunition. The most common cause of this embarrassing and highly dangerous situation was that the pilot had opened fire too soon, expending his valuable ammunition to no other purpose than to make the enemy aware of his presence. 'There should be no long range shooting. One should try to close to within 50 yards in order to do any damage.'[63]

If the pilot had the advantage of surprise and range, and had developed a reasonable skill at hitting the target, the final question which he had to consider was the angle of the attack. Traditionally, the image of a fighter attack during the Great War is that of two machines in line, the one at the rear being in close pursuit of the other, the pilot of which is weaving and turning as he desperately tries to throw off his pursuer. This was by no means always the case and was certainly not the approach advocated by Rees.

> If we attack a machine from directly in front or in rear the engine may cover the pilot's body or vice versa. This is the minimum target which the machine can present, and any shots hitting the target do damage, but there is a lot of room round the target in which shots which do not actually strike do no damage.
>
> Now, if we imagine a machine being attacked from the side, or straight from above or below, the target which we must aim for [the pilot] still remains the same small one, but now the rounds, which before were non-effective, will hit the engine and Observer, and will become effective.[64]

He summed up his ideas in a simple but rather lengthy list.

Open fire before the enemy.

Open fire at the shortest possible range.

Open fire under the most favourable circumstances.

Try to disable the enemy at once.

Close as soon as you can, so as to prevent the Enemy setting his sights and taking aim.

It is useless expecting to hit successfully at ranges over 400 yards.

Reserve your fire till within 100 yards of the Enemy, but if discovered open fire before the Enemy.

At ranges of 50 yards and under, if attacking from the flank, aim at the Enemy's leading edge as you see it (one or other wing top). This statement is only a guide.

If one must collide go straight up, as the enemy nearly always goes straight down. Then, if one hits the enemy one hits him with one's undercarriage.

Do not collide unless by accident. If the enemy pilot is disabled the enemy machine may travel quite normally for a long time, so that one runs the risk of wrecking one's own machine uselessly.

If it is necessary to change drums, dive under a tractor as that upsets his aim.

As a rule it does not pay to follow a machine down below 3,000 feet. At that height the machine guns from the ground become dangerous, and if the enemy machine is not disabled before that it will probably not be disabled at all.

It is dangerous to cross the tenches at heights below 2,000 feet.

If no enemy is in sight, never fly straight, even on our side of the lines. This prevents the enemy getting the size of the machine accurately. If the size is known it is very easy to get the range at short distances, as used in fighting in the air.

Do not take anything for granted. Work out all your own deflections, etc, for your machine.

No two machines fly normally at the same speeds.

Do not get put out when you find that your pet theory does not work.[65]

Almost obvious in its simplicity, Rees' manual also deals at some length with the actual mechanics of aerial combat; such items as the mechanics of deflection shooting, trajectory and sighting being dealt with in considerable detail and it is for this section in particular that *Fighting in the Air* deserves to be remembered.

By the beginning of 1916, the so-called 'Fokker Scourge' was having its effect over the Western Front. The Fokker *Eindecker*, the machine that Rees had encountered and destroyed on his first day in France with 11 Squadron, was appearing in numbers and, in the hands of skilled pilots such as Max Immelmann[66] and Oswald Boelcke,[67] was shooting down British machines in considerable numbers. The novice pilots of 1914 and 1915 had received only the most basic of training, learning how to handle their machines in routine flights and how to assemble and shoot their weapons. Nothing had been done to teach them how to fight. It was to take the arrival of a new type of aeroplane, the single-seater fighter, and new training courses, before Britain could feel she was sending men out to fight in the air with a moderate chance of success. Rees' booklet was the first attempt to impart to new pilots and observers the knowledge gained by experience, and his role in the development of a more efficient fighting force was to continue almost immediately, and was to last until the end of the war and beyond. *Fighting in the Air* remained in print for some time and was then republished in an amended format, but the content and message were the same and it was not superceded until 1918 when the manual *Bring Down Your Hun* appeared.

Notes
1. Later Air Marshal Sir Patrick Henry Lyon Playfair, KBE, CB, CVO, MC (1889–1974), a RFA officer. He qualified to fly on 3 September 1912. He succeeded Rees as AOC Palestine and Transjordan in 1928 and retired as AOC-in-C India in 1942.
2. Later Air Commodore Charles Curtis Darley, AM, (1890–1962) of Birmingham, a RFA officer. He had qualified to fly on 15 August 1913 and was shot down and wounded by the German ace Max Immelmann October 1915 and became a prisoner-of-war. In 1919 he was flying in a Vickers Vimy from England to Egypt, piloted by his brother, Cecil, and crashed in Italy. He attempted to rescue his brother from the blazing aeroplane but was unable to get him out of the pilot's seat. He was awarded the Albert Medal.
3. Later Air Commodore Andrew George Board, CMG, DSO, DL, (1878–1973), an officer in the South Wales Borderers, who had qualified as a pilot on 29 November 1910 (RAeC certificate 36) and came to 11 Squadron from the Central Flying School where he had been an instructor. In 1916 he was the OC 10 (Army) Wing who initiated the award of the VC to Lionel Rees. He retired in 1931 having served as Chief Staff Officer, RAF HQ Middle East. Like Rees, he re-joined the RAF in 1939 and served until 1941. Coincidentally, in his latter years he resided at Glan Gwna near Caernarfon, some two miles from Rees' od family home.
4. Later Wing Commander George William Patrick Dawes, DSO, AFC, Ld'H (1881–1960), he was an officer in Royal Berkshire Regiment and served in South Africa. He learned to fly in 1910 (RAeC certificate). He was a flight commander in 2 Squadron in 1914 and, on 22 August, when acting as an observer to Major Longcroft, encountered the first German aeroplane of the war. In 1916 he was given command of 16 Wing RFC in Macedonia.
5. 'The First Fighter Squadron' by AJ Insall, *Popular Flying*, February 1935. Algernon John Insall became one of the founders of the Imperial War Museum Photographic Department and a noted aeronautical writer between the wars. He published his memoirs of the Great War under the title *Observer*. He retired to live at Pen-y-Bont, near Llandrindod Wells whee he was an enthusiastic trout fisherman. He was the brother of Gilbert Insall, VC.
6. *Observer, Memoirs of the RFC, 1915–1918*, AJ Insall, London, 1970.
7. Later Group Captain Thomas O'Brien Hubbard, MC, AFC (1882–1962), he had been the Honorary Secretary of the Royal Aeronautical Society 1908–12, obtained his RAeC Certificate (222) in 1912, and joined the RFC Special Reserve. He became an instructor at the CFS in 1914 and then a flight commander in 3 Squadron. He commanded 11 Squadron (1915–16), 75 (HD) Squadron (1917), 44 (HD) Squadron (1917), 73 Squadron

(1917–18). Served in Egypt, Palestine and Iraq during the 1920s. Hubbard wrote a number of books on early aviation and was a noted collector of Cypriot antiquities.

8. LWB Rees, 'My Personal Experiences,' article published in the American magazine *Air Travel*, October 1917.

9. Corporal John Ditchfield (2123) was commissioned a second lieutenant in the RFC in August 1917. Extract taken from a personal letter written by Lieutenant Ditchfield, held by 11 Squadron, RAF, seen by the author in 1986.

10. RFC Communique N° 1, 25–27 July 1915.

11. 11 Squadron crossed to France in two groups. Travelling by air (and led by Lionel Rees) were: Captains LWB Rees and PHL Playfair; Lieutenants CC Darley G Allen and WB Hargreaves; Second Lieutenants MT Sandys, LA Tilney, REAW Hughes Chamberlain, HVC de Crespigny, GSM Insall, HT Kemp and LA Pattinson. Travelling by sea to Boulogne were: Major GWP Dawes; Second Lieutenant AE Snape (Assistant Equipment Officer); Second Lieutenants (Observers) JR Burns, E Gowring, AJ Insall, AL Findlay, J Cemlyn Jones, CW Lane and A Murray; Flight Sergeant (Observer) Hargreaves. Letter from the War Office to GOC RFC, dated 22 July 1915, National Archives AIR 1/2148/209/3/1919.

12. This aerodrome's name was taken from that of the nearby farm and the spelling Vert Galant (as opposed to Vert Gallant or Vert Galland) is that used in the current issue of the Michelin road map.

13. Glaswegian, regular soldier Flight Sergeant James McKinley Hargreaves (1883–1963), Service N° 1232, later qualified as a pilot having obtained a RAeC certificate (1887) on a Farman biplane on 13 October 1915.

14. LWB Rees, 'Some Flying Stunts in the First Two Years of the War,' published in the USA in the *Georgetown Gazette*, 3 July 1917.

15. The Fokker E.I monoplane was a development of the Fokker A.III single-seat, reconnaissance monoplane, introduced onto the Western Front in June 1915 following the invention of the interruptor gear by Dutch engineer Anton Fokker which enabled a machine gun to be fitted to the aircraft which fired forward through the arc of the propellor. *Eindecker* is literally translated as single decker or monoplane.

16. The surviving records of 11 Squadron at this early period of its service are limited. The account of this combat is taken from the description written by Rees himself when in the USA during 1917 and published in the *Georgetown Gazette*, 3 July 1917. The official records record that this aeroplane was 'Driven down', meaning that its destruction was unconfirmed. There is no record of any German pilots being killed on 28 July 1915, so one can assume that the pilot did manage to retain sufficient control of his machine to survive the crash landing. At this time, there were fewer than twenty Fokker E.Is in service on the Western Front. Of these, a number were further south, near Verdun, and the dearth of German records makes it impossible to identify the pilot who was in combat with Rees.

17. AJ Insall, *Observer, op cit.*

18. AJ Insall, 'The First Fighter Squadron', *Popular Flying*, February 1935.

19. Major Lanoe George Hawker, VC, DSO (1890–1916), a Royal Engineers' officer, qualified as a pilot in 1913. He served with 6 and 24 Squadrons. He became the first British 'ace' of the war. He was shot down and killed by Richthofen on 23 November 1916.

20. Major Hubert Dunsterville Harvey-Kelly, DSO (1891–1917), Royal Irish Regiment, qualified as a pilot in 1913 and was the first RFC pilot to land in France following the outbreak of war, flying with 2 Squadron. He was shot down by *Leutnant* Kurt Wolff of *Jasta* 11 and died of his wounds on 2 May 1917.

21. Probably a reference to Cecil Arthur Lewis, MC (1898–1967), who flew with several squadrons during the war and was the author of *Sagittarius Rising*, the classic account of aerial combat.

22. 2Lt Herbert Ambrose Cooper (1887–1916) of Raglan, New Zealand, qualified on 27 January 1914 and was the first New Zealander to serve in the RFC. He was killed in a flying accident on 21 June 1916.

23. Later Captain Albert Ball, VC, DSO**, MC, L d'H,OStG (1896–1917), Sherwood Foresters, who served in 11 Squadron during 1916.He achieved a combat score of 44 victories.

24. AJ Insall, 'The First Fighter Squadron' op cit.

25. Corporal John Ditchfield, op cit.

26. AJ Insall, 'My Most Thrilling Flight', *Popular Flying*, December, 1934.

27. LWB Rees, article 'Some Flying Stunts in the First Two Years of the War,' published in the USA in the *Georgetown Gazette*, 3 July 1917.

28. ibid.

29. 2Lt Lane had only just joined the squadron and Rees took him on this mission to show him the ropes. Rees was convinced from the manner in which he flew that the German pilot was also a novice – LWB Rees, article 'Some Flying Stunts in the First Two Years of the War,' op cit.

30. Archie was the nickname given by the RFC to the German anti-aircraft defences and is believed to have

originated from a popular music-hall song of the time *Archibald, Certainly Not!*.

31. Combat account written by Rees and published in 'Some Flying Stunts in the First Two Years of the War,' op cit. This is also mentioned briefly in RFC Communique N° 3, 31 July–4 August, 1915.

32. This was probably an LVG C.II biplane, built by the *Luft-Verkehrs-Gesellschaft* company as a two-seater reconnaissance / light bomber. The observer had a ring-mounted machine gun in the rear cockpit. Powered by a 160 hp Mercedes engine, it had a maximum speed of 81 mph. It has not been possible to positively identify the pilot of this particular machine although the squadron history of *Feld-Flieger Abteilung 32* would suggest that it may have been *Unteroffizier* Weickert who, accompanied by *Leutnant* Albert Münz, was involved in a thirty-minute combat with what is described as a 'Farman', a similar pusher machine to the FB5. The German machine, however, was not shot down, nor did it crash. I am indebted to American air historian AE Ferko for this information.

33. The .303 Lewis gun was designed in the USA and manufactured under licence in Britain by BSA. The air-cooling sleeve was removed to reduce the weight of the gun and the ammunition was fed from a drum which held 47 rounds. It had a rate of fire of 500+ rounds per minute.

34. 11 Squadron records and RFC Communique N° 8, 28 August–5 September 1915.

35. German casualty records would suggest that this aircraft crashed near Hendecourt and the pilot, *Offizierstellvertreter* Erich Tornack, was killed. The observer appears to have survived.

36. LWB Rees, article 'My Personal Experiences,' op cit.

37. ibid.

38. This is the spelling of Esterre in the official documentation of this mission. However, as Esterre is located over 50 miles north of Peronne, it would appear to be an error. It is more likely that the target area was between Peronne and Estrées-Denieourt, which are only some five miles south west of Peronne.

39. Article by James Hargreaves entitled 'My Most Thrilling Flight', in *Popular Flying*, August, 1933.

40. The mistake made about the number of engines was the result of the design of the machine which had one engine located behind the pilot which 'pushed' it forwards through the air. Each of the tail booms extended forward slightly beyond the leading edge of the lower wings and was enclosed in what can only be described as a streamlined casing, giving the appearance of an engine. Once again, it has not been possible to identify the exact machine involved in this combat. AE Ferko informed the author that *Feld-Flieger Abteilung 23, 1(B)* and possibly 27 had AGOs at this time.

41. Supplement to the *London Gazette*, 16 November 1915. 'For conspicuous gallantry and skill on several occasions, notably the following: — On 21st September, 1915, when in a machine armed with one machine-gun and piloted by Captain Rees, a large German Biplane armed with two machine-guns was sighted 2,000 feet below. Our machine spiralled down and engaged the enemy, who, being faster, manoeuvered to get broadside on and then opened fire. The attack, however, was pressed, and the engine of the enemy's biplane was apparently struck, for after a quick turn it glided down some distance and then fell just inside the German lines. On 31st August Captain Rees, with Flight-Serjeant Hargreaves, fought a powerful German machine for three-quarters of an hour. They then returned for more ammunition and went out again to the attack. Finally the enemy's machine was brought down apparently wrecked.'

42. Supplement to the *London Gazette*, 29 October 1915. 'For conspicuous gallantry and skill on several occasions, notably the following: — On 21st September 1915, when flying a machine with one machine gun, accompanied by Flight-Serjeant Hargreaves, he sighted a large German biplane with two machine guns 2,000 feet below him. He spiralled down and dived at the enemy, who, having the faster machine, manoeuver to get him broadside on and them opened heavy fire. In spite of this, Captain Rees pressed his attack and apparently succeeded in hitting the enemy's engine, for the machine made a quick turn, glided some distance and finally fell just inside the German lines near Herbécourt.

'On 28th July he attacked and drove down a hostile monoplane in spite of the fact that the main spar of his machine had been shot through and the rear spar shattered.

'On 31st August, accompanied by Flight-Serjeant Hargreaves, he fought a German machine more powerful than his own for three-quarters of an hour, then returned for more ammunition and went out to the attack again, finally bringing the enemy's machine down apparently wrecked.'

Rees also received his first Mention in Despatches in the same issue of the *London Gazette*.

43. The only reference to this encounter is in the article 'Some Flying Stunts in the First Two Years of the War', op cit.

44. The Albatros C.I was a single 150 hp tractor-engined, two-seater aeroplane which made its first appearance in 1915. Armed with a ring-mounted machine hun in the rear cockpit, it was used as a scout, reconnaissance and bombing machine.

45. 'My Personal Experience', op cit.

46. Casualty details obtained from *Casualties of the German Air Service*.

47. Lieutenant William Arthur Skeate (1893–1976) of Vine Farm, Worplesdon, Surrey was an officer in the West Yorkshire Regiment. He learned to fly in March 1916 after service as an observer with 1 Squadron. He transferred to the RAF in 1918.

48. Observer 2nd Lieutenant Reginald James Slade, Army Cyclist Corps, attached RFC, of Wanstead, Essex. He was shot down on 25 October 1915 by *Oberleutnant* Max Immelmann while flying with Captain Charles Curtis Darley in FB5 (5462) and both became prisoners of war.

49. Letter from Major TO Hubbard, nd, to HQ RAF, BEF, National Archives, History of 11 Squadron, AIR 1/688/21/20/11.

50. Flight Sergeant Raymond is unidentified.

51. Lieutenant Gilbert Stuart Martin Insall (1894–1972), the brother of Algernon John Insall, also served with 11 Squadron as a pilot. Later Group Captain VC, MC.

52. 1st Class Air Mechanic TH Donald, DCM (3022), *London Gazette*, 22 January 1916).

53. Later Major Robert Edward Aylmer Werge Hughes-Chamberlain, AFC (1887–1972). Interview recorded with air historian Barrington Grey in 1971, preserved at the Imperial War Museum, IWM 23153.

54. Captain Albert Ball, VC, DSO, MC (1896–1917) op cit.

55. Major Edward Corringham 'Mick' Mannock, VC, DSO with two Bars, MC and Bar (1887–1918).

56. Later Wing Commander James Ira Thomas Jones, DSO, MC, DFC and Bar (1896–1960).

57. Later Wing Commander Gwilym Hugh Lewis, DFC (1897–1996), author of *Wings Over the Somme 1916–18*.

58. *Cavalry of the Clouds*, broadcast by HTV in 1987.

59. *Fighting in the Air*.

60. *Cavalry of the Clouds*, op cit.

61. Later Air Commodore Ferdinand Maurice Felix West, VC, CBE, MC (1896–1988), Royal Munster Rifles, flew with 8 Squadron in 1918. He later became managing director and chairman of J Arthur Rank Film Distributors. Interview recorded for *Cavalry of the Clouds*, broadcast by HTV in 1987.

62. *Fighting in the Air.*

63. Ibid.

64. Ibid.

65. ibid.

66. *Oberleutant* Max Immelmann (1890–1916), *Der Adler von Lille* (The Eagle of Lille), the first German airman to be awarded the *Pour le Merit* (the Blue Max). He developed the flying manoeuvre known as the Immelmann Turn and was credited with fifteen aerial combat victories.

67. *Hauptman* Oswald Boelcke (1891–1916) was considered the father of air fighting tactics, advocating formation fighting rather than single combats. He taught Manfred von Richthofen how to fly and fight in the air. He published his rules of aerial combat *Dicta Boelke* in which he said:

Try to secure the upper hand before attacking. If possible, keep the sun behind you.
Always continue with an attack you have begun.
Open fire only at close range, and then only when the opponent is squarely in your sights.
You should always try to keep your eye on your opponent and never let yourself be deceived by ruses.
In any type of attack, it is essential to assail your opponent from behind.
When over the enemy's lines, always remember your own line of retreat.
If your opponent dives on you, do not try to get around his attack, but fly to meet it.
In principle, it is better to attack in groups of four or six. If fights break up into a series of single combats, pay attention that several comrades would not go after one opponent.

Gwilym H Lewis regarded Boelcke as 'a gentleman, who always fought a fair fight'.

IV

32 SQUADRON, RFC
(1916)

FOLLOWING HIS RETURN FROM FRANCE AND AFTER A SEVEN DAY LEAVE, Rees was promoted to the rank of temporary major on 28 November and posted as an instructor to the Central Flying School where pilots who had been taught the basics of flying at one of the numerous service or private flying schools, were taught to fly service machines and underwent additional classroom training in aeronautics, navigation and mechanics. The school had been established in 1912 on a 2,400 acre site, two miles from the village of Upavon in Wiltshire, close to Lark Hill. The airfield was located on a rather bleak plateau and was a puzzle to many who saw it, being exposed to every wind, from every direction, and it quickly acquired the nickname 'Siberia.' Nevertheless, the CFS prospered and throughout the war and for many years afterwards, successfully turned out thousands of qualified airmen for the RFC and RAF.

Due to the increasing numbers of aerial combats which were taking place over the Western Front, the War Office decided to establish several single-seater squadrons. Often referred to by the misnomer of 'Scout' squadrons, they were to set the pattern of future fighter development. The French pilot, Roland Garros[1] had, the previous April, succeeded in shooting down a German machine using a machine gun which could be fired through the arc of the propellor; damage being avoided by means of Sauliner deflector plates which were fitted to the rear of each blade. The weakness of the system was that when bullets struck the deflector plates there was no guarantee where they would go and they could cause damage to the machine from which they were fired. Garros went on to score two further victories before being forced to land through engine failure behind enemy lines where his machine was captured intact. Within two days, the Dutch aviation engineer Anthony Fokker, who was employed by the Germans, had developed a synchronized machine gun that fired forward through the arc of the propellor without the need for deflector plates. This mechanism was fitted to the Fokker EI *Eindecker* and on 15 July 1915, the first Allied machine was shot down using it. This quickly caused considerable consternation among Allied airmen who encountered a Fokker, and the

Germans appeared to have gained the upper hand in aerial combat. In reality, however, the Fokker had a very limited flying performance and British pilots who flew a captured machine under test conditions in April 1916 reported that, despite a very well-manufactured engine, its speed was '… the same as that of a 80 hp Morane Scout, but the climb is not nearly so fast. The lateral control is distinctly bad. The machine pulls up well in a very short distance after landing.' It could be dived very steeply and, showing an air speed of 115 mph, came out of a dive with complete ease. However, as a reconnaissance machine it was very poor and had no armour protection. Its average maximum speed at ground level was 86.4 mph.' The Fokker's only significant advantage over comparable Allied machines was the forward-firing gun which, when coupled with the numerous British incursions over German territory, led to losses which would have equally affected the Germans had they crossed the front line in comparable numbers. This information was revealed in 1916, but in the meantime, enemy propaganda made the most of the opportunity and created a totally unwarranted reputation for the Fokker, turning it into something of a 'super' aeroplane. Their despatches emphasised British and French losses, whilst ignoring their own, and bore no relationship to the real situation. Even today, the term 'Fokker Scourge' is still used to refer to the losses inflicted by the *Eindecker* during the summer months of 1915 and through the winter of 1915–16. It may be recalled, however, that on his very first day in action with 11 Squadron, Rees and Flight Sergeant Hargreaves had brought down an *Eindecker* and the type held no particular fear for the men of the new British fighter aeroplanes. British aircraft losses during the four weeks of January 1916 totalled thirteen, whilst the Germans lost nine, with two others probably destroyed; hardly a 'scourge' for which the RFC had no answer.

There were two distinct categories of fighting machine flown by pilots in the Great War. The first was an aircraft designed around the pilot's field of fire and the unobstructed view of the airspace around him. The second was the aircraft designed for performance in the air irrespective of its actual fighting abilities. Among the former, the 'pusher' biplane was viewed as the ideal, with the engine positioned out of the way behind the pilot who then had a clear view of the sky ahead of him. In 1915, this type of machine was exemplified for the British by the Vickers FB5 and for the Germans by the AGO C.I. In the latter category, the 'tractor' type was paramount, with an engine fitted in front of the pilot, which had a performance far superior to anything that could be fitted into a 'pusher' machine. Unable to develop their own effective forward-firing gun system, the British and French had either to use a pusher aircraft with a gun fitted to fire over the top wing (such as the Nieuport Scout) or at an angle of some 45° from the fuselage alongside the engine housing (to avoid bullets striking the propellor blades). Neither of these designs were ideal for aerial combat due to the great difficulties encountered when trying to aim the gun, particularly with a deflection shot. Consequently, the RFC relied heavily upon the pusher machine and squadrons equipped with aeroplanes such as the FB5 were able to achieve a measure of success in destroying the enemy when he was willing to stand and fight it out.

In January 1915, the aeroplane designer Geoffrey de Havilland, working for the Aircraft Manufacturing Company (Airco), had produced the prototype DH1, a two-seater pusher machine very similar in appearance and performance to the FB5. In June, de Havilland unveiled a development from this machine, a smaller, single-seater fighter designated the DH2. As a flying machine it had the typical characteristics of a 'pusher.' The 100 hp Gnome Monosaupape rotary engine produced a great deal of torque which necessitated the pilot holding the stick hard over to counter its effects in order to fly straight and level. The aircraft's very high power to weight ratio meant that careless handling could easily result in a spin when the engine was switched off. To avoid this potentially cataclysmic problem the pilot's natural reaction was to raise the nose, but this merely accentuated the difficulty which, if it occurred near the ground, would be disastrous. Instead of the normal fuel supply system, the aircraft had a hand controlled needle-valve which meant that there was no throttle and therefore no means of controlling the speed; the engine either ran at

Airco DH2, one of the two original machines supplied to 32 Squadron for training purposes in 1916.

The 100 hp Gnome Monosaupape rotary engine, showing a cutaway of the upper cylinder and the crank case. The whole of this engine rotated with the propellor around the crank. A single spark plug can be seen on the outside of each cylinder case, with a tappet and con-rod emerging from the top.
[Aeronautics, Handbook of the Collections Illustrating the Propulsion of Aircraft, MJB Davy and GT Richards, 1930]

full power or was cut out by switching off the supply of petrol or cutting the ignition switch. According to the men who flew it, the DH2 had three speed settings: full speed, dud speed (when a fault occurred) and stop. This meant that the machine's landing speed had to be regulated by switching the engine on and off, or 'blipping' as it was called. This in turn caused the machine to lurch to one side, an effect which the pilot had to be prepared for if he was to avoid a crash.

Although the DH2's pilot had excellent visibility and was positioned away from the engine fumes, his exposed situation at the front of the machine made him feel very cold. The renowned fighter pilot James McCudden[2] recorded that, 'I didn't care whether I was shot down or not, I was so utterly frozen. I liked this machine, but knew that I should have to fly it for a long time before I became its master.'

Rees (left) and an unidentified officer standing alongside a DH2 in which he would appear to have made a bad landing, losing its under-carriage and smashing the propellor. Photographed at the CFS in 1916. Rees is wearing a long leather flying coat and helmet to combat the extreme cold suffered while flying a pusher machine. This DH2 does not appear to be fitted with a gravity feed fuel tank.
[© RAF Museum, BF/PC97–52/003]

Whilst having an inferior performance to many other types, the DH2 did have one great advantage in its ability to turn very sharply without losing height and, if able to close on an enemy machine, it could hold its own in combat. It was armed with one forward-firing .303 Lewis gun, with up to seven drums of ammunition (each containing 47 rounds), which with practice could be changed in about five seconds but necessitated the pilot taking both his hands off the controls. The DH2 was not the type of machine in which any pilot was expected to build up a high score of enemy machines destroyed. Irrespective of an individual's skill, the enemy could invariably escape by diving away as German machines were, almost without exception, faster in level flight and had a better rate of climb.

All of these problems aside, the DH2 was still a great improvement on what had been available before and its only real rivals in the Allied armoury of aeroplanes were the Nieuport Scout and the Sopwith Pup, both tractor-engined machines, neither of which became available to RFC pilots until later in the year. The squadrons that were equipped with the DH2 were expected to achieve great deeds when they arrived in France and they did not disappoint.

After minor modifications, the DH2 was evaluated by Captain Robert Maxwell Pike[3] of 5 Squadron and his report to the OC 2 Wing RFC was dated 29 June 1915.

Sir, I have the honour to report that I received an order from the War Office to proceed to Hendon on June 21st and 22nd to inspect and if possible try out this machine. On 21st the machine was ready and had been flown a few minutes previously, but difficulty arose in the pressure feed system and the machine did not fly that day. On 22 June I again proceeded to Hendon and saw Mr de Havilland try the machine in bumpy weather. She seemed to behave well but was flying rather nose heavy. The tail plane was adjusted one notch and I took the machine up. I found that she climbed exceedingly well and is apparently capable of a climb to 3500 feet fully loaded in well under 5 minutes. The speed without streamlined wires is about 85 mile per hour. The machine was flying a little nose heavy and the tail fin had not been adjusted to counteract the torque, also there was a good deal of vibration which I believe to be due

Captain Robert Maxwell Pike, RFC.

Lionel Rees seated at the controls of one of the two DH2s delivered for evaluation to the CFS in January 1916. This machine (either 5917 or 5918) was fitted with a two-bladed propellor and had the gravity fuel tank under the upper wing.This was almost certainly the machine upon which he based his handbook for the DH2. [© RAF Museum. BF/PC97–52/001– 002]

to engine and propeller being out of balance. There were a few main alterations to be made. I strongly advise wing skids and drift wires to the front of the nacelle which should prevent vibration of the instrument board. Also the fin required to be put well over and a slight alteration be made to the tail plane. Even without these alterations, which will make the machine more comfortable to fly, she will be of enormous value out here. With practice one should be able to use the gun effectively and the range of fire is very large, and the vision greater than any other machine I have flown. The alterations are to take about a fortnight and the machine will be ready to take to the Front, should approval be obtained. Streamlined wires have to be obtained and it is estimated that the speed will be increased by nearly 5 miles per hour in consequence. The seat was a little on the high side or appeared so after the Vickers. The gliding angle is surprisingly good and the machine can be landed slow enough for all ordinary purposes a little under 50 miles per hour. The day was not a good one on which to try a new machine but she seemed to go through the bumps without paying much attention to them. There is a suitable telescopic mounting for a Lewis gun fitted in the machine. I have not seen a German machine which can equal this Scout for speed and climbing power.[4]

The first production machine (4732) was delivered to 5 Squadron in France for combat evaluation, but was lost when Captain Pike was shot down on 9 August and his DH2 captured almost intact by the Germans. The first order for operational service with the RFC was delivered in late November. Two machines (numbered 5917 and 5918) were allocated to the CFS where Lionel Rees was given access to one which he tested and evaluated. As soon as he was able to familiarize himself with the new single-seater scout, in addition to writing *Fighting in the Air* and a manual on the Gnome Monosaupape engine, Rees set about writing *Notes on the De Havilland Fighting Scout (DH2)* which was published during the summer of 1916. Although very basic in nature, this manual covered all aspects of operating the new aircraft, sometimes in considerable detail.

The Nacelle

The nacelle consists of an ash framework strutted with spruce, except where the main planes are attached to the nacelle, where there are steel tubes.

The bottom of the nacelle is braced with three-ply in front, and with 20 cwt cable in the rearmost bay. The sides are braced with 12-gauge HT steel wire, and the two bays under the engine bearers with 2½ ton cable.

The bottom struts of the nascelle carry the fittings for the attachment of the rudder bar and the control lever.

On each side, at the ends of the steel tubes, are brackets for the attachment of the main planes.

Rees' sketch diagram of the frontal view of the DH2 published in Notes on De Havilland Fighting Scout (DH2). *[Imperial War Museum Library Box 69/8/I]*

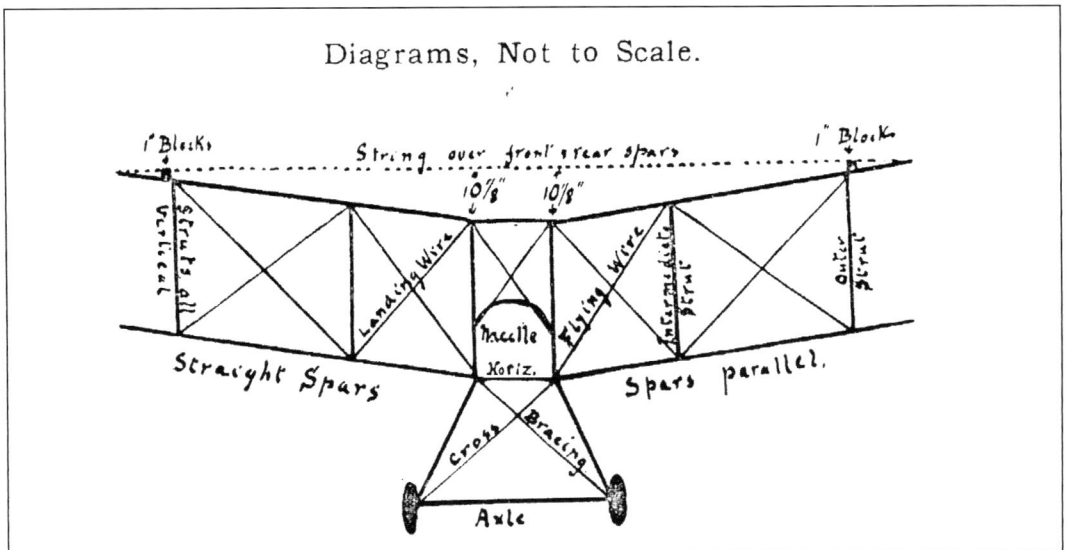

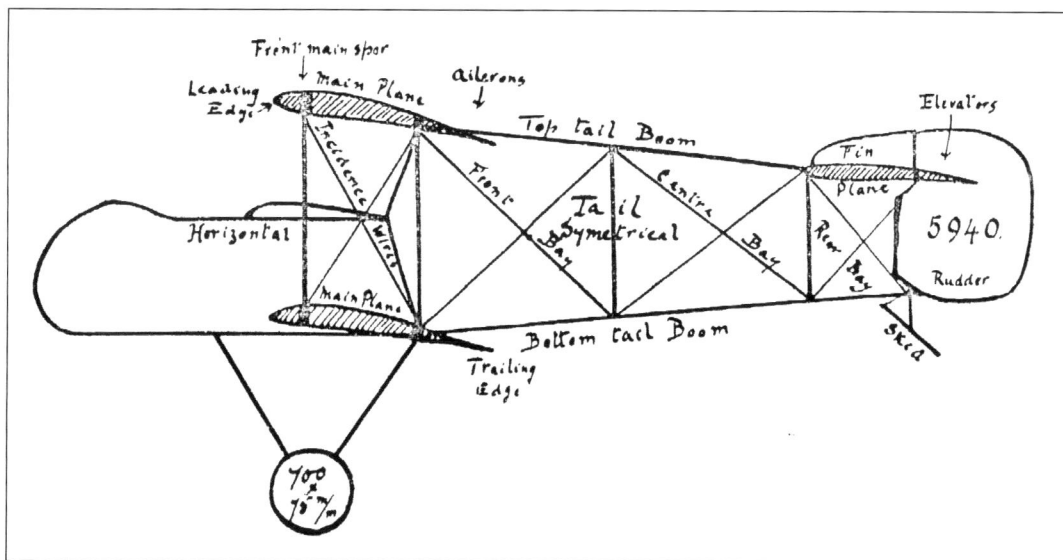

Rees' sketch diagram of the side view of the DH2 published in Notes on De Havilland Fighting Scout (DH2). *This diagram bears the registration number 5940 which was a machine delivered to 29 Squadron.* [Imperial War Museum Library Box 69/8/I]

Brackets project below the nascelle for the attachment of the under-carriage.

The adjustable gun mounting is fixed in the front of the nascelle. The front and top of the nascelle are covered with thin aluminium, and the sides with fabric. Aluminium should be free from dents and painted with a slightly matt paint, so that the machine cannot easily be seen when it is in the air. The fabric covers should be tight and well varnished so that the skin friction is small.

The fairing at the rear of the nascelle on the left side is covered with metal so that it will not be burnt by the hot exhaust gasses.[5]

In addition to the technical detail which he provided on the DH2, he gave advice on how the machine was to be rigged and how it should be dismantled for servicing and transportation by road. He gave details of how to correctly dope the wings, repair tears in the fabric and clean the aircraft, and even went into great detail about the gauge of every type of wire and cable that the machine was fitted with and the correct angles that the wings and tail should be stressed to.

Rather than convert an existing tried and tested squadron to the DH2, the RFC decided to create three new units which would go into action for the first time equipped almost exclusively with the untried machines. The first of these was 24 Squadron, which had formed at Hounslow on 1 September 1915, taking a nucleus of pilots from 17 Squadron,

Major Lanoe Hawker, VC.
[RAeC via Ancestry.co.uk]

Major Eric Conran.
[RAeC via Ancestry.co.uk]

and was intended as a two-seater fighter squadron until it was completely equipped with the DH2 in January. The renowned fighter pilot, Major Lanoe Hawker, VC,[6] was placed in command and immediately had to overcome a prejudice for the aeroplane which had developed following two fatalities whilst training. The small single-seater fighter was already being given the nickname of the 'Spinning Incinerator'. On completion of their training, the pilots flew their DH2s to France on 7 February and, following Hawker's example, the squadron quickly built up a reputation as an aggressive, successful unit.

The second DH2 unit was 29 Squadron which was formed at Gosport on 7 November (from a nucleus taken from 23 Squadron) and took delivery of its aircraft on 17 March, crossing over to France one week later under the command of Major Eric Conran.[7]

The third unit was 32 Squadron which was originally to be formed at Montrose in Scotland and the War Office issued orders to this effect in December 1915, but they were cancelled on New Year's Eve, and the squadron was to be formed at Netheravon from a nucleus of surplus personnel from 21 Squadron which was on the verge of proceeding overseas. Two or three trainee pilots and some ground crew, placed under the command of Captain SG Gilmour,[8] and allocated an assortment of Vickers FB5s and Farmans, formed the basis of the squadron on 12 January. On 1 February, command of the new unit was given to Lionel Rees with orders to prepare the squadron for active service in March.

The selection of Hawker, Conran and Rees to command the new scout squadrons is an interesting one and confirms not only their status in the RFC, but also acts as a clear indicator of what their superiors were looking for in the role of the fighter pilot. All three had already been highly decorated for aerial combat. Some years later AJ Insall wrote:

Hawker was a regular sapper, and he brought to the RFC all the calculating science of the engineer allied to the spirit of a gay cavalier. It was the debonair spirit more than anything else

An unidentified DH2 of 32 Squadron with its undercarriage having collapsed during landing. Located on top of the upper wing is the gravity fuel tank which had originally been positioned below the upper wing. [The late Gwilym H Lewis]

that, in my opinion, marked the difference between Hawker and that other great DH2 fighter, Major LWB Rees, VC. Rees was a gunner, a great strategist and a great tactician. Speaking as an observer – and observers had opportunities not given to all to judge of a pilot's capabilities – there was no one in the RFC with whom I would sooner have shared the ups and downs of a close fight than Rees. It was always my regret that, although we were in the same squadron for many months, the chance never came my way. One felt in Hawker's case, on the other hand, that he had been born to fight single-handed, and it was hard to realise that he had once flown BEs with a passenger to do his fighting for him. I have often tried to make up my mind which of the two, Rees or Hawker, was the greater; and I have never succeeded. Certain it is that both, given a machine of equal performance and neutral ground to fight over, would have made rings around any contemporary enemy pilot. Rees was the better shot – he could pick off a visiting card, right or left handed, with his service revolver at twenty-five yards. Hawker the more dashing pilot, the more capable of the unexpected manoeuvre that can decide an issue in a split second.[9]

The official historical record of 32 Squadron clearly showed why Rees had been chosen to command.

Major Rees had little to learn concerning the Monosaupape Gnome engine or the pusher type of aeroplane. As the senior Flight Commander in Nº 11 Squad-ron during the greater part of

2 Lieut Gwilym H Lewis

1915, he had become a recognised expert in matters affecting the pusher biplane; his own Vickers Fighter in that squadron had put to shame many an official performance sheet. In the actual handling of the aeroplane as in the fighting of it, he was a past master.[10]

On 13 February, Rees travelled to Hendon to take delivery of the squadron's first allocated DH2 (5941) which he flew to Netheravon. This machine, and a second DH2 (5942), were used to instruct the pilots. Apart from Rees, the only squadron member who had some previous experience of the DH2 was Captain Gilmour.

There can be little doubt that Rees had a clear vision of what he was looking for in the young men he was charged with training for combat – pilots who were aggressive, thoughtful and willing to take the fight to the enemy. Three experienced men, Captains Gilmour, Hellyer[11] and Allen,[12] were appointed as flight commanders and the remaining places were filled by unattached pilots and newly qualified men coming from the nearby CFS. One such aspiring youngster, who was typical of all the young pilots going through training at that time, was Second Lieutenant Gwilym Lewis,[13] formerly of the Northamptonshire Regiment, who had gained his RAeC certificate at Hendon on 27 November. He had then been sent to Farnborough where he flew an 80 hp Caudron 'which I think they wanted me to crash, but which I managed to keep in one piece' and then to the CFS for instruction on a BE2a 'which would spin as soon as look at you. I flew it very carefully and got through the course. I was then put on a BE2c in which I determined to do a loop. I then went on to flying a Vickers FB5 before being awarded my "wings".' He thought his chances of being selected by Rees for 32 Squadron were remote to say the least. 'Most of my friends had gone to another squadron and I thought that I would go with them. Thankfully, I did not as they were all killed.'[14] In a letter to his parents, written shortly after his arrival at Netheravon, Lewis recorded his opinion of his new commanding officer.

Major LWB Rees is in command and it is he who makes the squadron mostly ideal. He has got permission to go out as a flying commander, and he can teach every member of the squadron how to fly. He has published a booklet on how to rig the DH2 and was this evening giving a lecture on the Mono engine. He knows the job thoroughly and, above all, is a perfect gentleman. I shouldn't be surprised if he comes home with a VC; he has already got an MC. Half the reason why I am so keen to go out is because I know several of the fellows well: however, I feel the chances are remote.[15]

Seventy years later, Lewis' boyish enthusiasm of 1916 had been tempered with the moderation of maturity, but the pride of having been a member of 32 Squadron and serving under Rees, still showed through.

Rees was a very competent commanding officer and a very experienced aviator. He was very senior to the rest of us in the squadron (I was only eighteen and the baby of the unit, known to my colleagues as 'Cherub', and he was in his thirties), and full of guts. He was exciting to serve under, always very keen to have a go at the enemy and an expert at his job. Unusually for a commanding officer at that time, he knew as much as anybody about engines and the rigging of aeroplanes, so it was no use anybody trying to pretend that there was anything wrong with their machine – he would have very quickly found them out.

He had a very quiet, pleasant personality and was always smiling. He never shouted at anyone and was always the perfect gentleman. It was he who developed the squadron's philosophy – always have a go at the enemy. One felt quite instinctively that he was a courageous man.[16]

Throughout the last weeks of the winter and into the spring the novices trained, and Rees and his senior officers did all they could to dispel any fears the younger pilots may have had about the stability of their new machines. The 'Spinning Incinerator' stories had been passed on from 24 Squadron and few held any real hope for the DH2 pilots against the Fokker, until the source of the fire problem was discovered in March – the Gnome Monosaupape engine. As had been found with the Vickers the previous year, rough handling, which was part and parcel of active service, was diagnosed as the root cause of the problem. Once the ground crews and the pilots were made aware of this, the reputation of the DH2 as a serviceable fighter aircraft was re-established. One of Rees' former colleagues in 11 Squadron, Captain Robin Hughes-Chamberlain,[17] then serving as a Flight Commander in 24 Squadron, was fortunate to have survived the effects of an unbalanced engine.

I had just been sent off on a stand-by patrol and had climbed to a height of some 4,000 feet by the time I was nine miles from Bertangles [the base of 24 Squadron]. Then, without any warning, one cylinder left the engine. It knocked off one propellor blade at the root and sailed through the top mainspar of the aircraft. You always had your ears pinned back for engine trouble in that squadron and I managed to switch off the petrol and ignition almost immediately.

The loss of the propellor blade was causing very serious vibration as the remaining blade [the DH2 he was flying had a two-bladed propellor] made the engine windmill in the slipstream. The aircraft appeared to be shaking to pieces. The damage to the mainspar dislodged one of the centre struts which carried the control lines to the ailerons and elevator. I looked round to see the mainspar sagging and, at the same time, noticed the ammunition drums, which were fitted at the side of the fuselage, flying away and bursting through the fabric of the wings.

I had little time to consider the damage caused by the drums because at this moment the mainspar gave way and dropped down some six inches. My control stick was almost useless. You usually manoeuvred by moving the stick only a few inches in any one direction, but I found that I had to swing the stick round about two feet to get any response from the aircraft. The vibration was making the Lewis gun – which was mounted in front of me – hop around madly and I had little forward vision.

I realised that if I couldn't get the aeroplane to the ground soon, it would disintegrate in the air. In fact it was disintegrating already. Luckily, I had not been very high and managed to pull off a very good landing in a nearby field. I stood up in the cockpit and rested my head against the top wing for some time after I had landed, and then almost had a relapse when I realised that the tail booms, which carried the whole tail assembly, could be waved about quite easily with one hand. The aircraft was considered a complete write-off.[18]

Lieut Coleman seated in his DH2 with his rigger (in charge of the airframe) and fitter (in charge of the engine) ground crew. A rack for two spare Lewis gun drums can clearly be seen outside the cockpit (another similar rack was fitted on the starboard side).
[The late Gwilym H Lewis]

Capt Gerald Allen

Capt Stanley G Gilmour

Capt Francis Hellyer

Lieut Philip GB Hunt

Lieut Edric P Henty

Lieut Reginald A Stubbs

Lieut Sturley P Simpson

Lieut William E Nixon

Lieut John C Simpson

2 Lieut Francis H Coleman   Lieut Charles H Nicholas   Lieut Owen V Thomas

2 Lieut Hugh G Corby   Lieut Charles L Bath   Lieut Herman von Poellnitz

Previous page and above – some of the officers of 32 Squadron who flew to France in May 1916.
[RAeC via Ancestry.co.uk]

Hughes-Chamberlain had been lucky and, as the mechanics mastered the problems of servicing the Gnome engine, the reputation of the DH2 changed dramatically. The nickname 'Spinning Incinerator' was heard less often and Gwilym Lewis had no recollection of ever hearing it used in 32 Squadron.

To Rees and his flight commanders training the squadron must have seemed rather a thankless task as they turned novices in something approaching competent pilots only then to lose them. No sooner were they proficient than they were posted to fill the gaps in other squadrons, particularly 29 Squadron based at Gosport and 24 Squadron already in France. According to Rees, the squadron effectively trained all its own pilots and mechanics, and even the flight commanders, with the exception of Captain Gilmour, had no previous knowledge of either the 100 hp Mono engine or the DH2 machine.

Being a more manoeuvreable machine than the Vickers FB5, the DH2 was capable of being flown in formation, something which Rees had been advocating for some time as being essential for combat. With 11 Squadron he had only experienced machines flying patrols alone until relieved by another aircraft. The greater flexibility and responsiveness of the DH2 enabled him to develop small combat formations based upon his own hard learned theories.

> When machines fly in flights they can fly in a line, diamond formation or echelon. I rather prefer the echelon formation with the Flight Commander well out to the front.

X Flt Comdr

X

X

X

> If this formation is used, any disabled machine can easily turn out of the formation without interfering with the others.

> The Flight Commander can be seen by every machine.

> In attack, the flight Commander can use his distance to the front in order to gain height, so that, if a single enemy machine is attacked, the flight can bring a crossfire to bear from the sides and from the top.

Lieut Herman von Poellnitz at the controls of his DH2. This view clearly shows the Lewis gun which has a forward sight ring and a telescopic sight in front of the pilot, above the 1½" back sight ring. The light coloured fairing under the nose was a modification made during the summer of 1916 to catch spent cartridge cases from the Lewis gun, apparently replacing the canvas bags issued by Rees. [The late Gwilym H Lewis]

Capt Francis Hellyer, OC A Flight, 32 Squadron, with one of the unit's two Vickers ES1 Scouts (5127). This machine had been to France before returning to Britain and being reissued to 32 Squadron. 5127 was damaged on the ground on 3 June by Hellyer. [The late Gwilym H Lewis]

If the enemy are also flying in formation, because the shooting is at present bad, I do not think there would be much extra danger if the enemy machines are singled out and attacked one after the other.[19]

In addition to inadequate flying training before being posted to a squadron, few of the pilots had ever fired a machine gun in the air, or even on the ground, and a great deal of time was expended enabling them to get as much practice at this as possible over Salisbury Plain.

Major Rees and all the other pilots would fly across the open Salisbury Plain to a special ground target and fire their Lewis guns. They had a good view as the gun was a fixture right in front of them. We were watching the practice taking place when we saw Major Rees' plane make a hurried landing. The propellor had been split apart by the bullet cases flying back when the guns were fired at a fast rate. So he gave orders for canvas bags to be made and placed where the cartridge cases fly out (no more broken propellors).[20]

Range firing also resulted in modifications to the Lewis guns themselves and the DH2s of 32 Squadron were fitted with a non-standard 1½-inch ring backsight and a Bowden cable which connected the trigger to the joystick, something which became a standard feature in all later RFC machines.[21]

Divisional manoeuvres on 28 April saw two of the squadron's machines taking part, but with little success as one was forced to make two landings due to a plug cutting out and one of the ignition wires being broken by a small piece of rubber which had fallen from the pilot's pocket. At the end of the month the squadron took delivery of the first of the new DH2s which, as soon as it was up to full strength, it was to take to France.

After April, while the other pilots in the squadron flew DH2s, Rees and Captain

The Vickers ES1 Scout (known as the Bullet), serial number 7758, flow by Lionel Rees in France during June 1916. Only three of these machines were built as, despite their advanced design appearance and their being fitted with the Vickers-Challenger interrupter gear which allowed the machine gun to fire through the arc of the propellor, the pilot had a poor view both above and below. This Mark II version had a cut-out in the upper wing to improve visibility. It was sent to 1 Aircraft Depot, St Omer on 22 June.
[JM Bruce/Stuart Leslie Collection]

DH2 (5954), seen here fitted with a two-blade propellor, was originally delivered to 32 Squadron but, according to the Squadron War Diary, it left Netheravon for service with another squadron on 27 April.
[JM Bruce/Stuart Leslie Collection]

Hellyer spent most of their air time at the controls of prototype Vickers 'Bullet' Scouts. This experimental aircraft (its official designation was the Vickers ESI – Experimental Scout I), although powered by a tractor engine and of an advanced design for the period, was handicapped by its rather bulbous shape and the positioning of the upper wings above part of the cockpit and the lower wings beneath the cockpit, greatly reducing the pilot's visibility. It was also described as being difficult to fly and land, although Vickers claimed it could reach 118 mph and gain height during a loop. Official records show that probably only four or five of these machines were actually built.[22]

Although the war gave the impression of being fought a long way away, the introduction of aeroplanes had, as early as 1916, brought it much closer than the average civilian realised. A perfect example of this occurred on 26 April when the squadron diary recorded that 'Major LWB Rees left for overseas. Captain Hellyer took over temporary command of the squadron.' The following day, the adjutant noted that 'Major Rees returned this day, leaving later in De Havilland N° 5954' and, on 28 April, 'Major Rees returned from overseas.'[23] Whether Rees made two visits to France during this three day period is unclear (it was probably only one), nor is the purpose behind the trip recorded although we can speculate that it was for a dual purpose, namely to ferry a machine out to one of the squadrons already at the front and to prepare the way for 32 Squadron's own overseas posting.

The loss of pilots to other squadrons continued almost right up until 32 departed for France, a state of affairs which made preparation for active service very difficult; on 1 May, five pilots were transferred to 60 Squadron at Gosport and three to 35 Squadron at Thetford. During the second week of May, Brigadier-General Trenchard[24] visited the squadron at Netheravon where he inspected the aircraft, followed three days later by Brigadier-General Sefton Branker.[25] As the day of their departure for France drew ever closer, the first members of the squadron went on pre-embarkation leave on 16 May and, two days later, the orders for posting to France were received, Even at that late stage, one flight of pilots was selected to be left behind to form the nucleus of 24 Reserve Squadron which was about to be formed and Lieutenant McNamara was posted to 1 Reserve Squadron and Crook Rogers to a Sopwith Flight at Farnborough. According to Rees, the squadron had 'passed out some 20 to 30 pilots first solo [on the DH2] without a single crash.'[26]

It took until 20 May for the pilots of 32 Squadron to receive their full complement of DH2s, most of them having flown to Hendon to pick up their own machine. Five days later, the last of twelve aeroplanes described as 'War Machines' was serviced and examined and the final two Vickers FB5s which had been used for training were struck off the

Lionel Rees with Capt CF Gordon, MC, (N
Staffs Regt/RFC/RAF) Adjutant of 4 Wing
(later served as an observer on the Western
Front and in Russia, OBE, DFC, CdeG),
Netheravon, 28 May 1916.This photograph
was taken just before Rees took off for
Folkestone en route for France. He is wearing
what appears to be a well buttoned-up
raincoat over his normal RFC uniform. His
service cap is tucked into his belt ready for
wearing when he reaches his destination.
[SK Taylor]

squadron's books and transferred to 19 Reserve Squadron. In addition, preparation of the two Vickers 'Bullets' (5127 and 7758) was also completed.

Finally, on 26 May, the squadron transport, under the command of Lieutenant Corbett,[27] left for Avonmouth where they boarded the SS *Santa Isabel* the following morning. The remainder of the ground staff left Netheravon on the 27th, spent the night in a rest camp, and boarded the SS *Duchess of Argyle* at Southampton the following evening. JC Simpson had wrecked DH2 (6001) on 26th when, after take off and in an effort to avoid flying into the sheds, he began a turn too close to the ground and his wing tip hit a lawn mower. Simpson was unhurt. The departure of the pilots and machines from Netheravon, scheduled for early on 28 May, was delayed by mist over Wiltshire and, after last minute engine testing and a group photograph, they eventually took off at 11.00 hours and flew a cross-country course to Folkestone. En route, Lieutenant Hunt[28] had to make a forced landing at Guildford, wrecking his machine, Lieutenant Henty[29] made a safe descent near Battle after his engine had failed and von Poellnitz[30] suffered some damage to his propellor and a broken rocker. The remainder of the squadron reached the coast, landing at RFC Folkestone without incident and, after a short drive for lunch at the Hotel Metropole on the sea front, they left for France at 15.00. Rees and Hellyer made the journey in their Vickers Scouts (7758 and 5127 respectively).

Any aerial crossing of the English Channel in 1916 involved a high element of risk. Rees was the first into the air and made the crossing alone in order to make arrangements for the squadron's accommodation in France. As the remainder of the machines took off, von Poellnitz and Corby[31] were left behind while the others made a safe crossing in three formations, eventually landing at the RFC Depot in St Omer, some twenty miles behind the front line, where they were complimented on their efficiency by Brigadier-General Trenchard. Lewis recalled 'I had only done 4½ hours on the DH2 when I flew across to France in a rotten aeroplane. As I flew across, the engine was popping and I was constantly watching out for a ship that I could land alongside in the event of an emergency.'[32]

The following day, Bath,[33] who had been left behind in England, made the crossing to rejoin the squadron. Some distance out over the Channel, a tappet rod in his engine seized up but, fortunately, he had sufficient height to enable him to reach the French coast and attempt a landing on the cliff top. As he touched down he realised that he was moving too fast and, as the aircraft had no brakes, ran over the edge of the cliff. Either by luck or judgement, or a combination of the two, he managed to retain control of the DH2 and made a successful landing on the beach below. Unfortunately, despite this remarkable

The pilots of 32 Squadron, photographed at Netheravon on 28 May prior to taking off for France.
Standing (back row): Charles Bath, Herman von Poellnitz, Eric Henty, Gwilym Lewis, John Simpson,
Charles Nicholas. Seated (back): William Nixon, Sturley Simpson, Owen Thomas.
Seated (centre): Reginald Stubbs, Gerald Allen, Stanley Gilmour, Lionel Rees, Francis Hellyer.
Seated (on the ground): Francis Coleman, Hugh Corby and Philip Hunt. [The late Gwilym H Lewis]

escape, the following day, whilst trying to take off, he ran into a concealed wire and his machine was written off, although he himself appears to have escaped injury.[34] Of the fourteen machines that left Netheravon, nine arrived safely at St Omer, which was regarded as a fine effort (29 Squadron had only managed to arrive with four machines intact when it made the crossing).

The contingent aboard the *Duchess of Argyle* arrived at Le Havre in the early hours of the morning of 29 May, and from there made their way to a rest camp at Rouen to await the transport. Two days later, they were at the docks to supervise the unloading of the stores and left the following morning to rejoin the pilots who were still at St Omer, arriving there at noon on 2 June.

By the summer of 1916, the Royal Flying Corps was a considerably larger organisation than it had been on the outbreak of war. Each of the four British armies out in France was allocated a supporting RFC brigade which was made up of two wings, a Corps Wing and Army Wing. The former provided air support for the troops on the ground through reconnaissance and artillery ranging and spotting; the second was the offensive wing, providing bomber and fighter aircraft. Each squadron was theoretically equipped with eighteen aeroplanes and crews (a significant increase on the twelve machines which had gone out with each squadron in 1915).

32 Squadron was placed in the 10th (Army) Wing of I Brigade, under Lieutenant-Colonel Philip Herbert[35] which flew in support of the First and Third Armies on the Arras Front. On 4 June, an advance party was sent on ahead to prepare accommodation for the whole unit at the small mining village of Auchel where the airfield was already occupied by FE2Bs of 25 Squadron under the command of Major Cherry.[36] Rees took off and arrived at the airfield at 09.40 and when the road transport arrived, additional canvas hangars were erected for the eleven DH2s and two Vickers Scouts. The remainder of the squadron, totalling sixteen pilots, arrived from St Omer after lunch. Their stay in Auchel was intended to give the pilots the opportunity to become accustomed to the area and life on active service but, for two days, the wet and windy weather prevented any flying. On 6 June, Lieutenant Simpson arrived flying a replacement DH2 (5986). At 07.40 hours the following morning, Captain Hellyer and Second Lieutenant Nixon[37] took off on the squadron's first war patrol over the front, an uneventful flight which lasted about an hour, and later that day the squadron moved to Treizennes, near Aire-sur-la-Lys. There, they were put to work almost immediately, replacing 27 Squadron, whose Martinsydes had that same day moved to André-au-Bois.

While the DH2s went on regular patrols over the lines, Rees continued to fly the

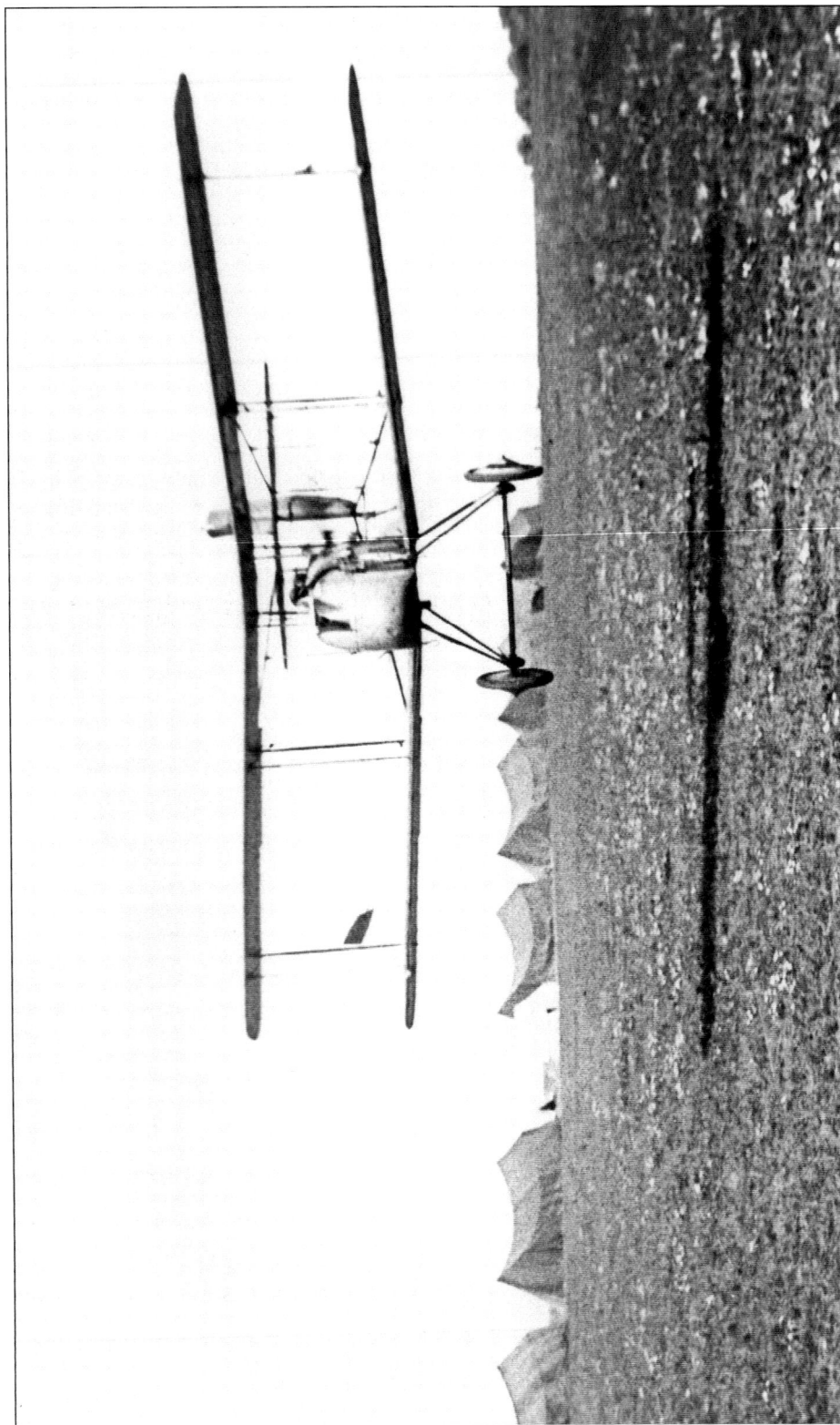

A rare photograph of a DH2 airborne, with Lieutenant von Poellnitz at the controls, making a low pass over Vert Galant airfield, 1916.
[The late Gwilym H Lewis]

Vickers, which had by this time been fitted with a Vickers-Challenger gun synchronizer, allowing it to fire a machine gun through the arc of the propeller. As squadron commander he was forbidden to fly beyond the British front line and therefore most of his flights were carried out in co-operation with the local anti-aircraft batteries, trying to intercept any intruders over the British side of the front. At the same time, he was tasked with providing RFC headquarters with a full evaluation of the Vickers as a front-line machine.

His first patrol (in Vickers (7758), accompanying DH2s flown by Sturley Simpson (5999), Owen Thomas (6012) and Gwilym Lewis (5979), occurred at 03.20 hours on 8 June, and lasted for an uneventful two hours and twenty minutes. Before take off, each machine was allocated a specific area to patrol and '… Hell was raised if a Hun gets through on your sector.'[38] The pilots of 32 Squadron were now involved in the real war and, as if to remind them of this fact, they suffered their first fatality that same day when Second Lieutenant Reginald Stubbs[39] took off in DH 6005 on his first patrol over the front lines. Observers on the ground noted that he was seen flying into a considerable concentration of anti-aircraft fire, but he appeared to have got through unscathed. Later, whilst returning to an aerodrome further south, flying at about 100 feet, his machine was seen to lurch upwards and crash. Stubbs was killed instantly and, when Rees arrived at the scene some time later, he was informed that, despite two minor wounds, probably caused by the anti-aircraft fire, there was no apparent reason for the crash. The official verdict recorded on the squadron papers was that Stubbs had fainted at the controls of his machine. Far more likely, however, is the possibility that some small but vital component on his machine had been damaged by the anti-aircraft fire and, when that part finally broke, Stubbs had neither the time, the height nor the experience to bring the aircraft down safely.

The same day, Lewis had the squadron's first encounter with the enemy. On patrol at about 08.15 hours, he spotted a machine flying towards him on the British side of the line. Unable to identify it as either friend or foe, he continued towards it trying to see its markings. Suddenly he spotted the black crosses and, as the two machines drew closer, he opened fire from a range which he insisted to his dying day, was no more than forty yards. The German broke to the left and he gave chase, firing the occasional burst whenever the opportunity arose. Certain that he had hit the German observer who was seated in the rear cockpit, his last view of the German machine showed the gun pointing up into the air and no attempt was made to return his fire. The pilot, however, used his superior speed and safely re-crossed the lines. On landing, Lewis discovered that a report of his action had already been made and the official record stated that he had opened fire from a range of 300–400 yards.

DH2s of 32 Squadron in line at Vert Galant airfield. This photograph was taken shortly after Rees left the squadron and his successor as CO, Major Cairnes, can be seen standing on the right.
[The late Gwilym H Lewis]

My CO wasn't at all pleased … and told me I had lost a chance. He is such a fearful fighter himself, and a wonderful pilot. However, better luck next time, it was only my tactics that were wrong. It is a most extraordinary game. Better than football yet something of the same. It is the same feeling to charge a Hun who sees you as it is to collar one of the biggest chaps in the school scrum.[40]

Despite Rees not being permitted to cross the front line, he seemed to fly a patrol at least every other day. He undoubtedly did this as an example to those under his command, to get a feel for the conditions in which his men were flying and to keep his own flying and fighting skills well honed. Usually these flights were in the Vickers Scout, but he also flew DH2 (5993) on a test flight when it arrived in the squadron on 12 June and similarly DH2 (6015) on 24 June.

The squadron quickly made its mark on its sector of the front and Lewis wrote regular letters to his father:

But what would surprise you more is the respect we get out here as a DH squadron. We are absolutely 'the ones' here. The DH has practically scared the Huns off the front. Occasionally they manage to steal over at about 15,000 but even then they hesitate whether they dive on a DH or not, if he happens to be below them. The FEs complain that they can get no fights hardly now; it is awfully amusing. Of course the DH's job is to attack and away he goes at any Hun he sees.[41]

The squadron's second casualty was Captain Hellyer, the senior flight commander. On 15 June, taking off in the machine (5979) normally used by Lewis, in order to carry out an engine test and patrol, his engine stalled whilst he was trying to clear some high trees. The machine side slipped and crashed into a nearby field. The engine, mounted behind the pilot, broke loose from its mountings resulting in Hellyer sustaining several broken ribs and a broken ankle. As a consequence, he was invalided home. Why he had decided to test Lewis's engine is unrecorded; it was certainly not the normal procedure for a flight commander. A pilot from 25 Squadron was allocated as Hellyer's replacement and sent to St Omer to complete a course on flying the DH2, having previously flown the FE2B. Before he could complete the course, he was also involved in a crash and invalided home; the DH2 was still proving itself to be something of a handful for an inexperienced pilot.

Throughout this period of the squadron's baptism of fire, Rees flew regular patrols in his Vickers but, despite spotting enemy machines on several occasions, he was not involved in any combats. More often than not, the weather prevented any successful patrols with the cloud level regularly below 5,000 feet which meant that no enemy activity could be observed either in the air or on the ground. Duty pilots waited on stand-by for up to twelve hours each day, ready to take off at a moment's notice should the weather clear sufficiently for a patrol to be mounted. On 16 June in response to a telephone message that a German machine was flying over Annequin, Rees took off in the Vickers but saw nothing. The following afternoon, whilst patrolling the front line he spotted a German machine being fired at by British artillery north of Armentières and set a course to intercept it. Before he was able to get within striking distance, the German pilot crossed back over to the German side of the front line and Rees abandoned the pursuit. Some ten minutes later he spotted another German machine (or possibly the same one) again being fired at by anti-aircraft guns south of Arras, but this also managed to recross the lines while still about a mile ahead of the Vickers.

The first really fine day since the squadron's arrival was 17 June and every possible patrol was mounted as the General Staff, in the midst of their preparations for the imminent Somme offensive, demanded information about the enemy's positions opposite the Fourth Army's front. Reconnaissance machines were sent up with 25 and 32 Squadrons providing protection when they crossed over in the area Laventie–Souchez and, at the same time prevent the Germans flying similar missions to observe the British build up of men and equipment. Whenever possible, the two squadrons alternated their patrols to ensure maximum cover of the area and, during one of these, Owen Thomas[42] (flying DH2 6012) caught up with a large formation of enemy aircraft and, although hopelessly outnumbered, closed with them and opened fire on a two seater. The ensuing fight lasted for thirty minutes as both pilots tried desperately to get into a position whereby he could get a clear shot at his opponent and bring him down. It was not to be, however, and the German pilot eventually broke away and headed back towards his own territory and Thomas made his way home.

During the afternoon, Sturley Simpson[43] (flying 5999) climbed to attack five Aviatiks which he spotted flying above him. Emerging from the middle of the enemy formation, he opened fire and the German observers quickly reciprocated. Simpson, however, used up all his ammunition and failed to achieve any noticeable success and was forced to break off the fight. Rees himself gave chase to two German machines in the Bullet, but both made a successful escape across the lines, either because of their extreme range or possibly their superior speed.

In an effort to counter the effectiveness of the new scout squadrons, the Germans regularly sent over formations of between five and twelve machines. Consequently, contact became more frequent, but 32 Squadron was still unable to claim any confirmed destruction of a German machine. Spurred on by Rees' leadership and example, the young pilots ranged the sky over the Fourth Army front, rivalling each other in their efforts to be the first to score a 'kill.' Their failure to do so was not due to lack of effort or skill as they were successful in preventing any infiltration of their sector. Instead, their lack of a score was caused by the enemy's refusal to fight, turning tail whenever they spotted a

Aviatik C III two-seater armed reconnaissance aircraft which was introduced on the Western Front during 1916. The pilot sat in the forward cockpit and the observer in the rear manning a 7.92mm Parabellum machine gun. It had a maximum speed of 88 mph and could climb at 255 feet per minute to a ceiling of 11,500 feet. [ME Schmeelke Archive]

A DH2 of 32 Squadron with its ground crew, photographed in France (possibly Treizennes) 1916. The wheel markings identify this aircraft as being part of C Flight. [The late Gwilym H Lewis]

DH2. Always quick to adapt to changing circumstances, the Germans had soon learned that discretion was the better part of valour as far as single-seater scouts were concerned. If a combat was to be entered into, then the reconnaissance machines which crossed over the German lines every day were very much easier targets.

The fact that 32 Squadron was eager to fight and had absorbed Rees' principles of aerial combat, was clearly illustrated by Lieutenant Nixon who, on 18 June, ran into a formation of five Aviatiks at 11,500 feet over Lens.

I closed with the rear one who opened fire at about 100 yards, and I commenced firing at about 50 yards. After firing my second drum I was hit in the arm. I then observed a De Havilland Scout about 100 feet below me attacking another Aviatik, so went to help him, but he turned away as if his gun was jammed.

I attacked the hostile machine and fired my third drum at him from underneath. When my drum was finished I observed that the German's gun was jammed. I was unable to change my drum owing to the wound in the right arm, so I returned to the aerodrome.[44]

Upon examination of his aeroplane, Nixon discovered that it had been hit in several places with damage recorded to spars, rudder, tail and several wires shot away, confirming that Rees' philosophy of aggressive action with the enemy was being taken to heart by the men under his command.

As the June days slipped by, it began to appear that the squadron's pilots would be put out of action, one by one, without any apparent loss to the enemy. Perhaps Lewis' comments about the status of the DH2s was erroneous. Three days after Nixon had been hospitalized, Sturley Simpson (flying 5127) misjudged his landing and came down on the edge of a cornfield to the east of the airfield, resulting in the machine overturning. Simpson sustained a severe cut to the head and injured his right shoulder. His machine had two badly bowed centre struts, the top main-plane attachment plates were broken, the front of the nacelle had been pushed right in, the rudder and propellor were damaged, two bottom tail booms were bent and one crossing-bracing wire was broken.[45]

By mid month, the pace on the Western Front began to 'hot up' as preparations for the forthcoming offensive moved towards their final stages. On Thursday, 22 June, after several days of bad weather, the sun broke through and 32 Squadron was able to mount twenty-six patrols. Several pilots reported enemy activity and it seemed that at last there was a strong possibility that a German machine had been destroyed, but as the action took place behind enemy lines, no confirmation could be made. Captains Gilmour and Allen, accompanied by Second Lieutenant Coleman,[46] had encountered eleven or twelve Albatros two-seaters over Lens and immediately went into the attack. Each officer fired two drums at different machines and Allen saw his tracers entering the fuselage of his opponent, just behind the observer. Coleman dived after a machine, firing as he went and, when he pulled out at 4,000 feet, he saw the enemy aircraft still falling until he lost sight of it at about 2,000 feet above Loos. Gilmour's Lewis gun jammed when he was in the midst of the German formation and he was forced to break away from the attack. Desperately trying to free his gun's mechanism, he released control of his aircraft and dismantled the gun but to no avail. When he landed, the bolt was found to be bent. None of the three machines were hit and all made a safe return to their aerodrome.[47]

DH2 (7907) also possibly photographed at Treizennes. This aircraft was part of B Flight.
[The late Gwilym H Lewis]

Second Lieutenant Owen Thomas was not so lucky when he suffered a broken gudgeon pin in his engine whilst on the evening patrol over Lens. The ensuing vibration forced him to switch off the engine and attempt to glide home. As he made his approach at 150 feet he tried a right turn but was unable to take the bank off afterwards with the result that the wing struck the ground causing the machine to crash. The DH2 (6003) was wrecked but, miraculously, Thomas was uninjured.

On 22 June, Rees, after mounting a two-hour patrol, returned his Vickers Scout (7758) to 1 Aircraft Depot and three days later collected a new DH2 (6015) from St Omer which was described as being 'in excellent condition.' This aircraft then became his own personal machine and, three days later, despite having had very little flying time, he had the engine changed for a new one; it was to prove a fortuitous decision and one week later almost certainly saved his life.

On the 23 June, the Allied artillery opened the most intensive bombardment of the war to that date, with the intention of destroying the German defences before the infantry launched their assault along eighteen miles of the Somme front one week later. For seven days and seven nights without respite the guns hammered out their message of destruction and the men of the RFC were given the dual tasks of ensuring that no enemy patrols crossed the lines to observe the preparations whilst also mounting patrols behind German lines to check on the effectiveness of the bombardment and the state of readiness of the enemy's defences.

Two days after the bombardment began, 1 Brigade RFC launched an assault on the German observation balloons in its sector. Five DH2s of 32 Squadron, flown by Gilmour, Allen, Nicholas,[48] Thomas and Corby, provided the escort for machines from 2 and 10 Squadrons which were to carry out the actual attacks. Rees accompanied them as far as the front line which he then patrolled to await their return. Several times the escorting scouts lost contact with the BEs due to cloud and, when they arrived over the target area, they discovered that the balloons had already been lowered and so the mission was aborted.

Despite the undoubted frustration felt by the pilots as the days slipped by without a confirmed victory, 32 Squadron's success in keeping its sector clear of the enemy was noted. On 27 June, Rees assumed temporary command of Tenth (Army) Wing, which covered 25 Squadron as well as his own, a clear indication that a staff appointment could be expected in the near future, but continued to prepare for the squadron's role in the great offensive that was about to begin. The next morning he took DH2 (6015) to St Omer ostensibly for some gunnery practice, but also as part of his duties as a wing commander.

F/Sgt Eric Henry Dobson (934). All the DH2 squadrons in 1916 had one NCO pilot. Dobson, from Edgbaston, Birmingham, joined 32 Squadron in France in June and was killed on 12 August 1916, aged 22. He has no known grave and is commemorated on the Arras Flying Services Memorial. [RAeC via Ancestry.co.uk]

The end of June brought several days of wind, rain and low cloud which severely hampered aerial operations, dulling the prospects for the opening of the British offensive. On the last day of the month, four machines, piloted by von Poellnitz, Nicholas, Hunt and Dobson,[49] mounted a patrol from Armentières to Laventie, acting as protection for six RE8s of 21 Squadron that were to bomb an ammunition depot and storehouses at the St Sauver Station in Lille. Again, no enemy machines intervened, although the aircraft were submitted to a terrific anti-aircraft barrage.

The following morning, 1 July, the pilots of 32 Squadron were up well before dawn as they, along with other RFC units, were scheduled to play their part in the opening hours of the British assault on the Somme front timetabled to begin at 07.30. The heavy concentrations of German aircraft over the French sector further south meant that the pilots and observers of the RFC were fairly confident that they had control of the air over their front line. Although 32 Squadron was engaged on the Arras front, some miles from the most northerly point of the impending British attack on the Somme front, they anticipated being fully occupied if only to provide protection for bombing missions and to act as a distraction and thereby prevent the Germans knowing the position of the northern flank of the assault. German rail communications in their rear areas were to be carefully watched and, if any traffic was observed, attacked. The weather was fine as the first machines, piloted by Thomas, Hunt and Henty, took off at 03.40, followed closely by von Poellnitz, Allen and Bath,[50] with orders to escort BEs of 2 Squadron and FEs of 25 Squadron on a bombing raid on the railway station at Don, and REs of IX Wing in a raid on Lille.

After the bulk of the squadron had left, Rees and the Canadian, John Simpson,[51] climbed aboard their DH2s (6015 and 7856) and prepared for a patrol of the front to prevent any German incursions. Rees would fly above the front line in accordance with the instructions laid down for commanding officers, and Simpson would patrol the area around La Bassée, Loos and Souchez. The two small aeroplanes flew together for about fifteen minutes until they reached the front line and then parted company with Simpson heading east across No Man's Land. The Canadian was generally regarded as one of the squadron's better pilots and a keen advocate of Rees' principles of aggressive flying. Although he had not succeeded in downing an enemy machine, he had flown numerous patrols and twice been forced to land with a faulty aircraft, the last time only two days previously when he made a forced landing near Les Harisoirs after one of the cylinders had blown off his Monosaupape engine.

It was not only the men of the RFC that were up and about their business early that morning. At an airfield near Valenciennes, some forty-five miles south-east of Treziennes, a formation of ten German two-seater fighter aircraft (mostly Rumpler C IIIs, but with some Albatroses[52]) of *Kampfgeschwader 3, OHL (Kagohl 3)* had also taken off to patrol the area over the mining town of Lens, close to the front line, just north-east of Vimy Ridge. The German machines were under the command of *Leutnant* Erich Zimmermann, an observer.[53]

Lieut John Clark Simpson, 32 Squadron, whom Rees accompanied on patrol on the morning of 1 July.
[The late Gwilym H Lewis]

Simpson, flying alone over enemy territory, saw a formation of aircraft ahead of him and, unsure as to whether they were friend or foe, began to close with them. As the gap between them narrowed, he must have realised they were German machines but, undaunted by their enormous advantage in numbers and following the philosophy laid down by the RFC at the time, he went straight in the attack. Three of the German machines then broke away from the formation and headed towards him. Whether Simpson ever opened fire is unknown, but in the brief combat which followed his machine was hit. Troops on the ground saw the DH2 descending, apparently under control from about 8,000 feet to about 3,000 feet from which point it appeared to go out of control and eventually crash on the British side of the lines. When Simpson's body was recovered it was found to have eight bullet wounds in the head so he must have been killed instantly and his aeroplane had flown itself away from the combat.[54]

Although Rees could not have been very far away when Simpson became involved in the combat, he apparently did not see anything. It was likely that, as Simpson left him to fly south-east over the lines, Rees had turned north to patrol the front. On reaching his most northerly point, he then turned back, acting like an airborne sentry, looking out for any aircraft heading his way. Fully aware that the British formations that had left earlier that morning would be heading for home before very long, he kept a careful eye over the German lines expecting to see them cross ahead of him. At 06.30, as he flew close to the famed coal-tip known as the Double Crassiers,[55] north of Lens, he spotted a large formation of aircraft flying above him in a westerly direction. His initial reaction was to assume they were a British formation returning from the bombing raids of earlier that morning and he turned his aircraft and commenced a climb in order to assist with escorting them home. Rees, however, was far too experienced a pilot to take anything for granted. As his DH2 climbed, he took a closer look at the formation through his binoculars and spotted their German markings. Realising that he was outnumbered ten to one by machines, many of which had forward-firing machine guns as well as observers capable of firing at him from a variety of angles, he could easily have banked and fallen away, leaving the enemy formation to continue on its way unhindered. Such a decision would, however, have been contrary to everything he had preached for so long and, ignoring the enemy's enormous numerical advantage, he continued his climb and made his preparations to attack.

The German formation was the same one that had shot down Simpson a few minutes earlier. When they saw a second DH2 climbing towards them they must have felt confident that he could also be quickly despatched in the same manner.

As I got nearer, at about Annequin,[56] the second machine turned out of the position and dived towards me firing his guns. I waited until he come within convenient range and fired one drum. This [sic] after about the 30th round I saw the top of his fuselage splinter between the pilot and the observer. The machine turned round and went home. This machine was marked with a big '3' and a small cross on the fuselage.[57]

The first round had gone to Rees and his success encouraged him to continue with the combat.

I then went to attack a second machine. When he saw me he fired red Very's Lights, and three more joined him. They fired an immense amount of ammunition but were so far away that they had no effect. The escort machines swooped down onto their own machine instead of me, and so shot past him and went out of the action. When I got to a convenient position, I fired

A Rumpler C III two-seater armed reconnaissance machine introduced in 1916. The pilot sat in the forward cockpit where his view was seriously obstructed by the position of the engine and its exhaust. Armed with two 7.92 Parabellum machine guns, one in the rear cockpit and one on the upper forward fuselage, the Rumpler had a maximum speed of 85 mph and a ceiling of 13,100 feet. [ME Schmeelke Archive]

one drum. After about 30 rounds a big cloud of blue haze came out of the nascelle in front of the pilot. The machine turned and wobbled, and I last saw him down over the lines under control. It looked either as if a cylinder was knocked off or else the petrol tank punctured.

I then saw 5 close together. They opened fire at very long range. I closed and fired one drum at very long range at the centre and the five dispersed in all directions. I then saw the leader and the two second machines going west. I overhauled them rapidly and, when I got near the lowest, he turned sharply to the left and dropped a bomb. He opened fire at long range. I closed, just as I was about to fire, a shot struck me in the leg putting the leg temporarily out of action. I fired another drum, but not having complete control of the rudder, I swept the machine backwards and forwards. I finished firing about 10 yards away, and saw the observer sitting back firing straight up into the air, instead of at me. I grabbed my pistol but dropped it on the floor of the nascelle and could not get it again. I then recovered the use of my leg and saw the leader going towards the lines. I got within long range of him. He was firing an immense amount of ammunition. Just before he reached the lines I gave him one more drum. Having finished my ammunition I came home.[58]

Rees, despite what proved to be a very serious leg wound, managed to fly his DH2 back to Treziennes where he made a near-perfect landing at 06.50. When the aircraft came to a stop, he managed to climb out of the cockpit and lower himself to the ground where he called for assistance. A stretcher was brought and he was immediately rushed to hospital for treatment to the wound in his left thigh, close to his knee.

As soon as he was able, Rees completed his combat report. Throughout the action he seems to have been in a calm and calculating frame of mind. Despite being heavily outnumbered, he was able to break up his attack into defined sections. As well as concentrating on flying the aircraft, defending himself and trying to inflict damage on his opponents, he was able to clearly see the overall picture, noting significant features of the enemy's machines and markings. He then added a technical report, giving details which might be of value to other pilots and to the higher command in trying to build up a picture of the German squadrons on the Fourth Army front.

I was using the Beliene sight fixed to the gun, but as the sun had only just risen it was not shining on the cross wires. Even without the cross wires the tracers appeared to be going very near the target simply through looking through the tube which is aligned on the axis of the gun. I met the enemy at 11,000 feet when I was at 9,000 feet. I had to raise the gun from its fixed mounting.

The Germans used their usual tactics of circling round and firing at an angle of 45 degrees between the tail and sideways. There were about ten machines flying in a ragged echelon – the leader well out to the front. The machines were of two types, probably LVGs and Albatrosses [sic]. The machine I got closest to had a fuselage very like a Nieuport. The pilot in front, observer close up behind, sitting back to back. The centre section, unlike a Nieuport, was solid and cut well away at the front. I did not recognise the observer's type of gun.[59]

Albatros C I, a two-seater armed reconnaissance/ fighter machine which first flew in 1915. The pilot sat in the forward cockpit with the observer behind him. With a maximum speed of 87 mph and a ceiling of just below 10,000 feet, the Albatros was armed with one ring-mounted 7.92 Parabellum machine gun operated by the observer. [Imperial War Museum]

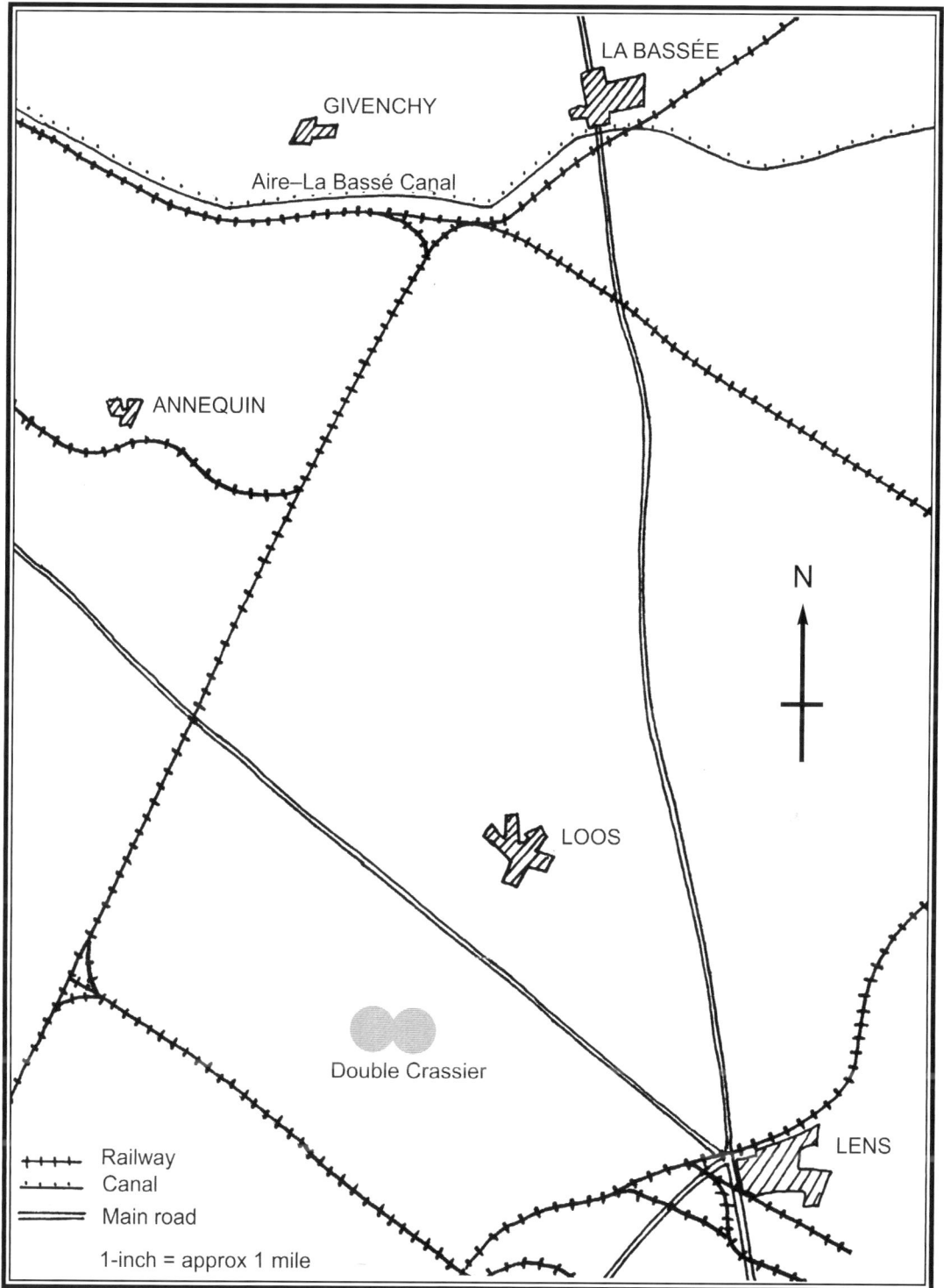

LA BASSÉE

GIVENCHY

Aire–La Bassé Canal

ANNEQUIN

N

LOOS

Double Crassier

LENS

	Railway
	Canal
	Main road

1-inch = approx 1 mile

Area over which Rees fought his VC action, 1 July 1916

An Albatros C I of Kagohl
3. *The crew are seated on
the wheels. The officer on
the left is wearing the
ribbon of the Iron Cross.*
[Michael E Schmeelke]

The entire action had been seen from the ground by the men of the 22nd Anti-Aircraft Battery. Captain TC Newton, RA, reported the next day:

On 1-7-16 about 6.30 am 10 hostile biplanes crossed our lines near the LA BASSEE Canal and headed West. A single de Haviland [sic] attacked them but was shot down. Another de Haviland then came up and fought most gallantly against 8 or 10 hostile machines. We were extremely busy firing and it was impossible to observe the exact sequence of events, but the net result was that a more or less compact body of hostile aeroplanes was completely broken up when about over GORRE. They began to wander about aimlessly in two or threes as if they had lost their leader and very soon retired without any sort of order. A BE2c also assisted, though apparently much below any of the other machines, and unless the enemy's object was merely reconnaissance of the country around GORRE and BEUVRY, one single de Haviland would appear to have completely broken up a raid of 8 or 10 hostile machines. Of these 2 were seen to retire damaged, one of them seriously as he dived very steeply over his own lines and gave every indication of being no longer under control.[60]

This report made its way to Lieutenant-Colonel AG Board,[61] OC 10 (Army) Wing and from him passed to Brigadier-General Duncan de Geyt Pitcher,[62] GOC 1 Brigade, RFC, who immediately filed a recommendation that Rees be awarded the Distinguished Service Order for his gallantry that morning. Basing his recommendation on the report from the anti-aircraft battery, he sent it through to Major-General Trenchard on 2 July.

On 1st July at 6.15 a.m. Major Rees, while flying a de Havilland in the vicinity of the Double Crassiers sighted what he thought to be a bombing party of our own machines returning home.

Extract from 'Colonel Brabazon Rees winning the VC', watercolour by Norman G Arnold. [Imperial War Museum]

He went to escort them. As he got near, about Annequin, he discovered that they were a party of enemy machines, numbering eight to ten. He was immediately attacked by one of the escort; this machine he fought and after a short encounter it was observed to turn and wobble down behind the enemy line. Five more enemy machines then attacked the de Havilland at long range but Major Rees closed with them, dispersing them in all directions. Major Rees seeing the leader and two others making off west gave chase and overhauled them rapidly, but just as he was coming to close quarters he was severely wounded in the thigh. The shock caused him to lose temporary control of his rudder but as soon as the numbness passed off he regained control of the machine and immediately closed again with the enemy, firing at a range of about ten yards. After using up all his ammunition he tried his pistol but unfortunately dropped it. He then returned home, landing the machine safely on his aerodrome and was then taken to hospital.

Lieut-Col Board, who initiated the gallantry award for Rees. [Royal Welsh Museum, Brecon]

The Officer Commanding N° 22 (Anti-Aircraft) Battery who witnessed the fight states that the net result of this fine performance was that a single de Havilland Scout appeared to have completely broken up a raid of 8–10 hostile aircraft, of these two were seen to retire damaged, one of which so seriously that he was observed to dive over his own lines with every indication of being no longer under control.[63]

Brig-Gen Pitcher, who recommended Rees for the DSO.

The eventual outcome of this combat (other than a realization that Rees had forced the entire German formation to turn back behind its own lines) was unknown for many years. Fortunately, the records of *Kagohl 3* have survived and confirm the account given by Rees. Two of the German machines were in fact brought down; the first was probably that which Rees recorded as having given off a 'blue haze', the details of which are unrecorded, but the second was that of the formation commander, *Leutnant* Zimmermann, who was killed, and his pilot *Leutnant* Wendler, who was severely

Maj-Gen Trenchard, who recommended Rees for the VC.

The grave of Leutnant *Erich Zimmermann. The inscription reads: 'Here rests in God our most beloved, cherished hero brother and brother-in-law Erich Zimmermann of Infantry Regiment N° 154, commander of a fighting squadron, knight of the Iron Cross II and I Class. Born 31 Dec 1899. Died 1 July 1916. Happy in his heroism, our proud brother fell in air combat for the Fatherland.' [Michael E Schmeelke Archive]*

wounded.[64] This aircraft was undoubtedly the machine which Rees noted as having an observer 'firing straight up into the air.' This latter machine was recorded as having crashed near Petite Hantay, a hamlet east of La Bassée.

To his subordinates in 32 Squadron, Rees' action on 1 July came as no surprise; it was what they expected of the Major. Gwilym Lewis wrote to his parents the following day:

… the Huns came over in one of their little bunches of eleven. JC Simpson, of Canada, met them and attacked them. Three detached themselves to attack. According to all trench reports he sent one of them down 'looping'[sic], then got his head in the way of a few bullets. … He was one of our cleverest DH pilots.

The Major happened to be up at the same time on a DH. I told you he was the bravest man in the world. He came across them a little later, and the archie's batteries say they have never seen anything so gallant or comic in their lives. The Huns were in a tight little bunch when he came along – after he had finished they were all scattered to twos and ones all over the sky; not knowing which way to go.

He landed in the usual manner – taxied in. They got the steps for him to get out of his machine. He got out and sat on the grass, and calmly told the fellows to bring him a tender to take him to hospital. I am afraid he has got a very bad wound, though he is lucky not to have had an artery in his leg shot, as I understand he would never have got back if he had.

Of course, everyone knows the Major is mad. I don't think he was ever more happy in his life than attacking those Huns. He said he would have brought them all down one after the other if he could have used his leg. He swears they were all youngsters on their first bombing lesson!!! I don't know how he does it!

SG Gilmour takes over the squadron for a few hours. He was in charge of A Flight before, but has been put up for his majority. He went to escort a bomb raid in the evening and landed nearby with his machine all shot about and a bullet through his ear. A rather cheery day for us on the whole.[65]

In hospital in Aire-sur-Lys, Rees wrote a letter to his sister Muriel, at the time in Australia, in which he appeared to trivialise both the aerial combat and his injury.

Yesterday I had quite a good scrap. I met 10 Huns altogether. The first I sent home. The second I wrecked completely. The third put a bullet through my leg so that I could not manoeuvre quickly, but he was sorry he met me before I finished with him. All the others went back across the lines & as I am not allowed to go across I helped them home at long range.

I am now in N° 2 Canadian Clearing Hospital. I am to go to the Base by the first train, stay there for a few days & then go to England. I should be alright again in a month.[66]

At RFC Headquarters, Trenchard gave careful consideration to the recommendation that Rees should be given the DSO. Also on his desk was a recommendation that another pilot, Second Lieutenant Arthur Lionel Gordon-Kidd[67] of 19 Squadron, should be awarded the Victoria Cross for his gallantry during bombing raids on 1 and 3 July. Trenchard approved the latter, but decided that the award of a DSO for Rees was inadequate for the gallantry which he had displayed on 1 July and he re-wrote the recommendation and upgraded it to a nomination for another Victoria Cross before passing it on to General Sir Douglas Haig, GOC BEF. On 7 July a letter was sent from Haig's headquarters to the Headquarters, RFC.

With reference to your remarks concerning the acts of gallantry performed by Captain (Temporary Major) LWB Rees, Royal Garrison Artillery and N° 32 Squadron, RFC, and 2nd Lieutenant ALG Kidd, General List and RFC, the General Officer Commanding-in-Chief has decided to recommend these officers for the honour of the Victoria Cross.

Will you therefore forward corroborative evidence of the acts of gallantry in support of the recommendation?[68, 69]

For whatever reason, Gordon-Kidd's recommendation was later downgraded to the award of a DSO. Rees' recommendation however was approved and passed forward to the King who granted it and it appeared in the *London Gazette* on 5 August. By this time Rees was a patient in the Countess of Pembroke's Private Hospital for Officers at Wilton House, the Earl of Pembroke's stately home in Wiltshire, having been admitted there on 10 July.

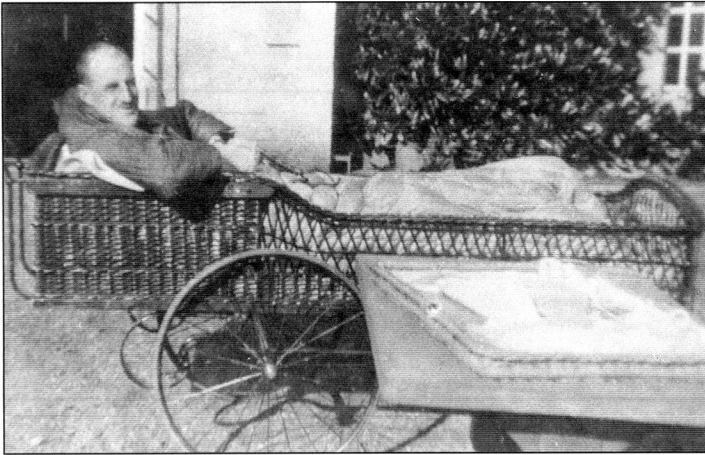

Rees as a patient at the Countess of Pembroke's Private Hospital for Officers, Wilton House, 1916. [Rees Family Archive]

I have got a lovely place. The view from the window is splendid, old trees, lawns, deer, trout streams, & the people are extremely nice. I have been here a week, but have had rather a temperature & have not been sitting up till today ... I expect soon to be able to wheel myself about.[70]

Far from being 'alright again in a month' as he had suggested to his sister, Rees was incapacitated throughout the summer, autumn and early winter of 1916. His leg wound had proved to be far more serious than it was first thought and was to result in his being partially incapacitated for the remainder of his life. The bullet appeared to have caused some damage to his left knee as well as the fleshy part of his thigh. Although eventually able to walk again, he often had to resort to a stick to assist him and his active service flying days were over. By the end of July when he replied to a letter he had received from Sergeant Batten, who had served under him in 11 Squadron, things did not look so promising.

Thank you very much for your letter. I have been unable to answer before as I had an operation and was not allowed to write. Even now I am tilted up, my feet above my head and a weight on my foot. I cannot imagine anything more uncomfortable.[71]

Indeed, his condition, far from improving was, if anything, deteriorating and two months later he was hardly any further along the road to recovery.

I have not written for ages but I have been in bed the whole time & it is very difficult to write in bed. Now I am beginning to get about again. I stood for the first time yesterday. Auntie Katie

& Nora[72] are still here & Auntie Katie pushes me about the grounds in a large perambulator.

I hope to get my medals presented as soon as I can walk well enough to get to London.

The hospital is moving next Tuesday from here to Longford Castle[73] which is about six miles

away & just the other side of Salisbury.

There is absolutely no news to tell.[74]

By the end of 1916, Rees was able to get about with the assistance of two walking sticks and was at last deemed to be fit enough to travel to Buckingham Palace where, on 14 December, he was invested with the Victoria Cross by HM King George V. By this time, his story was well known and a large crowd of pressmen gathered outside the Palace gates after the investiture in the hope that he might give them a brief interview or perhaps pose for a photograph. Rees, however, made every effort to avoid publicity and, by arranging a taxi beforehand, managed to escape their demands, shouting in reply to a request for a picture, 'Not if you were to give me a thousand pounds.'

Discharged from hospital, Rees went to convalesce at his aunt's house in Scotland. In February he wrote to Muriel:

I am still existing & getting extremely bored with everything. My leg is gradually getting bent, but it is so slow that I am beginning to be afraid that we will push in France before I can get out again.

I can walk with one stick now & one day I could walk without any help.[75]

Family and friends did all they could to keep him amused but the feeling that events were passing him by continued to lower his morale. On 25 March he wrote:

Things are going on much the same. Next Saturday I am due to attend another Medical Board, but whatever they say I am going to London to try and get a job of some kind. I am absolutely out of it here & am now simply wasting time.

The reverse of Rees' Victoria Cross showing rank, unit and date of VC action. [Eastbourne College]

Rees slowly recovering from his wound at his aunt's home, Greenhall, Blantyre, late 1916. [Rees Family Archive]

I am told that I will be able in time to bend my leg to a right angle, at present it does half a right angle & about half as much again if it is forced, but I can walk for a short distance without sticks & for long distances with one stick only.[76]

What his role in the RFC was likely to be whilst he was slowly recovering from his wound seemed to be anyone's guess. Having spent a great deal of time as an instructor in one capacity or another, some in the higher command felt that was where his future lay. He need not, however, have worried about his future employment. Events on the far side of the Atlantic were to bring his period of inactivity to an end much sooner than even he anticipated and lead his career off in a totally new direction.

Notes

1. Roland Georges Garros (1888–1918), pioneer French aviator. He is credited with the first aerial victory of the Great War when he downed a German dirigible on 3 August 1914. Taken prisoner in April 1915, he escaped in February 1918. He was killed in action on 5 October 1918. The Paris home of the French Open Tennis Tournament is named after him.
2. Major James Byford McCudden, VC, DSO & Bar, MC & Bar ((1895–1918), one of the highest scoring British pilots with a total of 57 enemy machines confirmed destroyed. He was killed in a flying accident in July 1918 having served under Rees at 1 School of Aerial Fighting.
3. Temporary Captain Robert Maxwell Pike (1886–1915) of County Carlow, Ireland. Educated at Harlow, midshipman Royal Navy 1902–07, enlisted RFC 1914 (RAeC certificate number 905, 21 September 1914). Served 5 Squadron. Following a combat on 9 August 1915, he crash landed his DH2 near Zonnebeke, Belgium. The aeroplane appears to have been undamaged in the combat but Pike received one bullet wound in the head which proved fatal.
4. www.rootsweb.ancestry.com/~irlcar2/Captain_Pike.htm.
5. *Notes on De Havilland Fighting Scout (DH2)* by Major LWB Rees, RFC & RA, N° 32 Squadron, 4th Wing, RFC Salisbury, nd (probably 1916).
6. See Chapter III, fn 19.
7. Later Squadron Leader Eric Lewis Conran. MC (1887–1924), an Australian, he served in the County of London Yeomanry and qualified as a pilot on 22 October 1912. He went to France with 3 Squadron in August 1914. He was an instructor at the CFS when he was appointed as CO of 29 Squadron. He was awarded the MC in the first group of awards (London Gazette, 1 January 1915).
8. Captain Stanley Graham Gilmour (b. 1889), Argyle & Sutherland Highlanders. He qualified on 15 December

1914. He served with 5 Squadron in 1914 and 97 Squadron in 1918. Shot down and taken prisoner in August 1918.

9. AJ Insall, *Great British Fighter Pilots*, War in the Air.

10. History of 32 Squadron, RAF, 1916–1930, National Archives, AIR 1/691/21/32.

11. Later Wing Commander (Hon) Francis Edgcombe Hellyer, OBE, MiD (1889–1950), of Farlington House, Havant. He was educated at Winchester and Trinity College, Cambridge. He qualified on 2 March 1915 RAeC Certificate 1131. Articled solicitor with his father, enlisted 9 Hampshire Regiment. Served in 4 Sqn 1915.

12. Captain Gerald Allen (b.1894) Connaught Rangers, of Dublin. He qualified on 11 March 1915. He returned to his regiment at the end of the war and served in India. Retiring he bought a smallholding in Kent then moved to farm in Jersey where he was during the German occupation of 1940–45. Farmed in Co Cork, Ireland where he died in 1974.

13. Later Wing Commander Gwilym Hugh Lewis, DFC (1897–1997), Northamptonshire Regiment (TF). He qualified on 27 November 1915 and later served in 40 Squadron and was credited with 12 confirmed victories. Recalled to the RAF in 1939, he served in the Cabinet War Rooms under Whitehall until 1945. He was the author of *Wings Over the Somme 1916–1918*, published in 1976, with a new revised and much expanded edition in 1994.

14. Interview with the author, 1986.

15. Lewis, *Wings Over the Somme*, letter dated 9 May 1916, .

16. Interview with the author, 1986.

17. Later Major Robert (Robin) Edward Aylmer Werge Hughes-Chamberlain, AFC (1887–1972). He qualified on 20 February 1915. He later commanded a flight in 24 Squadron.

18. Interview with Robin Hughes-Chamberlain, recorded by air historian Barrington Grey in 1971, preserved at the Imperial War Museum, IWM 23153.

19. Rees, *Fighting in the Air*, p.31 and 'Notes on Flying in Flights' by Major Rees, RFC, NA Air 1/920/204/5/885.

20. Letter to the author by Mr R Beach, dated 1 September 1986, who served as a fitter with 32 Squadron on its formation in 1916. Rees' innovative ideas seem to have stuck in the minds of those that encountered them. In 1939, his former colleague in 11 Squadron, AJ Insall (by then head of Photographic Records at the Imperial War Museum in London) wrote in a letter to the *Times* [published 6 April 1939] — 'The writer recollects an ingenious attempt at 'misrepresenting camouflage' put into practice during 1915 by an officer of the Royal Flying Corps in France. This officer, Captain LWB Rees … flew a Vickers Fighter of No 11 Squadron over certain known and respected anti-aircraft batteries behind the German lines with complete immunity, and when asked for a possible reason, explained that he had intentionally flown with 'one wing down,' thereby completely upsetting the calculations of the enemy's range-finder personnel, who had, as a result, grossly over-estimated the British machine's height. Unfortunately, the method was one that could not usefully be standardized.'

21. The Bowden cable was a flexible tube through which a length of fine wire rope could pass allowing a movement at one end to be transmitted to the other as in a bicycle brake cable.

22. The author is indebted to the late Wing Commander William Fry, MC, for particulars of this machine. He was probably the last survivor of the handful of pilots who flew the Bullet during the war.

23. 32 Squadron War Diary, 28 April 1916, NA Air 1/1494/204/387.

24. Later Marshal of the Royal Air Force Hugh Montague, 1st Viscount Trenchard, GCB, OM, GCVO, DSO (1873–1956). He qualified on 31 July 1913. OC Military Wing RFC 1914, 1 Wing November 1914, OC RFC (France) 1915, Chief of the Air Staff January 1916, OC RFC (France) April 1916.

25. GOC Northern Training Brigade and then Director of Air Organisation, he was eventually Air Vice Marshal Sir Sefton Branker, KCB (1877–1930).

26. Letter from LWB Rees dated 9 January 1919, regarding the history of 32 Squadron, NA Air 1/1494/204/38/6.

27. Lieutenant R Corbett, the squadron intelligence officer.

28. Captain Benedict Philip Gerald Hunt (1894–1958), 2/1 Shropshire Yeomanry. He qualified on 14 December 1915.

29. Later Major Edric Perceval Henty (1893–1966) of Melbourne. He qualified on 27 October 1915.

30. Later Major Herman Walter von Poellnitz (1891–1918), of Sidcup, the son of Baron Arthur James McKenzie von Poellnitz, born in Italy. Educated Repton and Sandhurst. Commissioned 2 Lincolnshire Regiment (wounded 1914). RAeC certificate 20 October 1915. Served in 32, 24 and 72 Sqn. He died of injuries received in a motor car accident in Mesopotamia on 11 May 1918 and is buried in Baghdad (North Gate) War Cemetery (X.F.8).

31. 2 Lieutenant Hugh George Corby (1896–1937), Royal Munster Fusiliers. RAeC certificate 2182, 2 December

1915, seconded RFC February 1916.

32. Gwilym Lewis, interview with the author, 1993.

33. Lieutenant Charles Lambert Bath (b 1894–1952) of Uplands House, Swansea, emigrated to Ontario, Canada. Served in Eaton Machine-Gun Battery, CEF. He gained his RAeC certificate on 8 February 1916.

34. There would appear to be some confusion over the identity of this pilot as some records indicate that it was Lieutenant Bath, whilst others state that it was Second Lieutenant Hunt.

35. Later Air Commodore Philip Lee William Herbert, CMG, CBE (1882–1936) Sherwood Foresters. He qualified on 16 July 1912.

36. Later Brigadier Robert Graeme Cherry, MC (1886–1974) Royal Field Artillery, attached RFC. He qualified on 30 April 1915.

37. Later Captain William Eric Nixon, MiD (1897–1917), of Derbyshire, educated at King William College, Isle of Man and Sandhurst. Served King's Own Scottish Borderers attached RFC in 32 and 40 Sqn. He was wounded three times and KiA7 May 1917, buried Mansy, near Douai.

38. Lewis, *Wings Over the Somme*, letter dated 9 June 1916.

39. Second Lieutenant Reginald Arthur Stubbs (1890–1916), 4 Royal Munster Fusiliers (TF). Before enlisting, he had been an undergraduate at Oxford, intending to take holy orders. He qualified on 5 December 1915. He is buried in Quatre-Vents Military Cemetery, Estrée-Cauchy (grave II.A.1). WO/339/32097

40. Lewis, *Wings Across the Somme,* letter dated 9 June 1916.

41. Ibid, letter dated 4 June 1916. Lewis' father, Hugh Davies Lewis, was knowledgeable about flying having obtained his RAeC certificate in January 1916 (2269), aged fifty. According to his son, Hugh Lewis had been determined not to fight in any trenches should the Germans ever land in Britain and thought that possession of a pilot's certificate might enable him to play a part in the air defence of the country.

42. Later Captain Owen Vincent Thomas (1895–1918), Royal Welsh Fusiliers. The son of Brigadier-General Sir Owen Thomas of Llanfachell, Anglesey. He was killed as an instructor on 29 July 1918. His two brothers, Trefor and Robert, were also killed during the war. Buried in St Alban's Churchyard, Epping.

43. Later Air Vice Marshal Sturley Philip Simpson, CB, CBE, MC (1896–1966), Bedfordshire Regiment, he qualified on 12 December 1915. He commanded 18 Group during the Second World War.

44. Combat report in 32 Squadron War Diary, NA Air 1/1494/204/37/7.

45. 32 Squadron War Diary, 18 June 1916, NA, AIR 1/1494/204/38/7.

46. Second Lieutenant Francis Henry Coleman (1894–1975) 15 Middlesex Regiment, a native of Guernsey. He qualified on 14 January 1916.

47. 32 Squadron War Diary, 22 June 1916, op cit.

48. Later Air Commodore Charles Henry Nicholas, DFC, AFC (1894–1966), 3 South Wales Borderers. He qualified on 14 January 1916. He became OC 5 School of Aerial Fighting in 1918, RAF Hornchurch in 1939 and Air Commodore HQ Air Defence of Great Britain 1943.

49. Sergeant Eric Henry Dobson (934) (1894–1916) of Edgbaston, a former corporal in the RFC, he qualified in France on 13 August 1915. Missing in action 16 August 1916. Arras Flying Services Memorial.

50. Lieutenant Charles Lambert Bath (1894–1952) of Swansea and Toronto, gained his RAeC certificate on 8 February 1916.

51. Lieutenant John Clark Simpson (1890–1916) of Guelph, Ontario, son of James Howard and Leila Ada Simpson

52. Rumpler C III had been developed from the C I and introduced on the Western Front in 1916. With a maximum speed in level flight of 85 mph, it was armed with a fixed forward-firing machine gun operated by the pilot and a ring-mounted machine gun in the rear cockpit operated by the observer. The Albatros C V was a two-seater reconnaissance aircraft was introduced in early 1916 and had a maximum speed in level flight of 110 mph and was armed with one ring-mounted machine gun operated by the observer.

53. *Leutnant* Erich Zimmermann (1893–1916) of Göritz, *Infantrie-Regiment* 154, Iron Cross 1st Class.

54. Lieutenant John Simpson was buried in Vermelles British Cemetery (grave IV.F.24). The village is mid-way between Bethune and Lens. He was 26 years of age.

55. These two coal tips still survive and can clearly be seen to the north-east from the Canadian National Memorial on Vimy Ridge.

56. Annequin is a small village four miles east of Béthune.

57. 32 Squadron War Diary, 1 July 1916, op cit.

58. Ibid.

59. Ibid

60. Report on attempted hostile air raid. National Archives, AIR 1/993/204/5/1216, Recommendations for Honours and Awards, RFC in the Field.

61. See footnote 3, Chapter III.

62. Brigadier-General Duncan de Geyt Pitcher, CMG, CBE, DSO (1877–1944), Indian Army, He had qualified on 29 August 1911 (125). He served with 4 Squadron in France and was then appointed as an instructor at the CFS, rising to commandant in December 1915. GOC 1 Brigade April 1916. Retired as Air Commodore, AOC 22 Group, 1926.

63. Dated 2 July 1916, National Archives, AIR 1/1479/204/34, Recommendations for Honours and Awards, RFC in the Field.

64. *Leutnant* Zimmermann is buried in Göritz, Germany. *Flugmeldebuch – Armee Oberkommando* 6, July 1916, via Michael E Schmeelke.

65. Lewis, *Wings Over the Somme*, letter dated 2 July 1916.

66. Letter to Muriel Rees, dated 2 July 1916, Imperial War Museum, Document Box 69/8/2.

67. Temporary Second Lieutenant Arthur Lionel Gordon-Kidd (1893–1917). He qualified on 30 December 1915. DSO awarded in 1916 'For conspicuous gallantry, skill and determination. On one occasion he dived his machine from a height of 7,500 ft. to 900 ft. and placed a bomb on the enemy's ammunition train, which set it on fire and blocked the line. A few days afterwards he performed another very hazardous undertaking well within the enemy's lines, whilst exposed the whole time to all descriptions of heavy fire.' He was later promoted to Captain and placed in the Dragoon Guards, attached to the RFC. He was awarded the Silver Medal for Bravery by the King of Montenegro on 31 October 1916. He died of wounds received when shot down by the German ace, Werner Voss, on 23 August 1917.

68. National Archives, AIR 1/1479/204/34.

69. National Archives, AIR 1/993/204/5/1216, Recommendations for Honours and Awards, RFC in the Field contains another recommendation, dated 16 August 1916, also signed by Brigadier-General Pitcher, for the award to Lionel Rees of the Russian Order of St George, 4th Class. This award does not appear to have been approved, presumably because, at the end of the recommendation it was stated that 'This officer has been awarded the Victoria Cross,' although it was not unknown for such recipients to receive both decorations.

70. Letter to Muriel Rees, 17 July 1916, Imperial War Museum, Document Box 69/8/2.

71. Letter to Flight Sergeant Batten undated, 1916, held in the archive of 11 Squadron.

72. Auntie Katie and Nora were Rees' aunt, Mrs Catherine Moore, and cousin, Nora Moore, of Greenhall, High Blantyre in Lanarkshire. Catherine Moore appears to have become a surrogate mother to him after the death of his mother in 1911.

73. Longford Castle, the home of the earls of Radnor.

74. Letter to Muriel Rees, dated 29 October 1916, Imperial War Museum, Document Box 69/8/2.

75. Letter to Muriel Rees dated February 1916, Imperial War Museum, Document Box 69/8/2.

76. Letter to Muriel Rees dated 25 March 1917, Imperial War Museum, Document Box 69/8/2.

Temporary Major Lionel Rees, VC, MC. A studio photograph taken just before his departure for the United States in the spring of 1917. [Author]

V

WASHINGTON DC
(1917)

ON 6 APRIL 1917, AT A SPECIAL SESSION OF THE UNITED STATES CONGRESS, President Woodrow Wilson declared that a state of war existed between the United States and the German Empire. In Europe, the Allies rejoiced at the thought of the addition of America's power being added to their cause. Now, at last, there might be some light at the end of a very long tunnel and victory seemed assured so long as America's resources could be brought to bear with the shortest possible delay. Time was running out for the Germans and the onus lay with them to launch an offensive which would win the war before the US forces arrived in Europe and tilted the balance away from them forever.

The Allied leaders had taken the greatest care not to be seen publicly encouraging America's entry into the conflict and, as late as 10 March, Wilson's advisor, Colonel House,[1] a staunch supporter of the Allied cause, had written to Prime Minister David Lloyd George.

Tell your people to take no steps to hasten matters directly or indirectly; it only hinders instead of helping us. Let us alone and we will go all the faster. The only thing I fear is you trying to push us, the strongest pro-Allies resent this.

Tell them we are with you to the finish of our resources in supplies, money and men. We are prepared to go the whole hog. They have no idea how soon we can raise a big army; many thousands of young men have the necessary training – cadets in our military schools and State institutions. Texas alone has 200,000 men who can ride and shoot, and other Western States are in proportion.[2]

Despite such a proud claim, there were few on the eastern side of the Atlantic who did not regard the Americans with some scepticism – there had been little opportunity to take part in cavalry charges since the opening days of the war. Nevertheless, the will was there and it was felt that the Allies should take the earliest opportunity to make the Americans fully aware of the true facts of life on the Western Front. The British War Cabinet had already agreed in principle to send a military mission to Washington DC and on 5 April, the Foreign Secretary, Arthur Balfour, was nominated to serve as its leader, subject to agreement by the US government. As a former prime minister, Balfour's name carried sufficient kudos for the mission to gain admission to the highest levels of the US administration.

Balfour was briefed to impress upon the Americans the need to send a small force of trained soldiers to Europe as soon as possible as an act of good faith, and to commence the training of a large army which could, if necessary, complete its training in France. Any assistance which the US government might need was to be given. Balfour was to be supported in his task by a team of specialists who could advise both him and their American counterparts as required. They would also be expected to act as public relations emissaries to give the American public a clear picture of what their forces would be up against in Europe and how the existing allies had dealt with the demands of the war up to that time.

One of the main areas in which the US authorities lacked experience and knowledge was that of aerial warfare. Although powered flight had been initially developed in the United States (following the first successful efforts made by the Wright brothers at Kittyhawk, North Carolina in 1903), the US Army had proved to be equally as short-sighted as their European military counterparts with regard to aeronautics. Before August 1914, such an oversight might have been forgiven when one considers America's geographically isolated position in relation to other military powers. After 1914, however, to ignore the developments which were taking place over the battlefields of Europe was foolish in the extreme. The war had clearly shown the potential of air power but, despite this, the War Department in Washington had learned nothing. A few stalwarts had been experimenting with military aviation since 1909 and in March 1916, 1 Aero Squadron had been ordered to accompany a force of 15,000 men, under the command of Brigadier-General John Pershing, which was to cross the border into Mexico and there destroy the rebel forces under the command of Francisco 'Pancho' Villa. From their experience in this brief campaign, the airmen themselves had learned a great deal, but the General Staff appeared to have learned nothing. Perhaps the greatest lesson that should have been learned was that the machines then being used by the army were totally unsuitable for military flying, even under the best of conditions. Two years after the outbreak of hostilities in Europe, the Americans were ignorant of the knowledge which was being gained daily in the skies above France and Belgium and, to a lesser extent, Italy. In April 1917, when Wilson declared war, the Aviation Section of the US Army Signal Corps had about 100 trained pilots and 125 aeroplanes, the latter being totally unsuitable for combat. General Pershing, who was to command the American forces in Europe, recorded in his memoirs that of the fifty-five training machines operated by the US Army at its training airfields, '51 were obsolete and the other 4 were obsolescent.'[3]

America had not even sent a single military observer to Europe to gather what would have proved, with the benefit of hindsight, to be essential technical and operational knowledge. As one of the leading industrialized nations which could have benefitted greatly from the development of an aviation industry, America had failed to grasp the

Lieut-Col Henry 'Hap' Arnold

opportunity and, although the Allies had drawn heavily upon her for the supply of many of the weapons of war, there had been no approach for the supply of aeroplanes as the means to manufacture them simply did not exist in America.

If the situation before America's entry into the war was a cause for considerable concern, the response afterwards verged on the comical. The French premier, Alexandre Ribot, requested the US government to send 4,500 aeroplanes, 5,000 pilots and 50,000 mechanics to France by the spring of 1918. Remarkably, this did not seem to the US War and Navy Departments to be an unattainable target, and by the early summer of 1917 they had set their own even higher targets of producing 22,625 aeroplanes, 45,000 aero engines and providing basic flying training for 6,210 pilots. Needless to say, these figures were not achieved.

The professional airmen in the US Army were under no illusion about their facility for waging war in the air. Lieutenant-Colonel 'Hap' Arnold,[4] who had learned to fly in 1911 and been involved in military aviation ever since, wrote about the meetings with the European airmen in 1917 in his memoirs:

In the Airplane Division, we couldn't do much about it … even when we did get the rare chance to give advice, our lack of experience prevented our making clear-cut, conclusive recommendations. Our Signal Corps superiors, though they didn't always listen to us, certainly listened intently to the comments and criticisms of those foreign commissions. The British, French and Italians naturally wanted everything we could send immediately — men and machines — and all of them disagreed on every point except one: we, American airmen, didn't know anything. They had been fighting the war and we hadn't.

We had no theories of aerial combat, or of any air operations except armed reconnaissance … we hadn't a single bomber. Such things as formation flying … were unknown to us. It was quite a shock to look at Europe that year and remember that ours was the country of the Wright brothers and Curtiss ….[5]

Amongst other roles, the Balfour Mission particularly hoped to be able to assist with the development of air power, seeing this as perhaps the quickest way that the Americans could contribute to the Allied war effort. The man chosen to serve as the Mission's military aviation advisor was Lionel Rees, who was certainly at the forefront of British airmen in having not only experience of combat, but also having spent a great deal of time in various roles within the training establishment. He was also fully conversant with both the mechanics of aeroplanes and the demands placed upon them by modern warfare. His celebrity status as the recipient of the VC and the MC, coupled with an affable personality made him the ideal officer to fulfil the public relations aspect of his duties.

The personnel of the mission assembled in London and left Euston Station on 4 April under the greatest veil of secrecy possible, travelling by train to Dumfries in Scotland where they were delayed for twenty-four hours by the presence of a U-boat off the coast of Northern Ireland.[6] The following day, they embarked at Greenock and made an uneventful crossing to Halifax, Nova Scotia where their ship docked on 20 April and the emissaries boarded a train for New York City.

Arriving in the city they were driven through cheering crowds along streets decorated with the Stars and Stripes and the Union Flag, to a house on 16th Street which had been put at their disposal by the owner. They reached Washington DC two days later and there commenced a hectic round of official and social functions. The British party was followed by similar missions from France (arriving on the 24th and led by former premier René Viviani and Marshal Joffre) and then Italy, Belgium, Russia, Romania and Japan.

With the exception of Balfour himself, and Major-General Bridges,[7] it was Rees who seemed to capture the imagination of both the American public and the press, which referred to him in glowing terms wherever he appeared. In her memoirs written many years later, Mrs Wilson, the First Lady, recorded a dinner given to the principal members of the mission – '… among the younger members of the party was an 'aviator' who had brought down seven [sic] German planes. Looks little more than a boy, and is very lame poor fellow.'[8]

Although the mission was primarily concerned with preparing the ground for the future and stimulating goodwill, a great deal of useful work was achieved and, in just over a week, a report was sent to the Chief of the Imperial General Staff in London which outlined the progress they had made. With regard to the air service, the following decisions had been reached.

• Twelve American officers were selected for an intensive course at Toronto where they were to be trained as instructors but would not fly operationally.

• Fifty US Army cadets were to proceed immediately to Toronto (with the rank of sergeant) to be trained with a view to obtaining commissions.

• As soon as possible, up to 1,000 mechanics were to proceed to Toronto for training. It was believed that in three months units would be formed from the above personnel, provided with transport and tools, but with no machines. The US Government was desirous of buying aerodromes near to those already in use by the British as well as aircraft for the use of American airmen.

• It was proposed to send to England complete personnel of squadrons with partially trained pilots who could then be trained and used by the RFC and RNAS until required by the US. These would be in US uniform and receive American pay. The Air Service was proving to be very popular in America and the volunteers were plentiful and of a high standard.

• With regard to aircraft, it was thought that American motor factories would manufacture engines for Britain.

Strange as it may seem, the entry of the United States into the war did not ease the pressure on European industry which was working to meet the apparently insatiable demands of the armies at the front. In terms of aircraft production, the Americans were in no position to assist at all and in fact placed an additional burden upon the British and French airframe manufacturers. Those, like Rees, who were fully aware of the conditions imposed by combat flying, considered every existing American design to be obsolete. Even when European designs such as the DH4 were handed over to the Americans to produce under licence, the manufacturers could not fulfil the demand and, by the end of hostilities, only 417 American-built DH4s had been used in combat operations in Europe.

As well as examining the situation with regard to military aviation and reporting his findings to the British government, Rees was also involved in the public relations exercise which was intended to win over the American public to the Allied cause. When one considers his natural modesty and reticence, his success in this role was surprising and was given weight by the appearance of his name in numerous newspapers and magazines across America. Every effort was made to show the Allies in a good light, whilst every opportunity was taken to destroy the image of the Germans. When one reads the propaganda which Rees released to the US press, it is important to bear in mind that April 1917 was to go down in the history of the RFC as 'Bloody April', a month when the Corps lost more men and machines than at any other time during the war. There was no hint of this in the report published in the *New York Times*.

Washington, April 30. How the British and French are maintaining practical control of the air over the western battlefront was graphically described today by Major LWB Rees …

Whilst the Allies' operations are conducted almost entirely beyond the German lines, the Major said, the German machines now cross the Allied lines only rarely in raiding parties. The Germans have given up all attempts to guide their artillery by airplane and seek only to smash up the Allied reconnaissance over their lines … Major Rees gave it as his opinion that the British had defeated the Germans in every way in the air and deprived them of valuable reconnaissance power … The Major stated that the purpose of his coming with the war mission was largely to tell American aviation experts the results of England's two and a half years of experience in flying. All the patents and designs used in British machines will be available for the Government with any other information in the possession of the British Flying Corps.[9]

Where possible, Rees' own gallant service record was used to boost the image of the mission. Indeed, his decorations, personality and the limp which was visible evidence of his wound must have seemed a godsend to both the mission and the American press.

THE MODEST TALE OF REES VC – WHOSE MIDDLE NAME IS MODESTY

In the good old days when every press agent was a poet and every poet consequently had a chance to make a name for others whilst making a living for himself, wars bred heroes as thickly and inevitably as a compost-heap breeds flies. Without some such expert co-operation, it is extremely hard to make the bravest and most desperate of deeds seem as heroic as it really is. Take the case of Major LWB Rees … to look at him you would never think he was a hero, for he is only twenty-eight years old [sic] and strikingly boyish and unwarlike in appearance. Yet he is one of the few living men who has the great distinction of wearing the Victoria Cross … and the Military Cross. … It was Major Rees who, single handed and alone, performed what experts call 'the best bit of air fighting' of the war, which means of course, the most desperate and thrilling piece of fighting any human being ever took part in.

Would you like him to tell about it? Very well, ask him and watch him turn red in the face, stutter and look furtively about him for some way of escape … you will soon realise how much he needs a press agent.[10]

The man said by many to be the greatest British airman living has steadfastly refused to have himself made much of. Now, however, he has put aside his dislike of personal publicity … as a service to aviation and the cause of the Allies.[11]

Such adulation must have caused Rees to cringe with embarrassment, but it would have been just what the War Office and the British government would have wanted in terms of propaganda and public relations. He had obviously made his mark on the American public and the military authorities in the capital and, when the Balfour Mission prepared to leave Washington and return to Britain, the US Army intervened.

Please permit me to make this acknowledgement of the services rendered the United States by Major L Rees, RFC, in connection with the air service of the United States Army. Understanding that it is your intention to return Major Rees to England, I take this opportunity of expressing the hope that you will allow Major Rees to remain in the United States for duty in my office, that he may continue to assist us with the development of the air service of our army.[12]

This request was granted and Rees, who had been promoted to temporary lieutenant-colonel with effect from 1 May, was transferred to the personnel of the British War Mission which commenced its duties under the chairmanship of Lord Northcliffe at the end of May. Allocated an office in Washington DC, he was given Major Lord R Innes-Ker[13] as his assistant, provided with a car and ordered to give the Americans every assistance. During this second phase of his time in the United States, Rees moved away from the propaganda role which he had fulfilled during April and May and played a significant part in aiding the Americans to meet the revised request, sent initially by the French prime minister, Alexandre Ribot, for 8,000 planes in the line by 1 May 1918 (out of a total of 20,000 machines which were to become available) in addition to a heavy monthly output of engines. He was also to use his experience of training to encourage both the American authorities and volunteers to fill the enormous quota of airmen who were estimated to be needed by 1918 (including 6,200 pilots as well as 38,500 mechanics).

The remainder of the Balfour Mission left the US capital on 23 May, and the following day Rees left for Dayton, Ohio where, two days later, after visiting a new aerodrome at

Maj Hiram Bingham III

Fairfield, he had lunch at Moraine Farm with the aviation pioneer Orville Wright. This was followed by a four-day tour of various cities in the states of Michigan and New York, the first of a series of similar tours which were to take him to every part of the USA, turning him into a nationally-known celebrity. Much of the time he was accompanied by Major (later Lieutenant-Colonel) Hiram Bingham, the noted explorer turned military aviator, who was tasked with organizing the US Schools of Military Aeronautics at eight universities.[14] Bingham had been set a difficult task.

I think General Squier[15] expected more of us than we could possibly perform. He had seen what miracles were being done in England and France, and had the greatest optimism regarding American youth. Our Chief followed the principle of giving his subordinates the widest possible authority and permitting them to make decisions of the greatest importance. Seldom did he deny our requests. Our opportunity was tremendous and our responsibilities increased from day to day. His optimism was contagious, and his belief in the great future of the American pilot spurred us on to work at high speed early and late. Holidays were welcome because they meant a freedom from callers and the opportunity to accomplish more constructive work than on ordinary week-days.

The universities co-operated to the utmost of their ability, and showed unusual patience with the frequent changes of plan and curriculum that were necessitated by military exigency. Just as we would get comfortably settled in one course of study, word would come from General Pershing, urging that more stress be laid somewhere else. The truth was, that the General Staff knew practically nothing about Military Aeronautics. Neither then, nor for many months afterwards, was there a single General Staff officer in Washington who had attended a flying school, or who understood through practical experience the needs of a School of Military Aeronautics. We had to work out our own salvation – and keep going at the same time. Fortunately, we had the constant aid and assistance during those difficult six months, of Colonel LWB Rees of the Royal Flying Corps … [who] had been used in England as an instructor, so his advice was particularly valuable. We learned to turn to him on all doubtful questions. That we did not make more mistakes was due chiefly to his long experience and good judgement.

On my first tour of inspection of the cadets in the ground schools, I had the good fortune to be accompanied by Colonel Rees, and to witness the enthusiasm which his presence aroused among the cadets and the eagerness with which members of the various faculties plied him with questions both before and after his lecture. Merely to get a glimpse of him across the campus and to realise what he had done was enough to increase appreciably the zeal of the cadets.

It was only with the very greatest of difficulty that one could get Colonel Rees to speak of his great fight [of 1 July 1916], even in private.[16] His lectures were confined to discussion of recent developments in aerial tactics and amusing stories of mistakes that had been made by British pilots, due in some cases to inability to read maps, and in others to disobedience of specific instructions. His readiness to help us in the minutest details was particularly appreciated by Lieutenant John C Farrar[17] whose duty it was to collect for the use of the schools all the latest information concerning military aeronautics … We continually received the very latest confidential information prepared by the Royal Flying Corps. Its use in the courses at the ground schools was of great psychological value. It raised the morale of the cadets and made them take pride and interest in the course of instruction. Unfortunately, it could not get them to the Front any sooner.[18]

Most of June and July was spent on a tour of the USA during which Rees lectured on military aviation to cadets at the military camps which had been established at universities and other centres of learning throughout the country. Commencing in Columbus, Ohio, the tour included Urbana and Chicago in Illinois, Berkeley, San Francisco and San Diego in California, San Antonio and Austin in Texas, and Atlanta in Georgia. Much of the subject matter included in his lectures appears to have been based upon the combat tactics outlined in *Fighting in the Air* and the manual itself was serialized in the *Air Service Journal* during July 1917. The tour ended with Rees addressing the US Congress on 11 July, when he described what he had seen at the various training camps. His report, in the best traditions of the diplomatic service, said very little, and certainly nothing that might offend.

It was conceded by British officers who visited our schools in the summer and fall of 1917 that some of them were quite as good as the similar schools of the Royal Flying Corps. Perhaps they were trying to flatter us, but remembering that British officers have very poor reputations as flatterers, we were greatly encouraged. The school which particularly aroused the praise and admiration of our visitors was that maintained under the auspices of the University of Texas at Austin.[19]

*Lionel Rees (centre) with Majors Henri Dourif (left) and Raphaelo Perfetti at the
Chicago Athletic Club, Michigan Avenue, Chicago. [Rees Family Archive]*

He was more frank in a letter which he sent to his aunt in Scotland.

We went to San Diego … right on the Mexican border. There was a fiesta going on when we
arrived and a lot of Mexicans were in the town. There was a decorated parade of cars and troops
of all kinds were in the streets. I think they might have been better employed. The hotel we
stayed in was not too dirty. I got a joy-ride around the aerodrome to see the size. I did not like
to say I was not impressed, as Salisbury Plain was 20 miles across, and a good landing place
all the way. We met a Swede at San Diego who built his own planes out of condemned
Government parts and then flew the machines. I expect he will come to a bad end in the near
future. He takes up people at ten dollars a time, and he has not killed many people yet.

At San Antonio … I lectured the officers of the post and they all came except the old general
who could not understand my English accent.[20]

The US government had initially intended to produce its own military aircraft in large
numbers for service in France. These were to be powered by engines that would be built
in America. Initially, it had been hoped that manufacturers could build tried and tested
Allied engines under licence in the United States, but this was found to be quite
impracticable and instead, the Liberty engine was designed and developed from scratch.
With regard to airframes, the reverse proved to be true and in July 1917, the designs for

the British DH4 two-seater multi-role aircraft, as well as one complete working machine, were shipped to the United States. Whereas there was already a large, engine-manufacturing capacity available, based upon the motor industry, the airframe industry was almost non-existant. The DH4, powered by the Liberty engine, went into production on 18 October but the first machine did not reach France until 17 May.[21]

In August, Rees was sent off to the west coast in the company of the heads of the French and Italian aviation missions, Majors Dourif[22] and Perfetti.[23] They inspected the forests and timber yards of Washington and Oregon and encouraged the men working in the timber industry to increase their output of spruce which was considered vital for the expansion of aeroplane manufacture. As usual, his personality endeared him to those that he met.

> That grin … the happiest, whole-hearted, most infectiously spontaneous one that hit Tacoma for a long time – it introduced Lieut Col LWB Rees … this morning as he limped his long, slightly drooping person up the long slip from the Seattle boat.[24]

Their arrival in Aberdeen coincided with the calling off of a lumber strike in the area, and, at the Grand Theater in that city on 10 August, they were greeted by a standing ovation from the capacity audience. As was usual at each public meeting held on the tour, Rees addressed the audience 'in his deliciously broad English brogue,' then showed a number of motion pictures illustrating the work of the Allied air forces in Europe.

By the autumn, he was back in Washington DC focusing again on the training of US airmen. He assisted with the preparation of an instruction manual for those volunteers then under training, the value of which when completed, Bingham summed up in a simple note of thanks which he sent to Rees.

> Permit me to congratulate you on the fine piece of work that you have turned out … I shall make every effort to have this made up into a little book which can easily be

Rees at Seattle in 1917. [Rees Family Archive]

carried in the pocket and shall try to see that every pilot in the American Army has one.[25]

The training methods adopted and adapted during the latter part of 1917, were designed to provide novice airmen (both pilots and observers) with basic flying skills. Prospective pilots entered the system as flying cadets and undertook a period of ground school training that lasted for up to twelve weeks during which time he learned the theory of flight, radio, photography, engine, airframe and machine-gun maintenance, meteorology and astronomy, all while being taught military drill, law, discipline and physical training. The university schools eventually graduated 17,500 cadets by the end of hostilities. Unfortunately, the practical flying training aspects of the course lagged far behind the theoretical as there were insufficient airfields and aeroplanes available. Consequently, part of the shortfall was made up by opening up the RFC facilities in Canada to the Americans which were used during the summer of 1917. In return, the Americans would allow RFC trainees the use of airfields in the southern United States once they became operational during the winter of 1917–18. By December, some fifteen American training bases were operational, all in the southern states where flying conditions were good all year round.

During the next stage, the initial flying training, US airmen made use of the home-built Curtiss JN4 (Jenny) to complete up to 50 hours of instruction before being awarded their wings. By the end of the war, some 8,700 cadets had qualified as pilots. The advanced flying training courses were to be carried out in either France or Britain.

Rees had played a significant role in the development and introduction of this training regime and by the final weeks of 1917, his time in the United States was almost at an end. Lieutenant-Colonel Arnold expressed the official military view of his services as the time came for them to part company.

You must realise the very deep and sincere regret it occasions all of us that your duties here are finished. Every officer of this Division shares with me the sentiment that it has been a privilege to have known and be associated with you. To see you later on the other side is something truly to be looked forward to.

On behalf of the Chief Signal Officer, I wish to express deep appreciation of the valuable service you have rendered here, and wish to thank you for your good cheer and extreme courtesy always.[26]

On a less formal level, the views of the American officers who had served under Rees were best summed up in a Christmas card which he received from a junior officer, Lieutenant Stephen Clement.[27]

I wanted to send this Christmas greeting to you, and to simply tell you how genuinely sorry I am you are leaving us. May I also, Sir, thank you very appreciatively for the hospitality you have always extended me and the many kindnesses you have shown me in the office. I shall never forget your patience at my constant interruptions in your work, and your generous spirit of helpfulness to us all in the Instruction Bureau – Good Luck always![28]

Sometime in December he had been considered for appointment as the commandant of the Imperial Flying School that had been established in Canada, but his wound had ruled him out.[29] He spent Christmas and the first few days of the New Year staying with friends in New York City before embarking aboard the RMS *Carmania*, along with a contingent of men for the American Expeditionary Force, and heading back to Britain.[30]

Notes

1. Edward Mandell House (1858–1938), a Democrat career diplomat from Texas was a close friend and advisor to President Woodrow Wilson. He played a key role in shaping America's foreign policy during and after the Great War. He had never served in the military and 'Colonel' was a courtesy title bestowed by the Governor of Texas.
2. Interview with J Allen Baker, 10 March 1917, who brought a message from the USA to David Lloyd George and Arthur Balfour. Quoted in *War Memoirs of David Lloyd George*, v1, 992, second edition (London, 1938).
3. *My Experiences in the World War*, John J Pershing, I, 17.
4. Later General Henry Harley 'Hap' Arnold (1886–1950) was a pioneer American airman who was taught to fly by the Wright Brothers in 1911. In 1917 he was the executive officer of the Aviation Division of the US Army Signal Corps. He became Chief of the USAAC in 1938 and GOC USAAF in 1942.
5. *Global Mission*, HH Arnold, 1949, p 52.
6. While the members of the mission were staying anonymously at the Station Hotel in Dumfries, their 'cover' was nearly ruined by no less a person that Balfour himself who gave his autograph to the hotel lift attendant.
7. Later Major-General Sir George Tom Molesworth Bridges, KCB, KCMG, DSO (1871–1939), governor of South Australia 1922–7.
8. Edith Bolling Galt Wilson, *Memoirs of Mrs Woodrow Wilson* (London, 1939).
9. *New York Times*, 1 May 1917.
10. *The World*, 10 June 1917.
11. *Air Travel*, October 1917.
12. Letter dated 18 May 1917 from Brigadier-General George Owen Squier, Chief Signal Officer and Chief of the Aviation Section of the US Army, 1916–17, to Lieutenant-General Tom Molesworth Bridges, CMG, DSO, a senior member of the Balfour Mission.
13. Major Lord Robert Edward Innes-Ker (1885–1958), youngest son of the Seventh duke of Roxburghe, Irish Guards. He became an equipment officer in the RFC and later served in the RAFVR.
14. American politician, academic and explorer, Hiram Bingham III (1875–1956), claimed to have discovered Machu Picchu in 1911. He was appointed a lieutenant-colonel in the Aviation Section of the US Signal Corps and the US Air Service in 1917, organizing the US Schools of Military Aeronautics at eight American

universities. He is believed to have been the inspiration for the fictional hero Indiana Jones.

15. Brigadier-General George Owen Squier, PhD, DSM, KCMG (1865–1934), later Major-General, Chief Signals Officer, US Army, member of the Aircraft Production Board. He founded what became the Muzak company.

16. Bingham eventually managed to persuade Rees to give an account of his VC action which still underplayed the events of the previous year. If his memory served him well some two years later when he recorded his memoirs, the account added a few more background details to the story.

'He was in charge of a squadron at the Front just before the Somme offensive. Annoyed, as he whimsically relates, by the continual ringing of the telephone and the repeated asking of unnecessary questions by junior officers at Headquarters, he decided to take a patrol himself. … While on his solitary patrol he saw a squadron of ten German machines headed for France. … With almost unparalleled daring, he attacked the squadron, broke it up, sent down at least three, if not four, of the enemy aircraft in flames [sic], and had the satisfaction of seeing the others hurry homeward in a demoralized state. During the latter part of the engagement, he was suffering from the effects of a machine gun bullet, which entered his right thigh and lodged near his right knee. This did not prevent him, however, from completing his victory by demolishing his last opponent and flying safely home to his own airdrome. He spent the next six months in the hospital, but eventually had the satisfaction of having the "VC" pinned on his coat by the King himself.' [*An Explorer in the Air Service*, pp 31–2]

17. John Chipman Farrar (1896–1974), American writer, editor and publisher, he served as an aviation inspector during the Great War.

18. *An Explorer in the Air Service,* Hiram Bingham (Yale, 1920).

19. Ibid, pp 31–2.

20. Letter dated 12 July 1917, from Lionel Rees to his aunt, Mrs Catherine Davids of Greenhall, Blantyre, Scotland.

21. Only 1,200 DH4s were operational with the American Expeditionary Force by the time of the Armistice in November 1918. The bulk of American airmen on active service in France and Belgium flew British or French built machines.

22. Major Henri Dourif, *CdeG* (1881–1967), a French engineer who had served in the field artillery and the French Aviation Service where he was responsible for developing a corps of aerial artillery observers. He was the French aviation representative on the mission with instructions to advise the Americans on increasing their production of aeroplanes. He later became a US citizen and co-founded the Standard Ultramarine & Color Company.

23. Major Rafaello Perfetti was the Italian aviation representative sent to the USA in 1917.

24. Newspaper cutting held in Muriel Rees deposit, Imperial War Museum, Document Box 69/8/2.

25. Letter from Lieutenant-Colonel Hiram Bingham to Rees held in the Muriel Rees deposit, Imperial War Museum, Document Box 69/8/2.

26. Letter from Lieutenant-Colonel 'Hap' Arnold to Lionel Rees, held in the Muriel Rees deposit, Imperial War Museum, Document Box 69/8/2.

27. Lieutenant Stephen Merrill Clement Jnr (1887–1943), a graduate of Yale University, he later became a well-known architect.

28. Newspaper cutting held in the Muriel Rees deposit, Imperial War Museum, Document Box 69/8/2.

29. *The Aeroplane*, 24 January 1917 (quoted from *The Canadian Gazette*).

30. Passenger Manifest, SS *Carmania*, 24 January 1918.

VI

Aerial Combat Schools
(1918–19)

DUE TO THE RAPID EXPANSION OF THE ROYAL FLYING CORPS during 1916 and the early months of 1917, new developments in military flying and dramatic changes in aerial combat illustrated in previous chapters, there was a steep rise in the casualty rate on the Western Front, particularly among newly qualified pilots. Losses in the air rose dramatically amongst the combatants of all nations from mid 1916 onwards and it became apparent to many senior airmen that, in addition to the normal flying instruction which had been designed to produce a competent pilot, special schools were required where pilots and observers could be taught more advanced skills which would help them stay alive once they were over the front line.

The first step in this development was to establish training schools where pilots could be taught to really fly and control their machines, rather than just get them up into the air and back down again. In December 1916, Major Robert Smith-Barry[1] was given command of 1 (Reserve) Squadron at Gosport where he put into practice training methods for new pilots that were regarded as revolutionary. As well as teaching novice airmen the basics of flying, Smith-Barry positively encouraged them to perform stunts, stalls and spins in order to master control of their machines. Not only did this method of instruction produce pilots that were far more competent, but it also trained them much faster than previously. A great deal of Smith-Barry's philosophy would have matched that which Rees had advocated at both the CFS and Netheravon twelve months earlier. The major drawback of this methodology, however, was the potential for flying accidents. Smith-Barry insisted that the young men under his command should be allowed to experiment '… limited only by the state of their own nerve. … If the pupil considers this dangerous, let him find some other employment as, whatever risks I ask him to run here, he will have to run a hundred times more when he gets to France.' To achieve these enhanced skill levels, Smith Barry emphasised the need from the beginning of the process for not only specially trained instructors to teach flying, but also the requirement for dual controls in training machines with the instructors being able to speak to the pupils whilst in the air via the 'Gosport' tube which he had fitted to each aeroplane. Earlier pupil pilots had been obliged to listen carefully while on the ground, watch their instructor in the air, and then remember everything whilst trying to master the controls of their machine. Gwilym Lewis of 32 Squadron recalled in an interview with this author, that in 1915 his first instructor had told him that he was ready to 'have a go,' gave him a flying manual (with the appropriate page showing how to land turned down in case he forgot what he had been told) and up he went on his first flight in a single-seater machine. While Smith-Barry's methods may have appeared dangerous – and indeed many pupils crashed and were killed while learning his techniques – those that achieved mastery of their machines stood a much better chance of surviving once they got to the Front.[2]

When the Germans introduced large formation flying for their *jastas* (*jadgdstaffeln* – fighter squadrons) in 1917, they quickly gained a level of mastery over the Western Front which they had not previously managed to achieve. In April 1917, as Rees arrived in Washington DC declaring that the Allies had supremacy in the air, the RFC and RNAS were suffering their heaviest losses of the war in what came to be known as 'Bloody April' when 245 aircraft were lost, 211 aircrew were killed or missing and a further 108 were taken prisoner.[3] It was evident that, having learned how to fly under the new Gosport system, fighter pilots in particular needed to be taught how to fight, and the knowledge of experienced pilots needed to be passed on to the novices *before* they were sent overseas. To this effect, training establishments were set up to train both pilots and observers (gunners) how to do just that. One such centre was 1 School of Aerial Fighting which was established at Ayr in Scotland on 19 September 1917 (2 Auxiliary School of Aerial Gunnery having already been established at Turnberry, some twenty miles to the south).

On his return from the United States, Rees appears to have had a period of inactivity during January and early February. The fact that he had been ruled out of taking command of the Imperial School of Flying in Canada because of health issues would suggest that he was still not fully recovered from his leg injury, and he may well have undergone further treatment at this time. Although the records do not show him as holding any official position until 7 March when he was appointed to command 1 School of Aerial Fighting, there is surviving evidence that clearly shows him as being present at Ayr several weeks earlier. A number of American airmen, mostly former members of the First Yale Unit of volunteers who arrived in Britain in late 1917, passed through Ayr at this time and recorded Rees' presence as *de facto* commandant of the school as early as February. The decision to give him this appointment was undoubtedly influenced not only by his abilities as an instructor and commanding officer, but also by the fact that a sizeable percentage of the airmen who were passing through Ayr would be Americans and there was no other officer in the RFC who had his experience of dealing with the young airmen then training in the USA. His leg injury and senior rank, made an active flying command in France unlikely, although he would have been eligible for the command of a wing or a staff appointment. In these circumstances, the offer of the role of commandant at Ayr, with its emphasis on flying, would have greatly appealed to him. Lieutenant David S Ingalls, USN, wrote a letter to his mother, dated 21 February, 'We arrived at Ayr last night. This morning we reported to Col Rees.'[4] This 'early arrival' at Ayr would suggest that Rees may have been sent to

Lieut David S Ingalls, USN.

the school to make some sort of appraisal of the courses being run there, and was then given formal command with the brief to make significant changes. Certainly, life as experienced by the pupils at Ayr and Turnberry during the late winter and early spring 1918 was very different to that experienced by their successors during the late spring and early summer. Another American naval aviator, Lieutenant Kenneth MacLeish[5] arrived at Turnberry on 7 February and described his daily routine at the gunnery school in a letter home:

There's work to be done here. … We start at about eight-thirty, get ten minutes off for a smoke at ten-thirty, quit at noon, lunch at half-past, start again at one thirty, get a few minutes off at three, and finally stop at four to four-thirty. But that isn't all. Then the work begins! We're given pamphlets (they're really libraries) to copy notes from. One gets to bed just in time to get up for breakfast. But not a second is wasted. It's all wonderful 'dope,' that we all must know, and its taught in the quickest, most efficient way. There isn't a great deal of flying, and what there is done in heavy, slow machines for the most part, though I understand there are scouts here too. The course is over in two weeks at the outside, and twelve days is an average. From here we go to another station [Ayr] for aerial fighting and formation flying. That course is about the same length.[6]

Rather than being a hotbed of aerial combat-flying training, Turnberry was full of '… only young, inexperienced cadets, slews of them, as this is practically a nonflying course with cadets spending their days 'sitting on hard wooden benches in sorts of classrooms, studying twice as hard as I ever did in school.'[7]

For the last two weeks we attended lectures, … shot every sort of gun, studied and handled machine gun stoppages. We learned all about those darn guns; I think I can take one down and put it up in my sleep now. I find that a machine gun is darn hard to shoot, not like playing a hose, and the gears, which synchronize the propellor and bullets and the sights for deflection, etc, are pretty complicated.[8]

The young American aviators who had attended various courses of instruction in the US and, from December to February at Gosport, found the Turnberry course most valuable. When they arrived, they viewed their future with trepidation, checking the daily list of postings to combat units. After supper each evening the Americans, and the other pupils at Turnberry, rushed to check the overseas posting list. Ingalls recorded in his diary on 5 February that he appreciated '… the feelings of those in the Bastille, or wherever they kept the poor French devils en route to the guillotine, when the jailer came in with the list of those to be honored.'[9] Writing to his father on 21 February, he noted, 'Although at first the course seemed very monotonous and boring, now I am enjoying it immensely and it is most interesting.[10] All RFC/RNAS pilots and gunners were obliged to complete a gunnery course, but only those selected to be scout pilots went on to the aerial fighting courses at Ayr and elsewhere.

The targets were placed among the sand dunes so that the bullets would not go straying over the countryside, for each day some 10,000 rounds of ammunition were fired in these practices. The machine guns were mounted on a framework which was pivoted in such a manner that it could be balanced only by manipulating the controls as one would in an aeroplane. Thus, when firing, it was necessary to swing the whole contrivance about as one would when in the air & hold it steady, often getting the sights on the target.

The greater part of the practise was devoted to deflection aiming. When firing at a machine which is moving at an angle across the line of flight of the attacking plane, it is necessary to aim some distance ahead of it to allow for the speed it is travelling. For instance, if a plane is moving at 100 miles per hour at right angles to the line of flight of the other, and they are 200 yards apart, it is necessary to aim 37½ feet in front of it so that the bullets & the 'target' will arrive at the same point simultaneously. … However if the target is moving across the path of the attacking plane at less than a right angle, one must use his own judgement as to the amount of deflection to allow. This varies from full deflection at 90 degrees, to none at all when the 'target' is moving directly in the line of flight of the attacking plane. Quarter and half-size models of aeroplanes were built & put on quarter & half-sized ranges. Then, when firing a deflection practise, the bullets passed thru a sheet of paper erected on a wooden frame to the front of the model 'target.' In this manner, one's ability at judging deflection was checked up. There was one other interesting deflection practise in which we did not actually fire the gun but, instead, after aiming, it was clamped in place & the deflection checked up by measuring the distance from the nose of the model 'target' to the point where the bullets would have passed had they been fired … a time limit was placed on the aiming operation … We sat behind a curtain with the gun while the model was being set at an unknown angle, then the curtain was drawn aside for 5 seconds during which time we must aim & clamp the gun. Later we were allowed but 3 seconds, then 2 & finally only one second. To our surprise, we made the best scores when only 1 second was allowed.[11]

On 20 February, MacLeish moved to the School of Aerial Fighting a Ayr, noting in a letter home 'in the past four flying days there have been twenty-three crashes, and I'll be very lucky if I get a chance to fly. If they keep this up they'll have the factories working day and night.'

As well as restrictions upon flying laid down by the nature of the course, pupils' experience in the air at both schools was also curtailed by the weather. On 23 February MacLeish wrote: 'There's been no flying here for eight days on account of this beautiful Scotch weather, but I'm in hopes that we'll have a good day before the war is over.'

Once they had been signed off at Turnberry, those airmen who were destined for scout squadrons were transferred to Ayr for their final course. The airfield at Ayr was located on the racecourse to the east of the town and comprised one large aeroplane shed, some technical buildings and fifteen canvas hangars, sited on the north side of the site. There was no accommodation on the airfield itself, the pupils under instruction being lodged in the large houses and hotels close to the sea shore from where they were transported to their duties aboard red, double-decker buses. The routine was similar to that at Turnberry, pupils being expected to be at the aerodrome by 08.30 hours. Each morning was taken up with flying instruction until 11.00 hours, followed by a one-hour lecture, one-and-a-half-hours for lunch, then flying instruction until 17.30. The instructors were all very experienced airmen who had completed at least one period of duty with a front-line squadron before being recalled to Britain in order to pass on their accumulative knowledge to others, and their decorations amply demonstrated their experience and success and greatly impressed their pupils.

The pace of life at Ayr seems to have increased after Rees had been officially placed in command, and the nature and style of the courses changed. Each course lasted approximately one week, during which relatively short time the school achieved a remarkable rate of success that can be measured in part by the decline in the casualties amongst newly qualified pilots arriving in France. In addition to the obvious advantages for the pupils, there was an added benefit in that the instructors learned a great deal about the problems facing newly qualified pilots so that when they (the instructors) eventually resumed their duties with a service squadron, they were far more sympathetic to the novices and therefore devoted more time to the induction of replacement pilots into their units.

The object of the school was quite simple – to teach pilots and their observers to fly and shoot in combat in such a way that their manoeuvres became reflexive, eliminating any delayed reaction which could give an enemy precious seconds in which to destroy them. Once an individual had mastered the basic fighting skills, he was taught to use them in conjunction with other members of the same squadron. It was hoped that pilots, having obtained the much prized 'wings' brevet awarded at the end of their flying course, would learn how to survive in the air and, most importantly, work as part of a team. As Ingalls noted, 'The course was subject to frequent changes as the advances in aviation are made, and every effort is devoted to make the school as complete, up to date, and efficient as possible.[12]

Upon their arrival at the school, all pupils were given instruction in gunnery, and pilots were tested to ensure that their flying skills were up to the minimum required standard. Once this preliminary stage had been passed, all the pupils were taken up in a two-seater machine and, with an instructor at the controls, carried out a mock combat against another aeroplane. Throughout the time in the air, the instructor was meant to keep the pupil fully informed of everything that was happening and why (utilising the Gosport Tube). This was followed by the pupil flying a service machine in mock combat against the instructor, a procedure which was repeated until the pupil was able to demonstrate that he had mastered the necessary techniques. Instructors would then lead a number of pilots into the air in order to teach them the basics of formation flying and the various manoeuvres which they would be expected to be proficient in when joining their service squadron. Pupils also flew in mock combats against each other before being issued with fully-armed machines which they used for firing practice against stationary and moving targets, both on the ground and in the air. Rees himself took a regular part in the aerial activity at the station and, on 4 March, MacLeish wrote:

I certainly had an exciting time today. A big bunch of machines were attacked by another big bunch. I was in the bunch trying to break through a defense, and we had the best old shamfight you've ever seen. I hope never to be mixed up with so many machines again. They were on top, below, in front, behind, and on either side of us. The air was just black. We were convoying and our group got through without being attacked. I got into four separate fights, one with the colonel [Rees] here. He has a Victoria Cross … and a Military Cross. Of course, he put it all over me after we got started, but when we began the first picture I took of him with my camera gun was a dead hit, and I got four more of him later.[13]

2 Lieutenant Rodney D Williams recorded the training that he was given.

The object of the flying in this course was to teach all the little tricks in flying that had been found successful at the front. At first one went up in a two-seated machine to demonstrate his ability at stunting & manoeuvering. If he was not doing the operation in the best possible manner, the instructor would show him how. Then formation flying was practised & 'tight' formations were insisted upon, that is the machines were required to fly within ten or fifteen yards of each other. When the pupil was considered fairly proficient he went up in a single-seated 'scout' & one of the instructors went up in another & they engaged in a regular battle only that they used camera guns instead of machine guns. Sometimes whole formations would be sent up to attack one another & every week a big 'show' was staged in which every machine on the aerodrome (some sixty in all) took a part. To keep the work right up to the mark there was always a high class pilot straight from the front to lecture on the very latest 'tips'. While I was there, Maj McCudden … was the chief instructor. Not only did he lecture on fighting, but he demonstrated it as well. … He emphasized two points only in his lectures, one was 'work' and the other 'opportunity'. By 'work' he meant the care of our machine so that it would always be ready when the 'opportunity' arrived & by 'opportunity' he meant not the kind one waits for so much as the kind one creates by studying the habits of that most methodical of all creatures 'the Hun'. He told us how to get 'on the tail', for that is the position from which one could fire at the enemy without being fired at, and how to stay there. Then he would go to the aerodrome & get into a machine, then sending someone else up in a 'two seater', he would demonstrate what he had been telling us.[14]

Pupils were taught not only how to attack the enemy but also, most importantly, how to defend themselves against an

Lieut Rodney D Williams.

Maj Cyril Foggin, a senior instructor at Turnberry, 1918.

attack. They were encouraged, within the limited time available, to get in as much practice as possible, in any and all aspects of combat flying, particularly those which they considered to be a weakness. Straight forward flying was frowned upon as a waste of valuable time. It was a firmly held belief at the school that a successful pilot required discipline and that without it, he would endanger not only himself but also his comrades. This discipline was not a passive, regimental obedience to orders, but rather personal self-control. As an example of this, pupils were actively encouraged to carry out stunt flying and to get as much practise at low-level flying as possible, both activities that had been viewed with great disfavour at the CFS. It was clearly pointed out to them that any 'stunts' which they carried out should not cause any concern to others, either on the ground or in the air. It was firmly believed that a pilot who was comfortable in his machine, who knew its characteristics and limitations in every possible situation, was far more likely to make a good fighter pilot and, consequently, was more likely to survive those crucial first weeks at the front.

All the flying here is stunting and we have service machines. Every time we go up, we are supposed to find another machine and have a dog fight with it. The Colonel stays in the air a lot and is the best at scrapping – he and Foggin[15] and Atkinson.[16,17]

Life at Ayr could prove to be as dangerous as that of a pilot with a service squadron, as one American witness recorded in his diary.

March 20. Cush Nathan killed.[18] He was flying an SE and the wings came off at five thousand feet. He went into the roof of a three-storey house and they dug him out of the basement. A real fine fellow. I liked him. So did everybody.

March 26. George Vaughn[19] cracked up an SE in splendid style. The engine concked with him over the town and he pancaked in a vacant lot and climbed up on top of a building. Later on, somebody wanted a picture of the crash and wanted him in it. He got back in the seat and the Fuselage collapsed and the whole thing toppled over. Pansy[20] ran into a chimney with a Camel and scored one complete write-off.[21]

The school's emphasis on personal self-discipline applied equally to staff as well as pupils and, as many of the instructors were famous combat pilots, it was to be expected that the pupils would look up to them and try to emulate their behaviour. For this reason the instructors were required to present a good example at all times. One breach of this discipline which might have had tragic consequences, but in reality was only highly embarrassing, concerned Captain James McCudden[22] who had arrived at Ayr shortly after being decorated with the Victoria Cross in recognition of his combat record. Instructors were permitted to make use of service machines for private flying in the belief that the pupils would gain confidence by seeing aeroplanes used as part of the day-to-day life of the senior pilots. His biographer, Christopher Cole, described how McCudden was invited by Captain JD Latta,[23] a fellow instructor, to visit his family at Failford House some six miles away and, after finishing work for the day, they both took off in an Avro 504, landing a few minutes later on the front lawn of Latta's home. During the course of the evening, Mary Latta, the sister of the pilot, managed to persuade McCudden to give her a short flight in the Avro, a practice which was strictly against the rules. After about ten minutes in the air the engine suddenly stopped and would not re-start, forcing McCudden to attempt an emergency landing in a field. All went well until the final moments when, after touch down, the Avro ran into a concealed depression in the ground which caused the machine to tip over onto its back. Fortunately, neither McCudden nor his passenger were injured, but the pilot had the embarrassing task of reporting the problem to Ayr so that some transport could be sent to pick him up and a guard provided for the aircraft until it could be recovered the following day.

There was no disguising the circumstances leading to the crash and the following morning the young 'ace' was summoned to appear before the commanding officer to face the consequences. All who knew about the incident waited to hear the outcome of the interview and wondered whether McCudden's status and image could protect him. Rees was certainly not amused and, as a fellow holder of the VC, felt not in the least bit intimidated by the younger man, and proceeded to give him what was described as a first-class dressing down, making it crystal clear that the rules of the school were to be obeyed by everyone, irrespective of rank, reputation or public esteem; there were too many casualties among the pupils and instructors for any civilians to be added to their number.[24]

On 1 April 1918, after a lengthy process of investigation, discussion and very careful planning, the government merged the two flying services, the RFC and the RNAS, to form the world's first independent air force, the Royal Air Force. All the Army and Royal Navy

Lieut Ira Thomas Jones,
DSO, MC, DFC & Bar, MM.
[Author]

personnel who had served in either before that date were allowed to continue serving in the new force, albeit many of them were only on temporary attachment to the RAF.

Not all pilots who passed through Ayr as 'pupils' were novices. Many were highly experienced flyers who came to Ayr as members of a new squadron which was about to be posted to France. One such man was Captain Edward 'Mick' Mannock,[25] who commanded A Flight of 74 Squadron and was already well on his way to becoming the top-scoring British pilot of the war. With him in 74, and himself destined to soon become a distinguished destroyer of German machines, was Welshman Ira Jones,[26] who later recalled his short time at the school.

Most of the fliers chosen for 74 Squadron were sent to Ayr in Scotland for a course in aerial fighting. The school was commanded by the Welsh VC Colonel Rees, and amongst the instructors were the famous Major James McCudden, VC, Captain Gerald Maxwell,[27] late of 56 Squadron, Captain Atkinson, late of 29 Squadron, and one-eyed Captain Foggin, who was tragically killed a few months later in an accident in France.

The course was simple. The instructor showed the pupil what to do and not to do during a fight. Besides practising fighting, trainees were encouraged to throw their aircraft around with abandon, in order to gain the maximum confidence in the machines. It was an excellent course. Its teachings saved my life more than once in actual combat. At the end of it every pupil had to appear before Colonel Rees and explain not only what he had learned, but what stunting he had carried out. To the latter question one pupil replied: 'I climbed up to 15,000 feet sir, and zoomed.' N° 74 Squadron was to be equipped with SE5 single-seater scouts. While at Ayr I did all my flying in this type of machine. Pupils who were to go to France with Sopwith Camels – rotary engined, single-seater scouts with exceptionally fast manoeuverability – had to fly that type. The accidents were many, I remember seven funerals in one week as the result of the right hand turn close to the ground. Dozens of pilots were killed by the Camel.[28]

As Jones pointed out, the most difficult of the new breed of fighters which the pupils had to master at Ayr was the Sopwith Camel which had developed a reputation as a difficult machine for the newly-trained pilots to fly.

The Sopwith Camel single-seater fighter which was introduced into front-line service in 1917. It was a difficult machine to fly but became the most successful fighter of the Great War, its pilots claiming the destruction of nearly 3,000 enemy machines. [Author]

The planes [Camels] were equipped with two Vickers machine guns, firing through the propeller, and we fired on ground targets – planes silhouettes laid on the beach away from the airfield. We also had camera guns that we could fire when fighting each other. The films from these showed how close you came to making a kill.[29]

One pilot, Harry Harnett[30] of the RNAS, described the machine as '… a buzzing hornet, a wild thing, burning the air like raw spirit on the throat.' On the whole, casualties among the pilots at Ayr were rare with the exception of those who flew in C Flight which was equipped with Camels. Ensign Frederick Hough of Chicago was injured following a spin from 300 feet. 'One second it was OK, the next it just disappeared with an explosion and then there was a little pile of debris. We pulled Hough out. His legs were badly [injured], very badly, but no other injury. He may lose his legs though.'[31] He died of his injuries on 13 March. On 7 March, the very day that Rees officially took command of the school, two Americans were killed, one of them an instructor of considerable experience,[32] followed by a third the following day.[33]

Six [sic] American pilots were sent over from France to take the course here [Ayr]. They thought Camels were as easy to fly as the Hanroits they had been flying in France, and they wouldn't

Instructors at Turnberry, late 1918. L–R: Capt Philip Edmund Mark Le Gallais, AFC (of Jersey); Capt Edward Dawson Atkinson, DFC, AFC (10 victories); Capt Gerald Joseph Constable Maxwell, MC, DFC, AFC (26 victories); Capt Stanley Wedgwood Taylor, MC, AFC (of South Africa) and Capt John Leacroft, MC & Bar (22 victories). The aircraft is a Bristol M1 Scout monoplane. [The late Chaz Bowyer]

Turnberry airfield. This rather poor quality aerial photograph (looking east) shows the line of the railway, with the golf course dotted with bunkers in the foreground and the airfield and hangars centre left. [Turnberry Hotel]

listen to any advice from the instructors here. Three of them were washed out in one week.[34]

The problem with instructing pupils to fly the Camel reached such a pitch at one stage that it was in danger of becoming destructive to the morale of the pilots who viewed the machine as something of a jinx. Discovering the cause of the difficulty was simple; like in the DH2 two years earlier, the rotary engine which powered the aircraft meant that the cylinders rotated around the fixed camshaft creating a number of issues, paramount of which was the torque which resulted from such a design. This, combined with the Camel's very forward centre of gravity, made it a

P/O Harry Harnett, RNAS.
[RAeC via Ancestry.co.uk]

'… one sided, feverish and vicious' machine until the pilot was taught to recognise the problem and counteract it. As he taxied for take-off, the pupil had to ensure that he applied full right rudder in order to counter the aircraft's natural desire to attempt a loop while still on the ground. As soon as the tail lifted, the rudder had to be straightened very quickly to prevent a sudden left turn which would inevitably result in the wing tip hitting the ground causing the machine to crash. Once airborne, the pilot had to remember to cut the choke immediately and then continually move the fine adjuster and throttle as he gained height. As the torque built up with the increasing engine revolutions, the nose would be forced down in a right-hand turn. If, in order to counteract this the pilot pulled back too far on the stick, the nose would come up very quickly and the engine would stall. If he then tried to put the machine into a dive, the torque would try to set up an outward loop. Captain Norman MacMillan,[35] an experienced combat pilot, recorded his first, and very nearly his last, flight in a Camel.

I thrust the control stick forward hard against the dash, exactly as we did in the old two-seaters. My little mount answered instantly, rose up under me, and plunged straight back downwards towards the ground over the vertical and partly on her back. As she went she projected me outward and forward from the cockpit. My belt was an elastic-sided contraption and expanded so that I slid through. When I felt myself going, I clutched downward to grab the seat. My fingers missed the seat but caught the petrol adjusting tap, which I had screwed off just before pushing the stick forward. My fingers closed around the tap, but the acceleration was too much for that flimsy resistance, and I shot out of the cockpit on to the guns along the top of the

Capt Norman MacMillan,
MC, AFC.
[The late Chaz Bowyer]

fuselage, where I lay for a moment with my nose feeling very much like being grazed by the propellor.

For an instant I lay while the acceleration died out and left only the terrific dive to earth with my plane partly on her back, and I literally standing on my head. Inch by inch I forced myself backwards and upwards towards the cockpit until, with my right land, I found the ring at the top of the control column and pulled myself into the machine again. I got in, found the rudder bar with my feet, and gradually pulled the plane out of the headlong plunge.I levelled out at two thousand five hundred feet, having fallen head down for nearly a mile.[36]

As this account clearly shows, even an experienced pilot could easily find himself in very serious difficulties when flying the Camel; newly-qualified pilots would have had very little chance of surviving in a similar situation. The issue had reached such a pitch at Ayr that Lieutenant Ingalls wrote on 10 March, '… there was a strike today. All pupils refused to fly any more Camels. It does look like sure destruction. There are only a few machines left anyway.'[37] To resolve this growing fear, Rees decided to repeat something which he had done with the DH2 at Netheravon in 1916. Without informing anyone of his intentions, he decided to take a Camel up for himself. One must bear in mind that he had not flown a combat machine in anger since July 1916, and had little experience of flying Camels, other than what he may have picked up since his arrival at Ayr. Selecting one of the machines on the airfield, he waited until there were sufficient numbers of pupils and staff around to see his performance, and took off at full power, climbed to 500 feet and immediately commenced a flying display the like of which few of those on the ground had ever seen before. If anyone had harboured any doubts as to his skills as a pilot, they were dispelled that day. He made the Camel do everything the machine was capable of, and deliberately put it into situations that brought on all its worst characteristics, handling them all with masterly skill. To the large numbers watching from below, he demonstrated beyond any question that the Camel could be mastered and turned into the most manoeuvreable fighter of the war. One of those present said that it was '… a wonderful exhibition' as, never climbing above 500 feet, he '… certainly did fight the treetops and he wouldn't come out of a spin above fifty feet.'[38] On landing, he climbed out of the cockpit, limped away to his office, then ordered all the instructors to repeat the performance, for performance is what it had surely been, and from then on, although pupils still eyed the little fighter with wary concern, they were in no doubt that the instructions given by the staff of the school worked and that those who gave out the orders were also quite capable of carrying them out. Ingalls wrote:

> So this afternoon the instructors went up in what remained [of the Camels] and stunted all over to inspire the poor devils. I never saw such marvelous flying; it was simply superb. And was without an accident. The only marring element was that two Avros hit head on at about 100 feet. However, no one was hurt.[39]

A sad postscript to this tale was that several of the pupils were so impressed that they took off almost immediately to try and emulate the display. Within minutes, the Camel had claimed another victim. However, despite the accidents, the American airmen at Ayr felt themselves privileged to be there.

> Everybody here wants to get out of the US Army and join the RFC where they'll get a square deal. We certainly have gotten a rotten deal from the USA and the British couldn't have treated their own Field Marshals any better. We owe the British a lot and have a lot to get even with our own army for.[40]

Certainly Rees appears to have played a part in establishing these cordial relationships and was held in high regard by the 'Yanks'. Not long after he arrived at Ayr, Elliott White Springs found himself in the commandant's sights, the Americans having already acquired a reputation among the pupils for the quantities of alcohol they consumed.

> Everybody had gone crazy over eggnog … . The next day they made five gallons and it lasted ten minutes … Springs's father sent him ten pounds of sugar and we had three cases of brandy. It must have made fifteen or twenty gallons. Everybody from the Colonel down came over to drink it. By lunch time every officer in Ayr was full of eggnog.
>
> We all went out to the aerodrome after lunch and tried to fly. They are short of magnetos and the only way they can get more is to steal them off crashes. There were three Spads, so Capt Foggin asked for Spad pilots. He sent Springs up in one hoping he would crash it. He had a quart bottle of eggnog and took it up with him to drink. The motor conked all right, but he made a nice landing in the field with a dead stick without crashing, so Foggin put him up in another one.

Springs decided he'd steeplechase. The field is an old racecourse so he came down wide open and ran his wheels on the track. He tried to bank with the track for a turn but they had put up some heavy wires and his top wing caught them. He went straight up three hundred feet and stalled and fell out of the stall right into the middle of the field. God certainly took over the controls. He wasn't hurt but the Spad was a write-off and Foggin got one mag.

Springs was mad as a hornet because he had the bottle of eggnog in his pocket and when he saw he was going to crash he threw it out to keep from cutting himself up.

The Colonel sent for Springs to bawl him out, 'Ah, listen here,' said the Colonel, 'I really have enough trouble running this school without you youngsters interrupting my telephone connections. Don't do it!'[41]

On 11 May, 1 School of Aerial Fighting was closed down at Ayr and the staff and equipment moved to Turnberry some twenty miles south where they were formed into 1 Fighter School, expanding their activities to incorporate those previously carried out by 2 Auxiliary School of Aerial Gunnery. This amalgamation of roles may well have reflected the changes proposed by Rees in order to bring the school up to the required standard. The change of location was clearly brought about by the expansion in the duties of the new school which could develop at Turnberry – in addition to the type of instruction which they had carried out at Ayr, the school's staff now had to instruct the crews of two-seater fighters, both pilots and observers, and the crews of bombers. The airfield was situated right on the coast where the weather made flying conditions equally as hazardous as they had been at Ayr, but unhampered by not being in close proximity to any urban centre. The choice of Turnberry as a training station may have appeared rather strange as, although situated on relatively flat ground – the airfield was located on the famous golf course – it was only a few miles from the mountains and this, coupled with the potential danger of sea mist, provided a perfect recipe for disaster should a pupil become lost or disorientated whilst in the air. However, due to its relative remoteness and coastal location, it was well suited for the practice of air-to-ground and air-to-air gunnery, and its ease of access to a railway line was a distinct advantage. The staff and pupils were accommodated in the luxury of the Turnberry Hotel, overlooking the golf course.[42]

1 Lieutenant Robert Todd[43] of the Aviation Section, US Signal Corps, recorded his rather comfortable stay there:

After reporting in [at Turnberry] we were assigned sleeping quarters in the Turnberry Hotel, a very fashionable vacation spot. The adjoining golf course had been turned into an aerodrome.

The hotel sat half way up the side of the mountain, looking out over the aerodrome and into the bay, a most beautiful spot … across the bay we could see Ailsa Craig. All our meals were served in the main dining room.

The aerodrome was the golf course, complete with bunkers, sand traps and a dandy water hazard that circled the whole field. This was a brook. … The prevailing wind came off the sea which was not bad for take offs, but to land we had to come down the mountain where the hotel was and sideslip in for a very short landing strip to avoid the brook and other hazards. We played billiards and cards for recreation.[44]

Lieut Robert Miles Todd.

As at Ayr, the new school was divided into three training flights and a pool, and commenced work on 14 May. The first flight had three Bristol Fighters and five or six Avro 504s; the second fifteen Sopwith Camels and six Avro 504s; the third four or five SE5s and three or four Avro 504s. There was also a fourth flight, acting as a pool, which was equipped with three or four Sopwith Camels, two SE5s, a Bristol MC1, several DH2s and two or three Avro 504s. In addition, the school also had at least one RE7, SPADs, Sopwith Pups and a captured Albatros Scout. Each machine had a fitter and rigger, and each flight had a flight sergeant. Pupils began each course with intensive instruction in ground gunnery (similar to that previously carried out at the School of Aerial Gunnery) which was followed by aerial combat exercises. A target was moored out at sea in order to provide air-to-ground firing practice and camera guns were used to record the pupil's success, or lack of it, for examination at a later time. Air-to-air firing practice was provided by RE7s which cruised the sky towing large flags through the air. Twice weekly the pupils were pitched against the instructors in a dog-fight with camera guns recording the results.

Now the pupil is ready to unite formation flying and fighting. One instructor therefore leads a flight across the line patrolled by several flights and a battle takes place as soon as the patrolling flyers catch sight of those crossing. For this purpose, here, the coastline offers a splendid line of defense, and the attacking party endeavors to outwit the defenders by making use of clouds, inequalities in the land, etc, and cross the line unobserved, when, if successful, they rise and show themselves offering battle. As many as possible of these maneuvres are carried out, the two parties dividing upon a given signal, and repeating the performance. Each pilot is given at least two opportunities of engaging in this work. Some time during the latter part of the

Staff Officers, Turnberry, April 1918.

Front row (L–R): Capt GC Maxwell, MC; Capt WD South; Capt SW Taylor, MC; Capt KH Marshall; Lieut-Col LWB Rees, VC, MC; Capt JW Woodhouse, DSO, MC; Capt F Paterson; Capt JB McCudden, VC, DSO, MC, MM, CdeG; Lieut FM Thomas. Second row (L–R): 2 Lieut RJ Sladden, DCM; Captain ADC Browne; Capt JD Atkinson; Lieut JR Bost; Capt LAF Foers, MC; Lieut HAD Edwards; Lieut DJ Rollo, CdeG; Capt JM Burd, MC; Lieut IM Harris. Third row (L–R): Lieut RM Makepeace, MC; Lieut EL Zink; Lieut JRG Rowden; 2 Lieut RW Farquhar; 2 Lieut HW Elliott; Lieutenant D Sutherland; Lieut HL McNaughton; 2 Lieut RW Weatherby; Lieut HB Redler, MC. Fourth row (L–R): Lieut DH de Burgh; Lieut WAG Young; Lieut FM Howard; Lieut H Jones; Lieut A Armstrong. [Alex Revell] course a large bombing raid is engineered in which everyone takes part. All the men training form two flights, led by an instructor. These are the bombing machines. Two large flights of scouts are also led by an instructor, one to convoy each set of bombers. All the Bristol Fighter pilots, the men in the pool and the remaining instructors form the defense. The latter, the instructors, fly all types of machines, including a German Albatross [sic] and several types of English machines, including one or two of the latest, or even experimental machines.

Some town or city nearby is selected as the objective. The defenders leave the home aerodrome first and get in position. Shortly after they leave, the two attacking forces go off in a wide, roundabout way, having beforehand determined upon a certain time at which they will attack the city from different sides. As close as possible to the predetermined time both parties of bombers and escorts attack. The convoying scouts endeavor to keep the defenders from the bombers, which in close formation dive upon the city and fly over the points to be bombed. All the machines, about 35 or 40 in all, then engage in a tremendous battle. After about ten minutes of this, when the bombers have flown back and forward over the city several times, a signal is given and all the machines return. Then a flight of pupils alone is sent in formation and each leads the flight in turn.

Afterwards all pilots and instructors are called together, and each flight commander reports his objective, its success or failure, and gives advice on his flight's actions. Then the CO [Rees], who always is overseeing, all while flying among the defenders, gives a talk on the different points of the raid and raids in general.[45]

Rees ran the school efficiently and with a firm control, but was not opposed to the staff and pupils letting off steam and a rivalry soon developed between his own command and the men of the North Western Area Flying Instructors' School[46] which had moved into the airfield at Ayr, and there were regular raids which kept both stations on their toes. The instructors were also often involved in spectacular aerial stunts, a particular favourite being to fly past the Turnberry Hotel, below roof level, in an inverted position. It was a practice which had to be discontinued after one pilot died whilst attempting it. The local residents, despite the obvious dangers and annoyances caused by the school, appear to have gone out of their way to make life as pleasant as possible for the airmen and several memoirs make reference to visiting private homes in the area whilst stationed at Ayr and Turnberry. Rees himself spent much of his free time at a house he had rented near the airfield, where his aunt, Mrs Katie Moore, acted as hostess and to which place he would often invite junior officers serving in his command.

Among the few documents that have survived that relate to the School of Aerial

Lieut George Squires
[http://www.maybole.org]

Fighting are three letters written to the mother of 1 Lieutenant George Squires, one of four United States servicemen who died whilst training at Turnberry.[47] They are worthy of being quoted here at some length as they not only describe some of the training undertaken by the students, but also the care and concern expressed by the staff and the general public when a tragedy did occur. The first was written by Rees, albeit in the 'third person':[48]

It is with the very deepest regret and sympathy that I have to confirm the news, which you have no doubt received by telegraph, of the death of your son, 1st Lieut George Squires, who was at the time attached to this School for a Course of Instruction in Aerial Fighting and Gunnery. I beg to give you the following brief particulars of the fatal accident and of the funeral arrangements.

On Saturday May 18th, at 10:30 in the morning, the machine of 1/Lt G Squires, who was carrying out practice in certain fighting evolutions, was seen to circle slowly and begin descending, the descent taking place apparently normally until the machine dived at a steep angle and crashed to the ground. Your son was in sole control of the machine, no passenger being carried on the type he was flying.

A Court of Inquiry investigated the circumstances on the following day, and it was not established from all the available evidence what was the definite cause of the accident. There was no structural defect suspected in the machine, as the latter had been reported in perfect condition and 'OK' for flying on its descent from a flight undertaken by one of the instructors immediately before the fatal one.

In view of the evidence given by a farm hand who witnessed the accident, it is considered almost certain that your son was endeavouring to make a forced landing owing to engine failure, and that he lost flying speed (the speed sufficient to maintain a machine in the air) at a height which did not permit him to recover from the ensuing dive. The fall took place about 1,000 yards south of Kirkoswald Village, Ayrshire, at a point almost exactly two miles eastward of and inland from this aerodrome.

Immediately upon the report of the accident happening, the motor ambulance with Medical Officer proceeded to the scene, and found 1/Lt Squires dead, having been extricated from the wreckage by a local resident who was first on the spot.

The cause of death was fracture of the base of the skull, both thighs had been fractured and there were other injuries, and it is considered that death was practically instantaneous upon the machine striking the ground.

Units of the Royal Air Force are not permitted to telegraph or cable direct to the next-of-kin in cases of fatalities occurring where the nearest relatives reside out of the country, but you no doubt heard as soon as possible, after our reporting the accident to the proper British and American authorities.

In regard to funeral arrangements, the interment took place at Doune Cemetery, Girvan, at 2 pm on Tuesday, May 21st. Girvan is the nearest town of any size, and is about 5 to 6 miles distant from this Station.

The burial service was conducted by the Rev GB Allen, the Church of England Chaplain to the Forces stationed here, and the following American brother officers of the Aviation Service acted as pall-bearers:- 1/Lt JA Roth, 1/Lt E Hollander, 1/Lt AM Roberts, 1/Lt RL Paskill, 2/Lt HR Smith,[49] 2/Lt LT Wyly.

A large number of other American Officers and British Officers of the School attended, the latter including the Commandant, Lieut Col LWB Rees, VC, MC.

A firing party accompanied the cortege, firing three volleys over the grave at the conclusion of the service, after which the 'Last Post' was sounded by the bugler. The coffin was covered with the American Flag and three floral tributes from the American brother officers of your son, the officers of the staff of the School and the Camp YMCA authorities.

The position of the grave is No 6, Section M, Fast Division, Doune Cemetery, Girvan, Ayrshire. … As a temporary measure a plain white wooden cross of the pattern prescribed for a British officer or man, is being placed above the grave, pending later arrangements for memorial.

The interment took place in brilliantly fine weather, which, indeed, prevailed upon the day of the accident,

If there is any further information which I can furnish, will you please let me know, and be assured that any assistance which it is, in my power to afford will be most willingly given.

The second letter was from Mr LS Balkie, headmaster of Kirkoswald School, who took a great interest in the airmen at Turnberry and who was a civilian eyewitness at the crash scene:[50]

I happened to be about half-a-mile away when your son came down. He was circling slowly down from a fair height when, as it appeared to me, he lost flying speed and nose dived. I heard the crash and ran for the place where it appeared to me [that it] had fallen. Poor fellow!

when we got there he was past help. A farm worker Robert Lawrie was there a couple of minutes before me and had your son removed from his seat; he cut the fastenings. We had him on the road side and made a pillow for his head. We despatched a phone message for a doctor and ambulance. He was still breathing and we did not then quite realize the extent of his injuries. A crowd was there by that time. I got the men there to take off their coats which we put over and under him. As I said before, we were more than half-a-mile from anywhere, but we ran [and] got tepid water and bathed his wounds. He, however, never recovered consciousness. When the doctor arrived he pronounced life extinct.

Altho' he received multiple injuries, the only noticeable wounds were one on the left cheek and another gash above his left knee. I was assured [that] medically he suffered no pain; also, that he could not have lived. This worried me greatly … in respect that the man was lying here, too far away from a house to be removed to one and we could do so little. What little we could do we did. After the arrival of the Ambulance he was gently lifted on to a stretcher and put inside.

He was flying in a single-seated Sopwith Camel machine, I think of about 130 hp. The military will know better than I do what went wrong, but it appeared to me he had engine trouble and probably miscalculated his distance in trying to land to have things put right.

It was a pathetic sight. Your son's face will haunt me as long as I live. It is however a consolation to me to have been there; we did what in us lay to soothe his last moments.

Thirdly, Lieutenant Ralph Gracie,[51] a friend of the deceased, wrote summing up the feelings of the American students at Turnberry with regard to the tragic fatal accident and to the training which the students were receiving.

… I happened to be in the air myself at the time of George's accident and when I came down and learned the horrible news, it was almost as hard to believe as that the sun would not shine again.

George had done about thirty hours flying in 'Camels', the type of machine he was up in. He really liked to fly them and could fly them better than any of our other fliers that [I] have watched. I am flying 'Camels' myself and know to what extent he surpassed me in handling what is really one of the most difficult machines to fly. He was feeling his best that morning, I know, as I had sat beside him at the table.

He had asked a number of times for a machine that morning and had made several flights besides the necessary ones for the course in fighting which we were engaged in.

He came down some distance from, the drome and the only actual witness was a laborer, who was questioned at the 'inquiry'. He had heard the sound of an aeroplane overhead and told of a sound which the flying officers present interpreted as a stall on a turn and a spin into the ground, from what height we have no very definite idea.

George had been working particularly at rolls, half rolls and the 'falling leaf stunt' and the machine, as I said before, being a most tricky and treacherous one, it does not take long to come to grief. He was a splendid pilot and apparently physically fit, and what happened is what is liable to happen to any one, no matter how long his experience at this game. There is, of course, the possibility of something wrong with the machine, but at that station they are much better and better maintained, and any that I had up were a pleasure to fly compared to the average.

Lieut Ralph Gracie

… We have now lost four of the fliers who came over with our squadron to train in England.[52]

There can be no doubt that the School of Aerial Fighting and the Fighter School were very successful and played a significant part in the establishment of Allied air supremacy over the Western Front during the summer of 1918. While little glamour was attached to the training of pilots, those who were involved were only too aware of the risks which their duties entailed, both for instructors and pupils, and the staff of training establishments played a vital role in the history of the air war. It could be argued that Rees' contribution as the commandant of Ayr and Turnberry was of greater significance than anything else which he had done since 1914 and certainly countless British and American airmen owed their lives to the skills they learned in Scotland. So often one hears criticisms of courses of all kinds, but there was never anything but praise for those run by Rees.

Rees remained at Turnberry right through to the end of the war and on into 1919. Much to his surprise, he had survived the first conflict to be fought in the air and ahead of him lay the peace which for many was a time of reconstruction and taking stock, but for him and the others who were desirous of remaining in the fledgling Royal Air Force, it was a period of uncertainty that faced them.

Instructors and Staff, Turnberry, on the occasion of a visit by General Caley, CB, 1918.
Rees is sitting fifth from the right. [JM Bruce/G Stuart Leslie Collection]

Notes

1. Later Lieutenant-Colonel Robert Raymond Smith-Barry, AFC (1886–1949) of Mayfair, London. Undergraduate of Trinity College, Cambridge. RAeC certificate 1911 and joined the RFC in 1912. Served 5, 60 and 1(R) Squadron. Full details of his career can be found in his biography, *Pioneer Pilot. The Great Smith Barry Who Taught the World How to Fly*, F D Tredrey, London, 1976.

2. The generally accepted figure for RFC pilot fatalities during the war is 14,166, of which approximately 8,000 were killed while training.

3. These figures vary according to how they were calculated. Full details can be found in Peter Hart, *Bloody April: Slaughter in the Skies Over Arras, 1917*, London, 2005.

4. Geoffrey L Rossano (editor) *Hero of the Angry Sky. The World War 1 Diary and Letters of David S. Ingalls, America's First Naval Ace*, (Ohio, 2013), hereafter referred to as Ingalls. Ensign David Sinton Ingalls, DSM, Legion of Merit, DFC (GB), Legion of Honour (France) (1899–1985), a native of Cleveland, Ohio, and a former Yale undergraduate, became the only US Navy 'ace' of the Great War. He was later a US Congressman and Assistant Secretary of the Navy. He was Commander of Pearl Harbor Naval Air Station during the latter part of the Second World War. He was also a director of Pan American Airways, a lawyer and newspaper publisher.

5. Ensign Kenneth MacLeish (1894–1918), of Glencoe, Illinois, was a member of the First Yale Unit of aviators who volunteered for military service in the Great War. He was killed in action flying a Sopwith Camel with 213 Squadron, RAF. He was' last seen attacking about seven Fokkers single-handed' near Ostend in Belgium. He was awarded a posthumous Navy Cross.

6. Geoffrey L Rossano (editor) *The Price of Honor, the World War One Letters of Naval Aviator Kenneth MacLiesh*, Annapolis, 1991, hereafter referred to as MacLeish. Letter dated 7 February 1918, 94.

7. Ingalls, op cit, 116.

8. Ibid, diary 5–15 February 1918, 116.

9. Marc Wortman, *The Millionaires' Unit the Aristocratic Flyboys Who Fought the Great War and Invented America's Air Power*, London, 2006, 175.

10. Ingalls, op cit, 120.

11. 'Memoirs of a World War 1 Ace', unpublished manuscript written by Rodney D Williams (1896–1972) of Delafield, Wisconsin, hereafter referred to as Williams. After instruction in Canada he became a pilot with the 17th Aero Squadron, attached to the RFC, and completed his training in the United Kingdom. He later downed four German aeroplanes and one balloon and was awarded the Silver Star and a Mention in Despatches (GB). His manuscript is held at the Wisconsin Veterans Museum, Madison, Wisconsin, and was sourced via the

Wisconsin Aviation Hall of Fame.

12. Ingalls, op cit, 133.

13. MacLiesh, op cit, letter dated 4 March 1918, 109.

14. Williams, op cit.

15. Major Cyril Edgar Foggin, (1891–1918), of South Gosforth, he qualified in 1912 and became a professional aviator. Flight sergeant RFC, he was commissioned in September 1915. He served with 1 and 40 Squadrons, losing his eye in 1916. He was killed in a motor car accident in France, 30 July 1918 and is buried in St Riquier British Cemetery.

16. Later Squadron Leader Edward Dawson 'Spider' Atkinson, DFC, AFC. Indian Army Reserve of Officers, he transferred to the RFC in 1916. He flew with 1, 56 and 64 Squadrons, achieving a score of ten victories (one balloon, four aeroplanes destroyed and five driven down out of control).

17. Elliot White Springs, *War Birds, diary of an unknown aviator* (New York, 1926), hereafter referred to as Springs. Springs was a North Carolina businessman who volunteered for the American Air Corps in 1917 and was trained in Britain by the Royal Air Force, attending a course at the 1 School of Aerial Fighting. He ended the war as a captain with a 'score' of sixteen enemy aircraft destroyed. He wrote *War Birds*, which was based upon the diaries of his friend John McGavock Grider (1892–1918) of Grider, Mississippi. A farmer, Grider enlisted in April 1917 in the Aviation Section. He served in 85 Squadron, RAF, and was killed in action on 18 June. He is credited with four aerial victories. A film of the same name, released in 2003, was based upon this book.

18. 1 Lieutenant Thomas Cushman 'Cush' Nathan (1897–1918) of Dorchester, Massachusetts, who was a student at the Massachusetts Institute of Technology for one year before enlisting in March 1917. He trained at Miami and Berkeley before embarking for Britain and was killed on 20 March 1918 while testing a SPAD aeroplane when the wing collapsed.'Considered the best American pilot to ever attend the school at Ayr.' Buried in Ayr Cemetery.

19. Lieutenant George Augustus Vaughn, Jnr, DSC, DFC, Silver Star (1897–1989) of Brooklyn. He learned to fly at Princeton University. Served with 84 Squadron (RAF) and 17 Aero Squadron (USAS), credited with a total of thirteen victories. Author of *War Flying in France* (New York, 1980). Corresponded with the author 8 April 1989.

20. 'Pansy' was the nickname of an unidentified American pilot.

21. Springs, op cit, 89.

22. Major James Thomas Byford McCudden, VC, DSO and Bar, MC and Bar, MM, *Croix de Guerre* (France) (1895–1918), Royal Engineers, of Gillingham, Kent. He enlisted in the RE in 1910 as a boy bugler and transferred to the RFC as a mechanic in 1913. He flew as an observer with 3 Squadron before qualifying as a pilot in 1916 and serving with 20, 29, 66, 56 and 60 Squadrons. He is credited with 57 aerial victories. He died of injuries received in a flying accident. Author of *Flying Fury, Five Years in the RFC* (1918).

23. Later Squadron Leader James Douglas Latta, MC (1897–1974), London Scottish, he transferred to the RFC in 1915 and served in 5, 1, 16, 60 and 66 Squadrons. Awarded an MC in 1916, wounded in 1917. He is credited with the destruction of two balloons, one aeroplane and two aeroplanes driven down out of control. He became OC 602 (City of Glasgow) Squadron, RAuxAF in 1925–7. Chairman of Scottish Stamping & Engineering Co Ltd.

24. *McCudden, VC*, Christopher Cole, London, 1967, 181.

25. Later Edward Corringham 'Mick' Mannock, VC, DSO & two Bars, MC & Bar (1887–1918). A former telephone engineer, he joined the RAMC in 1915 and after being commissioned in the RE in 1916 he transferred to the RFC. He served in 40, 74 and 85 Squadrons. He was killed in action in July 1918 and was officially credited with sixty-one victories (although his actual score may have been significantly higher).

26. Later Wing Commander Ira Thomas 'Taffy' Jones, DSO, MC, DFC and Bar, MM, Cross of St George (Russia) (1896–1960) of St Clears, Carmarthenshire. He served briefly in the Welsh Regiment (TF) before transferring to the RFC as a mechanic and gaining his first gallantry award, the MM, in 1916. He served for a period as an observer before commencing flying training in 1917. Posted to 74 Squadron, he ended the war with 37 victories. He served in Russia with the White Russian forces before receiving a permanent commission in the RAF in 1919. He retired in 1936 only to be recalled in 1939 and commanded a number of training units until the end of the war. He wrote several books, including *King of the Air Fighters, Tiger Squadron* and *An Air Fighter's Scrapbook* He died following a fall from a ladder at his home in Aberaeron.

27. Later Wing Commander Gerald Joseph Constable Maxwell, MC, DFC, AFC (1895–1959), of Inverness, son of 10th Lord Herries of Terregles and nephew of Lord Lovat. Served with the Lovat Scouts in Gallipoli 1915, then transferred to the RFC in 1916. Served 56 Squadron. Achieved a score of 26 victories (12 destroyed and 14 driven down out of control). Transferred to the RAF and resigned 1921 to become a director of Maxwell-

Chrysler Motors. Served RAuxAF. OC RAF Ford 1941–5. At the end of his career he flew Meteor jet fighters. Deputy Lieutenant of Hampshire.

28. James Ira Thomas Jones, *Tiger Squadron* (London, 1955), 63–4.

29. *Sopwith Camel Fighter Ace*, Robert Miles Todd (Falls Church, 1978).

30. Petty Officer Harry Wakefield Harnett, RNAS, (1890–1966) of St Giles, London, a police officer, enlisted in the Royal Navy in April 1915 for service with the Royal Naval Division. He qualified as a pilot in May 1918 and eventually transferred to the RAF on 1 April 1918. He was an officer in the City of London Police.

31. Ingalls, op cit, diary 3 March 1918, 127.

32. The instructor was 1 Lieutenant Andrew Carl Ortmeyer (1886–1918), Aviation Section, US Army Signal Corps, A native of Chicago and a Yale graduate, he was killed on 7 March when his Camel span into the ground from 300 feet. He had over 300 hours experience in the USA where he had instructed on the Curtis biplane. The other pilot killed on the same day was Ensign Harry Glen Velie (1893–1918), US Navy, also of Chicago. Both are buried in Ayr Cemetery.

33. Lieutenant Thomas Sydney Ough Dealy (1896–1918), Australian Flying Corps was killed on 7 March 1918 when his Camel (B7418) went into a spin at 800 feet from which he failed to recover. He is buried in Stonyhurst College Burial Ground.

34. Springs, op cit, 87.

35. Later Wing Commander Norman MacMillan, OBE, MC, AFC, DL (1892–1976) of Cambuslang, Lanarkshire. Served as a soldier in 5 Highland Light Infantry (TF) and was commissioned and transferred to the RFC. Qualified RAeC 1917. He served with 45 Squadron. Author of *Into the Blue*. Served as a war correspondent during the Second World War with the rank of wing commander.

36. *Into the Blue*, Captain Norman MacMillan (London, 1929), p 113.

37. Ingalls, op cit, diary 10 March 1918, 129.

38. Springs, op cit, 87.

39. Ingalls, op cit, diary 10 March 1918, 129.

40. Springs, op cit, 86. It would appear that the American pupil pilots had a great deal to be dissatisfied about. Having been among the first US servicemen to cross the Atlantic, many had not been commissioned. The American commander in Europe, General Pershing, had decided that pilots did not warrant even warrant officer status and he wanted them all to be sergeants. He was also in favour of abolishing flying pay. Some of those who had been commissioned were threatening to resign unless the same privileges were given to their comrades.

41. Ibid, 87–9.

42. Turnberry was established as an airfield at the famous Turnberry Golf Club, between the hotel and the coast, and alongside the present day A719. The Turnberry Hotel was used as the officers' mess and as a hospital for airmen injured during training. During the Second World War, when Turnberry was again used as a training station for pilots, a number of fatal accidents occurred and it was rumoured that shortly before each crash a ghostly biplane fighter had been spotted over the area.

43. Later Colonel Robert Miles Todd, USAS, (1897–1988) of Cincinnati. He volunteered in August 1917 and trained in Texas and Canada before crossing the Atlantic. He served with the 17 Aero Squadron, under RFC command, and was credited with five 'kills'. Wounded in August he became a prisoner of war. He served in the USAAC during the Second World War.

44. *Sopwith Camel Fighter Ace*, Robert Miles Todd (Falls Church, 1978).

45. Ingalls, op cit, 131.

46. The North Western Area Flying Instructors' School was established at Ayr in July 1918 as an extension of Smith-Barry's school in Gosport. Two of the original hangars at Ayr survived until recently, the last, a Belfast hangar, was demolished in 1989 and the site is now occupied by a superstore.

47. Lieutenant George Squires of St Paul, Minnesota (1896–1918) was killed on 18 May when his Sopwith Camel, (B9218), stalled on a turn at 100ft and crashed south of the village of Kirkoswald. During his initial training in Canada in August 1917, he had been involved in a mid-air collision with Stephen H Dorr; both pilots had been on their first solo flight. Squires was cleared of all blame for the accident.

48. Letter reproduced from the website www.worldwar1.com/dbc/ukburials.htm.

49. 2 Lieutenant HR Smith was killed whilst training at Turnberry.

50. Letter reproduced from the website www.worldwar1.com/dbc/ukburials.htm.

51. Lieutenant Ralph Gracie of Bemidji, Minnesota, was reported missing on 12 August 1918 and was believed to have crashed into the sea off the coast of France following a combat with German aircraft.

52. Letter reproduced from the website www.worldwar1.com/dbc/ukburials.htm.

VII

RAF College Cranwell
(1920–25)

THE GENERAL ELECTION OF DECEMBER 1918 BROUGHT WINSTON CHURCHILL the dual portfolios of the War Office and the Air Ministry. It had been Prime Minister Lloyd George's original intention that the two ministries should be merged as the first step towards the disbanding of the RAF, a move which would have pleased both the Admiralty and the War Office. Other events took precedence, however, as the world's statesmen met to begin drawing up the peace treaties with Germany and the other members of the Central Powers block, a matter which was to take until the summer of the following year to resolve. This delay proved to be the salvation of the RAF for, by December 1919, the government had reviewed the situation and decided to maintain an independent air service. The position of Chief of the Air Staff had seemed to be destined for Sir Frederick Sykes, who had held the post at the end of the war, but internal manipulations led to it being offered to Hugh Trenchard who was given orders to drastically reduce the strength of the RAF from its wartime high of 185 operational and 200 training squadrons to a financially more realistic peacetime service. By the end of 1919, the RAF had been reduced to 26 squadrons of all types.

The restoration of peace had found Rees with the rank of lieutenant colonel, still serving as commandant of 1 Fighter School at Turnberry. Clearly, his expertise as a former commander of a front-line squadron, trainer of airmen and an administrator placed him in an advantageous position when the senior commanders began to select from the wartime RAF officers those who would be offered permanent positions in the peacetime service. In April 1919, he was appointed Inspector of Recruiting just as the RAF began to drastically cut its manpower. Still officially a regular officer in the Royal Artillery, Rees was promoted to the rank of brevet lieutenant-colonel (the RAF had yet to finally settle on its own rank titles) and then, on 25 July, to lieutenant-colonel (aeroplanes), and given the command of 2 Fighter School, South East Area. One week later, his application for a permanent commission in the RAF was accepted and he relinquished his Army rank of lieutenant-colonel to become an RAF wing commander. There had been no doubt in his mind where his future lay; eleven years of peacetime soldiering in the RGA had brought him little advancement and to return, after an absence of four years, at a time when the services were contracting, would have been foolish in the extreme. On the other hand, his service in the RFC and the RAF had raised him to the position of a well known and highly respected officer with a proven record as a man who was willing to accept any challenge, with the ability to carry it through to a successful conclusion. A future in the RAF seemed to offer infinitely better prospects and he eagerly seized the opportunity.

In December 1919, Trenchard published Command Document 467 entitled *Permanent Organisation of the Royal Air Force* in which he emphasised the 'Extreme Importance of Training.' If the strength of the RAF was to be dramatically reduced, then great care had to be taken to ensure that the service retained its ability to train new pilots upon whom its future would depend. Training was to be specialized and carried out in specific training units, and he recommended that pilots should be trained as distinctive fighter, reconnaissance and bomber pilots. Although the RAF was less than two years old, he wished to preserve as many as possible of the traditions which had been built up over four years of war. In Command Document 467 he emphasised that,

> The present need is not, under existing conditions, the creation of the full number of Squadrons we may eventually require to meet strategical needs, but it is first and foremost the making of a sound framework on which to build the service, which while giving us now the few essential service Squadrons, adequately trained and equipped, will be capable of producing whatever time may show to be necessary in future.[1]

Clearly, the establishment of flying-training establishments was of paramount importance and Trenchard was cognizant that great care needed to be taken to ensure that the officers who were accepted into the new service were capable of not only instilling the correct ethos to future students, but also had the right attitude with regard to flying training. Rees fulfilled all the criteria laid down by Trenchard for the new peacetime service. His abilities as a pilot could not be questioned and the decorations which he wore placed him firmly in the category of a builder of tradition, a man whom younger officers could look up to and respect. His long-time association with the dynamic training methods introduced during the war also made him an ideal candidate for a significant all-important training position.

The other figure in the RAF who appeared to perfectly fit the mould of the future officer was Lieutenant-Colonel Robert Smith-Barry who had been advocating revolutionary training methods since 1916. The flying training system he had established at Gosport, was the standard method of flying training throughout the RAF by 1919. In 1918, Smith-Barry had produced a short book entitled *Flying Instruction*, which outlined the methodology then in place. He advocated that students should be allowed into the air at the earliest opportunity, ideally in 'bumpy weather'; they should never fly simply in order to gain more flying hours, all flights should have a purpose; they should be encouraged to get into, and out of, difficult situations without interference from the instructor until the last minute.

> … good and bad morale, confidence and the lack of it, are more easily caught than the most contagious of physical diseases, and the new pupil will be immediately infected with either one or the other by Instructors and advanced pupils. … The words 'danger' and 'nerves' must not form part of the Instructor's vocabulary. Nothing that a pilot may do in the air is dangerous if he knows what he is doing and what the result will be. Almost all accidents are caused by ignorance, and if, instead of telling a pupil that a manoeuvre is dangerous, he is taught how to do it, his instinct of self-preservation will do the rest.[2]

Smith-Barry had refused to conform to the wishes of his more senior officers in the service and had openly opposed many of Trenchard's proposals during the latter part of the war. Consequently, he did not remain in either the RAF or the Army after the war, but retired to the life of a country gentleman. Rees, however, was the ideal officer to fulfil Trenchard's vision for the future RAF. His natural shyness and modesty endeared him to all whom he met, but in the background was that determination which had brought him so much success during the war. RAF Cadet Wilfred Freebody[3] recalled him at this time of great changes.

> He never appeared to be career minded, nor did he make capital out of his undoubted achievements. He was quite diffident about his decorations … very polite and kindly and in this respect stood out in contrast against those of his contemporaries who thought themselves to be in the 'up and coming' category. He was modest and fun-loving and made jokes at his own expense.[4]

The pace for establishing the peacetime RAF was a rapid one during 1919 and, on 18 September, after less than two months in command of 2 Fighter School, Rees was again moved to take over the command of RAF Eastchurch on the Isle of Sheppey, a station where he had first served in 1914. Established in 1912 as a the Royal Naval Air Service flying instruction camp, Eastchurch had been that service's equivalent of the RFC's Central Flying School throughout the war, until it became the RAF's Air Gunnery and Bombing School. Amongst those stationed there in 1919 was Boy Mechanic Walter Dawson,[5] who had enlisted for training as an aero engine fitter at Halton in February and, shortly afterwards, had been drafted to Eastchurch for technical training.

> Parts of it seemed strange to even RAF eyes. For example, the Station Warrant Officer was in the uniform of a naval CPO (old uniforms could still be worn out) – that was a 'fore and aft' without crowns, anchors or stripes, and he was a chap who threw his weight about considerably, so half a dozen of my draft were in the guardroom before we discovered the status of this unpopular type. The Station Adjutant wore the uniform of an RFC Captain. We lived 20 boys to a hut and each hut's occupants formed a class who moved together – marching to school or workshops or parades, etc and each hut was in charge of a Boy Corporal who, to my surprise, wore full corporal's stripes under the Boy's 'cartwheel.' I became the Boy Corporal of A5 Class. Wing Commander LWB Rees was the Station Commander and the course was a 6 months 'cram', probably a hangover from the wartime need for quantity at the expense of quality.[6]

It was at this time that Rees added to his collection of honours. In addition to the VC and MC, he was awarded the newly instituted Air Force Cross, in recognition of his services to flying training during the war, particularly at Ayr and Turnberry.[7] He was also made an officer of the newly-established Order of the British Empire, in recognition of his work in the United States during 1917.[8] However, the honour which probably meant the most to him and made him particularly proud was the Freedom of the Borough of Caernarfon.

His home town, like almost every other town in Britain, had suffered severe losses during the war and felt that it needed to do something to commemorate the deeds of local men who had made a significant contribution to the final Allied victory. Most were in agreement that nothing could be done to repay the massive debt that was owed to those who had made the supreme sacrifice, but it was a matter of some concern to many that those who had survived should not feel that their services were unrecognized. In Caernarfon, the Borough Council decided to further honour those men who had received decorations for their gallantry and devotion to duty. A civic reception was planned for all of the identified men, where one man would be singled out as the focus of public attention and as a representative of all the men involved. The members of the Borough Council had little difficulty in selecting that individual. Although there were a large number of men who had received gallantry awards, only one, Lionel Rees, had received Britain's highest decoration for gallantry as well as the MC, the OBE and the AFC.[9] There would have been little debate as to how they should recognise his achievements and he joined the very short list of men who had been created Freemen of the Borough.[10] The ceremony was held on 15 January 1920, at the Guildhall, a building which had been built at the behest of his grandfather, where Rees was also presented with a Sword of Honour, a suitably inscribed dress scimitar, in recognition of his gallant service.[11] In a speech, Councillor Abbot reflected

Rees receiving the Sword of Honour from the Borough of Caernarfon, 1920.
[Rees Family Archive]

the town's pride in Rees' achievements as was reported in the *Carnarvon & Denbigh Herald*.

… he had the greatest pleasure in seconding the resolution … enhanced by reason of the fact that they were honouring a Carnarvonite [sic], in other words a *hogyn o'r dre* [a town boy]. Though they were a small community, they had reared men who had become famous … not least of these was Wing Commander Rees, the worthy son of a worthy sire. It was said that 'a prophet is not without honour in his own country' but those proceedings that day belied that statement. They were honouring a prophet, not only in his own country, but in his own native town … the youngest ever to be admitted to the Freedom of the Borough, the highest honour that the people of Carnarvon could confer on anyone.[12]

In his speech of acceptance, Rees was his usual modest self, reminding those present that 'when he won the Military Cross, he had with him … one of the best observers in the Service.' And again when he fought the action for which he was awarded the Victoria Cross, '… he was lucky in the pilot who was with him.'[13] The first reference was obviously, and quite rightly, an acknowledgement of the role of Flight Sergeant Hargreaves, but the second reference, presumably to Lieutenant John Simpson, was clearly an attempt to play down the award as his action had in reality been single-handed. Finally, he showed another side of his personality when he announced that he had made arrangements for some 2,000 local children to be entertained at local cinemas the following afternoon. In addition to the free admission, each child was to be presented with a packet of chocolate. A simple gesture, but one that clearly showed his gentle nature and love of children, and which seemed to contradict all the gallant platitudes expressed by the assembled councillors.

Four weeks later, undoubtedly prompted by the award of the Freedom of the Borough, the Carnarvon Sailing Club (not to be confused with the Royal Welsh Yacht Club) voted unanimously that Rees be elected a Life Member.

Such pleasant, but undoubtedly highly embarrassing events were accompanied by more official events where he was asked to represent the RAF. On 26 June 1920, he was one of 310 VC recipients who attended a luncheon at Wellington Barracks before marching to Buckingham Palace for a garden party hosted by the King and Queen, the first ever VC reunion. Perhaps the most notable of these was his presence as one of the Guard of Honour at the burial of the Unknown Soldier in Westminster Abbey on 11 November 1920.[14] He was also the senior RAF officer present at the unveiling in 1923 of the memorial to those airmen who had died at Turnberry during the war.[15]

A major aspect of Trenchard's plan for the re-formed RAF was the establishment of a cadet college which would be the main route into the service for permanently commissioned officers. In Command Document 467 he had noted that,

...to make an Air Force worthy of the name, we must create an Air Force spirit, or rather

Rees with his dog in front of one of the administrative buildings at RAF College, Cranwell. [Rees Family Archive]

foster this spirit which undoubtedly existed in a high degree during the war, by every means in our power. Suggestions have been made that we should rely on the older services to train our cadets and Staff officers. To do so would make the creation of an Air Force spirit an impossibility, apart from the practical objection, among others, that the existing naval and military cadet and staff colleges are not provided with aerodromes or situated in localities in any way suited to flying training.[16]

As he noted, there was considerable pressure for entry to be via the existing cadet colleges at Dartmouth, Woolwich and Sandhurst, but the Chief of the Air Staff was adamant that flying instruction *must* be an integral part of all RAF cadet training and this could only be provided by a separate establishment which would build upon the training systems and

L–R: Wg Cdr Barratt, Air Cdre Longcroft and Wg Cdr Rees at Cranwell, c 1921.
[Rees Family Archive]

traditions developed during the war. The case was accepted and, on 1 November 1919, Air Commodore CAH Longcroft[17] was appointed Commandant of the Royal Air Force College which was to be opened at the former RNAS station at Cranwell in Lincolnshire.[18] The nucleus of such a college had existed for some time in the form of Headquarters 12 Group, also based in the same county. Cadets were to be taught general educational subjects, such as mathematics and languages, as well as receive professional training in such areas as flying instruction and aviation technology. The first senior flying instructor (the title chief flying instructor was not introduced until 1930) was Squadron Leader 'Peter' Portal, DSO, MC, who had commanded 16 Squadron on the Western Front and, since 1918, 24 Training Wing at Grantham.[19]

By 5 February 1920, the preparations were complete and the first cadet intake, comprising seventeen Royal Navy entrants and thirty-three direct entrants from schools, had arrived at the isolated and rather spartan college accommodated in former RN brick-built, bungalow-type structures. The members of the RN intake were only required to serve one year at Cranwell after which, if their performance was satisfactory, they would be offered permanent commissions. The schools entry, however, were to follow a two-year course and had been selected after sitting the same examination as candidates for Woolwich and Sandhurst. Unless an applicant expressed a preference for a particular cadet college, the first forty or fifty in the rank order of examination passes would go to Woolwich and the remainder would be offered places at Sandhurst until that college had reached its required quota. Cranwell then took those who remained. Flying Cadet Mills,[20] a member of that first schools intake recorded:

> At first our standard was low in comparison, for instance I was first for Cranwell, but only forty-fourth for Woolwich. This changed very quickly. On the other hand, our medical standard was much higher and kept out several who would otherwise have qualified easily.[21]

This initial structure for admission seems to carry traces of discrimination imposed by the two older services upon the potential RAF cadets. Rather than fight a perhaps lengthy battle to get the cadet college he had envisioned, Trenchard was perhaps being realistic, understanding that establishing the principle of an independent air college was of paramount importance. Once that had been achieved, steps could then be taken to ensure that in the future, potential cadets would be selected and trained to the high standard that he had envisaged all along.

Staff at RAF College Cranwell c.1923. Seated (L–R): Cadet George Mills; –?–; Kilner; Longcroft; Rees; –?–; –?–, c 1921. [RAF College, Cranwell]

Caricature of the senior staff officers at RAF College, Cranwell, November 1921. Presumably drawn for the Cranwell magazine, it was later annotated with the officers later ranks. L–R: Sqn Ldr England; Gp Capt Lionel WB Rees; Gp Capt Arthur L Godman; AVM Charles AH Longcroft; Wg Cdr Arthur S Barratt; Gp Capt Cecil F Kilner, DSO; and Flt Lt Rhodes, Cranwell. [RAF College, Cranwell]

The cadets for the new college came from similar social backgrounds as those who had traditionally entered the older military and naval establishments. The imposition of an invisible economic 'glass ceiling' meant that most young men, particularly from the lower classes of society, were automatically excluded by the £125 per annum cost of the course, but provision was made for a small number of cadets who were accepted on either reduced fees (usually the sons of deceased or serving officers) or free of charge (King's Cadets from the Boy Apprentice Schools). As official members of the armed forces all cadets were to be paid five shillings per day in their first year, rising to ten shillings per day in the second year. Amongst those who aspired for entry in that first year was Boy Mechanic Dawson at Eastchurch. The son of a draper's shop assistant from Sunderland, he would have had no opportunity to apply for direct entry to the RAF College and had been destined for a service career as a fitter.

Early in '19, the Air Ministry announced that they would soon be opening a cadet college at Cranwell on a similar basis as Sandhurst and Woolwich and subject to the same competitive exam, which included certain 'set' subjects and offered a choice of others – total marks to count so long as a qualifying standard was achieved in the 'set' subjects. I obtained entry forms and a couple of sets of past exam papers from the Civil Service Commission.

I had left school at fourteen but fortunately had attended night classes. I decided that if I worked hard enough I stood a chance in the main subjects. But one of the 'set' subjects was French and I knew nothing of that. But, I bought Hugo's *French Simplified* and set to work. A barrack block is not an ideal place in which to teach oneself French, but fortunately I made a very early application for leave to take the exam on the grounds that if I couldn't have leave it was no good working for it.

The Adjutant did his best to dissuade me, on the very understandable grounds that I would be in competition with Public School boys, many of whom would have been to a crammer, so I hadn't a hope and I would waste my entrance fee (£4 I think). Fortunately, the Squadron Commander came through the office, asked what was going on, said he would take over and took me into his office. He was Squadron Leader Chainey,[22] an ex-naval warrant officer, with a voice like a foghorn, apt to frighten the pants off the Boys, until we found him a fine commander and good friend.

I doubt if he had ever sat an exam, but he was no fool and I was closely examined as to how far I understood what I was taking on. He then gave me the sole use of an HQ office outside working hours and gave me valuable encouragement.

The great day arrived and I was dressed in my best uniform (still khaki in those days) an hour before I need leave, when a motor D[espatch] R[ider] arrived to say the Station Commander

Five Avro 504s of C Flight, Cranwell, c 1922. This was the RAF's basic trainer during the Great War and for many years afterwards. [RAF College, Cranwell]

wanted to see me immediately. So, a very worried Boy Corporal arrived at Station HQ. The Warrant Officer told me to report to the 'Adj' which I did and he said, 'Oh, yes, the Old Man wants to see you,' then he barged through the door to the CO's office and announced me. I heard a voice say 'Send him in,' and I was waved in. Startled at not being marched in. Still more startled when the CO said 'Pull up that chair to the desk and sit down.' I was fascinated by his top row of ribbons – the VC, the OBE, the MC and AFC.

He spoke to me quietly, asking about my home life, schooling, apprenticeships, night classes and specially about a scholarship to Sunderland Training College. He soon had me completely at ease and said I had a better educational background than he expected, but that I lacked experience of exams. 'This is a big one,' he said. 'I took an earlier version before going to Woolwich.' So he talked about exams, giving me practical and sensible tips, and made notes as he talked. Then he said he would not expect me to remember more than half he had said so he gave me his notes, with an order to memorize them and follow them in the exam. Then he wished me luck. The result was as I had forecast – a failure to qualify in French, but very satisfactory totals. I passed the second exam.[23]

When Dawson arrived at Cranwell with the college's second intake in September 1920 Lionel Rees was already there, having been appointed on 21 June to take command of the Flying Wing.

Trenchard had a crystal clear picture in his mind of what he wished Cranwell to become. Despite severe financial restrictions, the Cadet College was to provide a thorough all-round education for the future officers of the RAF. There was no place for anything other than excellence, particularly if such officers were to be accepted as the equals of their contemporaries in the naval and military academies. The cadets were required to study a wide range of subjects, both academic and practical, which included: barrack-square drill, physical training, flying, theory of flight, workshops, British history, RAF history, geography, English language and literature, wireless, law, sanitation, meteorology, armament, science, mathematics and the organisation of the Royal Navy and the Army.

Cranwell, located as it was in the heart of Lincolnshire, was well away from any large centres of population and provided little to distract cadets from their studies. Divided into two squadrons, A and B, the cadets were housed in wooden or iron huts and exposed to the rain, snow and cold winds which blew from the North Sea across the camp's elevated position. Each day began at 06.45 and they were expected on parade at 08.00. This was followed by drill and lectures which took them through to lunch at 12.30. An hour and a half later, they were all expected to take part in various organised activities which lasted until 16.30. Discipline was maintained on the whole by the cadets themselves, although major incidents would be dealt with by the college staff. A clear divide seems to have existed between the cadets and their officers and instructors. Theodore McEvoy, a cadet of 1923 recalled, 'I had the greatest admiration for Uncle Rees, but we as humble flight cadets, had only limited contact with the great.'[24]

Dermot Boyle, a cadet of 1922, had similar memories.[25]

We all held him [Rees] in high regard as a World War 1 ace, as the holder of the VC and as a courageous pilot. He was OC Flying Wing, but in fact I never met him to talk to and only saw him on parades. This was in no way unusual because of the great difference in rank and age and the fact that the cadets lived in a mess of their own. Had I broken flying regulations or become a doubtful pilot, I would have very quickly met OC Flying Wing.[26]

It was not only the cadets who regarded Rees with some awe and respect, amongst the other ranks a former AC2 Carpenter Rigger, Harold Jones, had fond recollections of him.

A warm, outgoing personality, showing the meaning of the saying an officer and a gentleman … strict, but fair, he would listen to reason and if he had occasion to punish, it was well deserved. One Sunday in the month he would have a barrack room inspection and on these occasions would often make critical remarks on items he had already passed, the people responsible would swear he had eyes in the back of his head.

The cadets under his command were given extensive instruction in the theory and practice of mechanics. One must assume his rating in that direction must have been very high. I recall seeing him floating down by parachute from a Vickers biplane. He had been taken up standing on a small platform at the foot of the rear interplane strut. The Vickers biplane was on the station to give the pilots the experience of parachuting – they were actually tugged off the aircraft when they opened the parachute. Despite his gammy leg, the Wing Commander took his turn and showed the pilots how it was done.

The same way, most mornings he took off in his Sopwith Snipe to make a weather test before giving the OK for flying training to commence.[27]

The enforced aloofness between staff and cadets did not however prevent the cadets forming an opinion of the character of Rees. Geoffrey Worthington,[28] a cadet in the very early days of the college, wrote;

Rees at the controls of his Sopwith TF1 'Snipe' at Cranwell. This design saw active service during the Great War and, because of its aerobatic qualities, became the RAF's standard single-seater fighter during the early 1920s. [The late Chaz Bowyer]

… he was a very senior officer at Cranwell and as a Flight Cadet I saw very little of him except on parade and very occasionally to talk to. When flying I saw mostly my instructor and Squadron Leader Portal … My recollections are that we all loved Daddy Rees and thought him a splendid chap.

He tested me for the Fellows Memorial Prize (which I did not win!) but I thought him very brave to sit in the gunner's cockpit of a Bristol Fighter and urge me to throw him about the sky.[29]

This reference to 'Daddy Rees' and the earlier description of him as 'Uncle Rees' appear in the recollections of many cadets from those early days at Cranwell. Different intakes appear to have bestowed upon Rees different relative nicknames, but always for the kindest of reasons. Air Vice Marshal Freebody believed that this was because,

… he appeared elderly, partly because he was bald and also had a bit of a stutter which was inclined to give the impression that he was dithering. In fact he was far from being a ditherer and was constantly surprising us all with exploits which would put much younger men in the shade.[30]

AD Gillmore added,[31]

He was certainly much respected by the cadets. My recollection of him was that he was a man

of high moral principle and that he adopted a somewhat grandmotherly attitude towards the

cadets. Indeed, he was affectionately known as Granny Rees in my time.[32]

Cadets were, to all intents and purposes, confined to the camp and its immediate environs until they were in the senior term when they were allowed to visit Lincoln. This almost school-like atmosphere did not meet with the approval of all the staff. SPB Mais,[33] professor of English at Cranwell, whilst thoroughly approving the nature of the college, felt strongly that the cadets were subjected to too much discipline and should have been allowed the same sort of freedom granted to university undergraduates. As part of their mechanical training, the cadets were provided with dismantled motorcycles which, when reconstructed, could be used for recreation and a free tankful of petrol was provided each week, although few were able to find anywhere to go on the machine; they not being allowed beyond a ten-mile radius of the college and Sleaford, the only town within that area, was out of bounds. Those that did venture out found that dare-devil escapades were the only use for the motorcycles and accidents (for the most part minor ones) became a feature of Cranwell life and the local population became accustomed to the antics of the cadets on the country roads around the college. Officialdom, however, did not always smile on such events and Sir Theodore McEvoy recalled Rees giving the cadets a 'stern harangue' during a Colour Hoisting parade about the evils of getting injured riding a motorcycle; he classed such injuries as 'unfair risks,' as against accidents in the hunting field which he regarded as 'fair risks.'

In 1920, the Flying Wing was divided into A, B and C Flights, with instruction being provided by battle-seasoned veterans of the Western Front. The basic trainer was the Avro 504, a two-seater, tractor biplane powered by the ubiquitous 100 hp Monosaupape engine. In addition, instructors and senior cadets also had available the Bristol Fighter, the DH9a and the Sopwith Snipe (the latter being reserved for the personal use of the senior staff only). In the early days, the actual flying training was limited and, even after graduation from the college, cadets were not awarded the coveted 'wings' of a pilot. The first trainees, the members of the Royal Navy entry of 1920 who had to complete the course in twelve months, had a knock-on delaying effect on the other members of the original intake who did not commence flying training until February 1921, flying three or four times each week so that most had gone solo by the end of April. Others were not so lucky and, as late as the winter of 1924, there were problems ensuring that the cadets had sufficient flying experience. Former cadet, Ellacott Ward recalled that '… our flying in those days was spasmodic – no more than once a week, and sometimes we went as long as a month or so without flying at all.'[34] The training method used at that time was the Gosport System, and Sir George Mills left a very clear account of his experiences as a member of the first intake.

I got very impatient and rather frightened as I began to feel ready to go, but felt quite calm when I was sent off alone. I lost my prop just before touching down, but that was forgiveable on a first solo and I was not too far from the tarmac.

After this, apart from frequent short checks by our instructors, we always flew alone. We would be told what to practice and for how long; anyone who landed late when someone else was waiting was very unpopular. Very soon we added aerobatics on our own, often egged on by hearing that someone else had tried. Some were shown how by their instructors, but I never was. This

Rees wearing the full dress uniform of a wing commander, RAF. [Rees Family Archive]

was in line with the Gosport doctrine that a pupil should be encouraged to find out for himself once he could fly reasonably safely. It could make you breathe a bit, making up your mind to do things, particularly for the first time! We never really spoke about being frightened, even amongst ourselves, but no doubt most of us were from time to time. In fact it was this mixture of fright and enjoyment that made flying such fun and so fascinating.[35]

All cadets were required to complete at least two cross-country flights, one to Lincoln and back, and the second a triangular journey, usually Cranwell–Duxford–Bircham Newton, and conducted in either a Bristol Fighter or a DH9a. With little by way of navigational equipment and no means of communicating with the ground, it was vital that cadets recognised familiar landmarks from the air, and sight of the 'Lighter than Air' sheds at Cranwell (which housed the airships) always brought a private sigh of relief to a pilot returning to the aerodrome.

The Commandant's Report for December 1921 gave details of the amount of flying carried out during the previous term when the cadets had completed a total of 770 hours and 50 minutes, of which 319 hours and 5 minutes were solo. The final term's cadets (who were also the first to complete the full Cranwell course) averaged 16 hours of solo flying each, having received an average of 8 hours of dual instruction before being allowed to go up alone. During the term there had been only one accident in which the cadet concerned was slightly concussed.

In March 1922, Rees was appointed as the successor to Wing Commander Barratt[36] as Assistant Commandant of the Cadet College and the following month the Flying Wing and the Ground Wing were amalgamated under his command. With the added control that went with this new position, Rees was able to implement a number of changes in the training procedures which he hoped would improve the quality of the trainees as well as increase the amount of flying available to them. Previously, cadets had not been allowed near the aircraft during their first term and it was only at the commencement of their second year that they were permitted to touch the controls. Rees changed the format so that cadets were sent into the air as soon as possible after their arrival at Cranwell, followed by instruction on the Avro as soon as they had completed their observer's course. In future, all cadets were to pass out on the Bristol Fighter and, if possible the DH9a. That this revised procedure was a success can be seen from the statistics recorded in the Commandant's Report for August 1923 which show that during the previous term cadets had spent a total of 2,063 hours and 3 minutes in the air, compared with 1,481 hours and 4 minutes the previous year – an equivalent gain of fifteen months in flying training during the previous six months.

Clearly, there had been a significant change of focus at Cranwell since the college had first opened. It would seem that the original selection and training procedure was heavily based upon those used previously at the naval and military academies and colleges. Prospective cadets' backgrounds appeared to have been far more important than what their abilities were. Once into the system, the cadets were expected to focus primarily upon the military aspects of the course, the drill and academic classes, and flying was almost a corollary after they had first been turned into officers and gentlemen. Failure to master the social aspects of RAF life seemed to have been sufficient to eliminate an individual from completing his training to become a pilot. Rees, with his great experience as a trainer of airmen, knew that young volunteers accepted for pilot training did so because of their desire to fly, not to march in formation around a parade ground. While recognizing the importance of military discipline for which he had always had a high

Five Bristol F2Bs and two DH9As of D Flight, with engines running (with two DH9s at the far end of the line), Cranwell, c 1922. [RAF College, Cranwell]

regard, he felt it was essential that cadets should get into the air as soon and as often as possible if they were to overcome their natural fears and become masters of their machines. The changes which he oversaw during his first three years at the RAF College paid immediate dividends once he had been given overall command and were to have a profound effect on the RAF throughout the years of government neglect up until the mid 1930s. It was the system established by Rees that trained the men who were to take command of the fighting units of the RAF at the commencement of the Second World War, and faced the strength of the Luftwaffe in 1940.

Remarkably, when one considers the novelty and precarious nature of flying in the 1920s, there were few serious accidents, and most bad landings resulted in both the pilot and his instructor walking away from the scene, as in the case of Cadet Beaumont[37] who crashed and totally wrote-off a Bristol Fighter in July 1923 and, although somewhat shaken, was uninjured. During Rees' tenure at Cranwell only two cadets were killed in flying accidents. This fortunate state of affairs was not the result of luck, but rather the high level of care taken by the instructors and staff. Former cadet John Franks recalled Rees' concern for cadet safety.[38]

He was forever in the air and I can see him in his old overalls with leather helmet and goggles. Occasionally he would decide to fly behind a Cadet to give him confidence. I remember when I was in hospital after a minor flying accident, he came to see me & show me a photograph album full of pictures of fatal crashes at the School of Aerial Fighting which he had commanded during WW1. He was technically interested in the cause of aeroplane accidents.[39]

Rees, Royal Tournament Foil Champion, 1923.
[Rees Family Archive]

Rees appears to have got on well with his colleagues at the college, perhaps life there brought back memories of his days at Eastbourne where he had been so happy nearly a quarter of a century earlier. The isolated location and comparatively small circle of officers and their families suited his personality. The Commandant, Air Commodore Longcroft, was a man after his own heart; a native of Cardiganshire and a former officer in the Welsh Regiment, he had been seconded to the RFC before the war and had quickly gained a reputation as an enthusiastic aviator. During the summer of 1912 he had established a number of endurance records for flights within Britain and had commanded 4 Squadron on active service. Interested in all aspects of physical activity, he was particularly keen on riding to hounds and his love of the outdoors endeared him to Rees who, according to Lady Joan Portal, was '… deeply interested in country life,' although there is no evidence that he ever took part in any form of equestrian sport.[40]

As for Rees' subordinate, Squadron Leader Portal, there can be little doubt that there was a common bond of respect and similar interests between them. A distinguished

wartime pilot, Portal was also keen on various field sports and it was he who first introduced Rees to the ancient sport of kings, falconry, which was to develop into something of a passion. Both men experimented with the use of birds of prey to remove other birds from the vicinity of the airfield at Cranwell; it was known that the mere presence of such a bird was sufficient to drive away other species. Today, most major airfields in the world use

'He was forever in the air and I can see him in his old overalls with leather helmet and goggles.' Rees next to a Bristol F2B of B Flight at Cranwell, c 1923. [Rees Family Archive]

birds of prey as a means of preventing air strikes by birds. FCT Rowe, a cadet in 1920, recalled that Rees and Portal '… both kept hawks which were (when not hawking) tethered to posts outside their respective offices. Both in features resembled their falcons and when roused could behave like the same!'[41] Lady Portal, often the general dogsbody of the two falconers when they required assistance with the birds, wrote,

I know he [Rees] and my husband had a great mutual interest in falconry. We kept peregrines and merlins & the airfield at Cranwell was full of partridges which flew in to feed on seeds in the uncut grass. Rees amazed the married quarters by trying to persuade merlins to catch an outbreak of sparrows and pigeons which made their roofs a mess.[42]

Rees with one of the falcons that he and Portal introduced to Cranwell to help prevent bird strikes on the aircraft.
[Rees Family Archive]

Rees was also determined to master the sport of archery and the occupants of the married quarters were further harassed when, after the failure of the merlins to catch the unwanted sparrows, he tried to remove them by firing arrows at the roof.

The college authorities encouraged the cadets to become involved in physical activity of every kind. By way of an example, Rees threw himself into the competitive sporting life of the service, representing Cranwell at Pirbright in 1921 and 1922 where he fired the .303 rifle and, in the former year, became the RAF revolver champion. In 1923, he came first in the foil and second in the sabre competitions at the Royal Tournament, and took third place in the officers' bayonet drill competition. In his free time, he took up skiing and went on an annual trip to Switzerland and, determined not to miss out on the limited time he had on the slopes, was regularly seen practising on the hills around Cranwell, irrespective of whether there was any snow, in order to ensure that he was in good physical shape before leaving. That he was a man of action had been clearly demonstrated during the war and this almost obsessive involvement in sport (he was by this time approaching his fortieth birthday) may have been a means of escaping from the comparative inactivity of his administrative post. The varied activities in which he became involved could all be done by a man who continued to have great difficulty bending his

Rees, RAF Revolver Champion, 1921. [Rees Family Archive]

left leg, and photographs of Rees at this period clearly show that his old war wound was still causing him significant problems.

There can be little doubt that Rees enjoyed his time at Cranwell and that he made a very significant contribution to the establishment of the college on a solid footing and generations of RAF officers who have passed through its doors owe him a great debt. Walter Dawson, the former Boy Corporal from Eastchurch, came across Rees again at Cranwell.

He sent for me and asked who was paying my fees. I told him I was, and he asked if I would object to the Air Ministry taking them over, since I had signed on for eight years and he held that they were responsible. They did, and refunded my first year's fees and waived the second – just as well because I had no means of paying the second year.

I always wished I had been able to thank Rees and tell him that I retired 41 years later as the senior officer employed by the RAF (there were no Marshals of the Royal Air Force employed at that time).[43]

This one cadet, plucked from the relative obscurity of an apprenticeship at Halton, retired from the RAF as Air Chief Marshal Sir Walter Dawson, KCB, CBE, DSO. There were many others who, like former cadet Richard Jordan,[44] had fond memories of Rees from their very early service days.

Rees (right) on one of his skiing expeditions to Switzerland. His leg injury from 1916 had by this time stabilized and he was able to walk without the aid of a stick, but would appear to have been unable to fully straighten his left knee. While this may have made flying difficult, it does not appear to have hampered him when skiing or fencing.
[Rees Family Archive]

He was a very shy man … with high standards of honour, efficiency and moral standards in life in general. I remember him damaging the undercarriage of a DH9a and writing out a report on himself in which he stated that he had been negligent & careless & should pay for the damage he had done out of his own pocket. This was typical of the way Rees expected the same standards for himself as he did from others. He was a very fine pilot & a great example to us cadets. Naturally, as young men, he was a hero to us, and has remained so all my life & I am now 85.[45]

The portrait of Rees which hangs on the main staircase at RAF Cranwell. It is based on a photograph of him taken in 1919 .
[RAF College, Cranwell]

With an almost obsessive fascination for gadgets and gimmicks (several of his adaptations to the combat aircraft that he flew in 1915 and 1916 had become accepted as standard equipment for RFC machines) and there can be no doubt that he came to be regarded as something of an eccentric by some of those under his command.

Two incidents … have remained in my mind. Rees was the first and only officer that I remember who had a motor scooter to get around the camp. He was, of course, pretty lame from war wounds. The other was his originality. His hut at Cranwell had a lawn with flower beds at each end & it was a great sight to see Rees and his batman gardening. This consisted of mowing the lawn & weeding the flower beds at the same time and was done as follows: the little motor mower would be sent on its way by Rees who would then start weeding & the batman at the other end of the lawn would stop weeding, catch the mower & turn it back & Rees would do the same thing. This I consider was the first time & motion study ever done & showed how original some of Rees' thoughts were.[46]

A mixture of admiration for Rees as a conventional RAF officer and his unusual approach to day-to-day problems was also illustrated by Air Vice Marshal Franks in the following memoir.

Rees, accompanied by his sister, Muriel,
attending a wedding in the 1920s
[Rees Family Archive].

I have very vivid memories of him, especially in regard to his influence upon our flying training in those pioneering days. Rees insisted that cadet flying should include the Bristol Fighter & DH9a, in addition to the Avro. His single interest was 'aeroplanes' and flying them.

He was a bit of a crank – I remember he was reputed to have designed a bed for himself in which he lay inside a wooden framework, so that bed clothes didn't touch his body!! To ensure sound sleep for pilots. It was not adopted by the authorities![47]

That Rees had made an impression on the young men in his charge was proven when, in 1926, the Old Cranwellian Association was formed and he was invited to become one of its two vice-presidents, an honour which he enthusiastically accepted. It was not only the cadets who viewed him with affection, the college staff also appreciated his many gifts and his ability to see the humorous side of life, particularly if the joke was directed at himself. Amidst the numerous papers preserved at Cranwell is a short verse by one of the officers who had served on the college staff in the early 1920s.

> Uncle [Rees] whose inventive brains,
> Kept evolving aeroplanes,
> Fell from an enormous height
> On our garden lawn last night.
> Flying is a fatal sport –
> Uncle's wrecked the tennis court![48]

Although the poetry leaves much to be desired, this short verse illustrates the affection in which Rees was held and more than one person has claimed that he was the most popular officer in the RAF.

By the end of 1925, he was one of the most experienced training officers in the service and, when he left Cranwell prior to his Christmas leave in 1924, was promoted to the rank of group captain and appointed deputy director of training at the Air Ministry in London on New Year's Day. Although a desk appointment, this very clearly showed the way in which his career was developing and, coming only a few weeks after his appointment as Aide de Camp to HM King George V, it seemed that his future was secure and that he was destined to attain the very highest ranks in the service.

Notes

1. Command Document 467, *Permanent Organisation of the Royal Air Force – Notes by the Secretary of State for Air on a Scheme Outlined by the Chief of the Air Staff.* This document is often referred to as 'Trenchard's White Paper', London, 11 December 1919.
2. Ibid.
3. Later Air Vice Marshal Wilfred Leslie Freebody, CB, CBE, AFC (1906–91), an aircraft apprentice entrant to Cranwell in September 1921, he became a flight cadet 1924 and was commissioned in 1926. He represented Cranwell at both fencing and skill at arms where he would also have come into contact with Rees.
4. Letter from Air Vice Marshal Freebody to the author, dated 12 March 1987.
5. Later Air Chief Marshal Sir Walter Lloyd Dawson, KCB, CBE, DSO (1902–94), a Boy Mechanic entrant to Cranwell in 1920. He was the last AOC Palestine (1946–8). Chairman Handley-Page Ltd. Dawson Field in Jordan was named after him.
6. Letter from Air Chief Marshal Sir Walter Dawson to the author dated 20 June 1987.
7. *London Gazette*, 2 November 1918.
8. *London Gazette*, 3 June 1919.
9. The other Caernarfon servicemen singled out for recognition by the Borough were: Col Cecil Allanson, DSO, CIE; Lt-Col John Evans, DSO; Maj J Price Roberts, DSO, MC; Maj Tom Armstrong, MBE; Maj George Brymer, MC; Maj H Gordon Carter, MC; Maj Ludwig SB Tasker, MC; Lieut Harold Owen Bodvel-Roberts, MC*; Capt Leslie J Fairchild, MC; Capt HT Finchett-Maddock, MC & Bar; Capt Reginald G Hayes, MC; Capt GE Lloyd Jones, MC; Capt R Parry Morris, MC*; Capt W Hilton Parry, MC & Bar; Capt Albert de Burgh Thomas, MC; Capt RA Williams. MC; Lieut GW Taylor-Morgan, MC; QMS J Hughes Bracegirdle, DCM*; Sgt-Maj John Hughes, DCM; Pte John Evan Jones, DCM; Cpl William Williams, DCM; Lieut AJ Williams, MM; Sgt DO Williams, MM; Sgt WF Lambert, MM; Cpl WR Hughes, MM; Cpl FW Warren, MM; L/Cpl William Flynn, MM*; L/Cpl Jack Hughes, MM; L/Cpl Robert Humphreys, MM; L/Cpl Fred O Jones, MM; L/Cpl CJ Bulkeley Williams, MM; CSM AC Pike, MM; Bmbr RH Fellows, MM; Bmbr WR Roberts, MM; Pioneer EJ Pugh, MM*; Pte John Hughes, MM; Pte John Hughes, MM*; Pte ER Jones, MM; Pte Roland W Jones, MM; Pte TJ Lewis, MM; Pte David Parry, MM*; Pte Walter R Roberts, MM; CSM Pierce M Davies, MSM; CQMS T Emlyn Williams, MSM; Pte Abram Davies, Croix de Noir; CSM CE Leak, Croix de Guerre; Pte Walter Roberts, Persian Medal. Each of these men (or a family representative) was presented with a pennant by the Borough Council. Those indicated as having died before 1920 are marked *.
10. The previous Freemen of the Borough of Caernarfon were: Sir William Preece; JH Bodvel-Roberts; Rt Hon David Lloyd George, MP, PC; Sir John Pritchard-Jones; Sir Charles Assheton-Smith, Bart; Mr Owen Jones.
11. This mameluke dress scimitar in a monogrammed red velvet scabbard was engraved on the blade with 'Borough of Carnarvon, January 15th, 1920. Presented with the Honorary Freedom of the Borough by the Corporation of the Borough of Carnarvon, to Wing Commander Lionel Wilmot Brabazon Rees, VC, OBE, MC, AFC, in testimony of its high approbation of the gallant services rendered by him to his King and Country during the Great War.'
12. *Carnarvon and Denbigh Herald*, 16 January 1920.
13. Ibid.
14. On 11 November 1920, Armistice Day, the body of the Unknown Warrior was borne in procession from Victoria

Station to Westminster Abbey. As it entered the abbey and was carried to its final resting place, it passed between two lines of 96 men who had been decorated for gallantry during the war, of whom 74 were recipients of the Victoria Cross. Coincidentally, all the ironwork of the coffin in which the Unknown Warrior was buried, was manufactured by the De Winton company of Caernarfon.

15. The inscription on the memorial, which overlooks the twelfth green at Turnberry reads: 'To the memory of the officers, non-commissioned officers and men of the Royal Flying Corps, Royal Air Force and the Australian and United States Air Services who gave their lives for their country while serving in the School of Aerial Gunnery & Fighting at Turnberry, MCMXVII–MCMXVIII. Their name liveth forever more.'

16. 'Command Document 467, *Permanent Organisation of the Royal Air Force.*

17. Later Air Vice Marshal Sir Charles Alexander Holcombe Longcroft, KCB, CMG, DSO, AFC (1883–1958), a native of Cardiganshire, he was commissioned into the Welsh Regiment. He gained his RAeC certificate in 1912 and was seconded to the RFC.

18. RAF Cranwell was established on 1 November 1919.

19. Later Marshal of the Royal Air Force Viscount Portal of Hungerford, KG, GCB, OM, DSO and Bar, MC (1893–1971). He served as a despatch rider in the Royal Engineers before being commissioned and transferring to the RFC in 1915 where he served as an observer and then trained as a pilot. OC 16 Squadron 1917 and 24 (Training) Wing 1918. Granted a permanent commission in the RAF as a squadron leader. OC British Forces, Aden 1934. Imperial Defence College staff 1936, air vice marshal 1937, acting air marshal 1939, C-in-C Bomber Command 1940, Chief of Air Staff 1940, Marshal of the RAF 1944. Retired 1945.

20. Later Air Chief Marshal Sir George Mills, GCB, DFC (1902–71), AOC Allied Air Forces Central Europe 1955.

21. 'Cranwell Cadet – 1920', Sir George Mills, *Cranwell Magazine.*

22. Squadron Leader George Barrett Chainey (1865–1927) was a former Royal Navy rating who had served in Egypt in 1883 and was later a Chief Petty Officer gunner before being commissioned in the RNAS during the Great War and eventually transferring to the RAF.

23. Letter from Air Chief Marshal Sir Walter Dawson, op cit.

24. Later Air Chief Marshal Sir Theodore Neuman McEvoy, KCB, CBE (1904–91), he entered Cranwell as a Flight Cadet in 1923 (awarded the Sword of Honour). As Assistant Chief of the Air Staff (Training) he oversaw he changeover of RAF training from piston-engined aircraft to jets. Letter to the author, dated 28 August 1985.

25. Later Marshal of the Royal Air Force, Sir Dermot Boyle, GCB, KCVO, KBE, AFC, CdeG (1904–93), he entered Cranwell as a Flight Cadet in September 1922. He became a Qualified Flying Instructor in 1927 and led the CFS flying display team. He became Chief of the Air Staff in 1956 and was Vice-Chairman of BAC.

26. Letter from Sir Dermot Boyle to the author, dated 2 September 1985.

27. Letter to the author dated 24 September 1987 from Harold Jones, an AC2 Carpenter Rigger, who was posted to Cranwell from Halton in 1923.

28. Later Air Vice Marshal Sir Geoffrey Luis Worthington, KBE, CB (1903–92). Like Rees, he was a former pupil of Eastbourne College.

29. Letter from Sir Geoffrey Worthington to the author dated 28 August 1985.

30. Letter to the author, op cit.

31. Later Air Vice Marshal Alan David 'Peter' Gillmore, CB, CBE (1905–96), he entered Cranwell as a Flight Cadet in 1923.

32. Letter to the author, dated 4 March 1987.

33. Professor Stuart Petre Brodie Mais (1885–1975) was a noted author, journalist and broadcaster. He graduated in English Literature at Christ College, Oxford and taught at a number of schools before being appointed to teach English at Cranwell in 1920. He left in 1921 following a disagreement over permitting cadets a free hand to criticize the authorities in their creative writing. He was the author of over 200 books, many about the English countryside, and was the original broadcaster of *Letter from America.* His recollections of his time at Cranwell were recorded in *All the Days of My Life,* published in 1937.

34. Later Air Commodore Ellacott Lyme Stephen Ward, CB, DFC (1905–91), entered Cranwell as a Flight Cadet in 1924.

35. 'Cranwell Cadet – 1920', Sir George Mills, *Cranwell Magazine.*

36. Later Air Vice Marshal Sir Arthur Sheridan Barratt, KCB, CMG, MC, DL (1891–1966) he obtained his RAeC certificate in 1914 whilst serving in the Royal Field Artillery. He was OC 6 Squadron, 49 Squadron and 3 (Corps) Wing during the Great War. He became OC School of Army Co-operation in 1926, Chief Instructor at the RAF Staff College in 1936 and was AOC British Air Forces France in 1939–40. He retired as Inspector General RAF in 1945.

37. Later Flight Lieutenant Francis William Lionel Collings Beaumont (1903–41), the son of the Seigneur of Sark

in the Channel Islands. He resigned his commission in 1928 and rejoined the service as a pilot officer in the RAFVR in 1939, taking up a career as a film producer. He and his wife were killed in the Liverpool Blitz in 1941.

38. Later Air Vice Marshall John Gerald Franks, CB, CBE (1905–95) he entered Cranwell as a Flight Cadet in 1923 and rose to be Senior Air Staff Officer at HQ Technical Training Command in 1955 and President of the Ordnance Board in 1959.

39. Letter to the author, undated, *c.*1985.

40. Letters from Lady Joan Portal to the author dated 4 September 1985 and 26 May 1986.

41. Later Wing Commander Francis Charles Thorne Rowe (1903–76), a native of Devon, he entered Cranwell in 1920.

42. Lady Joan Portal, op cit.

43. Letter from Air Chief Marshal Sir Walter Dawson to the author, op cit.

44. Later Air Marshal Sir Richard Jordan, KCB, DFC (1902–94) he entered Cranwell as a Flight Cadet in 1921. He retired in 1958 as AOC-in-C Maintenance Command.

45. Letter from Air Marshal Sir Richard Jordan to the author, undated *c.*1985.

46. Ibid.

47. Letter from Air Vice Marshal John Franks to the author, op cit.

48. Verse held by the Library, RAF Cranwell.

VIII

Palestine and Transjordan
(1926–29)

FOLLOWING THE PEACE TREATIES THAT WERE SIGNED between the Allies and the defeated Turkish Empire in 1919, the map of the Middle East had been dramatically transformed as various formerly Turkish-controlled territories were confiscated and handed over to the victors as what were termed 'mandated territories' – areas to be administered by them until such time as they were deemed to be capable of running their own affairs when they would be granted independence. Great Britain was given the mandate to run Palestine, Transjordan and Iraq, whilst France took control of Lebanon and Syria. To many, particularly the Arabs, the arrangement was seen as a betrayal, frustrating the nationalist dreams of independent Arab states. The change of control from the Turks to the British and the French was deemed to be merely the exchange of one relatively weak colonial power for two that wielded much more power and influence on the world stage. Britain was particularly anxious to become involved in the Middle East as a means of retaining control over the interests of British companies in the oilfields of the region.

As early as December 1919, the British Secretary of State for Air, Winston Churchill, had defended the future role of the RAF as an economic means of keeping the peace in a turbulent world.

> I must remind Honourable Members that we still have an empire to defend … we have all those dependencies and possessions in our hands which existed before the war and in addition we have large promises of new responsibilities to be placed upon us. The first duty of the Royal Air Force is to garrison the British Empire.[1]

Trenchard had argued with some conviction that the RAF was the most financially efficient force to police the more remote regions of the Empire, and he had been able to prove his point in 1920 when one squadron of bombers succeeded in destroying the power of Mohammed Abdullah Hassan (the 'Mad Mullah') in Somaliland,[2] something which the Army had been trying to achieve, at great cost in both men and materials, since the beginning of the century. He had also argued that Egypt was the logical centre for a sizeable RAF establishment as the weather conditions made it ideal for flying training. Consequently, control of the British mandated territories was handed over to the RAF in April 1922 and RAF Middle East Command was created, and in October 1923 Air Vice Marshal John Salmond[3] was appointed to command all military forces in the Middle East. Under his command were a number of RAF sub-commands, viz Egypt (with Air HQ in Cairo), Iraq (with Air HQ in Baghdad), Palestine and Transjordan (with Air HQ in Amman/Jerusalem) and South-West Arabia (with Air HQ in Aden). Of these, Iraq was initially the most problematic as a resurgent Turkey under the leadership of Kemal Atatürk began to flex its military muscles along the northern border. Palestine was also a potential area of difficulty as the British government tried to square the circle created by the Balfour Declaration of 1917 whereby it had stated its wish 'to look favourably upon the creation of a Jewish homeland in Palestine.' This had resulted in a post war influx of Jewish settlers into what was a predominantly Arab country. Riots had broken out in Jerusalem as early as April 1920 and in May 1921 95 people had been killed in rioting in the city of Jaffa. The military ground forces numbered 7,670 men at an annual cost of £3.5 million. In London, many felt that control of areas such as Palestine should lay with the Colonial Office, but the financial issues which this involved were not viewed as being beneficial by all concerned. In 1922, Winston Churchill (by then Secretary of State for the Colonies) had written to the Secretary of State for India:

> I think there is some misunderstanding in the India Office about the question of the Air Ministry acting as the controlling agency for military purposes in Palestine. You will recall the Cabinet decision of December that military control in Palestine should be transferred to the Colonial Office. I have not the necessary machinery here for the exercise of direct military control; and it would be both undesirable and extravagant to set up a large military establishment at the Colonial Office merely for the benefit of Palestine. I have accordingly invited the Air Ministry (and they have accepted my invitation) to act as my agents there in the same way as they are to act in Iraq after the 1st October. This does not imply that Palestine is to be controlled from the air, but merely that as a matter of convenience the administrative channel through which the military affairs of the country will be conducted will be the Air Ministry and not the War Office. [4]

The Air Ministry was therefore the controlling agency, giving military advice to the Colonial Office with regard to Palestine. Initially, the Army garrison there was headed by a GOC who was under the command of the Air Ministry but later, when the garrison was

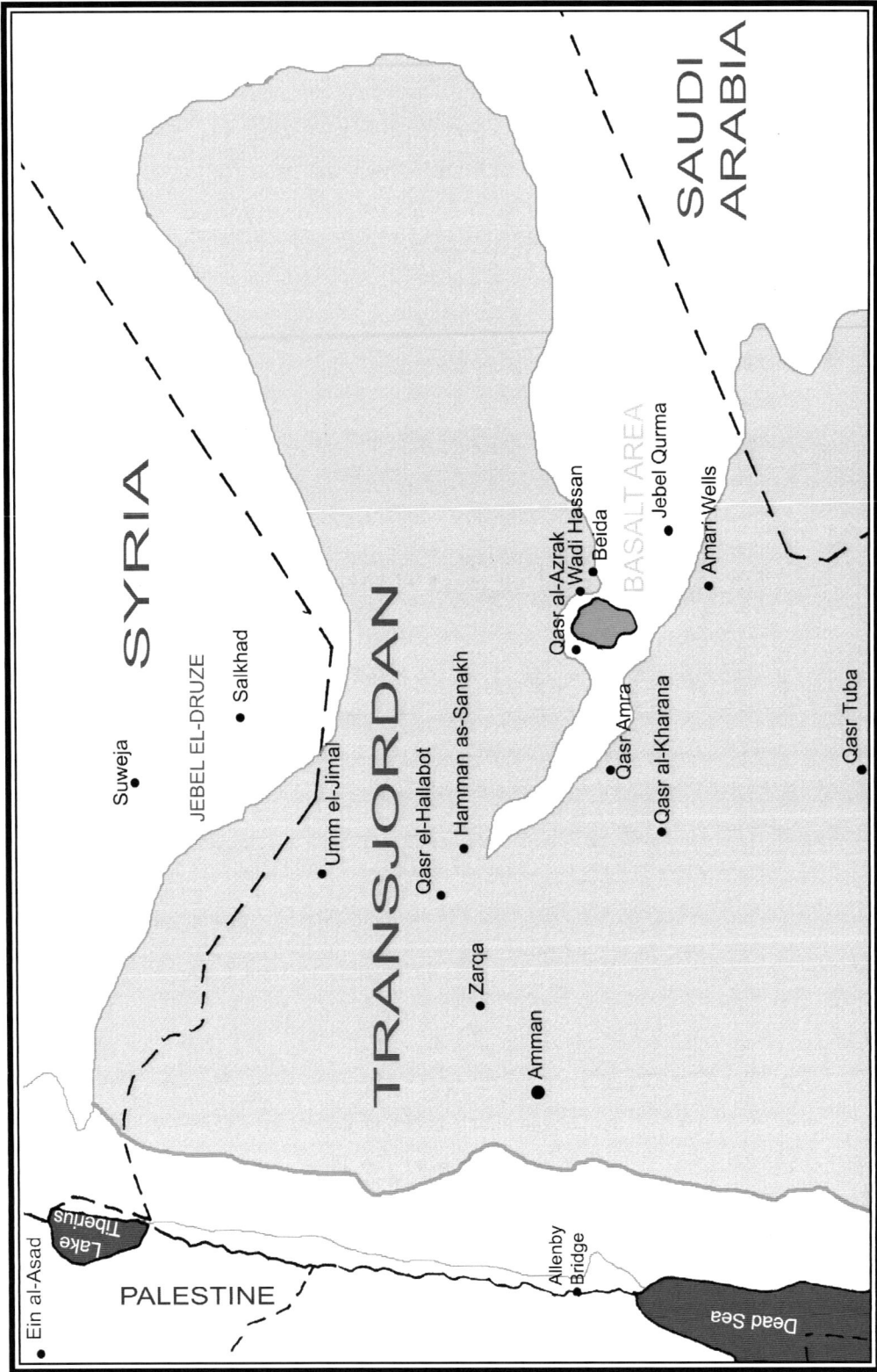

Sketch map of Transjordan c 1926

Approx. scale in miles

Over 1500' asl

reduced, the GOC was succeeded by an AOC. The Air Ministry was also to assume responsibility for Transjordan on the understanding that there would be a presence (particularly in Palestine) of what was described as a '*Gendarmerie*', a civil-based police force to control any potential unrest. Transjordan on the other hand, was deemed to be less developed than Palestine, with less of a potential for unrest and frontiers that could be more easily defended (particularly against 'desert tribes') and patrolled by the use of aircraft. By January 1925, the Colonial Office saw the role of the 'Imperial garrison' in Palestine and Transjordan as being,

> … the external defence … against a civilised enemy or against an organised attack from Central Arabia. It also has the secondary function of supporting the Palestine and Transjordan Governments in the maintenance of public security.[5]

To do this, the Colonial Office advocated the removal of all ground forces other than the purely civil police, which the Air Ministry most strenuously opposed, insisting that the '*Gendarmerie*' should *not* become a civil police and 'to rely for purposes of defence upon the local *Gendarmerie* with British officers and a proportion of non-commissioned officers, supported … by aeroplanes and armoured cars.'[6]

De Havilland DH9As of 14 Squadron, Transjordan, c 1926. Note the spare landing wheel strapped to the fuselage alongside the engine. [JM Bruce]

One of the armoured cars of 2 Armoured Car Company RAF (with Rees' staff car in the distance). The figure on top of the vehicle is a member of the TFF. [Author]

These arrangements were driven by the overriding desire to reduce the costs of defending the region. In October 1925, Field Marshal Lord Plumer of Messines was appointed to the civil post of High Commissioner for Palestine and immediately set about reorganizing the defence forces in the region. The civil *gendarmerie* was abolished, and a police force, which included 200 British officers, was established. The military *gendarmerie* (the Transjordan Frontier Force) was to be retained and used primarily in Transjordan for what was termed 'tribal control', in conjunction with the RAF forces. The Air Staff did not believe this change was for the better and that the aircraft deployed in the region could not be used to back the security forces should disturbances break out. Plumer had in fact requested that the existing two flights at Ramleh and one in Amman should be increased by at least two further flights. After a lengthy period of prevarication, the Colonial Office informed the High Commissioner in February 1926 that, due to the extra cost involved, no additional flights would be sent to either Palestine or Transjordan. Plumer's decision as regards ground forces was however implemented which meant that there was effectively no longer any serious military presence on the ground in Palestine, the whole focus of attention being concentrated upon Transjordan.

By 1925, it had become clear that aerial policing did not work and the RAF had to rely heavily upon its armoured car units, the police and the military *gendarmerie,* particularly should unrest break out in Palestine; experience had shown that trouble usually occurred in the urban areas where aircraft could not be used due to their indiscriminate and inaccurate use of bombs and machine guns..

In 1926, the position of AOC Middle East Command passed to Air Vice Marshal Tom Webb-Bowen.[7] and on 1 October, Lionel Rees took over the command of the newly-created RAF Headquarters Palestine and Transjordan, effectively an independent command with control, for operational and training purposes, over not only the RAF but also any ground forces stationed in the region, as well as the Transjordan Frontier Force (TFF). Based in

Amman, Rees had control over 14 Squadron, equipped with the DH9A light bomber, and 2 Armoured Car Company RAF, a unit that had been formed in 1922, equipped with the Rolls-Royce Type A armoured cars and a Morris wireless tender. The armoured cars were armed with a Vickers .303 machine gun in the turret and a ring-mounted Lewis gun on the open rear of the vehicle. The TFF, which was established at Sarafand on 1 April 1926, comprised three cavalry squadrons (each of 120 men), an infantry unit and a camel company.

Initially, the territories of Palestine and Transjordan were relatively quiet when compared to the unrest then prevailing in the Iraq command, and Rees' major cause for concern would seem to have been the ever increasing numbers of Jewish immigrants arriving in the region in pursuit of the Zionist dream of an independent Jewish state. In 1926, the numbers involved had not yet reached the massive proportions of the 1930s and late 1940s, and it was hoped that open conflict between Jews and Arabs could at best be avoided altogether or, at worst, contained by the civil authorities. The Turks were an ever-present threat, particularly to northern Iraq and the local tribesmen in Transjordan were well armed, highly mobile, relatively well organised and liable to spark off trouble anywhere.

Being given the command of Palestine and Transjordan was without doubt a feather in Rees' cap, clearly indicating that he was a man who was a likely to continue up the promotion scale of the RAF in the near future. His period as a combat pilot and commander of a fighting unit during the Great War had been relatively short and most of his RFC and RAF career had been in a training role. He had, however, displayed a talent for administration, diplomacy and innovation. His technical skills as an airman, soldier and engineer were ideally suited to the demands of the small force that would be under his command.

The artificial boundaries of the mandated territories followed convenient political lines which meant that in many cases they were culturally and historically meaningless, cutting across areas populated by one people who were in effect made citizens of two different countries. This problem was difficult enough within an area controlled by one foreign power, such as the boundary between Palestine and Transjordan, but was made much more difficult when the boundary separated territories controlled by different powers, as was the case between Syria and Transjordan. The politics of the Middle East had always been a complex subject, but these imposed frontiers only served to exacerbate the situation. One clearly identifiable group who felt themselves to be aggrieved by the arrangements were the Druze of southern Syria and it was from this quarter that Rees' major problem emerged very soon after his arrival in Amman.

A complicated and mysterious association of peoples, the Druze had originated in Lebanon during the twelfth century when Ismail ad–Darazi took refuge in the mountains there after fleeing from Egypt following the assassination of his insane master, Caliph Hakim, who had proclaimed himself a god some three years previously. As one of the Caliph's most fervent followers, Ismail ad–Darazi was in grave danger if he remained in Egypt and, once in Lebanon, he began to preach of the divinity of his former master. He managed to attract a sizeable number of followers who formed themselves into a highly secretive community based upon a religious belief, the details of which were known only to the elders. This group, the Druze, came to play an increasingly important role in the life of the region and, as they were often compelled to defend themselves against religious persecution, they acquired a high reputation as warriors. After many centuries of rebelling against any form of authority they were eventually forced in 1861 to migrate to the mountains south west of Damascus, which became known as Jebel el-Druze.

During the early years of the French mandate in Syria, many Arab nationalists were compelled to either go into hiding or exile but, despite these difficulties, they managed to keep the flames of independence burning in both Lebanon and Syria with the result that numerous local uprisings occurred. The appointment of a conscientious, hardworking, but insensitive officer by the name of Carbillet[8] as governor of the Jebel el-Druze in 1923 resulted in considerable unrest. He believed that it was his duty to improve the lives of those under his control, whether they desired it or not. His reforms in Syria were numerous and on the whole were of great benefit to the local population, taking as they did the form of new roads, irrigation schemes, improved sanitation, new schools and courts, even a museum. To the Druze, however, these changes seemed to threaten their traditional way of life. Worst of all, Carbillet managed, for the first time in Druze history, to collect the local taxes in full. Power seemed to be passing out of the hands of the local chieftains and into the hands of the mandatory power and its democratically elected representatives. When a Druze deputation was dismissed by the French High Commissioner in 1925, and Carbillet was replaced by Captain Raynaud[9] (who could see no problem in the manner in which his predecessor had administered matters) tempers began to wear thin and delegations that tried to put forward the Arab case were either dismissed or totally ignored by the authorities in Beirut. Then, in early July, five Druze chieftains were summoned to appear before the French High Commissioner on the pretext that they could present their demands. Three arrived and were promptly arrested on the orders of General Sarrail.[10] Immediately, the most belligerent of the Druze leaders, Sultan al-Atrash, decided to come out in open rebellion against French rule. Within days, French aircraft had been fired upon, the town of Salkhad had been occupied and looted and, on 21 July, a column of about 200 French troops was cut to pieces at Kafr. The survivors of the column, some seventy in number, managed to reach Suwayda where they were besieged for two months.

The authorities still regarded the trouble as being of little importance and virtually nothing was done for a few days. On 2 August, General Michaud[11] left Azrak in Transjordan at the head of a force of 3,000 men with the intention of relieving the men trapped at Suwayda. That night, they were attacked by a strong Druze force and defeated. Over 800 men were either killed, wounded, captured or deserted. One

Sultan al–Atrash. [Wikipedia]

colonel committed suicide on the battlefield and Michaud was recalled to France. As a consequence of this action, the Druze took possession of 2,000 rifles, a battery of artillery and vast quantities of ammunition. Overnight, a localized Druze rebellion was changed into a national revolt and Sultan al–Atrash[12] was proclaimed as president of the Provisional Syrian Government as many groups seized on the opportunity to rid their country of colonial control. In reality, however, the uprising was a shambles and, lacking any clear political leadership or support amongst those members of Syrian society whose opinions carried the most weight, was doomed to failure.

The French government then placed General Gamelin[13] in command of the forces in the region and, by the use of airpower and tanks, he was able to relieve Suwayda by 24 September, but was unable to regain control of the Jebel el-Druze. There then followed many months of guerilla fighting with Druze attacks upon roads, railways, police stations and settlements that were believed to be pro French. In October, fighting broke out in Damascus itself resulting in the use of artillery against areas of the city where rebels were believed to be active. By November, the High Commissioner had been recalled to Paris but there was no indication of any solution to the situation which was to witness acts of great brutality from both sides. By early 1926, the rebels had failed to make any real gains and a new French High Commissioner, de Jouvenal,[14] visited London where he sought, and received, the support of the British government to bring the conflict to an end. In the spring, the government forces in Syria went on the offensive and the Druze began to lose ground. Repeated attempts were made to try and persuade the tribesmen to surrender, but they invariably elected to continue the fight, and by April yet another new French governor was in the Jebel el-Druze. Sultan al–Atrash, however, managed to evade the net that was closing in around him and continued to roam the region at the head of a substantial force of armed men, crossing the frontier into Transjordan as the need arose, in order to evade capture. This action contravened the agreement reached between the British and French governments who had decided that any Druze warriors that crossed into British territory would be compelled to return to Syria. If necessary, military force would be used to ensure their compliance.

A substantial number of the dependents of Druze tribesmen arrived in British territory during April and their leaders, based in Syria, contacted the authorities in Amman to request permission for these refugees to remain, under British protection and jurisdiction, in a camp which they hoped to establish near the old fortress of Qasr al–Azrak.[16] Permission was granted on condition that no Druze warriors were to enter Transjordan, that tribal chieftains would accept the responsibility for the good conduct of the non-combatant refugees and that they, the chiefs, remained in Syria. As a concession to the rugged and unpredictable nature of life in the region, the authorities granted the refugess the right to have a limited number of armed men in the camp by way of protection.

In Syria, however, events did not progress so peacefully. On 18 July, the French forces launched an attack against the area where the rebels were still harassing the authorities. Six columns, amounting to 8,500 men, supported by artillery, tanks and armoured cars moved into an area only fourteen miles long and eleven miles wide. They then commenced to drive the rebels (and anyone else who happened to be in the area) towards Damascus. There were acts of great barbarity, particularly by the Senegalese troops, who in one village killed every Syrian they came across, irrespective of whether or not they were involved in the rebellion. French troops entered and searched abandoned villages and shot, without any pretence of a trial, dozens of inhabitants whom they believed to be either rebels or harbourers of rebels. The Druze in return ambushed French forces wherever they could and took their revenge. This period of terror continued into October and, as a consequence, the British authorities realised that the agreed conditions concerning the refugee camps in Transjordan were not being adhered to and that substantial numbers of warriors were sheltered there, along with several chieftains, including possibly Sultan al–Atrash and other leading figures in the revolt. Despite protests from Amman and demands that the agreement should be complied with, there was no satisfactory response from the Druze camp. As the situation in Syria showed no

RAF aerial photograph of Qasr al–Azrak showing the palm trees growing around the wells and the old medieval fort. [University of London, Institute of Archaeology]

sign of being resolved before the onset of winter, it was decided that a show of strength on the part of the mandatory power would be necessary the following spring.

As the senior military official in the region, responsibility for the organisation and execution of this operation lay with Rees. Although the 'demonstration of military strength' would involve significant numbers of RAF personnel, it was to be mainly an exercise in the use of ground forces, and he gathered together a column which consisted of three sections of 2 Armoured Car Company, three companies of the TFF and the DH9A aircraft of 14 Squadron. One of the officers serving with the column, Stanley Vincent, who had been an instructor at Cranwell under Rees, had fond memories of the armoured cars which were to prove particularly effective in the months ahead.

I had many interesting experiences with the good old Rolls-Royce armoured cars. It was then 1926 and most of the chassis were 1912, and one 1920. These had been private cars for some years, then bought during the war and had four and a half tons of armour and extra leaves in

Lieut-Col Bewsher, CO Transjordan
Frontier Force. [Anon]

their springs to put on them. They would still do their 60 mph over a mud flat.[17]

Although the distance from Amman to the camp at Qasr al–Azrak was not great (fifty miles by air or seventy-five miles by the desert track), the expedition had to be planned with great care as the availability of water was always a matter of some concern. The usual watering place was El Dunni, near Qasr al-Kharana, where, by digging into the bed of the dried-up river, supplies could be obtained in great quantity, albeit slowly. This possibility was eliminated when reconnaissance patrols reported that the wadi was occupied by the Bene Sakhr and it was not advisable to drink their water at the beginning of the year. An alternative route had therefore to be found and numerous air and armoured car patrols were sent out which discovered a route that was considerably shorter ,with a good surface, something which could not be said of the traditional road.

On 12 April, Rees, accompanied by Lieutenant-Colonel Bewsher,[18] made a personal reconnaissance of the proposed route and decided that one five-mile section was unsuited to the weight of transport which they intended to use and further flights were ordered to discover yet another way of reaching Azrak. Fortunately, this revealed an excellent flat track along the Wadi Hoopoe which, despite the absence of water along the way, was selected as the route for the expedition.

On 13 April, the advance party, comprising one armoured-car section, seven lorries and seven tenders, covered the fifty-four miles and established camp at Qasr al-Azrak without incident. Two days later a water convoy transported 3,300 gallons to a 'dump' some fifteen miles west of Zarqa where the Transjordan Frontier Force was to water the following day. Leaving their headquarters, the TFF, accompanied by one section of armed tenders and escorted by one flight from 14 Squadron, reached the water safely having covered a distance of twenty-four miles. This force, comprising 450 mounted men, is recorded to have consumed 1400 gallons of water at the halt. After a further stop (when 2,000 gallons were consumed), the column arrived at its destination at 14.00 hours without any undue fatigue or injury to either men or horses. The heavy Leyland lorries, however, proved quite unsatisfactory for the transportation of supplies, and the RAF transport drivers reported that they were unable to carry the weight, the solid tyres cutting up the track in the three days so greatly that a new track had to be made. They were much too slow getting over bad terrain, even those places which the heavy armoured cars would consider normal, and could not keep up with them when the going was good. In addition to the ground transport, two Vickers Victorias (large, twin-engined biplane freight and troop carrying aircraft, based in Iraq) were used to convey supplies to the column by air using a hastily prepared landing ground at Azrak.

In his report on the opening stages of this operation, Rees commented that the 'Heath Robinson' system which he had adopted for supplying water was quite unsatisfactory and had only just managed to provide the desired amounts; had the columns encountered any real difficulties then they might have been in very serious trouble due to lack of adequate water supplies. In his opinion, any future operations of a similar nature should be supported by purpose-built water tanker lorries, preferably six wheelers or tracked, in order to negotiate the difficult terrain without any major problems arising.

On 18 April, an initial examination was made of the Druze camp and evidence was found of the movement of mechanised vehicles in the area which confirmed the belief that the Druze leadership had been seeking sanctuary at Azrak. A few chiefs actually called to see Rees and assured him that they were only too willing to comply with any request or order which he might make and, as a consequence, he issued a proclamation demanding that the terms of the Anglo-Druze agreement be complied with and, as a result, nearly all the leaders and about 300 men were seen to leave the camp heading for Syria.

The next step was to try to ascertain the numbers that remained in the camp. The mounted troops and one flight of aircraft carried out a detailed reconnaissance of the area, as a result of which it was estimated that there were 2,462 persons in the Druze camp, mostly women, old men and children, but including about 300 men, either traders or guards. When questioned, these men openly admitted that the agreement had not been adhered to, but that most of the 'illegal' refugees had now left: 650 men under Sultan al–Atrash himself had gone on 26 March, and 800 men under the command of Emir Adil Aslan on 15 April. These figures, apparently supplied quite freely, showed that the authorities had been quite justified in their concern, as together these two forces made up the majority of the Druze fighting strength and had, therefore, posed a serious threat to the region: their continued presence in Transjordan would, at best, have caused mistrust between the British and the French. It was also discovered that there were a number of non-Druze refugees from Syria or Palestine living in the camp. The use of aircraft to help estimate the numbers and location of the refugees had not only announced to the tribesmen that there were military aircraft readily available should any trouble break out, but they were also able to make an accurate calculation of numbers without the refugees being aware of what was happening – they would otherwise have almost certainly hidden away many of their warriors to prevent them being detected by ground units.

Concerned about the whereabouts of the departed tribesmen, Rees ordered that the area to be patrolled should be expanded for the next few days to ensure that the prohibited warriors were indeed back in Syria. Little of interest was discovered, but the land and air patrols made detailed reports of the terrain and its suitability for future operations should the need arise. The Druze that remained within the camp were issued with passes if they wished to carry arms for defensive purposes, and a number of illegal refugees were ordered to leave and return to the mountains, being watched from the air until they were at least eighteen miles away from the camp. It was probably hoped that these men would, when they returned to the main Druze force in Syria, report the situation in Transjordan and clearly point out the determination of the British forces to see that the agreement was complied with in future. Remarkably, Rees received a most unusual letter from Sultan al–Atrash himself, thanking him for his assistance in persuading the Druze to return to the field. He, their sultan, had failed to convince some of his men that they should return to Syria and recommence their offensive against the French, but the arrival of Rees' column at Qasr al-Azrak had caused them to change their minds and they had then gladly agreed to return to Jebl el-Druze!

The problem of identifying those who were entitled to be in the camp and those who were not was a difficult one and whenever a head count was taken and passes checked, a different total was reached. Determined not to be made to look foolish while endeavouring to establish the rule of law, Rees set up a series of courts martial which tried those found without a pass and sentenced those convicted accordingly. On the whole, the sentences were light and consisted of short periods of imprisonment followed by deportation back to Syria but, occasionally, the offence was of a more serious nature and carried a heavier sentence. Rees was not afraid to use his power when necessary and, when Hayle al–Atrash, a nephew of the sultan, was found without a pass, he was sentenced to be deported. Unfortunately, en route to Syria, he assaulted his guards and was brought before a second court martial which sentenced him to twelve months imprisonment. Despite the fact that all the Druze regarded the members of the Atrash clan as being 'privileged persons', and therefore above the common law, Rees confirmed the court's sentence, regardless of any possible backlash from the angered tribesmen.

For Rees and his officers, life in the camp, although undoubtedly more interesting than that in Amman, was basically a matter of administration and quickly settled into a routine of long periods of boredom broken up by short periods of activity and home-made entertainment. In his autobiography, Vincent recalled how the men of the armoured-car unit relaxed.

At Azrak were two 'lakes' in which it was nearly pleasant to bathe at the end of a hot, sticky and dusty day – the qualification 'nearly' being caused by mosquitos! We had our camp about half-a-mile away for this reason; to bathe we would put on our trunks in our tents, get into a Rolls tender and drive to the water's edge – run and dive in. Even then much splashing was necessary before putting one's head out! After ten minutes or so of good cooling, one of us would say 'All out – Go!' whereupon a rush would be made to the bank and so to the Rolls tender and away as quickly as possible, in a heap, without pausing to dry! [19]

Regular patrols were mounted by the men under Rees' command during which a number of arrests were made. Usually these were carried out by small numbers of soldiers who intercepted larger numbers of tribesmen who had been spotted from the air and, generally, such events passed without difficulty. The Druze treated these incidents as something of a joke and returned to their rightful location without comment. One cannot but wonder, however, what their reaction might have been had the armoured cars and aircraft not been so readily available. As Vincent noted, '… four armoured cars with Vickers guns trained on them are not things with which to trifle.' On 30 April, Major JW Smith[20] of the Transjordan Frontier Force, totally unarmed and accompanied by only one trooper and one horseholder, intercepted a party of eight armed men and arrested them all, later handing them over to the police at Azrak. After interrogation, they revealed the location of a further eight tribesmen who were also taken into custody without any problem – all very different to the manner in which the Druze had reacted to French attempts to control them in Syria.

Despite rumours that the Druze leaders, as the tide of war continued to flow against them in Syria, were preparing to return to Qasr al-Azrak with their armed followers, the early days of May passed without incident and Rees kept his men employed preparing the area for any future operations which might be required.

The chief duty of Nº 2 Armoured Car Company was the making of roads, in the first instance in order to deliver to a forced landed machine a new engine, and later on in order to allow cars and soldiers to arrive at tactical positions behind the inhabited area, should the necessity arise.

Reconnaissances were made to find out the extent of the basalt area, and it is established that no forces except those in the area could operate south of the Syrian 'Border actual' inside the area Umm el-Jimal, Hamman as-Sarakh, Azrak, Jebel Qurma, and to the east without overcoming difficulties which, with the means at their disposal, are practically insurmountable.

Air reconnaissance was useful in checking information as to the movement of herds, and as to the location of Abdul Ghaffer's Camp.

A daily Air Mail service was organised at Amman and many officers were transported.

The situation at Azrak is now completely under control, and is such that the 'Druze Committees' are asking for our help in order to keep affairs going on as they should.

Should trouble arise in the future the road Zerka–Azrak will provide a ready means of approach for some time to come, and tactical roads are constructed which will allow vehicles and soldiers to approach the inhabited area unexpectedly and will make it comparatively easy to occupy tactical positions of vantage in the basalt which surrounds Azrak Castle. [21]

Upon receipt of this report, the British High Commissioner, no doubt wanting to economize wherever possible, issued instructions that the forces at Qasr al-Azrak were to be reduced by 25 May. No sooner had Rees received this order than reports reached him of disturbances elsewhere in the territory. The Druze, natural rivals of the Rualla tribe, complained that the French authorities in Syria had given the latter a number of villages situated on the main route north of the Basalt and Azrak. They saw this as an act intended to provoke enmity between the two tribes as it would make communication between the Druze in Syria and those in Transjordan very difficult. They also claimed that the Rualla, acting upon instructions from the French, had attacked a camp west of Azrak, just outside the area covered by martial law. The camp, which belonged to Abdul Ghaffer Pasha, had lost all its tents, stores, cattle, guns and clothes. In addition, the attackers had killed a shepherd and a cousin of Sultan al–Atrash and taken the sultan's brother and several others away as prisoners. Fearful of further attacks, Abdul Ghaffer had moved his people into the area over which Rees had jursidiction and surrendered on 16 May. As the attack had taken place outside his administration, Rees could do nothing other than offer the Druze his protection and ensure, by means of aerial patrols, that the Rualla remained in French territory. Once they had been located, they were carefully kept under observation, Rees himself going up on at least one patrol to see them. 'The Ruella on the march were a fine sight, when halted they had 1,072 tents and camels without number. They occupied a grazing area of about 15 miles by 6.'[22]

The situation, although still relatively calm, was deteriorating, and it appeared to Rees that the root cause of all the problems that were building up in Transjordan was the activities of the French forces near the border. His operational diary entry for 23 May showed the changing situation.

On the 15th an incident occurred for which I can see no justification. A French column with an escort came to the ruined village of Semme inside our border near Nasib on the railway. Although our police asked them to refrain, the French galloped into Semme. Naturally the Beni Sakhr who were grazing in and around the ruins opened fire and this gave the French an excuse for machine-gunning the tents, quite at random, and killing some five men, a woman and a child. Not only this, but the French have apparently wounded and carried off one of our Arab Legion policemen.[23]

These disturbances and the reduction in the garrison of Qasr al–Azrak combined to cause a marked change in the attitude of the local Druze. On 26 May, Major Smith ordered eight men to halt in order that their passes might be inspected. They disregarded his orders completely and went back into the basalt area from where they had appeared. It was later discovered that a much larger group, numbering about sixty men, was gathering in the basalt and a troop of soldiers was fired upon when they attempted to arrest a small group of mounted men east of Ein al-Beida. In addition, a permanent camp was discovered in Wadi Hassan and large numbers of armed men were observed near a camp at Jebel Hassan. Major Smith led a force into the camp at Wadi Hassan only to find it deserted and when the Druze returned in the evening they behaved aggressively but were persuaded to move off south without causing any real incident. About an hour later, Smith heard the sound of gunfire coming from the direction in which the Druze had travelled and a restless night was spent before the small force moved off the following morning after destroying the tents, stores and ammunition that the Druze had left behind.

At the same time, a troop which had been sent to patrol the northern watering holes in the area of Ain Ankiyeh was fired upon by a band of armed men. This was repeated during the evening and Rees, who was with the unit, gave the order that warning shots were to be fired in the air. When this failed to have the desired effect, he ordered one of the attacking tribesmen to be shot and, as a consequence, one of the Druze had his leg broken and his horse killed and a second horse wounded. This demonstration of intent succeeded in persuading the other tribesmen to cease fire and move away.

Rees then had no alternative than to issue a proclamation warning the Druze that the situation which appeared to be developing would not be tolerated by the authorities.

Proclamation under Martial Law N° 10 [24] — Yesterday at 9.30 hours a band of Armed men opened fire on my troops east of Ain Beda. My troops fired into the air in order to make the band come in and surrender. In the evening my troops were again fired on at Ain Ankiyeh and it was not until dusk that direct fire was ordered. Numerous instances occurred during the day of armed bands moving in the Military Area refusing to obey orders to halt and adopting a threatening attitude.

I hereby give warning that orders have been issued to my troops to open fire on anybody

> a. who refuses to halt when called upon to do so.
>
> b. who endeavours to avoid capture after being challenged.
>
> c. who opens fire on my troops.

Realising that the situation could very easily get out of hand and that his force of one company of the TFF and one section of armoured cars was not sufficient to control any possible trouble, Rees sent a radio message to Amman at 03.00 hours on 27 May requesting reinforcements. An additional company and two more sections were able to cover the sixty-two miles, some of it in darkness, and reach his camp by 07.30 thereby proving the wisdom of constructing new roads.

To secure the area and to make the Druze fully aware that the British force in Azrak had been reinforced, Rees ordered his men to occupy every known water hole and thereby make it difficult, if not impossible, for anyone else to operate in the area. He also ordered that no passes were to be issued and that any unregistered horses found in the area under martial law would be shot.

The situation could have easily erupted into violence and Rees, with the relatively small force that he had at his disposal, would have been unable to do anything about it. Each of the warring factions, the Druze, the Rualla, the French, the British, or even the bands of uncommitted brigands who roamed the region, could spark off trouble. The only hope was to prevent trouble breaking out, which would be a very difficult task requiring a great deal of tact and diplomacy.

The root cause of the difficulties was clearly the hostility which existed between the Druze and the French authorities in Syria and, although the former had already been militarily defeated, the latter were refusing to allow the situation to stabilize until they had accounted for all the Druze warriors and their leaders. Towards the end of May, Rees contacted Colonel Arnaud of the French Army and set about trying to find a peaceful solution to the problem. He felt great sympathy for the Druze and believed that they had just cause for complaint, but also realised that they would never enter into negotiations with the French if they were ever to leave British territory and return to Syria. He asked Arnaud to allow them to return to Jebel el-Druze without fear of French reprisals and, in return, he would arrange for the construction of a good quality road along the northern edge of the basalt or, if that should be too expensive, an armoured car road along the same route. This would act as a deterrent to future incursions by the Druze into Transjordan and, indirectly, the French would also find it difficult to explain their wanderings into British territory. Arnaud agreed in principle, but asked Rees to delay his plans as it would cause the French grave embarrassment because they already had a column operating in the basalt area. Rees accepted the delay and in return the French promised to provide him with any intelligence which their column might gather during this operation. A second meeting was arranged at Umm el-Jimal when the French informed him that Sultan al–Atrash was back in Wadi Hassan with a sizeable force of armed men.

Rees and Arnaud then agreed to leave the northern border of Transjordan open and the British forces then began a drive with the intention of forcing al-Atrash and his men back to Syria. Arnaud, accompanied by other senior French officials, arrived at Qasr al-Azrak on 14 June to commence discussions with the Druze leaders, the British High Commissioner's representative, Alec Kirkbride,[25] and Group Captain Rees. From the start, the meeting seemed to be doomed to failure as Sultan al–Atrash made a speech which was clearly intended to inflame the French. Before Arnaud could break up the meeting, Kirkbride was able to calm the situation and the Druze appeared to divide into two groups, those that wished to continue with the negotiations and those that wished to continue fighting. When it became apparent that the latter could not be moved from their belligerent position, they were asked to leave and the remaining Druze negotiators were given assurances of their safety and treatment should they decide to return to Syria. The offer was accepted and the authorities gave them a deadline of 1 July, by which date they were to have left the area that was under martial law.

Those Druze who had rejected the French safeguards then began a propaganda campaign to try and dissuade their comrades from leaving. Fearing that if this was successful, all the negotiations might be endangered, Rees ordered all refugees who did not hold passes, or who were not members of the group returning to Syria, to leave the camp immediately. This seemed to have the required effect and, when Colonel Henry, governor of the Jebel el-Druze, arrived at Azrak on 21 June, most of the tribesmen present in the camp accepted the terms for their return to Syria and, four days later, there were only three tents remaining.

The dissidents, however, had not mellowed, and fully aware that Rees had every intention of using military force to ensure that his orders were carried out, they had moved out of the Military Area and were forming a new camp at Amari Wells some fifteen miles further south. Al-Atrash declared that he and his followers (who numbered about 1300 men) had every intention of attacking the French at the first opportunity and would remain at Amari Wells unless ordered to move on, despite the fact that there was a grave shortage of grazing there for their animals. Atrash had selected the spot very carefully and, by using the tribe's considerable wealth, was able to transport food by road from Amman. He was also able to launch raids into Syria without hinderance from Rees' force as the water holes on the route were too scattered for him to be intercepted.

Such a situation was clearly in open defiance of Rees' orders and could not be tolerated. If Rees allowed Sultan al–Atrash and his men to remain at Amari Wells, then all the agreements with the French might be endangered and, not only would the British be accused of harbouring rebels, but also those Druze who had been promised a safe return to Syria might find that the authorities had changed their minds in view of the continuing attacks. If however he moved a British force against the new camp, he might rekindle many of the troubles of the previous month. In order to try and preserve the peace, Rees decided to give the Druze the option of leaving without the obvious threat of military force. This would enable the sultan to preserve his dignity while maintaining cordial relations between the British and French authorities.

On 3 July, Rees issued a proclamation stating that the boundaries of the Military Area had been extended to include the area around Amari Wells. Al-Atrash and his followers were informed of the new boundaries by means of leaflets dropped over their camp by British aircraft. Rees gave the Druze two days to consider their changed circumstances then issued a further proclamation.

> Whereas it has come to my knowledge that there is an assembly, including a number of Druze Combatants, at Amari in the area under Martial Law, I hereby order that all persons there assembled who are not habitual residents of Transjordan shall leave Transjordan territory on or before the 16th instant, after which date I shall take measures as appear to me to be necessary to enforce compliance with my order.[26]

This, whilst clearly stating the position of the Druze at Amari Wells, gave them sufficient time to move out of British territory without fear of being attacked by the authorities and the result was more than satisfactory. RAF air and ground reconnaissance units reported that the Druze had immediately begun to search for a new location for their camp, deciding to settle at Hassiedat in Nejid territory, outside the expanded military area. A column of cars was seen to travel from Amman carrying food for the move, and two hundred camels from Amari carried the possessions of the Druze towards the new camp site. To speed up the evacuation and guarantee that all the tribesmen left, Rees ordered that all food convoys were to be prevented from entering the camp at Amari Wells and diverted to the new site. As it was estimated that there was only sufficient food at Amari to last a month, the tribesmen would be compelled to leave by 25 July and the deadline for their departure was extended to that date in order to avoid any possible cause for confrontation.

Patrols kept a watchful eye on progress throughout the month and their reports indicated that the Druze were making every effort to comply with Rees' orders. Two days before the deadline expired, Amari Wells was reported to be clear and an armoured car sent to the new camp stated that all the Druze were there, a fact which was confirmed by aerial reconnaissance on 25 July. On that date, Rees ordered all his forces to withdraw from Qasr al-Azrak and return to their normal stations. As a gesture of goodwill and by way of recognizing the Druze compliance with the authorities, all prisoners confined in British prisons by the orders of military courts were released. Each week, to ensure that the rebel tribesmen remained in the Nejid territory, an armoured car was sent through the Military Area and aerial patrols checked the roads. Any raiding parties that were observed were then reported to the French authorities.

The British forces in Transjordan, and Rees in particular, had handled the situation with diplomacy and tact. The excesses which had taken place in Syria could very easily have overflowed across the border, but Rees' policy had been to avoid confrontation whenever possible in the belief that open fighting solved nothing and only created further problems for the future. Throughout the period of the disturbance, no member of the British forces was killed and only one policeman was wounded (by the French) and the Druze only suffered one man wounded; a remarkable achievement when one considers the large number of casualties sustained by both sides inside Syria. The authorities' faith in giving Rees his own semi-independent command had been more than justified and he had demonstrated his ability in yet another field of military activity.

The Druze Rebellion in Syria, although serious, had not captured the attention of the world outside of the region, apart from the colonial departments in Paris and London. The main focus of British attention during this period had been on Palestine where the conflict between the indigenous Arabs and the increasing Jewish population was always simmering just below the surface. Rees, fortunately, does not seem to have had to deal with a great deal of trouble from that quarter and his period in command of Palestine and Transjordan appears to have fitted neatly in between two periods of disturbances in the former territory. Stanley Vincent, however, recalled one incident in Jaffa, which turned out to be of little long-term consequence.

> A riot started in Jaffa over some political squabble … and I was sent with my section of armoured cars to quell it. I asked Group Captain Rees … if I had to fire to stop the trouble, whether I should fire over their heads, or shoot to kill? He replied, 'Vincent, that can only be decided by the man on the spot, but I assure you that whichever you do, you will certainly be court-martialled'! [27]

Fortunately for the RAF, the local population and Rees, the presence of the armoured cars had proved to be sufficient to persuade the rioters to return to their homes. This, however, had not always been the case. When the French had attempted to relieve Suwayda in the Jebel el-Druze, their armoured cars had been surprised, turned over and destroyed and, as a consequence, the Druze captured the French supply column 'and thus obtained enough machine guns and ammunition to conduct a two years' war.' As a result of his experiences, Rees put together his own theories on how such forces could be handled in an RAF context.[28]

The forces under his command included air units, armoured units, motorized infantry and support aircraft and vehicles. He examined the lessons learnt when similar forces had been utilised in the Middle East in the distant past (citing events as far back as 1400 BC) and the near past and drew a number of conclusions —

- the ability of any controlling power to be able to operate in a potentially hostile region was dependant upon advance information.
- armoured vehicles could only use their speed and power against an enemy if there were adequate road links through the proposed area of operations.
- adequate expenditure in times of peace on military materials and an infrastructure on which they could operate could prevent the outbreak of hostilities.
- the commander of the controlling power's forces should never despise his enemy no matter how weak or obsolete the enemy's force might appear to be.

The main problems of operating in territories such as Transjordan fell into two categories – the nature of the enemy and the terrain over which a military command operated. Mastery of the second was essential if mastery of the first was to be achieved. The potential enemy was accustomed to operating in the region and had adapted his forces to suit the terrain. Rees saw a direct lesson that could be learned in the raid on Ziza by the Wahabi tribesmen in 1924[29] when a force of 3,000 tribesmen had been able to enter unobserved territory that was ostensibly under the control of British troops and operate there for some time before eventually being driven out by superior weaponry, most notably aircraft and armoured cars.

Rees outlined how he saw the role of each element of his command in Transjordan should be developed, both in preparation for potential hostilities and after those hostilities had broken out.

- all military units should endeavour to learn and understand the geography and terrain of the region in which they would operate. Whenever possible, opportunities should be taken to prepare maps and then keep them up to date.
- regular reconnaissance should be carried out and aerial photography utilised to expand the knowledge of the region and its peoples.
- a network of roads should be constructed and maintained to allow the rapid movement of ground forces.
- all ground combat units should be supplied by both air and ground support units.
- all ground and air combat units should endeavour to inflict casualties on the enemy and also seize property and key individuals in order to reduce his ability to continue with operations against the controlling power.

He also drew up detailed schemes for training, and outlined the exact equipment that was needed for combined air/ground operations in a country such as Transjordan.

Notes

1. Winston Churchill, addressing the House of Commons, 15 December 1919.
2. Mohammed Abdullah Hassan (1856–1920) had been a thorn in the side of Britain since 1900 when, at the head of a Dervish armed force he had raided British protected areas in the Horn of Africa. During 1901–04 he managed to inflict a number of defeats upon British, Italian and Ethiopian forces. The fighting continued up until the outbreak of war in Europe and Hassan controlled a considerable area until Britain re-focussed her attention on him in early 1920.
3. Later Marshal of the Royal Air Force, Sir John Salmond, GCB, CMG, CVO, DSO. See Chapter II, p 31, fn 30.
4. NA AIR 9/19 Quoted letter from Winston Churchill to the Secretary of State for India, 24 February 1922.
5. NA AIR9/19 Quoted letter from the Colonial Office, 8 January 1925.
6. NA AIR 9/19 quoted telegram from Colonial Office to the High Commissioner, Sir Herbert Samuels, 19 July 1924.

7. Later Air Vice Marshal Sir Tom Ince Webb-Bowen, KCB, CMG, DL (1879–1956). A native of Pembrokeshire, he was an officer in the Middlesex Militia, then the Bedfordshire Regiment and served in India. He gained his RAeC certificate in 1912 and transferred to the RFC, becoming assistant commandant of the CFS and OC 2 Squadron and 3 Wing. He retired in 1933. His brother, Captain Hugh Ince Webb-Bowen, Royal Welsh Fusiliers, had been killed serving in Gallipoli in 1915.

8. Captain Gabriel Marie Victor Carbillet, who served as Governor of Jebel el-Druze 1924–5, became notorious for the cruel manner in which he treated the Syrian people under his control.

9. Captain Antoine Raynaud, provisional governor Jebel el-Druze, generally recognised as a member of the right-wing faction in the French officer corps. He was one of a group of disaffected officers who leaked information about Captain Cabrillet's activities in Jebel el-Druze to the *Echo de Paris* in 1925.

10. General Maurice Paul Emmauel Sarrail (1856–1929), GOC VI Corps 1914, he served in Salonika 1915–17 and was dismissed for his failure to achieve success and his socialist views. He was brought out of retirement in 1924 and appointed High Commissioner of Syria. He was recalled to Paris in 1925 after ordering the shelling of Damascus.

11. General Roger Michaud, former chief-of-staff to General Sarrail in Salonika during 1916–17. Appointed GOC Armée du Levant, he ignored information obtained by air reconnaissance regarding the location and strength of the Druze forces and moved his column from Izra towards Suweyda (a distance of some twenty miles). His force was ambushed seven miles from its destination.

12. Sultan al–Atrash (1891–1982) had been a prominent leader of the arab military forces deployed against the Turks during the Great War and had been appointed a general in the Syrian army of Emir Feisal. The creation of Syria as a mandated territory under French control and that country's apparent mistreatment of Syrian Arabs, resulted in 1922 in al–Atrash leading an attack on a French convoy in an attempt to free prisoners. He was forced to flee to Transjordan (a British mandated territory) but was allowed to return and was pardoned. In 1925, he led what came to be known as the Syrian Revolution. He later became a prominent figure in the Syrian independence campaign after the Second World War. More than a million people attended his funeral in 1982.

13. General Maurice Gamelin (1872–1958), replaced Michaud as GOC *Armée du Levant*. He was C-in-C of the French Army in 1939–40.

14. Senator Henri de Jouvenal (1876–1935), politician, journalist and diplomat, was appointed the first civilian High Commissioner of Syria following the recall of Sarrail in December 1925.

15. Later Air Vice Marshal Stanley Flamank Vincent, CB, DFC, AFC, DL (1897–1976). He had qualified as a pilot in 1915 and served with 60 Squadron and was one of Smith-Barry's staff at the School of Special Flying at Gosport in 1917. OC 110 Squadron, he was unemployed in 1919 but re-joined the RAF and became a flight commander at RAF College, Cranwell before being posted to Iraq in 1923. In 1948 he was AOC 11 Group and retired in 1950.

16. Qasr al–Azrak is a stone fortress located by an oasis in the middle of a large open area of desert in Transjordan. Originally built by the Romans, it was rebuilt by the Arabs during the period of the Crusades, and had been used by TE Lawrence as an operating base in 1917–18.

17. *Flying Fever*, Stanley Vincent, London, 1972.

18. Later Brigadier Frederick William Bewsher, DSO, OBE, MC, (1886–1950), OC Transjordan Frontier Force 1 April 1926–1928. He had served in the 5 London Regiment (Royal Fusiliers) and was the author of the *History of the 51st Highland Division 1914–1918* and *The Reformation and the Renaissance (1485–1547)*.

19. *Flying Fever*, op cit.

20. Later Captain (acting Major) JW Smith, OBE, Transjordan Frontier Force.

21. Rees' report to the Chief Secretary in Jerusalem on the occupation of Azrak, 14 May 1927, National Archives, AIR 5/203, Air operations in Trans-jordania and Palestine and Jebel Druze revolt, Syria, 1925.

22. Ibid.

23. Ibid.

24. Proclamation under Martial Law No 10, National Archives, AIR 23/796, Military Reports: Palestine.

25. Later Sir Alec Seath Kirkbride, KCMG, CVO, OBE, MC (1897–1978). After war service in the Middle East (part of the time with Colonel TE Lawrence (Lawrence of Arabia), he served as the British High Commissioner's representative in Amman and was eventually appointed British Resident there in 1939. He wrote a memoir of his diplomatic service in the Middle East *A Crackle of Thorns*, published in 1956.

26. National Archives, AIR 5/203, op cit.

27. 20. *Flying Fever*, op cit.

28. Rees' findings on armoured car/air operations in Transjordan were submitted in the form of an essay for the

1929, Gordon-Shephard Memorial Prize. In addition to the topics extensively quoted here, he also dealt with issues such as supplies, reserves, casualties, vehicles, intelligence, training of officers and crews and tactics. The essay was awarded the second prize, the first going to Wing-Commander Wilfred Ashton McClaughry, DSO, MC, DFC (later Air Vice Marshal McClaughry).

29. The Wahabi tribesmen, under the command of Ibin Saud, launched operations in March 1924 to wrest control of the Hejaz from King Hussain.

IX

ARCHAEOLOGY
(1926–29)

THE BARREN WILDERNESS OF WHAT WAS OFTEN REFERRED TO AS NORTHERN ARABIA has captivated many of those who visited the region and Lionel Rees was no exception. In quiet moments during the period he was in command in Transjordan, he wandered about the apparently empty landscape and noticed signs that hinted at early human habitation. When he occupied the camp amongst the ruins of the old fort at Qasr al–Azrak, maintaining a watchful eye on the activities of the Druze tribesmen, his mind must have drifted to that other great castle on the banks of the Menai Strait, in the shadow of which he had spent so much of his childhood. The inscriptions at Azrak fascinated him and he wondered as to their origins. On long walks alone in the surrounding desert, he collected flints and other small rock fragments which clearly indicated, even to his untrained mind, that the area had at some point in the distant past been inhabited by more than just a small garrison at the fort or the occasional passing nomad. Like a fish drawn to some irresistible bait, he became hooked on the ancient history of the Middle East, a fascination which was to remain with him for the rest of his life.

The utilization of RAF aircraft in the Middle East, primarily for military purposes, had a profound effect upon the archaeological understanding of the region for, not only could great distances over inhospitable terrain be covered very quickly, but also details of the landscape, often invisible on the ground, could be seen from the air; landscape features which had previously been only visible in small sections, if at all, could now be viewed in their entirety and, most importantly, photographed.

The pioneering work of linking together aerial photography and archaeology had commenced almost as soon as the Great War had ended when Lieutenant-Colonel Beazeley[1] published some views on the subject in the 1919 and 1920 issues of *Geographical Journal,* but few recognised the potential which this new facility offered, and aerial photographs were, on the whole, only used to provide a new perspective of already identified and studied sites. In 1925, one of Rees' former subordinates in 11 Squadron, Gilbert Insall, VC, whilst flying over Salisbury Plain, took an aerial photograph which he realised showed a feature of the landscape which was unnoticeable from ground level. Archaeological investigation based upon Insall's photograph led to the discovery of what became known as 'Woodhenge,' a major early Neolithic site.[2] The potential for the use of aerial photography in archaeology was then recognised by a small group of scholars who saw tremendous scope for its use in the relatively unknown deserts of Mesopotamia and Transjordan, regions which had only recently come under British control.

Rees' successful involvement in the early aerial photographic work conducted by the RFC in 1915 had sparked in him an interest in this activity which was reawakened when he arrived in Transjordan where some of the men under his command were involved in carrying out surveys of the region in order to construct landing grounds for aeroplanes and routes for land forces needing to pass through the previously unpenetrable basalt-rock strewn landscape. Whenever possible, Rees endeavoured to combine military patrols with his new found interest, and tried to enthuse others who accompanied him – not always successfully, as a young pilot of 14 Squadron, John Franks[3] recalled,

His [Rees'] hobby was flying & motoring about the Sinai & Transjordan deserts by day & by night with a large scale map & a Bible finding places of biblical interest. An ADC sitting in the back of a motor car in which he was taking round a rather bored French colonel from Damascus, told me of an amusing incident, when [Rees] was pointing out the spot on the steep mountain track where it was mentioned in the Old Testament that Jacob had wrestled with the Angel who had put his thigh out of joint. His pidgin French confused the colonel whose reply was '*Ah, Je comprende, accidente automobile.*' Nobody even smiled! [4]

The American anthropologist Dr Henry Field[5] had visited Transjordan in 1926 as part of a joint Field Museum of Chicago and Oxford University archaeological expedition and had found sufficient evidence, in the form of prehistoric flints to the east of the Damascus–Maan railroad, to warrant a second expedition the following year. As part of the preparation for this second visit to the region, Field was obliged to contact the British government for fear that the Druze uprising would debar the Americans from entering the area. Following this contact, the Secretary of State for Air, Lord Londonderry, and Air Vice-Marshal John Higgins of the Air Ministry, sent instructions to Rees to assist the expedition which was to be in the area south and south-east of Amman during November 1927. Where, when and if the team was to be permitted to visit would be at Rees' discretion 'provided that no local disturbance or tribal uprising prevented the start of the expedition.'

By 1927, the RAF had established landing grounds (complete with fuel dumps) throughout the region which were charted and identified as LGA, LGB, LGC, etc. These airstrips had been cleared of all major obstacles that might impede the landing and taking-off of an aeroplane, and had been linked by rough tracks which had also been cleared of basalt rocks and marked by means of a ploughed furrow which was visible both from the ground and the air. These landing grounds were regularly patrolled from the air (utilising the DH9A aircraft of 14 Squadron) and from the ground (by small maintenance units in lorries, often escorted by the Rolls-Royce armoured cars of 2 Armoured Car Company). The relative lawlessness of the desert regions, particularly at the time when the issues regarding the Druze had still to be resolved, made it evident to Rees that the only way the American scientists could travel around the region would be if they were attached to a regular RAF patrol which would serve as both guide and protector.

Henry Field and his small party arrived at Rees' headquarters in Amman in a desert-equipped Cadillac provided by the Nairn Overland Transport Company. After a short period of consultation, the party (accompanied by Flight Lieutenant Silcox) was attached to a convoy of four small RAF lorries that was to leave Amman on 11 November for a short five-day trip to Bayir Wells. All went as planned and the expedition found ten new prehistoric sites. On its return to Amman, the expedition was then attached to an RAF convoy of two trucks and two armoured cars which left Amman on 19 November to visit all the landing grounds as far as LGR. Rees, who had already acquired considerable knowledge of the archaeological evidence in the region, decide to accompany the convoy,

A group of basalt stone circles, described by Rees as 'villages'. [Dr David Kennedy]

A series of basalt rock structures which Rees described as 'cairns'. [Dr David Kennedy]

The oasis and castle at Qasr al–Azrak with the ancient stone circles visible in the foreground. [Field Museum]

The western walls of Qasr al–Azrak. [Field Museum]

travelling in his own Rolls-Royce staff car, acting as an unofficial guide, and no doubt anxious to discover more archaeological information himself. From the outset, the expedition began to find ample archaeological evidence.

On the morning of November 18 at 11.10 hours we left Amman … following the road to Zarqa. Just before reaching Zarqa we stopped at Hadid. … There is a Roman fort of the usual square type and another fort with a circular ditch on the side of a small wadi. A few flint flakes and some fragments of pottery were collected.

We then proceeded across country in a northeasterly direction until we reached the wadi which runs into Hammam as-Sarakh. At a point about 20 miles from Amman and 6 miles south of Hammam as-Sarakh, where the road branches to Qasr al-Azrak, we found some worked flints. We halted at Hammam as-Sarakh which lies about 37 miles from Amman. The next stop was 40 miles from Amman at a small, square, ruined building with low walls of basalt boulders situated on a mud flat east of Hammam as-Sarakh.[6]

They camped the first night seventy-nine miles from Amman. Rees was in his element and made every effort to assist Field with his research.

On the morning of November 19, Group Captain Rees and I walked along the road running south from the mud flats … and collected flints from 3 sites before breakfast. Three and a half miles from camp we saw some graves made from faced stones. Toward Ein al-Asad at Azrak, a small trench had been excavated by Group Captain Rees and the pottery sherds excavated were presented by him to the Field Museum.

After breakfast we visited the 'kite' on the south end of the basalt south of Qasr al-Azrak. There was no flint in the 'kite' but some flakes [were found] near a cairn east of it. This 'kite' which lies about 2 miles south of Azrak is readily seen in aerial photographs of Azrak.[7]

Many travellers who had visited Qasr al–Azrak, the centre of activity of the Druze incidents of 1926–7, had been struck by its unexpected beauty, an oasis of loveliness amidst a barren desert region. The renowned archaeologist OGS Crawford,[8] who visited Transjordan in 1928, described it in his memoirs as

… one of the most romantic sites I have ever seen. For some sixty miles one motors over rolling desert, which is covered by brown carpets of flints that chinkle under the wheels. There were mirages everywhere looking exactly like lakes, but at last we came to a real lake, with bright green reeds growing on the margin. It was a strange site in such a desert. The scenery was most beautiful; at the back of the lake were some purple covered mountains that looked exactly like the heather covered hills of Killarney, and a clump of palms at the north end of the lake were the blue towers of a Roman [sic] fort.[9]

Located at the northern end of the ancient caravan route through Wadi Sirhan, on the western edge of the Arabian Desert, the oasis had long been of strategic importance. The fortress, once an imposing structure of black basalt was, by the 1920s, only an empty shell. Inscriptions on the stones dated the building to the thirteenth century, but other inscriptions indicated that its origins may have been much earlier, either Roman or Byzantine; some even argue that the site was used by the Nabatheans in the second century BC. That it had been in constant use throughout the centuries was the result of its location next to a plentiful supply of water in the form of large pools and marshes, fed by freshwater springs. TE Lawrence, who had used it as his headquarters during the final assault on the Turks, had described it as a '… luminous, silky Eden' and, as the only permanent source of water in 12,000 square miles, it attracted a great deal of both human and animal attention.

On 21 November, as the expedition was crossing rough boulder-strewn terrain east of

LGE, two RAF DH9As were spotted circling above them. When the column stopped, the observer in one of the aeroplanes dropped a message streamer which, when retrieved, was found to contain a message from RAF Headquarters asking Rees to return immediately. The column moved on to LGF near Ras Teida where the aircraft had landed to await them. Rees then left the expedition to return to Amman in order to attend to RAF business, and Field and his colleagues reached LGR on 25 November and from there eventually Baghdad.

After the scientists had left, Rees continued with his own private research in the region and when the Field party returned for a third time in April 1928, he again accompanied it into the wilderness. Numerous sites of archaeological interest were visited and recorded, particularly in the area around Qasr al–Azrak where the Druze were still in residence and where their reception gave a clear indication of their relationship with the RAF and with Rees in particular.

> April 26. We drank coffee with their leader. The Druze permitted us to measure the walls of their buildings provided that we did not disturb their womenfolk. When it became necessary to enter a building to obtain dimensions of a room belonging to the women, they were moved to another part of the building until our work was completed. Undoubtedly they considered us insane as we solemnly measured walls and buildings in the heat of the sun instead of sitting in a cool, sheltered spot to drink coffee and tea with the tribal elders.
>
> April 27. We accompanied Group Captain Rees to a curious, elongated cistern group near the pools, and also the 'kites' and stone circles to the south.[10]

The party returned to Amman on 1 May from where Rees took them to visit Greco-Roman graves south of the city. A week later they accompanied him on a southern

A DH9A (J7889) of 14 Squadron at LGF prior to take off with Rees as a passenger, 21 November 1927. The Field Expedition's Cadillac and Rees' Rolls-Royce can be seen in the background. [Field Museum]

Qasr Tuba, located some fifty miles north of Bayir. [Field Museum]

reconnaissance, travelling in his Rolls-Royce and the Cadillac, escorted by two armoured cars and two trucks, visiting a ruined Roman town, mausoleum and wells to the south of Amman, travelling through an area rich in biblical history. Passing the remains of what appeared to be guard houses and silted-up reservoirs, they reached Qasr Tuba, ninety miles from Amman, where they made detailed notes of the brick-built fortress. From there they travelled to the wells at Wadi al–Ghadaf and Wadi Bayir, examining further ruined forts and water cisterns, before eventually returning to Amman on 17 May.

The following day, the expedition (again accompanied by Rees) attached itself to another RAF patrol heading back to Qasr Tuba and Amri Wells, searching this time for an unidentified fort which Rees had seen from the air and wells which had been missed the previous week. After crossing large areas of mud flats the patrol eventually reached Qasr al–Azrak, with Rees pointing out numerous previously unseen features of interest on the way. At Azrak, Rees was obliged to leave the party and return to his headquarters in Amman, with the scientists making their way to Damascus and then Baghdad, arriving there on 26 May.

Henry Field, later praised the arrangements and co-operation which the expedition had received.

Group Captain Rees … assisted the expedition in every possible manner … Himself a keen archaeologist, [he] was able to make valuable suggestions as to the probable localities where prehistoric man may have lived. Owing to the kindness of the British Air Force, the expedition was allowed to visit places which otherwise would have been totally inaccessible. [11]

As already noted, the general value of the RAF's aerial photographic work had been recognised by OGS Crawford and, in 1928, he followed the Field Museum Expedition to Transjordan, having also applied to the Air Ministry for permission to use the aerial photographs of Transjordan to assist with the identification of sites of interest on the ground. The RAF instructed its officers to assist Crawford in any way that they could, as long as no additional burden was placed upon the service's already stretched budget.

The result was very gratifying. An undertaking was given that, subject to certain obvious limitations, ancient sites might be included in the normal routine of practice [aerial] photography. Further, it was agreed that these, and many existing but obsolete negatives of sites abroad, should be handed over to the Director of the British Museum, to form the nucleus of a national collection. In order to set the scheme in motion, I decided to visit the countries concerned, and collect and bring back with me the first instalment of obsolete negatives.[12]

On his arrival in Amman, he was immediately impressed by Rees.

We landed at Amman at three o'clock and were met by Group Captain Rees. He was an enthusiastic amateur archaeologist and had collected a large group of wasms – small boulders with names chipped on them. He knew Transjordan thoroughly, and used to patrol the tracks in six-wheeled Morris trucks, to keep them usable – a defence precaution that was then necessary.

I stayed with Rees at Amman for three weeks that were crowded with interest. The day after my arrival he had to accompany the Acting High Commissioner for Palestine, Sir Harry

The third Field Museum expedition travelling across the flat, sandy region between Qasr Tuba and Amri Wells in April 1928. The vehicles are [R–L]: The Cadillac, Rees' Rolls-Royce (flying the Group Captain's pennant), a Rolls-Royce armoured car, RAF tender, second armoured car and second RAF tender.
[Field Museum]

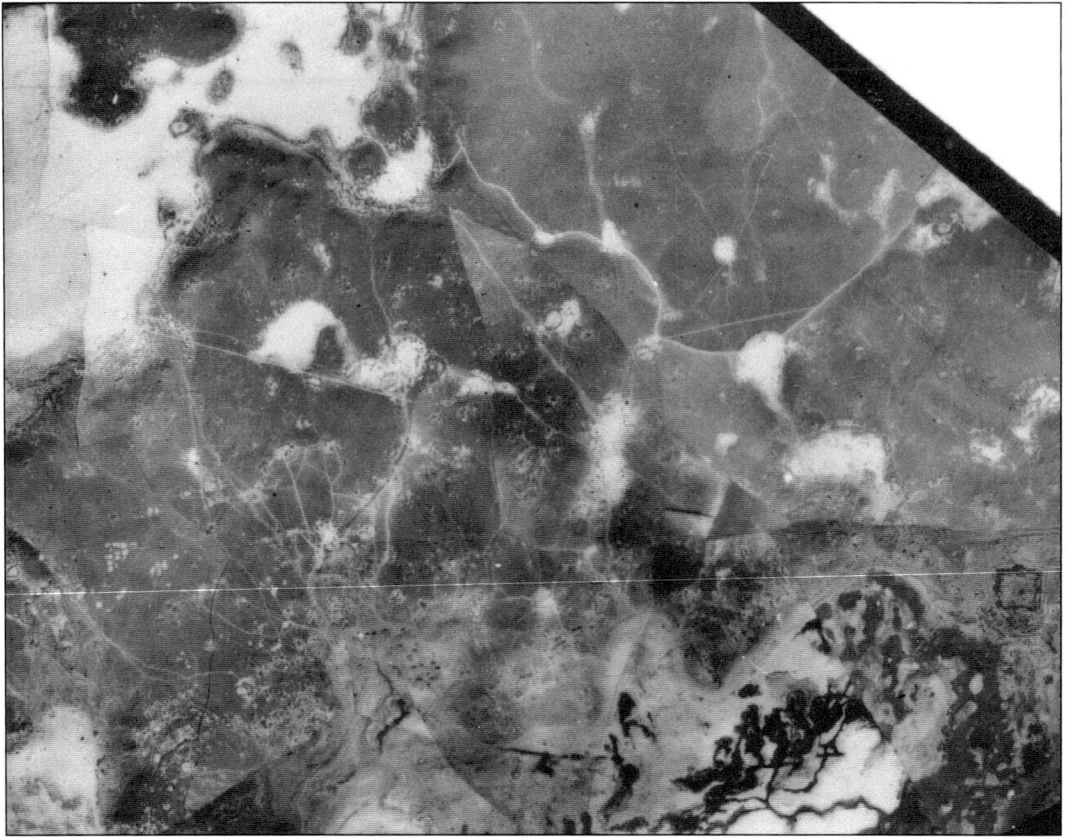

A set of RAF aerial photographs, taken c 1926, formed into a mosaic showing the area to the west of Qasr al–Azrak. The 'castle' can be seen on the extreme right, forming an almost perfect square, with the areas of fresh water seen in black to the south and south west of it. Some man-made circular features can also be seen in the light area in the upper left quadrant of the mosaic. [Dr David Kennedy]

Luke, on a tour of the frontier; though primarily intended to be administrative, the tour became in fact almost exclusively archaeological, for we were three enthusiasts.[13]

In addition to arranging field visits to notable sites, Rees allowed Crawford access to the sizeable collection of photographic negatives which he had already collected since the establishment of the command two years previously. He knew that the archaeologist would be pleased, as many of the plates had been taken with the purpose of recording interesting ground features, and anything which had caught Rees' eye had immediately become a target for further photographic missions.

The photographs were taken, mostly, as a matter of training. They are extraordinarily useful in showing new pilots the landmarks of the country, because in the desert there are often no landmarks except some of the old ruins. It is also important that pilots should know them.[14]

He had already made considerable use of these photographs to assist him with his own researches into the archaeology of the region and little did he realise how valuable they were to become years later. Recently, their value has been underlined by Dr David Kennedy,[15] who noted that if one were to examine photographs of Qasr al–Azrak, as a single example, they clearly indicate the enormous changes that have occurred during the past ninety years in such a remote and ostensibly featureless landscape. When the RAF began to photograph the region, it was much as it had been for hundreds of years, and the camps of both the Druze and the military were only temporary affairs.

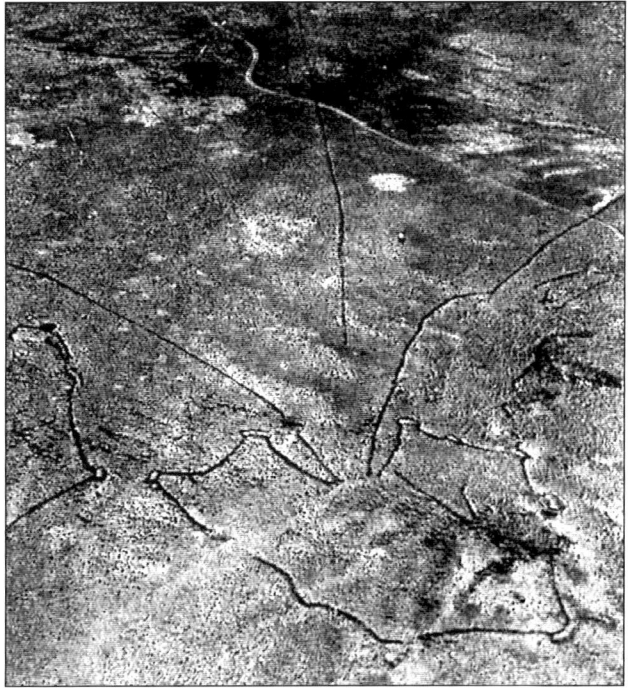

One of the aerial photographs taken during the 1920s which show features which were then known as 'kites,' which are now generally accepted as having been animal traps. Animals would have been herded into the ever-narrowing 'tail' sections (here visible in the upper part of the photograph) and into the large enclosure (seen in the lower part of the photograph) where they would have been killed. [Anon]

Today, however, there is a sizeable town of some 3,000 people on the site and the ground features have changed almost beyond recognition. For this reason alone, the RAF's work in photographing the area, and the preliminary archaeological work personally conducted by Rees (although rather naive and amateurish) were of immeasurable value to modern archaeologists.

East of Qasr al–Azrak lay the region known as the Basalt (or Harra), so called because of the large areas of basalt boulders which covered the surface. Rees had spent a considerable length of time studying the numerous cairn groups and stone circles which were located there, and discovered that they were not only evidence of ancient man's use of what is now a barren region, but that they also contained evidence of their use by a literate race of people at some period of their history. Inscriptions and/or drawings were to be found on or near to every large cairn that he examined, but were rarely found on the medium-sized cairns, and never on the smaller ones. Rees also noted that similar inscriptions were to be found on rocks that were remote from any cairns. As all these inscriptions were similar to those that had previously been discovered in the area of the Safa Depression, he dated them to the period known as the Safaitic period which extended from about the first century BC to the fourth century AD. He believed the inscriptions had been carved by the ancient Bedouin and other semi-nomadic tribes, and were very similar in style to those found in Southern Arabia, and the language used was closely related to Arabic, making them very distinct from the inscriptions of the settled people of the region who, at that time, were writing in either Aramaic or Greek. He made some interesting observations regarding the variations between those located in the north of the region and those found in the south, stating that the latter resembled very strongly similar drawings found in Africa, thereby suggesting that some sort of ancient cultural or even racial link may have existed with that continent. He even went so far as to attempt to read the inscriptions but, as he used a publication which had an incomplete script table for Safaitic, these are now viewed as having little value. Dr MCA MacDonald,[16] a leading authority in this field, summed up this aspect of Rees' archaeological work.

> His 'translations' of some of the names, though obviously *jeux d'esprit*, are pleasingly ingenious, thus the name 'Asad' (the common Arabic word for lion) is rendered 'Lionel', and so on. His contribution to Safaitic epigraphy lay in his discovery of the texts and his making them available to the scholarly world … His copies, though far from exact, are not at all bad, considering that he could not read the inscriptions at the time he was copying them. They certainly compare favourably with those of several other travellers and explorers. [17]

Rees labelled the stone circles 'villages' and believed that cattle could have been penned inside them. As they were located many miles from known sources of water, he concluded that there must have been a dramatic change in the water supply of the region, and that once that valuable and vital commodity had ceased to be readily available, the villages had ceased to be inhabited. He speculated that the cairns had also served as a form of defensive feature or guard houses for the Roman roads which, at that time, crossed the region. The larger cairns were all about the same size and contained a single chamber some eight feet by three feet in which it was possible to sit upright. They were circular in shape, built on a stone plinth and roofed over with six or seven flat stones. Some had a proper doorway, and each had a line of smaller cairns forming what Rees described as a 'tail,' which were in no way linked and had no means of access. These served no obvious residential purpose and he concluded that they were a flexible defensive feature, allowing the guard protection from whichever direction a threat might come.

The guard attacked in the rear could quickly slip round or between the small cairns … On a small hill – west of Kasr el Hallabat, the large cairn and part of the tail have been replaced by a Roman dressed stone breastwork wall.[18]

The noted French scholar, René Dussard was fascinated by Rees' findings as published in *Antiquity* and himself wrote an essay *'Les relevés du Capitaine Rees dans le désert de Syrie'*, which was published in the French journal *Syrie*[19] in 1929, in which he pointed out that Rees' discoveries of Safaitic inscriptions were clearly of importance. Previously, nearly all the many thousands of texts that had been uncovered were located in Syria. Rees, an amateur, had shown that the inscriptions also occurred in large numbers in Transjordan and that the Safaitic area therefore extend considerably further south than had previously been believed. Up to this time, archaeologists of the Middle East had devoted most of their attention to the regions surrounding Transjordan where there were obvious sites of great interest; to the west lay the numerous biblical sites of Palestine, and to the east the remains of the ancient civilisations of Mesopotamia. Little in the way of study had been made of the Transjordanian desert itself as it was popularly believed that such an inhospitable region could hardly have supported much in the way of human settlement. The generally accepted view was that the only people who could have survived in such a region were nomadic tribesmen who would have left behind little of interest to archaeologists. It was the enthusiasm and work of non-professionals like Rees that led to a change in this view and caused the region to become one of major interest by the mid-twentieth century. Dr MacDonald points out that 'Since Rees's day, and thanks to his lead, several epigraphic expeditions have been made to the Jordanian sector of the *barra* (basalt) and many thousands more Safaitic inscriptions have been found.'[20]

Certain sites were already well known and receiving attention by the late 1920s, but it was not these that caught the eye of the amateurs. Petra, the great Roman city, was certainly magnificent, but on a scale which was far too grand for men like Rees to become involved with. Instead, they turned their attention to the small items that others had ignored or failed to notice before the advent of the aeroplane. When Crawford visited Amman he noted obvious sites in his records, but also mentioned, albeit only in passing, the lesser discoveries made by Rees.

A camp during one of the Field Expeditions showing the RAF tenders and armoured cars parked along with the hired Cadillac on the far right. [Field Museum]

… we proceeded to the ruined but well preserved Roman town of Umm el-Jimal; the doors of some of the houses were formed of a solid slab of stone that could still be moved on its pivot. All around were the stone walls of the town's deserted fields, From there we went to Umm Keiss, an extinct volcano … from the top of which was a splendid view over the Roman town of Bosrah, whose field-walls are perfectly preserved, row upon row …. All around were the remains of habitations of unknown ages … we could see Qasr Amr, a group of baths built in the desert by Ommayad sultans early in the eighth century AD.

Our next excursion was in the desert. It was an ideal camping trip, for all the chores were done for us by our escort and we had nothing to do but enjoy ourselves. The tracks were fairly good … the weather was perfect and the desert air marvelously clear and sparkling, especially at dawn. We visited the remains of a fishing village beside a dried up lake, and some flint-sites of a much earlier date where flint implements and flakes were abundant.[21]

Rees' activities appear to have been mainly concerned with establishing that the region had, at one time, supported a substantial, permanently-settled population. He was convinced that there was ample evidence to support this hypothesis and that the region had only become an empty wilderness as a result of a dramatic change in the climate during the period of recorded history.

In 1927, one of the RAF officers serving in the Middle East, Flight Lieutenant Percy Maitland[22] had published an article in the very first issue of Crawford's archaeological journal *Antiquity*. Entitled 'The Works of the Old Men in Arabia,' it was the first attempt to describe and explain some of the archaeological features which were to be found in the desert east of Amman. In particular, Maitland was interested in the numerous walls and enclosures which could be clearly seen from aircraft flying over the Basalt. Rees, also interested in the same area of study, made numerous flights over the areas in question which were clearly divided by the walls, and also visited them on foot. His findings were published in *Antiquity* in 1929 and caused a minor sensation in the world of Transjordanian archaeology. Unfortunately, today, Rees' theories are discounted by some experts in this field who now have a great many more facts, as well as technology, available to them. Noted archaeologist Dr Alison Betts, however, did not dismiss Rees' contribution out of hand.

As to Rees' contribution to scholarship, I should not dismiss his work as naïve or old hat. To do so would be would be to do him a grave disservice. He went to an area about which very little was known (as is still the case to a great extent) and where no one else wanted to go anyway. For a long time there has been a general feeling that nothing went on in the desert areas … Rees showed that these areas had much potential for study. He reported his findings conscientiously, he also made special efforts to bring his findings to the attention of people who could comment on them with more authority – notably OGS Crawford and Henry Field, and helped them to examine the area for themselves. It is true that the interpretations in his publication are based upon a layman's background, but the information itself is of great value. I have certainly made use of the photographs for much of my work and it is unlikely that these features would have come to light until much later if it was not for Rees and Maitland.[23]

Rees had found the study of the ancient history of Transjordan totally absorbing, particularly his attempts at translating the pictographic languages of the Safaitic period. Recognizing the problems which he faced in this field, he began a study of the more 'standardized' languages of the region such as Greek, Hebrew and Arabic and he became, with practice, something of an expert on the oral and written tradition of the area.

Originating as he did from Wales, it is not surprising that, when he was appointed to the military command of Palestine, he began to feel a great awareness of the religious and cultural background which was common to both societies. He cannot have been unaffected by the close proximity of historical sites such as those in Jerusalem and the Jordan Valley which were as much a part of his own Welsh heritage as the castles of north Wales. Many of the settlements in Caernarfonshire had been named after places in the Holy Land; within a few miles of Caernarfon were Bethesda, Carmel, Nazareth, Caesaria, Hermon and Bethel among others. It was almost inevitable that the two interests, archaeology and the Bible, should blend together and develop into a fascination with the history of the Israelites as laid down in the Old Testament, a field of study which was to become something of an overriding passion to him, and yet another subject which he was to remain involved with for the remainder of his life.

Unlike his study of the stone remains in Transjordan, where he published his theories very quickly, Rees kept his biblical research very much to himself, only occasionally giving a lecture to small groups of interested listeners. It would appear that it was not until he had retired from the RAF that he gave his theories their first general airing with lectures and articles on the exodus of the Israelites out of Egypt.[24] Although the bulk of his papers have long since vanished, it is possible to construct part of the picture which he had created in his mind from what little that has survived.

When he had faced the problem of the Druze tribesmen seeking sanctuary in the territory under his command, pleading that they were escaping from the tyranny of the French authorities in Syria, he found that the situation equated in some ways with that faced by the kings of Bashan and the Amorites as related in the Book of Numbers (20: 14–21 and 21: 31–33.

And Moses sent messengers from Ka-desh unto the king of Edom. Thus saith thy brother Israel, Thou knowest all the travail that hath befallen us. How our fathers went down to Egypt, and we have dwelt in Egypt a long time; and the Egyptians vexed us and our fathers: and when we cried unto the Lord, he heard our voice, and sent an angel, and hath brought us forth out of Egypt: and behold, we are in Kadesh, a city in the uttermost of thy border. Let us pass, I pray thee through thy country: we will not pass through the fields, or through the vineyards, neither will we drink of the water of the wells: we will go by the king's highway, we will not turn to the right hand nor to the left, until we have passed thy borders. And Edom said unto him, Thou shall not pass by me, lest I come out against thee with a sword.

Thus Israel dwelt in the land of the Amorites. And Moses sent to spy out Ja-a-zer, and they took the villages thereof, and drove out the Amorites that were there. And they turned and went by way of Ba-shan; and Og, the king of Ba-shan, went out against them, he and all his people, to the battle of Ed-re-i.

Rees saw himself as the 'ruler' of the desert region of Transjordan and felt that the request made to him by the Druze was similar to that made by the Israelites. Rather than face unnecessary conflict with them he, unlike the kings of the Old Testament, allowed them restricted passage through his land, indeed the kingdom of the Amorites covered much of Transjordan, and the king's highway of biblical times was still in use in the early twentieth century and was the major routeway between Syria in the north and the Gulf of Aqaba in the south. The fort at Azrak was situated on this ancient route, and it was not surprising that Rees was drawn to the biblical precedent for the situation in which he found himself. 'I was faced with the problem that defeated Og, King of Bashan, and Sihon, King of the Amorites, and in order to find out where they failed, I read up about the Exodus.'[25]

This historical background reading of a modern problem stirred his methodical and military mind. The more he studied the story as related in the Old Testament, the less satisfied he became with the traditional interpretation. There is no evidence which would suggest that he had ever been an avid reader of theology, or that he was a great believer in the spiritual aspects of the Christian faith. Instead, being by nature a practical man, he found the miraculous events of the Exodus somewhat far-fetched and began to seek for more logical, scientific explanations. However, at no time did his theories contravene the essential facts or beliefs as laid down in the Bible; far from it, they attempted to explain the previously inexplicable and, it might be argued that in doing so, they strengthened the basic story.

Historically, most scholars have accepted that the Israelites left Egypt sometime between 1300 BC and 1200 BC. Moses is supposed to have kept a careful record of their journey, but this was very soon lost so that the details of the events which befell them only survived as part of an oral tradition which was not written down, in the form of the early books of the Old Testament, until some six hundred years later. Rees believed that this had led to a vagueness and lack of accuracy in the recording of the locations of certain events and, whilst the point of departure, Egypt, and the point of arrival, Caanan, are undisputed, the other places mentioned in the history are almost all open to question. He felt that one location above all was of the utmost importance if the route of the Exodus was to be understood with any degree of accuracy. 'As regards the route, the incidents on the march are clear only if Mount Sinai is put in the proper place; and … I intend to disagree with everybody as to its exact position.'[26] He argued that, at the time of the Exodus, and for many years afterwards, the location of Mount Sinai was of little significance to the Israelites. Although, as the place where God gave the ten commandments to man, it was a place of utmost importance to Moses and a place of shame to others who had reverted to their pagan rituals whilst awaiting the return of their leader. Rees totally rejected the traditional location for the mountain at the southern end of the Sinai peninsula, and brought evidence to support his theory.

About the year 400 AD, there was a growing unrest in the Transjordan desert which culminated over 100 years later in the birth of Mahommed. This unrest caused certain holy men in Jerusalem to feel that life in that town was not worth living, so they decided to go away into the desert.

They apparently turned to Deuteronomy, XXXIII, 2, which said that the Eternal had appeared on Sinai in the south; quite forgetting that when Moses sang that song he was well over to the east of the Jordan.

Whatever was the reason, they travelled south and came in due course to the end of the Sinai peninsula. When they arrived, even if they had not known it before, they found that the place was called Sinai and that it was a very holy place. There were the Turquoise mines that had been presided over by the Egyptian Goddess Hat-Hor, the mother of Turquoise; and a very ancient site where the Semitic people had worshipped Sin, the Moon Goddess.

The name [Sinai] means very little as on modern maps one frequently finds the same name in the forms Sinan and Snainerat. It merely means jagged or toothlike.

That it was always a holy site seems to me to make it impossible for it to be the Sinai of the Exodus. If Moses had wanted to worship the Moon Goddess, Pharoah would never have let the Israelites depart because everybody knew that for at least 400 years the Egyptians had oppressed the Israelites and the Moon Goddess had done nothing about it.

Even at the Burning Bush, Moses did not know to whom he was speaking and had to ask his name, and the name was quite a new one. Nevertheless, the Holy Men settled down there and a Monastery was built in 500 AD. [27]

He then went on to argue that when the Israelites reached Mount Sinai, the Lord appeared to them as detailed in the Book of Exodus [XIX, 16 & 18]

And it came to pass on the third day in the morning, that there were thunders and lightnings, and a thick cloud upon the mount, and the voice of the trumpet exceedingly loud, so that all the people in the camp trembled.

And Mount Sinai was altogether on a smoke, because the Lord descended upon it in fire; and the smoke thereof ascended as the smoke of a furnace, and the whole mount quaked greatly.

He saw this as a clear description of a volcanic eruption and the only volcanic region to the east of Egypt, within a range that the Israelites might have reached, was located in Transjordan and it was there that he located Mount Sinai, in the mountain range east of Aqaba.

Having accepted in his own mind that he had correctly identified the position of Sinai, he then commenced to place the other events of the Exodus in what he believed to be their correct geographical location. The crossing of the Red Sea he placed in the marshy area around Lake Timsah, near the northern end of the Gulf of Suez. The word 'Red' he said was a mistranslation and should have been 'Reed.' Unfortunately, the water features of that region had been changed beyond all recognition by the construction of the Suez Canal during the nineteenth century and, consequently, he was unable to pin-point the exact location which he was seeking.

> They crossed the Reed Sea in April on a night when a very cold and strong east wind was meeting the water laden air of the Delta. Such conditions ay this time of the year make for an exceptionally heavy thunderstorm, and the storm actually did arrive … storms may be quite local but the rain sometimes comes down so heavy and with such a definite edge that one can well describe it as a wall of water.
>
> Although the prevailing wind is north-west, at the beginning and end of the winter the wind sometimes switches over to an easterly direction and blows with gale force.
>
> After such a storm, the whole country becomes waterlogged and quite impassable to wheeled transport and animals. So the story of the crossing is literally true. The walls of rain water, not sea water, held the chariots till the sea swept back. [28]

Having crossed the Reed Sea the Israelites marched for three days in the desert of Shur, in the midst of which they found bitter water.

> In this dune country, all water, if any, is bitter. The sun sucks up the moisture and the salt dries out. Besides turning the water sweet by throwing in a tree, Moses ordered the well to be drained three times. That is still the way to find sweet water. You get down under the top crust of salt, drain away the salt water, and eventually, if you are lucky, reach fresh water. [29]

Had the Israelites then travelled south by the traditionally accepted route, as was suggested, then there surely would have been some mention of the sea (the Red Sea) which lay parallel to their route. There was no such mention and, he argued, this was because they were heading east, across the Sinai peninsula. It had been believed that for them to have selected such a course would have been the height of foolishness as it would have grave consequences should they have encountered any of the settled races who populated the area. This he asserted was not the case as, following on from the apparently miraculous escape from Egypt, Moses had told the Israelites that they had nothing to fear as the Lord was protecting them [Exodus XVI, 23–7]. If one can accept his theory that the Children of Israel headed out of Egypt by this easterly route, then many other mysterious facts in the story, such as that described in Exodus XIV, 21–2, suddenly become explicable.

> And the Lord went before them by day in a pillar of cloud, to lead them the way; and by night in a pillar of fire, to give them light; to go by day and night.
>
> He took not away the pillar of cloud by day, nor the pillar of fire by night, from before the people.

Here we have the suggestion that there was a great deal of urgency in their journey, that they were moving day and night, as indeed they would be, not only to escape from the Egyptians, but also to get across the wilderness as quickly as possible. The whole of the eastern seaboard of the Red Sea, their traditionally accepted route, was under Egyptian control, including the accepted location of Mount Sinai. Had they followed this route there would have been no special need for speed before reaching the mountain (where they remained for a lengthy period of time) as they would have been in danger for the entire journey.

If Rees' assertion that Sinai was in fact an active volcano is accepted, then the above verses make perfect sense. By day, a distant volcanic eruption would appear clearly, over a very great distance, as a tall column of smoke and, in the darkness of the night, that same eruption would be visible as a glow of light. He argued that this was therefore solid evidence that the Israelites followed the easterly rather than the southerly route, and that they were heading towards modern-day Jordan. He also stated that if this route was followed carefully on a modern map of the region then, not only could most of the names mentioned in the Old Testament story be discovered (by going back to their original meanings), but that they would also be found in their correct sequence. He felt that students of the Exodus story had simply to rid their minds of the prejudice created by the centuries-old belief in the southerly route down the Red Sea. By way of example, he highlighted that Old Testament references to the Wilderness of Sin (located in the south-west of the Sinai peninsula) helped to pin-point the traditional location of Mount Sinai. Might the true location have been the Wilderness of Zin, which name comes from the same linguistic root, but is located in the south of modern-day Israel, directly on the route which he suggested?

When the Israelites reached this barren region, Moses would have known that there was a strong possibility that they would find water due to the recent heavy rainfall. Travelling ever eastwards, they kept the 'Eternal' before them until they reached Mount Sinai. Somewhere in this region, perhaps at Kadesh-Barnea, they halted having found a plentiful supply of water.

The organisation of the Exodus and the problems facing Moses were similar to those faced by any military commander at the head of an army. Despite having initially been allowed to leave Egypt with the Pharoah's agreement, the Israelites had clearly seen their former masters change their minds and one attempt to recapture them had already been thwarted. It would have been obvious to Moses that his first priority was to put as much distance between his people and any renewed Egyptian pursuit. To do this, he contended that they *had* to head east, far beyond the frontiers of Egypt. To have followed the coastline south, through areas under Egyptian control, to a mountain that was an Egyptian shrine, would simply have publicized their progress and invited the Pharoah to give chase. It would therefore have been logical for Moses to decide to lead his people directly eastwards, *away* from Egyptian territory, even if it did mean crossing the inhospitable wilderness which we today call the Sinai Desert. Moses was an educated man and would have realised that it would be impossible to expect such a large group of people to navigate any form of accurate route across an often featureless landscape. Indeed, so great were the numbers of Israelites believed to have been, it would have been unlikely that they could have travelled in one mass. Some scholars of the Exodus have estimated that they have numbered as many as two million people, although such a high figure would seem highly improbable. Rees believed that their numbers were very much smaller, although still large enough to make their movement a major problem. The existence of an active volcano beyond the horizon would have provided a constant, or eternal, point of reference which even the most simple minded or uneducated people could follow. Moses is recorded as having spent some time away from Egypt before the start of the Exodus and Rees contended that this must have been what we would now describe as a reconnaissance mission to plan a route through the desert.

Rees believed that his theory, although far from perfect, was more acceptable than that which had hitherto been accepted as true. He had, however, one further theory for which unfortunately none of his evidence is known to have survived, but that would appear to have been the key to the whole story. To the east of his Mount Sinai location, there existed marks in the desert which, when he saw them from the air, he thought to be unique. Just below the mountain, there was some form of evidence which suggested that a large number of people had stayed there for some considerable time. Using a system of dating rocks by their colour (which has since been shown to be particularly inaccurate due to the movement of rocks over a period of time) he concluded that the site was so old as to be invisible at ground level where the rocks blended into their natural surroundings. Even he had failed to find the exact site on foot.

I like to think that this was the position of the camp at Sinai. It allows an excellent site for the
Dwelling, which could be seen for miles, and would give all the necessary conditions for the
incidents that happened at Sinai. [30]

Unlike his other archaeological theories, this location of the route of the Exodus was
not without a good background of scholarly research. For many years Rees made a careful
study of the Old Testament, wherever possible going back to as near the original texts as
practicable. He did not make use of the English or any other modern translation, prefering
to study the Greek account and then compare place names that he came across with those
shown on both modern and ancient maps of the region, and their traditional Arab spelling
and pronunciation. Unfortunately, as has already been pointed out, few of his papers have
survived and it is therefore not possible to check his sources and the 'route' which he took
to his conclusions.

Today, a sizeable body of learned opinion would seem to agree with his location of
Mount Sinai and regards this theory as somewhat routine. It must be remembered,
however, that when he first began to work on these ideas they were revolutionary and it
is unfortunate that nowhere does there appear to be any acknowledgement of his
pioneering work in this field.

While Rees may have given the impression that his time in Amman was spent indulging
his own interests and carrying out excentric activities, his theoretical work on the use of
armoured cars and ground units, and the practical application of the same while successfully handling the operation to contain and remove the Druze tribesmen from Syria,
clearly showed that this was far from the case. While no significant conflict broke out in
Transjordan during his period in command, he was able to draw upon his experience as
a junior officer in the RFA before the Great War, and the technical knowledge which he
acquired in the RFC and RAF, to create a new, effective, albeit small, military force based
upon the combined use of aeroplanes and ground forces. Everything he did had a military
logic behind it and in 1929, he submitted a paper to the Air Ministry for consideration for
the Gordon-Shephard Memorial Prize[31] in which he clearly laid out those ideas and tactics
which he developed during his period in Amman. This essay is quoted in its entirety in
Appendix III and clearly illustrates Rees' tactical, mechanical and training skills, all
melded into one report. In his overall analysis, he linked together not only the actual
military operations involved in dealing with a situation of conflict, but also the importance
of aerial reconnaissance and photography, air supply and the command of small units as

an effective means of maintaining control. He also saw the armoured car units as an ideal method of training junior officers, who mostly held short-service commissions, so that they understood the importance of knowledge of the terrain and how to independently command men. Just as he had done when he was first seconded to the RFC, Rees had also taken the time and trouble to learn as much as he could about the equipment under his control and adapted it for the particular use that he intended to make of it in order that it could be fully utilised in isolated and demanding conditions.

One might even argue that the *modus operandi* which Rees developed during his time in Palestine and Transjordan was to have a far-reaching effect on similar operations during the 1930s and the Second World War, particularly during operations in North Africa. He advocated a simple combined-operations organisation, that utilised several arms in a specialist role, something which came into its own with the establishment of 'Special Forces' in 1940–1.

Notes

1. Lieutenant-Colonel George Adam Beazeley, DSO, RE (1870–1961), a member of the Survey of India from 1897–1925. He served in Mesopotamia during the Great War where he used aeroplanes to carry out field survey work on the Tigris front. He was attached to the RAF after the war and is credited as one of the fathers of aerial photography in surveying, reconnaissance and archaeology.
2. Woodhenge is located in Durrington, Wiltshire, two miles north-east of Stonehenge.
3. Later Air Vice Marshal John Gerald Franks, CB, CBE (1905–95).
4. Undated letter to the author, *circa* 1986.
5. Dr Henry Field (1902–86), an eminent American anthropologist and archaeologist, worked for the Field Museum of Natural History in Chicago (named after his uncle, Marshall Field, who donated $1,000,000 to establish it in 1893). He made three expeditions to Palestine and Transjordan during the 1920s.
6. *North Arabian Desert Archaeological Survey, 1925–50*, Henry Field, Peabody Museum, Cambridge, Massachusetts, 1960.
7. Ibid.
8. Osbert Guy Stanhope Crawford, CBE, DLitt (1886–1957) was a Scottish archaeologist and pioneer of the study of aerial archaeology. He had served as an observer in the RFC during the Great War and was later employed by the Ordnance Survey to plot the location of archaeological sites. He founded the magazine *Antiquity* in 1927.
9. *Said and Done: The Autobiography of an Archaeologist*, OGS Crawford, London, 1955.
10. *North Arabian Desert Archaeological Survey, 1925–50*, op cit.
11. *North Arabian Desert Archaeological Survey, 1925–50*, op cit.
12. 'Air Photographs of the Middle East', OGS Crawford, *Geographical Journal*, v73, 6, 1929.
13. Ibid.
14. Ibid.
15. Dr David Kennedy, now Winthrop Professor at the University of Western Australia, Associate Member of the School of Archaeology, Oxford University, and founder of the Aerial Photographic Archive for Archaeology in the Middle East at Sheffield University.
16. Dr Michael CA MacDonald of the Oriental Institute, University of Oxford.
17. Letter from Dr MacDonald to the author, 2 December 1987.
18. 'The Transjordan Desert', LWB Rees, *Antiquity*, v3, 12, 1929.
19. 'Les relevés du Capitaine Rees dans le d´sert de Syrie', René Dussard, *Syrie*, 10, 1929.

20. Dr Michael CA MacDonald, op cit.

21. 'Air Photographs of the Middle East', op cit.

22. Later Air Vice Marshal Percy Eric Maitland, CB, CBE, MVO, AFC (1895–1985). Commissioned into the Royal Navy, he transferred to the RNAS as an airship pilot in 1915 and was based at Llangefni, Capel, Kingsnorth and Longside. He transferred to the RAF, and in the 1920s was a pilot in the Middle East and in the RAF Far East Flight. He retired in 1950.

23. Letter to the author from Dr Alison Betts, 30 November 1987. Professor Betts' PhD thesis was on 'The Prehistory of the Basalt Desert, Transjordan.'

24. Extant notes for a lecture given by LWB Rees at East Molsey, 2 February 1933, Rees family archive.

25. Ibid.

26. Ibid.

27. Ibid.

28. Ibid.

29. Ibid.

30. Ibid.

31. The Gordon-Shephard Memorial Prize was established by Sir Horatio Shephard in memory of his son, Brigadier-General Gordon Strachey Shephard, DSO, MC (1885–1918), the highest ranking officer to be killed in the flying services during the Great War. The subject of the 1929 essay was: 'Discuss the part which armoured and/or armed but unarmoured vehicles should take in the air control of an undeveloped country; their tactical employment; the types of vehicle and equipment which should be developed for this duty; and the training of the unit.'

X

Retirement
(1929–31)

THOSE INDIVIDUALS WHO KNEW REES AND CAME INTO DAILY CONTACT WITH HIM knew that his duties in the RAF were unaffected by his new found passion for the past, describing him as an enthusiastic and untiringly energetic officer. They all seem to have fond memories of him as a senior officer, colleague and, in a few cases, friend. He does, however, appear to have gone out of his way to cultivate his image as something of an eccentric, although it was probably more akin to what might today be described as a rather 'zany' sense of humour. The Assistant British Resident in Transjordan, Alec Kirkbride,[1] had very warm memories of Rees and his cheery disposition.

He and I spent several months reconnoitering and making our motor-tracks through the desert in Jordan which lay to the east of the Hejaz Railway. We used to go out with a couple of Royal Air Force armoured cars and some tenders; when we got lost, which was not infrequent, Rees used to infuriate the station at Amman by sending out a message such as this, 'We are lost somewhere within fifty miles of the Wells of Bair. Send an aircraft to find us and tell us where we are.' The column then just sat and sent wireless reminders until an aircraft did find us.

He loved to try his hand at making our position in the desert by means of observations of the sun and stars with navigational instruments. He would make long and complicated calculations with the oddest of results. One night he fixed our position to his entire satisfaction by the stars, and the next day, as we did not move on for some reason or another, he decided to check the result by solar observation. When he had finished, he looked across and said, with his cheerful smile that never faded, 'It is most extraordinary, I could have sworn that we had not moved, but, according to my results, we dropped three hundred feet in altitude during the night and went twenty miles further east!'

During one of our waits for an aircraft to tell us where we were, he announced his intention of getting up before dawn the next day and seeing what lay beyond a range of hills some miles away. He wanted me to go, but I refused, saying that there were more ranges of hills beyond, looking exactly alike for miles and miles; much further, in fact, than either of us could walk.

The DH9A which Rees crashed at Ramleh in Palestine. Note the spare landing wheel attached to the starboard side of the fuselage. Due to the spare equipment these aeroplanes had to carry, it is remarkable they managed to operate so successfully over Transjordan.
[JM Bruce/Stuart Leslie Collection via HG Crowe]

He would not be deterred and was gone when I woke up. When breakfast was ready, I looked across towards the hills to see if he was visible. I could see him running towards us, in his halting gait, clad in a pair of shoes and a pair of stockings; his shirt was in one hand and his shorts in the other. His explanation when he arrived was to the effect that it was much cooler that way.[2]

Rees' skills as a pilot certainly appear to have deserted him while he was in the Middle East, and he acquired a reputation as a habitual 'crash-lander' of aircraft. He was fully aware of the problem himself and, as a consequence, refused to carry any passengers in any machine which he was piloting on the grounds that the risk to their lives was too great. Despite this problem, which was probably caused by his old war injury (and undoubtedly compounded by the poor landing strips in the region), he was regularly airborne and appeared to be under some sort of divine protection. On one occasion, whilst attempting to land at Ramleh in Palestine, he was involved in what was described at the time as a spectacular crash. Those who saw the machine come to a halt in the middle of the runway were convinced that Rees could not possibly have survived and, when the crash tender and ambulance reached the machine, they were amazed to find him sitting in the cockpit, with no visible evidence of any injury, studying his watch. His only comment before climbing out of the aircraft was to criticize his would-be rescuers for their delay in reaching him, 'You should have been here two minutes ago!'[3] On another occasion he was not quite so fortunate as he struck his face on the aircraft's instrument panel and broke his nose, earning himself the local nickname of 'Bootnose.'

Being the senior officer in the region, Rees was not obliged to pilot himself anywhere and a junior officer would often be detailed to play the part of aerial chauffeur. Several times whilst flying the Group Captain over the desert, these young officers were horrified to hear him announce that they were passing over some feature of possible archaeological interest and that he was going down to take a look. Ordering the pilot to 'Cut the engine,' and with the parting instruction, 'Send transport,' Rees, clutching a spade (which he apparently always carried with him on any journey), would leave the aircraft, making the descent by parachute. He always assumed that the young pilot knew his position and, fortunately for him – and the pilot – such faith appears to have been fully justified and, every time it happened, a vehicle turned up a few hours later.[4]

Rees' amiability and total lack of pretentiousness endeared him to everybody and a anecdote from this period tells of him having wandered off alone into the desert when, far from any possible assistance, he met with two armed Bedouin who demanded his money. Assuring them that he had nothing in his pockets other than a handkerchief, he managed to turn their aggression into interest and then to sympathy. Before they parted company, the two arabs gave him, in the best traditions of Islam, a shilling to help him on his way![5]

That he had made a marked impression not only on his fellow officers but also on the NCOs and other ranks at Amman cannot be denied and when, in 1926, the Royal Antediluvian Order of Buffaloes established a lodge in the city, it was named after him.[6] To those nearer his own position, he proved a constant source of amazement as Alec Kirkbride recalled.

If anyone doubted his fearlessness, they had only to see his automatic shotgun in action. It was a weapon of which the bolt action came to pieces in about one in every ten shots. Rees said that he had bought it to encourage the makers, but I felt that they wanted discouraging from launching such a dangerous weapon upon the world.

He was a non-smoker and a fanatical tee-totaller. He was delighted when I opened my valise one evening to be greeted by a cloud of fumes from the whisky which had emptied itself onto the blankets from my last bottle. He enquired anxiously every night until we got back to civilisation as to whether I could still smell the whisky and, when I answered in the affirmative, said, 'Good, it should teach you to stop drinking the horrid stuff.'[7]

Harry Luke, the Acting British High Commissioner for Transjordan in 1928–9, became a close friend and wrote to the *Times* shortly after Rees had died.

Your notice of Group Captain Rees fails – I think inevitably – to shed light on the character of a rare and strange personality. I say 'inevitably' because Rees was a 'solitary' and hence not easy to know. I was fortunate in having been able to penetrate beneath the reserve of this unusual man whose highly original characteristics failed to endear him to his immediate superior in Egypt at the time. … This was in 1928 and 1929, when he was OC, RAF in Amman ….

I got to know Rees fairly well, partly through a shared love of the Syrian desert although I never approached his uncanny knowledge of that fascinating region, which he came to know as the palm of his hand. I remember our examining together, on our return from an expedition to Akaba, some inscriptions and pictographs which we discovered on a rocky cliff in the plain of the Khizmeh. The inscriptions were in an early South Semitic script unknown to me but promptly identified by Rees as Safaitic.

Rees, a batchelor, possessed of private means, was a man whose unselfish and generous instincts were matched by the monastic austerity of his personal life. Few, I fancy, of his brother officers knew at the time of which I write (and possibly also at others) he declined to touch his pay, preferring to divert it into various charities of the RAF.[8]

Luke appears to have touched upon a number of interesting points in this letter, perhaps most importantly when he mentions the attitude of Rees' immediate superior, the Air Officer Commanding the Middle East. From 1926–9 this was Air Vice Marshal Tom Webb-Bowen.[9] It would appear that Rees' involvement in archaeology was the root cause of the friction between them and, when he made a request for an extended period of leave in order to further his research, Webb-Bowen refused to sanction it and the relationship between them rapidly deteriorated. This serious difficulty does not, however, appear to have affected Rees' standing within the RAF although it may very well have coloured the way in which he saw his own future. When his period of command in Amman came to an end in December 1928, he handed over the reins to Group Captain Pip Playfair (who had commanded a flight alongside him in 11 Squadron in 1915), and returned to Britain on a 'long leave'.

In April 1929, Rees was appointed Officer Commanding the Inland Area Depot at RAF Uxbridge and, already serving as Aide de Camp[10] to HM King George V, became a regular visitor to Buckingham Palace whenever there was an investiture or other event involving RAF personnel.

The following January he was given command of 21 (Training) Group Headquarters, at RAF West Drayton near Uxbridge, his last career appointment in the RAF.

Rees had led a very active and varied life since enrolling as a cadet at the RMA nearly thirty years before and it is doubtful whether the life of a chairborne officer would have suited his personality. Although throughout his career he had worked alongside and under several men who rose to the most senior command positions in the service, there is no evidence that he ever made use of them to further his own prospects. The thought of a future as a desk-bound administrator would not have appealed to him at all. His next promotion, if it came at all, would have been to the rank of air commodore and would have meant an end to the active commands in which he seems to have flourished. One of his former Cranwell cadets, AD Gillmore, found nothing unusual in the fact that Rees went no further in the career structure of the Royal Air Force.

I am not really surprised that he left the Service before reaching Air rank. He seemed to me to be essentially a practical man, and the sort of high level staff jobs he would have had to take on with further promotion were not really his 'cup-of-tea' at all. I think he would have found them very irksome.[11]

Another Old Cranwellian felt much the same,

He never appeared to be career minded nor did he make capital out of his undoubted achievements … and studying Biblical archaeology was entirely in keeping with his character. I am sure he found more satisfaction in that pursuit than he would in reaching Air rank. I suspect the one contributory factor in him not reaching Air rank was that he did not positively aspire to the role.[12]

Rees' father died on 3 December 1930, while living with Muriel in Bromley, Kent. Despite being a solicitor, he does not appear to have left a will although one can assume that he would have made some sort of financial arrangement with his two children. It may have been such an inheritance which made Rees financially independent and finally prompted him to make the break from the RAF. Certainly, the fact that neither he nor Muriel had married meant that there was nothing to prevent him pursuing a totally selfish life in the years ahead. There was little prospect of the RAF being involved in any major conflict in the foreseeable future and the government was continually imposing financial constrictions upon the service under the continuing 'Ten Year Plan.'[13] Remaining in uniform would merely serve to ruin the memories of many happy and fascinating years. On 31 July 1931, he retired giving his intended place of residence as 3 Upper Hale Lane,

Edgware, although it would have been obvious to all who knew him that a sedentary life in suburbia could not possibly last for very long.

Notes

1. Later Sir Alec Seath Kirkbride, KCMG, Kt, CVO, OBE, MC (1897–1978).
2. *A Crackle of Thorns*, Sir Alec Seath Kirkbride, London, 1956, 116. This description appears in the chapter appropriately headed 'Odd Fellows'.
3. Ibid.
4. Ibid.
5. Letter from Air Commodore Thomas Bain Prickman, CB, CBE (1902–92) to the author dated 25 March 1897. This incident is also quoted by Sir Alec Kilbride, op cit, 117.
6. Membership certificate held in the Rees family archive.
7. Sir Alec Seath Kirkbride, op cit, 117.
8. 'Gp Cap. L W B Rees, VC' *Times* [London, England] 4 October 1955: 11. The Times Digital Archive. Web. 9 Nov. 2016. Letter written by Sir Harry Charles Joseph Luke, KCMG, DLitt, LLD (1884–1969).
9. Later Air Vice-Marshal Sir Thomas Ince Web-Bowen, KCB, CMG (1879–1956).
10. Air Aides-de Camp are technically assistants to the King, usually officers of the rank of Group Captain or above. They are distinguished by the wearing of aiguillettes (a braided golden cord) on their dress uniform. Rees would have participated at official ceremonies involving both the monarch and RAF personnel e.g. he would have been present at Buckingham Palace for the presentation of decorations.
11. Letter from Air Vice Marshal Alan David ('Peter') Gillmore, CB, CBE (1905–96) to the author, dated 4 March 1987.
12. Letter from Air Vice Marshal Wilfred Leslie Freebody, CB, CBE, AFC (1906–91) to the author, dated 12 March 1987.
13. The 'Ten Year Rule' was adopted by the British government in 1919 when the armed forces were asked to base their future spending plans on the assumption that Britain would not be involved in another significant war for at least ten years. As each year passed without any such war, the rule was extended for another year, so that by 1929 it was based upon the anticipation that there would be no major conflict before 1939. In 1919–20, the defence budget had been £766 million; by 1932 it had fallen to £102 million. If Rees' retirement in 1931 had been for this reason, it was perhaps precipitate as the 'Ten Year Rule' was abandoned in 1932 and there followed a period of significant re-armament, particularly for the RAF.

XI

The *May*
(1932–33)

WHEN LIONEL REES ACQUIRED MORE THAN A CASUAL INTEREST IN SAILING is unrecorded but, having spent his formative years in Caernarfon, there was undoubtedly an element of salt water in his blood from birth. Both his father and grandfather had been members of the Royal Welsh Yacht Club at Porth-yr-Aur in the town, although there is no evidence to suggest that either had ever owned a sailing vessel of any description. At the end of the nineteenth century Charles Rees had competed successfully in the annual regatta, but as an oarsman rather than a sailor. As already noted, Lionel had been made an Honorary Life Member of the Carnarvon Yacht Club in 1919 in recognition of his war service, but his adventures when attempting to navigate his way around the desert would indicate that he had never taken up marine navigation to any great level of proficiency. Following his retirement from the RAF, Rees went on an extended holiday to Scotland where he had spent so many happy days in the company of his mother's sister and her family. During this visit, he seems to have reassessed his circumstances and decided to purchase a sailing boat to fill the gap that existed in his life from not being gainfully employed. After carefully examining a number of boats, he decided upon a Loch Fyne class of ketch, named the *May*, a vessel which was to have a profound effect upon his life, literally taking him away to previously uncharted waters.

The *May* had been built in 1902 by Alexander Robertson & Sons at Sandbank in Argyll.[1] With an overall length of 34′ 6″, a 9′ 3″ beam, a fully laden weight of just over 12 tons, two masts and a two-cylinder Kelvin paraffin engine, she was a sizeable vessel for a novice to learn to handle and, despite her age, must have instilled a great deal of pride in her new owner.

Rees spent the summer of 1932 'playing about the Clyde' learning the basics of handling his new boat, before embarking on his first long-distance trip when he sailed south, through the Irish Sea to his home town of Caernarfon, where he moored alongside the Promenade and raised the ensign of the Royal Welsh Yacht Club. His stay in the town was short as his family ties had long since been severed and his natural wanderlust soon

The ketch May *in which Rees sailed to the Bahamas in 1933. [Rees Family Archive] The plaque was placed on the tower at Porth-yr-Aur, Caernarfon to commemorate this voyage. [Author]*

led him to prepare for a second voyage, south through the Celtic Sea, around Pembroke-shire into the Atlantic and then round the Cornish peninsula into the English Channel. He intended finding a convenient mooring on the south coast of England which would give him the opportunity to settle his affairs and during the winter present some lectures on the archaeology of the Bible. When he actually departed from Caernarfon is unre-corded, but it was almost certainly during September 1932. With a small group of local friends to see him off, he slipped out into the Menai Strait and, in a letter to one of those friends, Major Lloyd-Jones, he later recalled the event: 'As I crossed the Bar on that lovely evening, I looked back for the last time. The setting sun was lighting up the castle and the old walls with Twthill and the distant hills all bathed in a roseate hue. I shall carry this picture with me to the day of my death.' This romantic picture was indeed to be his last view of Caernarfon for he was destined never to return.

Reaching the English Channel without any mishaps, he moored the *May* in the

Beaulieu River on the Solent while he returned to his flat in Edgware and completed his programme of lectures. Then, according to Rees himself, the arrival of a postcard changed the whole course of his life; written by an old friend from Transjordanian days, Sir Richard Tute,[2] who had been appointed Chief Justice of the Bahamas. The message on the card suggested that Rees should call to see him at some future date '… if he were ever in the area.'[3] Thoughts of those far away islands set his mind to thinking about the possibility of making a crossing of the Atlantic in the *May*. It was the British climate that finally convinced him.

> One winter, *May* and I, finding it a little cold in the Solent, had sought shelter up the Beaulieu River (a beautiful place, worthy of its name). Whilst the thermometer stood below freezing, conditions were good; but one day the sun came out. A loud crash against the ship's side made me leap on deck; and the next moment I was rigging an ice-breaker as protection against the ice which was floating down from the duck pond further up the river.
>
> I said to *May* – 'What do you know about that?' and as she only groaned when a particularly large piece of ice hit her, I suspected that she thought just as I did about it.[4]

The more he thought about it, the more the idea appealed to his natural sense of adventure. Certainly, deciding to embark on a trans-Atlantic voyage less than a year after buying a boat and taking up sailing, must have required considerable deliberation, but his lack of experience does not appear to have daunted him at all. He finally made up his mind and, as winter passed into spring and spring into summer, he made his preparations. What his sister Muriel thought of the idea of him sailing single-handed across the Atlantic is unrecorded, but it can safely be assumed that she was becoming rather immune to the shocks brought on by Lionel's unusual schemes.

Having no real ties, he gave up his house in Edgware and set about disposing of anything which he felt was unnecessary or too valuable to risk losing should some mishap occur during the proposed voyage. As a man of independent means with a boat that was paid for and which would provide him with both a home and transport, he took his previously recorded generosity (having donated much of his salary to the Royal Air Force Benevolent Fund) one large step further when he also signed over his service pension, having determined to live on his savings and whatever he had inherited from his late father. His decorations and medals he presented to his old school, Eastbourne College.[5] The Sword of Honour given to him by the Borough of Caernarfon, he presented to the RAF College, Cranwell.[6] Clearly both institutions had made an indelible mark upon him.

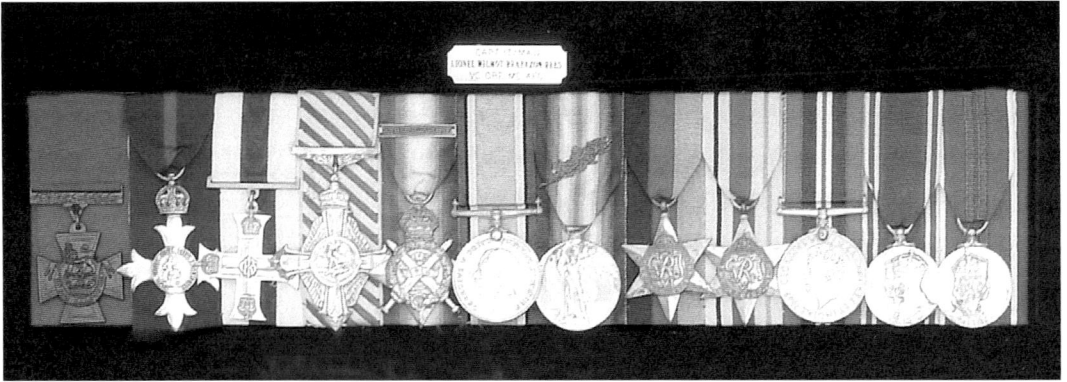

Rees presented his decorations and medals to Eastbourne College in 1933 and added his Second World War and Coronation Medals as he received them. L–R: Victoria Cross, Officer of the Order of the British Empire, Military Cross, Air Force Cross, 1914 Star (with Clasp), British War Medal (1914–18), Allied Victory Medal (with Oak Leaf), 1939–45 Star, Africa Star, British War Medal (1939–45), Coronation Medal 1937, Coronation Medal 1953. [Eastbourne College]

As the weather warmed and his boat was made ready for the voyage, Rees cast off from Beaulieu and set course westwards along the Channel coast to Falmouth in Devon and from there, on 2 July 1933, with sufficient supplies aboard to last for three months he set sail towards the south west. He kept a detailed diary of the voyage which not only tells the story of the voyage but also provides further insights into his personality.

A good north-easterly breeze took me well out of the Channel, past Ushant in two days. Having obtained a sufficient offing, I set square-sail and raffee; but no sooner was everything coiled down than a line squall, extending from horizon to horizon, came up from dead ahead. This was the first of many surprises, as hitherto I had always associated a line squall, with the change from bad weather to good weather, with a north-westerly wind.

There was nothing for it but to hand the square-sail and change over to fore-and-aft rig. Soon I was sailing close-hauled and reefed against an increasing south-westerly breeze. The sea had not risen very much, and progress was good, when suddenly the ship was lifted on to the top of a conical wave of the kind against which the Channel Pilot issues a special warning. Having no visible means of support, the little ship simply collapsed on to her beam ends in the succeeding trough. There was a loud crack as the starboard main shrouds chain plate gave way. It was a bad fitting anyway, and luckily there was no further damage, except that all the starboard rigging was strained – but not, apparently seriously. Most of the remainder of the day was spent in repairing the damage, and by the time the job was completed I was cold, wet and very miserable (a condition for which there should be some kind of yachting word).[7]

It was not an auspicious start to the voyage, but Rees was undaunted. Men with less confidence in their own abilities would have headed for the safety of a harbour where the boat could have been thoroughly checked, but he decided to continue.

> On account of the ship's rig and the scend of the sea … it was necessary to lay a course much further into the Bay [of Biscay] than was desirable. For nearly the whole of the next fortnight a series of small depressions passed at about a day's interval. In the mornings the course was no better than south (Mag[netic]), but in the afternoons it was possible to point towards the south west.
>
> Gradually, the general direction of the wind veered, so that the track on the chart shows a curve. During the whole of this period only one day was fine; and then there was so little wind progress was only 5 miles in the 24 hours. Even oilskins and sea-boots failed to keep out the weather, and the cabin was getting wetter and wetter. Usually, as a compensation, the wind moderated in the evenings, so that it was nearly always possible to enjoy a good, hot supper and a good night's rest.

Alone on the *May* (with which he conducted regular conversations), his only first-hand contact with the outside world were the small fishing fleets which plied their trade in the area. Occasionally, one of these boats would come alongside and a shouted conversation would ensure, but usually it was only a distant wave.

His first sight of land was Cape Ortegal in north-western Spain, but he was unable to get out of the wind and seek the shelter of its leeward side before nightfall and, the following morning, four exhausting hours were spent trying to beat to windward, but it was to no avail and he was forced to heave-to about thirty miles off the coast and await a change in the conditions which would enable him to get out of the Bay of Biscay and into the Atlantic Ocean.

At last, after several days' delay, the wind changed to an easterly breeze and, with the sun shining, the *May* escaped her prison and, with her square-sail set, began to head south down the Spanish coast. The good weather, however, did not last and by the afternoon he again had to heave-to as the wind gusted to gale force. The following morning he discovered that the leech (or edge) of his sail had been split in several places and he decided to steer a course for Corunna where he could carry out effective repairs and obtain a well earned rest.

In the morning the sound of a cock crowing awakened me to a glorious sunny morning. Through dreamy consciousness filtered the realization that usually seagulls do not crow, so I hurried on deck to find myself very close to a small Portuguese fishing streamer ... The morning was so fine I reconsidered my intention of putting in to Corunna and decided to make for the Azores. For the first time since leaving England it was possible to get out of oilskins and sea-boots and to open up and dry the cabin.

Soon the steamers' track was left far behind, and for the first time in my life I could sleep in the mornings as long as I liked. There was no more crowing, no bells, no striking clocks and nobody to interfere with me. On board I had food and water for about three months. I was free – entirely free.

This expression of delight at his isolation and the evident satisfaction at having survived the trials of crossing the infamous Bay of Biscay is totally in character. Rees was always at his happiest when facing, and overcoming, adversity by using his own resources. Major Lloyd-Jones wrote of him some twenty years later, 'He found it difficult to make friends and was always happiest on his own, flying high over the deserts of Arabia or sailing the sea.' Life aboard the *May* gave him the adventure and isolation which he had always sought. His survival depended upon his own wits and he owed nothing to any outsider. Social contact would be at his own discretion and when he felt the need to escape, he could simply weigh anchor, hoist the sail and be gone.

The Azores were ahead and a northerly wind carried the *May* towards the islands without incident. Conditions had improved so much that he was able to set a course, lash the wheel and relax or do the chores unhindered whilst the boat steered itself. About half-way between the mainland and the islands, as he approached the more tropical latitudes, the temperature began to rise and the miles slipped by more pleasantly. At 17.00 hours each day he would heave-to and then go below to listen to the events of the day on the BBC news broadcasts from Daventry on the radio receiver which he had aboard. Although he had no facility for transmitting, the radio was no mere luxury as he was able to use the Greenwich time signal to plot his position. Indeed, all his navigation instruments were somewhat unusual as he had to base his navigation upon the methods which he had been accustomed to in the air. An RAF bubble sextant was used to take a reading directly from the sun instead of the constantly moving horizon and, with an RAF slide-rule, the necessary calculations were speedily completed. Evidently he had become more adept at the art of navigation than he had been when wandering the deserts of Transjordan.

One need only look up the correction for height once when the voyage starts as it is quite easy to remember it. I used tablets only for amusement or for working out great circle courses, which were also amusement, as the wind would never allow me even to approximate to a great circle course. My wireless never failed to give me the Greenwich time signal but, as a matter of interest, I worked lunars for GMT, and found that I could get the time correct to within about 5 minutes.

I used the sextant the way we do when flying by night. That is to say, I bring the bubble in my level up to the sun or the star, but the *May* was jumping about too much for that, so I reversed the process and brought the level up to the sun.

As the boat ploughed her way south-eastwards, Rees recorded the beauty of the sights which he saw under different conditions. His fascination with and desire to understand everything that he experienced is evident in his record of the voyage.

My day commenced before sunrise, and one was always repaid for the early rising. One

The main cabin of the ketch May. *His radio can be seen on the right and barometer to the left of the door. The food storage system seen in the galley was purpose designed and built by Rees for the voyage and he wrote an article about it, entitled 'A Sea-going Galley, careful layout the secret of efficiency' in* Yachting World, *25 November 1932. [Rees Family Archive]*

morning was especially beautiful, about a third of the way across [from the Spanish coast to the Azores] when the whole seascape was covered with little detached rainstorms. There might have been about a dozen or more. As the sun rose, each separate rainstorm formed its own semi-circular rainbow, some having more than one.

After that swarms of di-atoms [microscopic algae] and for several days the sea was full of them. There were long ones and round ones, pearl necklaces and balls filled with diamonds, and all the rest of the little fellows.

A small fish appeared which for two days continued to rub his nose up and down the curve of the rudder with apparent enjoyment; and one evening two squid jumped aboard, leaving, much to my annoyance, great pools of ink on the deck. As the islands were approached, flying fish appeared, and turtles; even a whale showed itself for a short time one evening.

These days were nearly calm, and that made navigation very difficult. On one day the error was excessively great, and I found that it was due to a kind of double swell that was running. The swells were of two slightly different wave-lengths, which 'beat' at every fifteenth wave. The ship was therefore for several seconds above and then for several seconds below her normal level; and this was in addition to the level caused by the obvious waves which were passing. A few days later the same difficulty arose again.

His supplies of fresh 'greens' were, by this time, dwindling and, in order to compensate for this and maintain a balanced diet, Rees put some sprouting onions into a jar and used the green shoots which they produced in a salad.

His confidence in his navigation was rewarded as he approached the Azores. After thirty-one days at sea, he estimated that he should soon sight the island of Terceira, the most north-westerly of the group. In the late afternoon, the island appeared in exactly the right position and he sailed past it before heaving-to for the night within sight of Topo lighthouse on the island of São Jorge. The following morning he set a course westwards, between the islands, and using the engine arrived off the harbour at Horta two hours later, at sunset on 9 August. A pilot came out and guided the *May* to her berth, and by midnight, thirty-three days out of Falmouth, he was safely moored and went below to sleep for the remainder of the night.

His stay in the Azores was a prolonged one as, in addition to replenishing his supplies, a number of repairs had to be carried out to the boat. For nearly two weeks he worked on her each day, assisted by a gang of small boys, in return for a few cigarettes and some sweets. In the evenings he was feted by the British residents, an experience which he appears to have thoroughly enjoyed, and the news of his arrival on the island was even reported in the British press via the Reuter's correspondent.

At last, he felt that the *May* was ready for the next stage of the voyage and with the intention of following the route of Christopher Columbus who had sailed from the Azores in 1492, he prepared to set a course for the Bahamas. He awoke on the morning of 25 August to discover a gale blowing and was forced to remain in harbour to ride out the storm. Whilst there, *May* dragged her anchors and fouled the moorings of a large buoy and, as soon as the wind had abated, a diver came out who cleared the anchors in return for a bottle of beer. On Sunday, 27 August, with a light, favourable wind, the *May* sailed out of Horta harbour steering a course due west.

Almost as soon as he was out of the sight of land, the weather deteriorated and by afternoon cold rain was falling steadily, made worse by a contrary wind. By the following morning, however, the unpredictable weather had changed again and the ketch was speeding across the surface of the ocean.

> Things were going so well that I worked out a great circle distance to the Bahamas. This was a fatal step to take, as the wind immediately changed and I was virtually unable to make any westing for exactly one calendar month.
>
> Making the best of a bad job, I sailed southward as speedily as possible, so as to get into the Trade Winds. My problem was to get sufficiently far south to miss the equinoctial gales, and yet not to run into the hurricane belt before the hurricane season was over. The problem was complicated by the fact that the Trades are very uncertain during the hurricane season. In an endeavour to make the journey as short as possible I cut too closely to the edge of the Sargasso Sea, with the result that a lot of too calm weather was encountered.

Throughout September, the light south-westerly winds impeded his progress. Squalls were followed by periods of extreme calm but the falling rain reduced the threat of a shortage of fresh water and, in fact, there was sufficient for freshwater baths on board. In the area of the Sargasso Sea, large quantities of seaweed floated by, sometimes in sufficient quantity to enable small striped crabs to crawl about on the surface. At night, Rees kept a light burning (to avoid collision with any other vessel which might be in the area) and this fascinated the flying fish which appeared to aim for it and, consequently, landed on the deck where, in the morning, they were collected and cooked for breakfast. 'They are perfect little gentlemen. They taste excellent and they have no bones or nasty insides worth considering.' The marine life which he encountered, although not plentiful, he found fascinating to observe and he displayed an almost child-like interest in it.

On calm days the eddies under the stern would be full of 'goggle eyes', the food of the dolphin. They have a dreadful life. Every dolphin is full of as many of them as he is able to hold. Their little black eyeballs stick out as hemispheres; but even that, apparently, does not help them. The dolphin is a coarse fish to look at and eat, and appears at his best on a coat of arms.

For about a fortnight three shark pilot fish travelled a few inches in front of my bow. Every few moments they would shoot off to catch some food, and they increased in size visibly. One day they disappeared, but the next morning the largest of them came back leading a shark. The shark stayed a few hours, but as he got nothing to eat from me he soon got tired of staying around.

One or two types of seagulls were at times visible, but the most common bird was the bo'sun bird. He is most beautifully streamlined, like a marlin-spike, hence his name. He has a double tail; a small one of normal size, which he seldom spreads, and another consisting of a few long, tapered feathers. When he wants to hover, these feathers stick straight up, and give him stability, when by all the rules of flying he should be stalled and out of control.

The *May* did not reach the trade winds until she had passed through latitude 19 degrees North. In one month Rees had sailed 1,000 miles, but was only 500 miles west of the Azores. Toward the end of September, the winds increased and as he entered the hurricane belt, he logged distances of over one hundred miles each day. His wireless informed him that there were gales over England and that a hurricane was heading for Cuba, and it seemed that before long the weather in mid-Atlantic was about to follow suit. Concern about this made him set a new course which would take him some two hundred miles further north and, for two weeks, he was compelled to steer the boat manually as the wind direction made it impossible for him to lash the wheel to enable the *May* to steer herself. By the end of October, he was being carried along by the Caribbean Current and, hearing a hurricane warning on the radio, decided to abandon his plan to make landfall, like Columbus, at San Salvador and, as he approached the Bahamas, he headed straight for the capital, Nassau, on the island of New Providence.

His course meant that he would approach Nassau from the north-east, and he found himself too close to the shore of some of the more remote islands as light began to fall. Still worrying about the hurricane, he decided to spend the hours of darkness well out to sea, and it was not until noon the following day that he sighted the Hole in the Wall lighthouse. With a recorded speed of eight knots (the fastest of the whole voyage), he crossed the last stretch of open water and sighted the lights of Nassau at 22.00 hours. One hour later he was approaching the harbour and, despite some confusion over the harbour and buoy lights, he safely crossed the bar and entered the calm water beyond. At 02.00 hours on 21 October, sixty-five days out of Horta, he dropped anchor near the harbour offices in Nassau, no doubt a very relieved and contented man.

His arrival in Nassau caused considerable interest in the town and news of his voyage was flashed to news agency offices throughout the world and newspapers as far apart as London and Brisbane carried short articles giving brief details of his voyage. Today, when solo trans-Atlantic crossings are becoming commonplace, it is difficult to appreciate what Rees had achieved. He had just failed to become the first Briton to make the solo voyage in an east–west direction (against the prevailing winds and currents). On 17 June, the same year, Commander Robert D Graham, RN, had arrived in St John's, Newfoundland, in the cutter *Emanuel* after a twenty-four day crossing from Bantry in Ireland.[7] Rees' voyage, although in an area of the ocean that was generally considered to be calmer, had covered more than twice the distance travelled by Graham, and he had been alone at sea for a total of ninety-six days. In the pre radar, satellite-navigation and self-steering days of the 1930s, the crossing was a major achievement for any seaman, let alone an amateur with only just over one year's experience of handling a sailing boat. There is little doubt that Rees regarded this calculated adventure as his greatest achievement, something which far exceeded anything he had previously done.

A news reporter was one of the first to board the *May* after she and her master had been given a clean bill of health and had tied up at the eastern end of Prince George's Wharf.

As far as we could see everything was spick and span in the roomy cabin. For a man who likes his own company, Captain Rees [as he was to be known during his time in the Bahamas] has a comfortable craft … when you go on deck and see everything so small you wonder how any man had the vitality to face such a venture as a lone crossing of the Atlantic, but when you study the gadgets that are fitted up and hear the Captain's explanations you begin to realise how these things are done – if you like doing them.[9]

Chief Justice Tute, the apparent inspiration for the voyage, was aboard the *May* for two hours before leaving with Rees for lunch at his home, Breezy Ridge. As he left, Rees was asked about the crossing and why he had done it. He replied, 'Mr Tute asked me to come to tea, so I've come.'[10]

By the end of the month, *May* was in Symonette's Shipyard in Nassau undergoing an overhaul. The blistering Atlantic sun had taken its toll on the paintwork, but otherwise

Rees aboard the May *off New Providence Island, c1934. [Rees Family Archive]*

she was in remarkably good condition. On Wednesday, 8 November, she was back in the water and moored in the harbour, east of Fowler Street. Rees, however, was not yet satisfied and felt that having come so far it would be foolish not to complete the crossing of the Atlantic by sailing to mainland America, something which Columbus had failed to do. He spent the next few days making his preparations for this final stage, taking a break on Armistice Day when he was the guest of honour at the capital's Service of Remembrance.

At 07.00 hours on 21 November, Rees slipped quietly out of Nassau harbour bound for Miami in Florida. For two days the conditions were perfect as he steered *May* through the Berry Islands westwards across the famed Tongue of the Ocean which was over 2,000 metres deep. On the third day the weather deteriorated and he had to spend a worrying night amongst the shipping in the middle of Providence Channel, landing a little before dawn at Great Isaac lighthouse where he spent a pleasant day with the keepers. Preparing to set sail in the evening, he encountered some difficulty with his anchor which had become jammed under some coral and the moon was well up before he was en route for the Bimini Islands. As dawn broke, he was horrified to discover that he was in the middle of what appeared to be uncharted mudbanks and was compelled to retrace his course in an effort to get around them. It was some time before he realised that he was mistaken and that the mudbanks were in fact areas of deep water on the edge of the bank. Sailing along this edge he passed the entrance to Bimini Harbour and dropped anchor at Gun Cay, a few miles further south, where he spent the night.

The following morning he entered the Gulf Stream and, during the afternoon sighted the skyscrapers of Miami on the port bow. Using his engine, he entered the harbour at sunset but, as he moved towards the dock to enquire as to where he should berth, the

May ran aground. After sailing over 3,000 miles across one of the world's great oceans, his voyage ended a few yards short of his final destination because of an elementary error.

Once again, the local population expressed its admiration of his achievement and there was a seemingly endless stream of visitors to the *May*.

> I met several very charming people who showed me all the sights of the district. As far as possible I welcomed all visitors, and kept on board for them drinks and candies. One visitor … really did enjoy his visit as he stayed for 24 hours, going ashore only to sleep and bring off a friend. Towards the end of my few days stay, being so busy visiting and being visited, there was no time to buy even a fresh supply of sea stores! I left Miami at midnight without being able to bid *adieu* to those who had been so good to me.[11]

Rees does not explain his apparently hasty departure from Miami, but it was almost certainly brought about by his rather introverted personality; whilst it was delightful to be a celebrity, there was a limit to the amount of attention which he could tolerate.[12] By quietly slipping away in the middle of the night, he could return to the isolation which he had always welcomed and which, since the start of his voyage, he had become accustomed to. He enjoyed his own company and, if he wished for conversation, then *May* was a more than adequate companion as every movement and creak spoke

Blue Water Medal, 1934
[RWYC, Caernarfon]

volumes to him. His life had changed – gone was the discipline and order of military life, where everything was done by rote and to a well-established pattern. From the day he had sailed from Falmouth, he had become master of his own destiny. From now on he would do what he liked, when he liked. He could follow his many interests to his heart's content without a care or responsibility in the world. As he sailed back to the Bahamas, he had made up his mind about where he was going to start this new life which was to be as different from the old one as it was possible to be.

Notes

1. Alexander Robertson, the son of a crofter from Skye, completed an apprenticeship as a boatbuilder on the Clyde and set up his own business in 1876. He acquired an enviable reputation as the builder of high-quality sailing and motor boats.

2. Later Sir Richard Clifford Tute, KCMG (1874–1950), he had been a barrister in the Colonial Legal Service (previously Indian Service) and served as President of the Land Court in Jerusalem before being appointed Chief Justice of the Bahamas in 1932 (serving until 1939).

3. 'Sails Atlantic Alone', article in *Magazine of the Bahamas*, 1933.

4. 'A Cruising in the *May*', LWB Rees, *Nassau Magazine*, nd, *c*1937.

5. Eastbourne College retained the VC and medals until 2013 when they were sold for an undisclosed sum. The school's justification for this decision was –

   'During the year Council agreed to sell the medal collection of Group Captain Lionel Rees VC to the trustees of the Ashcroft VC colection. Group Captain Rees gave his medals to the Charity in 1931 on retiring from the RAF with the hope that they could be displayed. Given the value of the collection, it has not been possible to display it securely at the College for many years and there is no prospect of this situation changing. The medal collection will now go on permanent display in the Ashcroft Gallery at the Imperial War Museum (IWM), London. The Rees VC will join over 230 VCs beloging to Lord Ashcroft and IWM in what is today the national collection of medals for extraordinary gallantry.

   The Trustees decided to sell the medal collection after a careful review of Rees's intentions with respect to his medals, the needs of the Charity, and the duties of trustees under the law. They have acted after very full deliberation and after taking legal advice from specialist charity lawyers and an expert valuer.

   The outcome will be that Rees's name and deeds will be remembered by future generations of College students, as well as the general public, and the educational objects of ECI [Eastbourne College Incorporated] will be furthered. The Trustees firmly believe they are honouring his wishes by taking this action. The proceeds of the sale form part of the Charity's unrestricted funds. It is intended that there will be two Rees bursaries in perpetuity and that an appropriate space in the next building development at the College will commemorate Rees's gallantry.' [Eastbourne College Annual Report, 2013].

6. Rees' Sword of Honour was eventually transferred to the Royal Air Force Museum where it is held today.

7. 'To the Bahamas Single-Handed. Notes on a 6,000-Mile Cruise in a 12-Tonner,' LWB Rees, *The Yachting Monthly*, summer, 1934. The various quotes which appear in this chapter relating to this voyage are extracted from two long articles written by Lionel Rees which were based upon his own contemporaneous notes and diaries.

8. Commander Robert Douglas Graham, RN (1887–1957), of Bridgwater, Somerset, was the first owner of *Emanuel*, a 30-foot gaff cutter yacht built by Andrew Anderson and Son of Penarth, Glamorgan. He sailed her from Falmouth to Newfoundland and then south to Bermuda, returning to Britain via the Azores. Graham wrote an account of his voyage, entitled *Rough Passage*, which was published in 1936. *Emanuel* has recently been restored. Coincidentally, Commander Graham spent much of his Royal Navy service aboard HMS *Carnarvon*. He was awarded the Blue Water Medal (see footnote 12 below) in 1938 when he received the honour for sailing with his daughter from Ireland–Madeira–Bermuda–West Indies aboard the yawl *Caplin*.

9. *Nassau Guardian*, 21 October 1933.

10. Ibid.

11. 'To the Bahamas Single-Handed. Notes on a 6,000-Mile Cruise in a 12-Tonner,' op cit.

12. In 1934, Rees was awarded the Blue Water Medal by the Cruising Club of America for the most 'meritorious example of seamanship' of the previous year. This was later presented to the Royal Welsh Yacht Club and is today displayed in their clubhouse in Porth-yr-Aur, Caernarfon. Other noted recipients were Sir Francis Chichester (1960 & 1967) and Sir Alec Rose (1968). Also on display is the barograph which Rees had aboard the May.

XII

CRUISING
(1933–35)

REES SPENT THE WINTER OF 1933–4 CRUISING AMONG THE MYRIAD OF ISLANDS which make up the Bahamas group.[1] With Nassau as his base, he sailed on a number of short voyages, gaining experience in the waters of the area and visiting different settlements on neighbouring islands. His interest in everything around him had been evident in his detailed descriptions of even the most mundane of events during his crossing of the Atlantic and this again comes through in his writing from this period and, in a very short space of time, he managed to acquire an immense knowledge of the area.

Exploration [of the islands] is a little difficult, as the bush is so full of thorny creepers; and there are at least two kinds of poison wood that raises blisters whenever they touch the skin. Investigation is, however, well repaid as the whole colony is full of the remains of the pirates, buccaneers, early colonists and the old Lucayans. These latter come from Mexico way, and are especially distinguished by the fact that they bound the heads of the children between boards so as to distort the skull. They were still in the 'stone age' when they were killed off, or died off at the time of the pirates.

During the winter months the climate is as perfect as one could wish. There is very little rain, not too much wind and always a warm sun. The sea is very warm and even on the worst days one can stay in the water for as long as one feels inclined. Everywhere there are gorgeous colours that vary with each change of wind and tide.

I was most interested in the type of people. In height they are below the present English average, and their features are small but clear-cut. Their expression is one of determination amounting (I beg their pardons) to obstinacy. They are of the type I have always associated with my idea of the Pilgrim Fathers. May this little settlement long continue to thrive.

In letters to his sister and notes made for his own amusement and as a record of his activities, he passed comment on every aspect of Bahamian life. Something which he found to be of particular interest was the sponging industry.

Rees sailing the May, *c 1934. [Author]*

The sponging industry, in spite of the rubber substitute, is still important ... The sponges grow on rocks on the banks and a walk round the sponge market will soon make one familiar with the various names such as reef, grass or wool sponge. Many attempts have been made to cultivate the sponge, but although it is quite possible and is experimentally successful, it has never yet been done commercially. They are hooked up by teams of two men working in a dinghy; and a single sloop may serve as a mother ship to a dozen or more dinghies. Before being ready for sale the animals are squeezed, washed, dried, clipped to shape, and then baled.

The sloops are some 40 feet in length, and may carry a complement of two dozen or more. The mast, stepped very far forward, is rather longer than the hull and is stayed only up to a point several feet below the top, the upper portion being used only as a 'pretty' and to carry the ensign (sometimes two). The boom is about three quarters of the length of the mast and projects over the stern for some considerable distance.

The accommodation on the sponging vessels is very primitive. All the cooking is done on deck over a wood fire lighted in a wooden box. I do not know why the wooden box does not catch fire. This fire also acts as a navigation light to prevent collision.

The owners are very proud of their ships and some of them are well kept. The sloops that are usually in evidence, however, are generally in a dreadful state of repair. I have often seen a sail that consists more of hole than sail. The little inter-island sloops are awful; and are so loaded down with passengers and cargo that the dinghies tied on deck are floating when the ship heels over in a breeze. Surprisingly, these vessels seldom come to grief and I was informed that this fact was the cause of all the present trouble in Europe. Providence is so busy looking after Bahamas island sailors that he has no time for anything else.

So taken was he by the sponging industry that he decided to apply for the command of a new sloop then in the process of being built in Nassau. A short time later, however, he had changed his mind, explaining to Muriel that, although the sloop was just about ready to be launched, none of the improvements he had previously suggested to the boat builders had been carried out. He decided that the boat would probably be unsafe in Bahamian waters and that as 'an airman, the sailors do not listen to what I say.'

Part of his time in Nassau was spent at Symonette's Shipyard where he had taken upon himself the task of maintaining the yacht used by the Anglican bishop of the Bahamas on the rounds of his maritime diocese. The yacht had regular problems with both its engine and hull and for the former Rees recommended certain modifications to the manufacturers but, as in the case of the sponge sloop, his advice went unheeded.

By the summer of 1934, Rees felt that he had acquired sufficient experience of sailing in Caribbean waters which, when added to the high humidity of a Bahamian summer, made him think of further adventures on the high seas. This time he decided to set course for the island of Trinidad off the coast of South America, a distance, as the crow flies, of 1,350 miles. His record of this voyage, probably written with a view to publication in a sailing magazine, has survived.

Should anyone feel too old at forty (or any other age) and wish to put it to the test, I can recommend sailing a small ship, preferably single-handed, against the trade wind in the West Indies at the commencement of the hurricane season.

Last winter, the Bahamas had provided a most enjoyable experience, but in May nearly all my friends had gone home on leave, or had gone north for the summer. There was some delay about certain stores, and it was only in June that it was possible to leave the Banks.

July to October, inclusive, are considered to be the most dangerous hurricane months, although hurricanes have occurred in every month of the year. Usually in July the hurricanes seem to keep well east of the Caribbean Sea; but the trade winds in that and the succeeding months get stronger, and as somebody in Haiti said – 'Here in August, we seem to get a hurricane every afternoon.' I should hasten to add that no West Indian island admits to being in the hurricane belt lest the tourists should get frightened; and now-a-days the Islands suffer only from tropical depressions of a greater or lesser intensity.

Early in June I cleared for Trinidad, which is more or less south-east from Nassau in the Bahamas, with the trade wind getting stronger and more regular from that direction every day. The first evening out found my little ship in the sandy bay at the western end of New Providence Island. It is a beautiful place; and fish and crawfish are easy to catch.

Next day was hard work heading into a strong wind and in the evening, with no immediate prospect of shelter ahead, I ran to an anchorage behind a small cay to leeward. Bathing and fishing in the 'blue hole' in the middle of the cay whiles away a day or two. The 'blue holes'

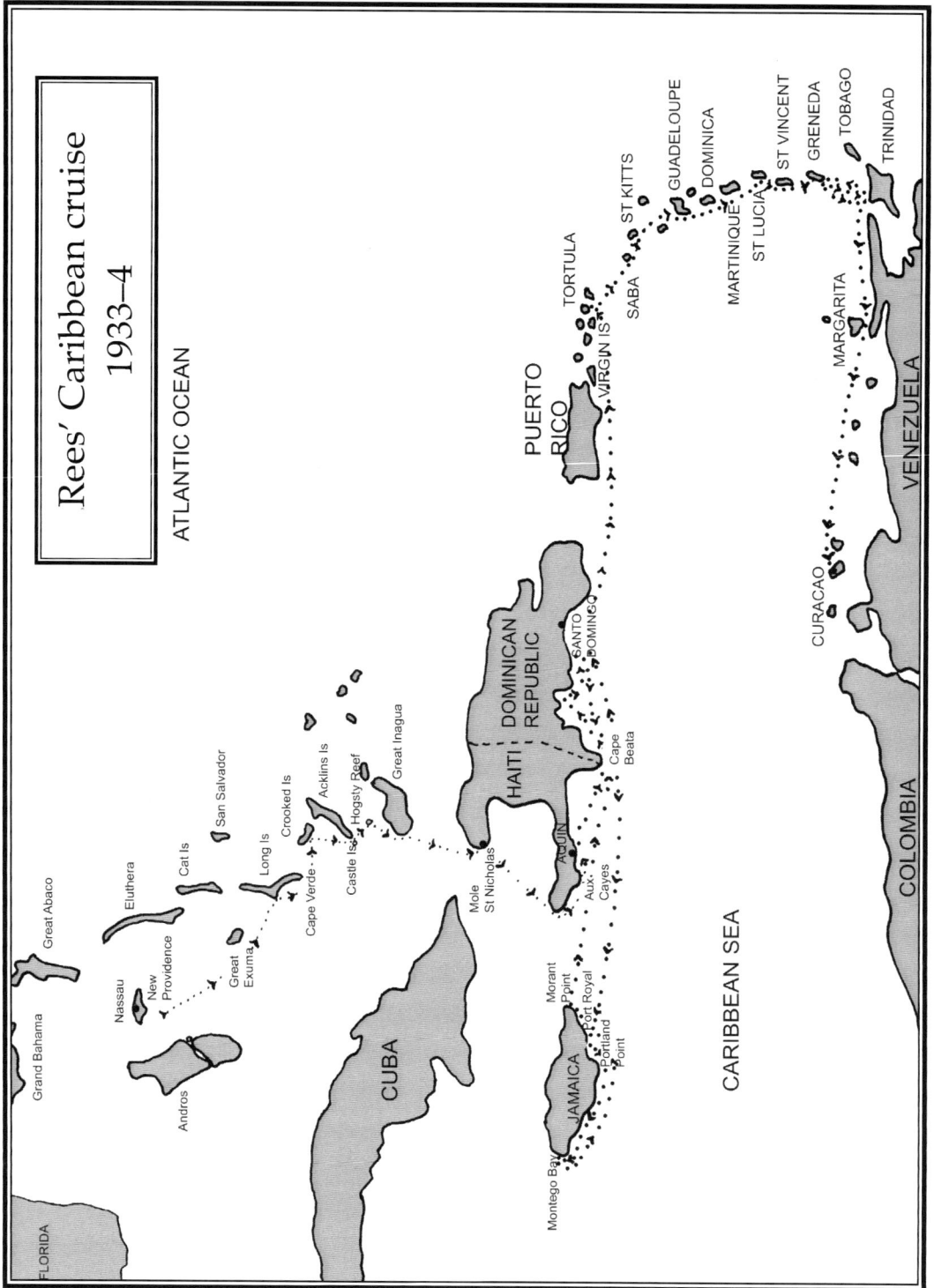

Rees' Caribbean cruise 1933–4

ATLANTIC OCEAN

FLORIDA

Grand Bahama

Great Abaco

Eluthera

Nassau
New
Providence

Andros

Cat Is

San Salvador

Great
Exuma

Long Is

Cape Verde

Crooked Is

Castle Is

Acklins Is

Hogsty Reef

Great Inagua

CUBA

Montego Bay

JAMAICA

Morant
Point

Port Royal

Portland
Point

Mole
St Nicholas

Aquin

Aux.
Cayes

HAITI

DOMINICAN
REPUBLIC

SANTO
DOMINGO

Cape
Beata

PUERTO
RICO

VIRGIN IS

TORTULA

SABA

ST KITTS

GUADELOUPE

DOMINICA

MARTINIQUE

ST LUCIA

ST VINCENT

GRENEDA

TOBAGO

TRINIDAD

MARGARITA

CURACAO

VENEZUELA

COLOMBIA

CARIBBEAN SEA

look like artificially constructed wells, but communicate with the ocean at a depth, it may be, of 50 fathoms or more.

As the wind showed no sign of either shifting or moderating, the next few anchorages were behind the reef on the western side of the Tongue of the Ocean which was the main route for the old galleons sailing between the Windward Islands and Florida. It was on that account that the pirates at one time (about 1719 AD) made New Providence their headquarters. Here Blackbeard (Teach) had a place, whilst the fort on the opposite corner of Andros is still named after Morgan. No galleon could pass out of the Tongue without being seen from one place or the other. Further south on Andros, the pirates had a big place on the mainland beyond Fleur-de-Lys Cay. From their lookout on the hill they could see right across the Tongue to Green Cay, so the southern end was also controlled by them.

What the pirates did to the old Lucayans, the original inhabitants of the islands, I do not know; but the commencement of the path leading to the fort [at Fleur-de-Lys Cay] was covered with Lucayan rock carvings. Near the patch is Money Rock, also covered with carvings. Two old (dusky) ladies guided me … to a Lucayan tomb … and as soon as we had dug up the first handful of bones they went into hysterics with fright. We had to quickly cover them up again till the old ladies had recovered. The tomb produced nothing but bones and a few bits of Lucayan pottery.

Money Rock was probably used for hauling down the old ships, as sailors had carved their names on it. A few years ago 'B BILL 1745' was to be seen, but nobody now knows where that inscription is.

The Tongue of the Ocean cuts through the middle of the bank, and ends in a vertical precipice. Here I met my first difficulties. Completely misjudging the strength of the tide, I was in deep blue water at nightfall. It was too dangerous to heave-to for the night with all the banks about, so I had to sail on for the channel over the bank. Soundings alter from 800 fathoms to 8 fathoms in a few yards, so striking the edge of the bank was quite exciting work. However, the job was successfully accomplished and as soon as the lead gave me three fathoms, I let go the kedge [a small anchor]. The wind was fairly strong and the seas steep, so the night was most unrestful.

Holding course along the edge of the bank, the succeeding day more than compensated for the uncomfortable night. The colours were wonderful. Here strips of yellow sand stretch across the white water of the bank and touch the purple edge of the ocean. One bank carrying a depth of only half a fathom, suddenly drops straight into 100 fathoms or so. That evening at Shark Spit, where I saw dozens of sharks, course was altered for Lark Channel [which] … is a blue lane between yellow sandbanks and navigation has to be done by eye. Beating into the wind and overestimating the strength of the current, I sailed unknowingly over the bar at the south

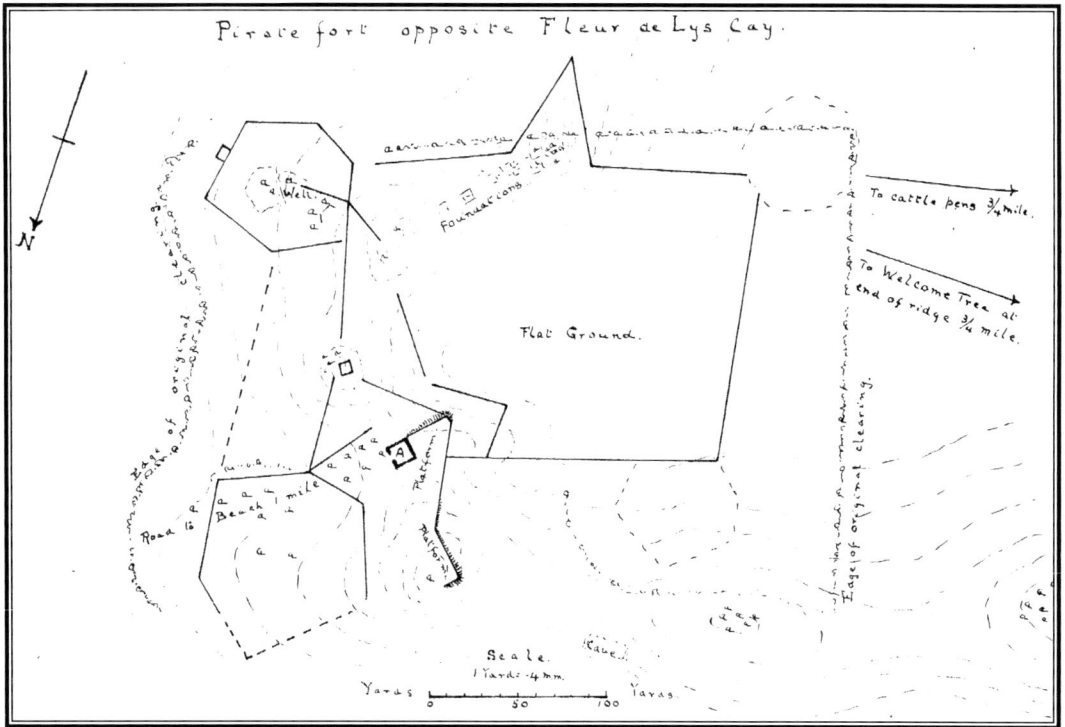

Wherever he travelled, Rees put to good use the surveying skills which he had developed as a Royal Artillery officer. This plan of the old pirate fort near Fleur-de-Lys Cay, Andros is one of only a handful that have survived in the family archive.

end of the channel at dusk. Groping about in the dark with the lead showed me what had happened. There was no going back again so, for a second time, it was necessary to kedge in the choppy sea in four fathoms and pretend to like it.

At dawn, not being sure of my position, a course had to be layed for Long Island by the method used by the Bahama spongers. They look at the sea, look at the sky and then spit in the water. What this disgusting action has to do with it I do not know, but on this morning it worked and I made my landfall with little error and without seeing a single coral head.

After some days of beating into the wind and sailing along the cays I was under the lee of the Cape Verde of Columbus. The colour impression of the land, consisting of sand and rocky cays, had been yellow, but this one was suddenly a vivid green. The wind took me around the point and then instantly deserted me. It died away so completely that there was a danger of being washed onto the reef, so the engine had to be requisitioned. In a few hours land had disappeared and, stopping the engine, I drifted slowly through a tropical noon. By mid-afternoon the current had taken me almost out of the Passage, so the engine was started again to take me into George Town on Fortune Island.

Here I arrived at dusk to find the recent hurricanes had destroyed all the landmarks – trees, huts and the wireless masts and leading marks. A Haitian gunboat, wrecked on the reef, was represented by a small black cone, which I mistook for the mooring buoy of the mailboat. Going in slowly by the lead in the dark, I felt the coral of the reef touch the keel, and then I backed out. By this time a policeman and the wireless operator were alongside and they guided me to a small sandy patch outside the reef. It was much too open for my liking and the ground much too foul, but I wanted a few stores and there was no choice.

One afternoon, the wireless operator offered to show me the sights. Almost as soon as we had started out, the wind shifted to the west, the sea on the reef began to rise and my little ship began to be thrown about. As quickly as possible I got on board, set sail and tried to get the anchor. Nothing doing – the cable was fast around the coral head. Being hove short made no difference, so I took in all the cable I could get and waited for a large wave. When it came along the chain lead on the bowsprit was shot off short as though by a catapult, and that on the stern severely bent.

After the next night in a delightful reef anchorage under the light of Castle Island, a gentle trade wind took me towards Hogsty Reef … which is of interest, being the nearest approach to an atoll to be found in the Atlantic. Evening found me becalmed, but the engine enabled me to spot the beacon on the reef at sunset. There being a bright, almost full, moon, I went in with the lead. It was a hopeless proceeding as the reef, about two miles long in its broadest diameter, was awash except for two small cays at the entrance, and it rises nearly vertically out of 1400 fathoms. However, I was able to pick up the loom of a sandy beach at the entrance and anchor safely.

The morrow was the hottest day I have ever experienced, being even hotter than Bond Street in July. There was no wind and no shade. Bathing from the larger of the little cays brought small relief as the water was tepid. In the evening a light trade wind arrived and under a bright full-moon I set sail for Great Inagua Island [which] … is largely salt ponds and swamps and almost at once I was able to smell it although it was at least 40 miles away. The island was well within sight at dawn and mid-day saw me moored in the open road off Matthew Town.

Here I experienced my first dealings with the Haitian authorities. Usually my Bill of Health was given me free, but the consul forced me to pay 5 dollars for it, and a further 3 dollars to have my passport visaed (total £1 12s 0d).

On the evening that I completed my arrangements, the wind began to veer into the roads, so under a bright moon I set sail for Haiti, which became visible at dawn, thousands of feet of it. Haiti means mountainous and the first view was most impressive. For several hours after dawn I was becalmed, but a good breeze took me into Mole St Nicholas during the afternoon.

I now became a heaven-sent opportunity. The local policeman came off to give me *practiqué*. I offered him a cigarette. He took the packet and, giving one to his boatman (who also came into my cabin), he pocketed the remainder.

Our conversation was in French, of which language I know little, and the situation was complicated by the policeman, who spoke only a patois, who enquired whither I was bound. I told him Trinidad. He repeated his question several times, asking if I meant Port au Prince or Jamaica. Having received the answer Trinidad each time, he settled the question by saying 'There is no such place!' and we went on to other business. After some time he went away to call the port authorities. They arrived and were the schoolmaster (who spoke English), the customs representative and a friend. The schoolmaster threatened to search the ship and then wrote out a requisition demanding some of my stores. They asked me more or less directly if I would like to be robbed officially or, as it were, between gentlemen. Being very tired and wishing to get rid of everybody, I chose the latter … having agreed to buy several pence worth of fruit etc for several pounds.

My visitors left but soon returned with the stores and my Bill of Health visaed. The first thing they did was to charge 6 dollars for the visa. They had looked such a lot of ruffians that I had put my pistol in my pocket and I nearly (literally) shot the lot of them out of the ship. Instead, I protested, pointed to my ensign [that of the Royal Welsh Yacht Club] and produced my Admiralty Warrant. They had never seen the ensign before and they certainly did not treat My Lords [of the Admiralty] with the respect that is their due. Then I had to meet the schoolmaster's requisition and as soon as they saw my stores the customs representative and the friend demanded an equal amount. When that was completed I paid for and took in the fruit. One thing amused me. I had agreed to pay 3 dollars for corn, expecting to get Indian Corn. What was delivered was a couple of dirty and damaged conch shells (cornes being the local French name). These I took without protest, owing to my unfortunate habit of keeping my word, and even the seller was surprised as he enquired for what purpose I required the dirty shell.

During the night the representative thought up some more reasons for getting money out of me and they were back again in the early dawn, ostensibly to give me a clearance (at a price) for other Haitian ports. I resisted several demands, including one for soap for their wives to wash themselves. The night's anchorage had already cost me seven or eight pounds but, as they were leaving, the representative demanded a present for their children and I handed over my loose cents, well pleased to be rid of them at any price. As soon as they were gone, I set sail, got out to sea, and then hove-to for breakfast and a rest.

For a long time I had wanted to go to Santo Domingo which was the centre of government [in the Dominican Republic] and is the best example of old Spanish fortifications on this side of the ocean. I therefore layed a course to take me along the western and southern coasts of Haiti.

Some delightful sailing weather saw me under the lee of Cape Dame Marie, the western corner of Haiti. I came in with the evening breeze and kedged under a small cliff in a sandy bay of a beauty that filled the eye to overflowing. On top of the little cliff was a small house, surrounded by its farm, nestling against a grove of palm trees, the whole showing up against a background of vivid tropical greenery. That evening, I was entertained by a display of flying by half a dozen pelicans, who dived after shoals of small fish, sometimes singly and sometimes in a formation that would not disgrace Hendon [the venue of the RAF's annual air display]. They never missed their objective.

From here to Santo Domingo is essentially a *Côte de Fer* [Coast of Iron]. The hurricane season was now well advanced and, although the weather was good, I got tired of reading in the Pilot – 'No safe anchorage during the hurricane months.' I tried to hurry, but the trade wind, affected by the high mountains, headed me off on each tack as I stood in or out from the shore. Being single-handed I dared not stand in at night. A gain of 20 miles a day was good going and the drop of wind at night entailed hours of excessive rolling in the long swell.

Although I had intended going straight through, I was enticed into the Baie Aux Cayes after a rough night off Gravios Point. With the best intentions the Pilot, who came to give me *practique* at Aux Cayes, directed me towards the inner anchorage. None of the pilots believe that I draw over 6 feet, as all the local boats are of comparatively shallow draft to take them over the coral heads. I could get in sufficiently far to shelter behind the protecting reef and spent several uncomfortable days in the rollers. There was a compensation that at night a gentle land breeze brought with it almost flat calm.

The Pilot had told me to make [sic] my number to the Customs house next morning at eight o'clock. I arrived on time to find most of the clerks chatting or reading the paper. One was sorting seeds, some of which he was putting in his tobacco pouch, which I thought a strange proceeding. The office clock, also, at that moment, although pointing to twenty minutes past four, struck eleven. I thought I had come to another Mole St Nicholas but, as soon as the Collector arrived things began to hum and I realised my mistake. The Collector was an American (USA) official. He was most efficient and helpful and, when he heard about my previous port of call, he promised to take the matter in hand at once.

Aux Cayes is a well laid out town of its kind … and very little inducement would have made me remain for a long time. Taking a few stores, I continued on my way. On the selected day, the sea breeze failed to arrive so, after drifting for some time, I used the engine to take me into the next sheltered anchorage. This was Aquin, an excellent place.

From Aquin there was a stretch of about 100 miles with no safe anchorage and the next few days found me continually being thrown about by the swell and making poor headway against a strong trade wind. As usual, the scenery was magnificent and, as the rains were on, there was usually a lightning display each evening, and marvelous cloud effects. One afternoon I spotted Cape Rojo, and that evening (it was becoming a habit) in the dark, I leaded [moved by checking the depth of the water by means of a lead weight] my way into the calm water under the lee of the cape. And I was very thankful to be there. Next day, during a make and mend, the sea breeze under the lee of the cape registered 26 (land) miles an hour by air speed indicator.

On the following morning I was under way good and early and the going was excellent. Suddenly, under the main-sail, a little Dominican motor gunboat appeared, full of sailors and bristling with guns. They shouted and waved, and I waved back. Then some of them took off their hats and I, endeavouring to be polite, also doffed mine till I remembered that I was clothed only in my hat. Then, much to my surprise, they uncovered the bow gun and trained it on me. As quickly as possible I hove to.

Two officers, heavily armed, came aboard and wanted to know where I came from. I replied 'OK,' thinking that this was the pronunciation of Aux Cayes, and it made them very angry. In return I protested against having a gun trained on me when I was wearing the blue ensign of my club, so we were quits. They wanted to see my papers, which I produced, and then they noticed that both my bunks were made up. I always sleep in the lee bunk, but the officers doubted that I was single-handed. Much to my amusement they began to search the ship for a hand (or perhaps a revolutionary agent), not a difficult task and they even peered into all the larger lockers. After all this palaver, we made our adieux as friends and then the interpreter begged for cigarettes. Was that the reason for my being held up?

My intention had been to find shelter under the lee of Alta Vela, the southernmost point of Santo Domingo [sic]. The wind was now quite strong and the gusts coming round the rock were stronger still. I had to reef right down and, in doing so, tore several hanks off the mainsail, split the headboard, damaged the side and jambed two slides in it at such a height that I could hoist only a double-reefed sail. Finding no decent lee at Alta Vela, I sailed to Beata Island and spent the afternoon repairing damage. During the delay, the current carried me several miles to leeward, back again under the lee of the island. It was too dark to go searching for an anchorage and, on account of the dangerous rocks, I could not heave to without keeping a watch, so I sailed out to safety into the open, through the Alta Vela Channel. About midnight, I had sufficient offing to allow me to lash the wheel so as to get supper and a rest. Although the wind had registered 28 miles per hour under the lee of the land and was now considerably stronger, there was no vice in it. The seas, however, were the largest I have ever seen, so large as almost to cease to affect the little ship.

At dawn I was miles out of the sight of land which only appeared again, when on the other tack, about midday. Suddenly I found the tiller lines chafed through and I had to reeve [thread a rope through] a new wire cable. Being on a directly lee shore the next few days were more uncomfortable than usual but, in due course, I made the landlocked harbour of Cadiera Bay [where] some odd jobs were completed and the ship cleaned up a bit.

Again, on the day of sailing, the sea breeze failed to come in so I drifted in light airs all day along the coast. At night, the land breeze and the engine speeded me well on towards Santo Domingo (the capital). It was an interesting sail as it was done by smell. Standing closely inshore I could not lay the course, and there was no unusual smell. Standing out, I would suddenly run into a belt, about a mile wide, where I could lay the course and where there was a strong and very agreeable scent of flowers. This was at the edge of the land breeze. Passing through the belt, I was in the trade wind where there was a very strong smell of the sea and where I was unable to hold the course I wanted.

At dawn, I was just entering Santo Domingo Bay, and at sunrise the wind dropped away completely and the swell subsided to an oily calm. Drifting whilst I got breakfast, I restarted the engine and proceeded slowly, as fast as my seven and a half horses would drag me, round the coast, reaching Santo Domingo in the mid afternoon.

As soon as I was inside the river, an English-speaking pilot parked me alongside the wharf at the customs shed and five hot and very heavily armed officers came off to give me practique. They were very polite and did their best to make it easy for me to comply with their regulations. They produced fountain pens, and ink spots still show on my settee covers. My shotgun and pistol, with all ammunition, had to be handed in to the Fort for safe custody. Two returns in quintuplicate were required, one showing the registered number of my arms and the other giving my name and destination. Much to my surprise, no charge was made for anything at this port. I found that I should have saluted the town fort on entry and that it was required that I should wear a Dominican ensign during my stay in their waters. Not being able to buy one I had to make it.

Santo Domingo is a very up-to-date and go-ahead town. All places of historical interest are well looked after. Everybody was very good to me and the place was well worth a visit. I wish I could have stayed there longer.

The main track was repaired. When I came to replace it I found that, as it was fitted in England in the winter, expansion would not allow me to get it back in place. It was not until after midnight, when the cool land breeze arrived, that it was possible to finish the job. How

Rees aboard the May in Nassau harbour, c 1934,
flying the ensign of the Royal Welsh Yacht Club.
[Rees Family Archive]

the expansion was, and still is, taken up I do not know, but it appears to be satisfactory.

The hurricane season was now still further advanced and, as the advice of the British Chargé d'Affaires agreed with my inclinations, I left Santo Domingo for the safe anchorage of Jamaica. The Trade Wind had won.

This first phase of Rees' Caribbean cruise is of interest for a number of reasons. Primarily, it shows what a practical man he was, sailing in a region where he had never previously been, yet adapting his still relatively new navigational skills to suit the changing weather and geographical conditions. Whenever difficulties with the *May* arose, he seemed able to turn his hand to the repair that was needed, often in difficult conditions. His personality and temperament were clearly shown in his encounters with the various officials en route. At no time does he appear to have lost his temper with the attempts of some to deprive him of as much money as they could, nor, when threatened by the gunboat, did he allow the crew to goad him into some action which he would later have regretted. It would seem that he admired almost everyone that he met for the manner in which they adapted to the circumstances imposed upon them. Rees, the former military man turned self-sufficient private sailor, was not a rebel, kicking against authority. Indeed, everywhere he went he did his level best to comply with the rules and requirements of the local officials. Had he lived until the 1960s, the era when people regularly 'dropped out' of society, it is doubtful whether he would have understood what was going on. His life choice during the 1930s was simply what suited his inquisitive but intensely private personality.

The trip to Jamaica, of no special interest, took rather over a week and, running mostly dead before the wind, I was rushing over the path along which it had been necessary to fight for every inch of headway only a few days previously. Being unable to obtain a chart of Jamaica, I had come to Port Royal by eye. As usual, here again I have found myself amongst friends. The Royal Jamaican Yacht Club kindly looked after my wants and my time was spent refitting and in day sailing.

There are many interesting places near[by]. One of the best is Portland Bight. Here, on Goat Island, are the ruins of a typical 'colonial' estate; it is said to have belonged to Sir Henry Morgan, the pirate and afterwards governor of Jamaica. Galleon Harbour to the north east is an ideal place, and the 'hurricane holes' cut into the mangroves for the old galleons, are still plainly visible. Just on the other side of the island is a small cay called Careening Island. It is kidney shaped, protected on the outside by a coral reef, but the inner angle is almost steep-to, and the old ships could have been tied up to the mangroves when they required to be hauled down for scraping. Old Sir Henry knew a thing or two about ships.

The tourist place, Montego Bay, was completely spoiled by the bad manners of the inhabitants (as is usual in all tourist resorts near here) and by a steamer who came in at night, dumped a lot of her fuel oil, and was away before dawn.

The most delightful anchorage of all was Ocho Rios, the Eight Rivers. The landmark is a waterfall, another waterfall drops into the sea at the mouth of the bay and there are streams all over the place. Being so well watered the place is very green and full of flowers. Not having a chart, I came in with the lead and the local blacks, not recognizing the blue ensign, thought I was a Norwegian spy. They were quite concerned about it. One drunk man followed me into a shop insisting that my ship was a yawl. I told him it was a ketch. After a great thought he suddenly said – 'I see what you mean. Your sails ketch the wind better.'

I had been stung in the ear by a jelly fish and at Port Antonio the matter seemed to be getting serious, the swelling would not go down and I was becoming quite deaf. A local black doctor looked inside the ear and said 'There is nothing wrong.' Even more surprisingly he said that he had done nothing and would accept no fee.

After a trip around the island, there were a lot of odd jobs to be done, and I left Kingston just before Christmas. A flat calm held me till I was from under the lee of the Blue Mountain, where they grow coffee. But, as soon as I poked my nose round the corner of the island, I got into a 'Norther.' The wind tore the cringle off the mainsail and I found that the ship, having dried in the sun, was leaking in several places. I had to put back into Port Morant for repairs.

The local blacks are a funny people. On the day I arrived [at Port Morant] some of the fruit company clerks shouted out that they were coming out to have tea with me. I did not want visitors just then, and did not pay much attention to what they said. In the evening five of them boarded me, went below and sat down. As politely as I could I pushed them back into their boat. Apparently they bore me no ill will as they all brought presents of fruit when they came to work the following morning and later on they sent me some recent daily papers which was good of them.

The last 'Norther' had brought a good current through the channel between Jamaica and Haiti and it took me three days to get across the 50 miles. Each morning I was back in the same place as on the day before. Even then, it was the engine that saved the situation. From now onward, I used the engine frequently to get me up against the wind, but this time as far as Tortola [in the British Virgin Islands]. I got into a strong counter current which held me along the coast. In a few days I was back in Santo Domingo capital. The conditions at Alta Vela were bad, as usual, but as soon as the wind saw I meant to get round the point it moderated, and I got excellent sailing conditions from now as far as Trinidad.

After Jamaica, my first real stop was in the Virgin Islands. At Tortola … I was being shown round one Sunday afternoon, and my guide said to a black man, who was leaning against his garden wall – 'You need to go to church regularly. I have not seen you in church for the last couple of Sundays. How is that?' The man replied, 'Oh, I was baptised a fortnight ago and am saved already. Therefore I need no longer go to church.' I liked all the people of Tortola. They are all pleasant proprietors and speak and act as such. They don't beg as the people in most of the other islands.

From Tortola I went to have a look at Saba, but it was too rough to land. At this island, which is simply a volcanic cone, there is no proper landing; it is necessary to jump out of the dinghy onto the steps cut in the side of the rock. A horse carries you up and down the steps. The people, who are Dutch, speak English and they live in a town on the top of a mountain called Botto. They are mostly sailors, build ships which they launch by lowering [them] over the side of the cliffs, and they have the only navigation school in the West Indies. Living on a bare rock, they grow vegetables for their own use, and also for export to the other islands. The place is well worth a visit.

I sailed on slowly and stayed in most of the large anchorages. At St Kitts I met RD Williams of Porth-yr-Aur [Caernarfon], who captains the fleet tanker *War Sirdar*. We talked a lot about olden times. At St Vincent I was surprised to find that the shore boats would not come nearer than shouting distance. The reason was given me by the officers of a schooner who called on me that evening. They were the Tough Captain and the Bucco Mate. Their conversation consisted entirely of the way in which they handled the crew. They had knocked them down the hold with a belaying pin and they had poured the hot soup over the cook whenever it or he had displeased them. That morning, the shore boats had annoyed the Mate who had taken pot shots at them with the largest revolver I have ever seen.

St Lucia is a very beautiful island. It had so many sandy coves, hidden anchorages with 'lone trees', etc, that I told myself tales of pirates for days after seeing the place. It was spoiled, as usual, by the people. Some of the shore boats came off and hurled foul abuse at me, quite unprovokedly. I have been called 'The father of a hat' by the *kafieh*-wearing arabs, and several other names in other parts of the world, but usually there has been some reason for it. Grenada was a good place and I stayed there several days. When I got to Trinidad, I disliked the longshoremen so much that I stayed only one day and decided to go back to Grenada to refit.

Leaving Trinidad, I got three days of calm and the current took me 150 miles to leeward. Not bad going if it had been in the right direction. Not wanting to make the large circuit of the islands so as to get back to windward, I turned round and came to Curaçao. I was well repaid by the decision. The conditions of my arrival would have delighted the heart of any boy of any age who likes tales of pirates. The visibility was none too good and suddenly I saw a line of steamers disappearing through an apparently blank wall. There were forts and guns about the refinery (the glare from which had been visible all night) was now apparently working overtime to produce a dense black smoke. When I reached the hole in the wall, I found a boom, the pontoon bridge across the entrance. As soon as I appeared the authorities had me in tow and I was tied up at the town wharf so quickly that I did not have time to even turn round and thank the pilot.

They have been good to me here, and I have done quite a respectable refit. For the last few days I have been tied up to the refinery wharf and crowds of children have been on board. They have broken and pulled off everything that could be broken and pulled off, so that I consider that I am now fit to ride out a gale; and the gale may be a hurricane as I leave tomorrow for the Bahamas.

Notes
1. All the extracts quoted in this chapter are taken from Rees' own contemporaneous notes which are held by his family.

XIII

WAR
(1936–42)

SHORTLY AFTER HIS RETURN FROM THE SOUTHERN CARIBBEAN, Rees decided to dispose of the *May*. She was a boat designed for the deep waters around the coast of Britain and had proved unsuited to the shallow banks around the Bahamas. Despite being fitted with a set of Bahamian sails which had greatly improved her handling, the depth of her keel caused her to run aground far too frequently with all the problems that entailed; so far he had been lucky, but this could prove to be a major difficulty should he run aground whilst alone on an isolated cay. The obvious solution was to purchase a boat designed for the waters around the islands, ideally a vessel built in the Bahamas.

In November 1936, Rees wrote to his sister that a young photographer, Stanley Toogood of Nassau, wanted to buy the *May*. He was an Englishman in his early twenties, who later recalled that he and Rees had '… a very congenial friendship … despite the differences in our ages.'[1] Coincidentally, Toogood, who had arrived in the Bahamas after Rees, had heard of the latter's plan to sail the Atlantic in 1933 and had written to offer his services as a crewman. The letter, however, arrived too late and Rees had already sailed.

Apart from the need to dispose of the *May*, Rees was also attracted to Toogood's offer of £500 in cash as well as another boat which he felt might meet his needs. After some negotiation, agreement was reached between the two; Toogood becoming the owner of the *May* and Rees taking possession of the *Aline B*.

The *Aline B* (or *Aline* as Rees was to call her) had been built at Johnson's Yard in Nassau in the early 1930s for a local man, Maurice Barbess, who intended to sail her across the Pacific. She had been named after Barbess' sister and, like the *May*, was a double-ended ketch, having the appearance of a prow both fore and aft. But there the similarities ended for the *Aline* was a much smaller vessel, finished to a much poorer standard than the *May*. Barbess had sailed her through the Panama Canal and westwards as far as the Galapagos Islands where he had been taken ill and forced to return to Nassau where he sold the boat to Stanley Toogood.

For the twelve months which followed his purchase of the *Aline*, Rees appears to have

The Aline B *as she was originally configured. Rees bought this boat because she was significantly smaller than the May and had been purpose-built for the waters around the Bahamas.*
[Stanley Toogood]

spent most of his time carrying out major modifications to his new floating home.

I decided to make a modernized copy of the *Goddess Isis* trading between Rome and the East.'Come down to the docks and have a look at the Goddess Isis. She has a mast seventy feet tall and they say that she carries enough grain to feed all Athens for over a year. Her captain is a little old man with a bald pate and a fringe of curly hair. He's an honest fellow and good company.' My ship is a little double-ender, and when we had re-decked it to represent the tarpaulin covering the grain, it looked like an egg; but when we had fitted port lights and verandahs to represent the rowers galleries, she looked more like a supercilious whale. She carries only a square sail and split rafee [small squaresail], so that she cannot go to windward. That is accomplished by a little engine to be used only in cases of emergency. The steering is done by rudder bar similar to an aeroplane.[2]

Rees at the helm of the Aline *after he had converted her into a new* Goddess Isis. *As well as having a very different profile, the boat was given a totally altered mast and sail configuration.*
[Rees Family Archive]

Only an eccentric individual like Rees could purchase a vessel because of her suitability for a particular purpose and her seaworthiness and then immediately modify her so dramatically. The reference to the Roman ship *Goddess Isis* and the rigging which he fitted on the *Aline*, indicate that a new interest had appeared in his life; not content with ordinary sailing, he embarked upon a life afloat which was to be difficult, to say the least, as he intended trying to match the achievements of the sailors from ancient and medieval times. His account of his Atlantic crossing had already shown his interest in the voyage of Christopher Columbus and it was now his intention to sail around the Bahamas in the wake of the Italian explorer, using a square rig similar to that which would have been found on the *Santa Maria* in 1492.

The *Aline* was ready by the summer of 1937 and Rees set sail for the island of Conception, where Columbus had landed and which lay directly south-east of Nassau. On the very first day out, he ran into difficulties as the wind drove him north-east to Harbour Island, Eluthera and from there, through Current Cut, to Hatchet Bay.

Last season, at this place [Hatchet Bay], I had gone half shares in a melon farm, and had watched the melons till they were nearly ready for market. Then I had to leave the Bay for a few days. On my return, my partner showed me a bare field and told me that the little red beetles had eaten all my melons. The little beetles only ate my melons. How did they know that those melons were mine?[3]

From there he sailed to Exuma Cays where one evening he '... dropped anchor in a little bay and was immediately hailed by a veritable cast-away. He was starving, and as I could not leave him on the cay, I had to sail all the way back to Nassau. So I was exactly where I had started after one month's travelling.'[4]

The next few months were spent trying every way to reach the south-eastern islands but to no avail. Rees found it impossible to make any headway against the wind and he refused to use the engine as it would invalidate his experiment. In the end, he had to admit defeat and re-rigged the boat with a fore-and-aft sail – 'The last few months have shown me quite clearly what the old navigators were up against, and I lift my sou'wester to them.'[5]

There now arose the matter of earning a living for the foreseeable future. Living on his capital was convenient enough but it was an ever diminishing asset and, in a letter to Muriel, he outlined his plans. 'I shall go seriously for growing sponges and build a shack on one of the cays in the creek where the sponge farms are situated. If you would care to come out I would build a two-roomed shack so that you could watch the sponges growing also.'[6] It was not to be. Not only had Muriel no intention of joining him in the Bahamas, but also the days of the sponging industry in the islands were themselves drawing to a close as a then unidentified disease was to all but wipe them out before the end of the decade.

There were to be no more long distance voyages for Rees. Living aboard the *Aline* he cruised amongst the islands, becoming something of a local celebrity, although few that met him ever really got to know the man behind the rather reserved, ever smiling, public face. Walton Smith, a fellow Briton, recalled a very shy man who avoided relationships with other people. He would often see Rees walking from Nassau, heavily laden with groceries but, despite the heat and the humidity of a Bahamian summer, he would always decline the offer of a lift in a passing car. To have accepted would have meant explanations and the barrier which he appeared to have built around himself would be slightly breached by each encounter. As with all eccentrics, the truth grows and takes on the form of a minor legend in which one finds difficulty distinguishing between the truth and the embellishments. Many of the Bahamian residents who knew of Rees at this time, did so following a lengthy account of him in the book *Out Island Doctor*, written by an American named Evans Cottman, who had initially met him in 1939. Unfortunately, much of Cottman's recollections would appear to have been either mistaken or invented.

Next morning Cavill[7] said he was going to take me to visit Captain Rees. The Captain, he explained, was a retired aide-de-camp of King George V and a holder of the Victoria Cross, won for gallantry as a pilot in World War One. Sometime in the late 1930s, Rees had bought a twenty-nine foot yacht and set out across the Atlantic alone. Originally he aimed for New York but at that latitude the prevailing winds were against him. When his motor conked out before he had gone 500 miles, he hoisted sail, turned south almost a thousand miles to catch the trade winds, rode out a hurricane, and eventually landed in the Bahamas.[8]

This opening paragraph is far from accurate, although it does show some remote link with the truth and would suggest that the information was obtained from some third party at a later date. It is highly unlikely that the information came from Rees himself, as it would appear that getting any facts from him about his earlier life was almost impossible. Many Bahamian residents knew him for many years before they became aware of his illustrious background. One such man, Lester Brown of Nassau, first met him during the 1930s and, as Rees was referred to as 'Captain', assumed he had a nautical background and had no knowledge of any RAF connection until some considerable time later. Eventually he discovered, but not from the man himself, that Rees was the holder of the VC and the story which he heard detailing how the award was earned was far from accurate.

He was a gentleman. Thoroughly well read and very interesting to talk to. He could discuss any topic and was a marvellous conversationalist. It is hard to imagine him as a man with such a distinguished war record as he gave the impression of being someone who would be unable to kill even a fly.[9]

Cottman's recollections of his actual meeting with Rees and the conditions aboard the *Aline* are littered with inaccuracies despite purporting to be a first-hand record of his lifestyle at that time.

We went in Cavill's sailboat, winding between a myriad of tiny uninhabited islands. Captain Rees was anchored off one of these called Mastic Cay [which] belonged to Mr Forsyth, and although there was no house on it, it had been planted with fruit trees and flowers until the island bloomed like a tropical garden. Rees' white yacht in the cove made the picture complete.

The Captain was a big, raw-boned Welshman; and if he deliberately lived a solitary life he made up for it when he had company. He was talking before we came alongside and he could get in more words per minute than a speed reader. He clipped the first syllable, or syllables, off most of them, and he spoke the others in such a Welsh accent that I could understand only half of what he said.[10] But obviously Cavill and I were welcome.

I never really appreciated the meaning of the word 'shipshape' until I stepped into Captain

Rees' boat. The cabin space was tiny, with every inch of it fitted to maximum use. There was a place for everything, and everything was exactly in its place. There was even a miniature machine shop with a lathe, on which Rees, still talking, turned out a new pipe stem to replace the one Cavill had broken.

The Captain invited us to stay for dinner and we happily accepted. The food was bully beef out of a can, but the service was something else again. The Captain brought out a complete set of sterling silver … and set to work polishing it. Meanwhile he talked, mixing in a wild collection of ancient British jokes with personal anecdotes about people he referred to only by their first name. It was a long time before I realised he was talking about various members of the British royal family.

Then, with bully beef ready and silver set, Captain Rees dressed for dinner. That is, he changed his torn shorts for an immaculate white pair. Perhaps in deference to his underdressed guests he did not add shirt or shoes.[11]

Rees had a personality and a kindness of approach which made him unforgettable, and people who met him only briefly during his early days in the Bahamas were well able to recall him fifty years later. The Reverend Hutcheson of Nassau remembered the time when, aged only twelve, he and his brother went aboard the *Aline* in Hatchet Bay, Eluthera, to try and discover what 'interesting thing the Captain was up to.'

The late Group Captain showed us how to pump air into the diving bell while he would be submerged in it, and told us that when we felt ourselves getting tired, we must call down to him and he would surface. He was not submerged too long before my brother and I, feeling ourselves getting tired, shouted 'Come up! Come up!' which he did, and he did not go back down.

He took an active interest in exploring, with a cousin of mine, a very large cave situated half way between the settlements of Hatchet Bay and Gregory Town on Eluthera, known as Crossing Hills Cave. After they had returned to the settlement my cousin said, 'I really had an experience today while exploring with Captain Rees. We went so far into the cave by using torch lights that we entered a room with so many pipes that it looked and sounded like a pipe organ when Captain Rees struck the pipes with the tools he carried. It was the most beautiful sound I ever heard.' As a smallboy I always held Crossing Hills Cave in awe because we were told by our elders that if we were to enter the cave we would get lost and never be found. Rees was a man I admired very much.[12]

It was at this time, when he was trying to establish some form of income for himself, that Rees took a job with the Erickson family of Great Inagua. The exact details are somewhat vague but were outlined by Margery, the wife of Jim Erickson, more than fifty years later. The Ericksons were an American family who had established a salt production company on the Bahamian island of Great Inagua in the 1930s. In late 1936, the company experienced some serious difficulties with the local store-keeper, shipping agent and justice of the peace, Arthur Lee Symonette, who saw his control of business on the island being threatened by the new entrepreneur. Historically, the Inaguan workers had been paid by the truck system (tokens paid by their employer which were only redeemable at recognised outlets) which meant that local employers and store owners had great influence over the local population.[13] The Ericksons tried to change these practices and there followed a series of strikes orchestrated by Symonette and other store keepers who were attempting to prevent them successfully expanding their business. The newcomers then imported unskilled labour from other islands and succeeded in taking over the steamship agency from Symantec.

Symonette then employed 'two Haitian toughs, George and Willis Duvalier' to aid him in a scheme to drive the Ericksons off the island. The Duvaliers quickly began to influence many of the workers and there was the potential for violence to break out. In December 1936 an Erickson driver, Charles Kaddy, drove his lorry into the side of Symonette's store and the incident escalated into violence. Jim Erickson sent to Nassau (370 miles to the north) to request police support for the solitary constable on Inagua, but believed that Symonette's son, the wireless operator never sent the message. Some of Erickson's loyal employees were assaulted by the Duvaliers, and George Duvalier was arrested and fined, to which he responded by stating in open court that 'if he were going to be fined two pounds every time he got into a street fight, he would kill the next time anything happened.'[14]

In August 1937, George Duvalier assaulted a man and was put on trial. He escaped from the courtroom and the police detective Corporal Edey gave chase. Willis Duvalier attacked Edey with a knife and wounded him in the shoulder and went on to assault Police Commissioner Fields. By this time, George had acquired a gun which he used to shoot the Commissioner in the arm, attempted to shoot Jim and Douglas Erickson, slightly injuring the former, and went on to shoot dead John Monroe, one of Erickson's employees. A riot then broke out and the Commissioner's house, the wireless station, a chemical store and part of a salt house were burned down. The Ericksons fled the island and sailed to Cuba, and for two days the Duvalier brothers controlled Great Inagua before fleeing to Haiti.

Jim Erickson and his supporters were arrested in Cuba and held for two weeks before being allowed to return. He then, on the recommendation of Chief Justice Tute, employed Lionel Rees as his personal bodyguard. Arriving on Inagua late in 1937, and armed with only his service revolver, he protected the family and their property while the search was mounted for the Duvalier brothers. By 12 October, both the Duvaliers had been arrested and brought to Nassau for trial before the Nassau Supreme Court. Rees' friend, Chief Justice Tute, presided at the trial and, on 3 November, both brothers were found guilty of murder and executed three weeks later. [15]

While working for the Ericksons, Rees impressed them 'as a very ingenious person … most interesting [but] a loner. [He] would not stay in our facilities, rather lived on the *Aline* hauled up on the beach in a cradle.'[16] With the exception of this short period of employment , Rees spent the closing years of the 1930s leading an idyllic existence amidst the tropical islands, pleasing no one but himself, unconcerned about material things and answerable to no one. This state of affairs was, however, destined to change. Even a remote island in the Bahamas was not immune to world news and, as war clouds began to gather over Europe, Rees felt his old loyalties beginning to stir and on the outbreak of hostilities in 1939, he was among the first to offer his services to the RAF. Now aged fifty-five, he was well beyond the age when such service was expected of him, but the idea of remaining in the peace and quiet of the Bahamas was unthinkable if there was the slightest possibility that he could be of any value to the war effort. Not surprisingly, he was judged to be too old and, in the eight years that had passed since he had retired, his ideas would have become outdated. The RAF which he had left in 1931 was a relatively small, budget-strapped service, equipped with aeroplanes that would not have looked out of place in the Royal Flying Corps of 1918. The service of 1939, equipped with modern, high-speed monoplane fighters and bombers, was undergoing a rapid expansion, and the introduction of modern technology, particularly radar, would have been a very unknown quantity to him. He must have rued his decision to leave the service as men who had been his juniors in rank now held positions of high authority, whilst others, older than he, were still on the active list and were about to play major roles in the conflict. Not one to give up easily, he sent letter after letter to the Air Ministry in London offering his services in any capacity and, perhaps by way of compensation, became involved in the recruitment of potential officers and men for the RAF from the volunteers who came forward in the Bahamas. Lester Brown and four other young men with private pilot's licences were among those accepted for the service, but told to remain in Nassau until they received orders to report to Britain. Friends who had admired them when they had volunteered, began to laugh as they saw them, weeks later, still walking the streets of Nassau. In desperation, they turned to the two most influential men that they knew, the Duke of Windsor, the newly-appointed Governor of the Bahamas, and Lionel Rees. Both promised to do what they could, and shortly afterwards they received their sailing orders. Brown recalls Rees bidding them *adieu* and assumed that the next time they would meet would be after the war was over. Surely, if young, trained pilots were finding it difficult to gain entry into the RAF, there was little hope for a man of Rees' age, irrespective of his past experience.

The fall of France during the summer of 1940 and the consequent preoccupation of Britain with keeping the enemy at bay on the far side of the English Channel, led Mussolini to believe that the time was ripe for Italy to make a move in North Africa. Believing it would only be a matter of weeks before the Germans were in London, the Italian Prime Minister and dictator determined to take the opportunity to seize British controlled territory in Egypt and Somaliland. The government in London was fully aware of the threat to Britain's lifeline, the route through the Suez Canal to the priceless oilfields of the Persian Gulf, and determined to defend Egypt with whatever resources could be spared.

Under the command of General Wavell, British troops faced Italian forces which outnumbered them by more than four to one. Initially, the Italians met with some success and managed to drive the British out of Somaliland, but this was short lived and, in early December 1940, the Middle East Command launched its counter strike which resulted in the expulsion of the enemy's forces from Egypt and East Africa early in the New Year.

While ground forces in Britain were relatively inactive during the second half of 1940, awaiting the expected German invasion, Dominion and Empire troops were available for operations in Africa. The same could not be said for the RAF which was fully occupied attempting to stem the tide of enemy attacks against Britain and her maritime supply lines, and the strength of the Dominion air forces was negligible at this stage of the war. Although large numbers of recruits were undergoing training in Britain and overseas, there was a severe shortage of senior officers to fill administrative posts as a stop-gap measure until others could be released from more active duties. This shortfall was partly made up by the recall to active service of officers who, because of their age, had previously been regarded as unsuitable.

By Christmas 1940, Lionel Rees found himself in uniform and back in Britain. At his own request he had relinquished the rank of group captain and was re-employed as a wing commander. His considerable experience in the Middle East made a posting to that theatre of operations inevitable and, on 25 January, four days after his return to the Active List, he arrived at Heliopolis in Egypt as a temporary supernumerary officer. Early the following month he was appointed to command RAF El Adem, twelve miles south of Tobruk in Libya, where he remained for only weeks before being recalled the HQ RAF Middle East until 26 March when he took over as OC RAF Helwan, fifteen miles south of Cairo. Helwan was the most important RAF station in Egypt and was also a major staging post for new air and ground personnel and units arriving in the theatre prior to posting to the Western Desert. Few remained at Helwan for any length of time and, whilst personnel came and went, engineers proceeded with the construction of a permanent runway capable of taking the very latest military aircraft. Designed to accommodate fewer than 1,000 men, the station was often overcrowded and this, added to the high turnover of officers and men, was a perfect recipe for administrative disaster. Throughout the spring of 1941, the airfield was a hive of activity and the volume of work tested the efficiency of the station personnel. At the end of June Rees recorded that,

> During the past month there have been on the Station about 1300 airmen, continually changing. Some of these were units re-fitting to go out to the Desert, and some were the men back from Greece and Crete waiting for re-posting. The result of this floating population was a great deal of disorganisation. … The numbers on the last day of the month had been reduced to 800, with which the Station could easily deal.[17]

Rees' role as the station commander was a purely administrative one and he very quickly found that it was almost impossible to maintain any continuity in his staff officers and that most of the administration fell to him. He seems to have been everywhere, doing everything and anything, while all the time trying to create as pleasant an atmosphere for the young men who were under his command, many of whom were on their first overseas posting. Wing Commander HE Rossiter, then a young RAF officer, remembered clearly the first time that he came into contact with Rees.

> We arrived at Helwan in a minor sandstorm, after a journey from Suez, very hot, very dusty and very thirsty. This figure marched up to us and said, 'Drop all your kit gentlemen and follow me.' He led us to the Officers' Mess where pints of cool beer were laid out. We were all pretty dehydrated and the beer was nectar.
>
> My first personal encounter with him was later when I and my detachment of airmen were having great difficulty in erecting the tents with which we were issued for accommodation.

A new conflict, a new battlefield, but an old rank. Wg Cdr Lionel Rees when commanding RAF Helwan, Egypt, 1941. [The late Chaz Bowyer]

An imposing figure came striding up to me. I remember my first impression was the rows of medals commencing with the VC … I had seen nothing like it before, nor indeed since. This figure then, in a most kindly voice, said, 'Excuse me my boy. I know that you are new out here, may I show you how to pitch a tent in the sand?' He then proceeded to do so, effectively and efficiently, all by himself. I thanked him and then a gust of wind lifted his Wolseley Helmet and sent it tumbling across the sand. I dashed after it and returned it, whereupon he said, again in a kind and fatherly voice, 'Thank you my boy, but again, I hope you don't mind me advising you … if your topi blows off in the desert, never run after it and pick it up.' Expecting some weighty advice about the dangers of sunstroke, I said, 'Why is that, sir?' whereupon he replied, 'Because some other bloody fool will do it for you,' and strode off leaving me dumbfounded and at a complete loss for any form of repartee.

From my own recollections I would certainly describe Rees as kindly, considerate and, to a very young officer, a typical RAF/RFC 'Uncle' figure, able to command because of his bravery and eccentricity, rather than as a disciplinarian. Whether he was efficient as a station commander I would query. He seemed to be just anxious to do all he could to help the war effort in any capacity. Indeed, he seemed to take on all the extraneous duties to relieve other junior officers of the work. He was PMC, Bar Officer, Mess Secretary, etc … I went to pay my mess bill on being posted … he was then sitting in the Mess Secretary's office typing out mess bills, one fingered, on an old battered typewriter. He thanked me for having the courtesy to pay during normal duty hours as so many others had kept him working into the night to settle up. He was one of the last great eccentric characters for which the pre-war RAF was noted.[18]

Although some considerable distance from the front line, Helwan was not always a peaceful station. Following the evacuations from Greece and Crete, those Egyptians who were pro-Axis in their sympathies felt that the time was ripe for them to show their true colours and the station came under fire from snipers, resulting in the death of one civilian worker. As the British and Dominion troops began to meet with some success, particularly after their advance into Syria where they destroyed the Vichy French forces, the sniping ceased as abruptly as it had started. Occasionally an enemy aircraft would venture over and attempt to drop bombs on the numerous military targets in the area, events which were dreaded by Rees' adjutant as, instead of taking cover during the raid, the Wing Commander would insist that they drive around to plot any bomb damage, particularly to the runway. Fortunately neither was injured and the adjutant was quite relieved to be posted away.

During the early summer, British operations in Syria and Iraq were supported by supply convoys sent from Helwan and, as a result, the sniping and bombing ceased. However, at the end of July, a detachment of one officer and twenty cadets arrived from Turkey en route for the UK, reporting that their ship had been attacked by a French submarine off the coast of Syria resulting in the death of several cadets.

By November, the construction work had been completed, but the airfield could not become operational as it was discovered that the runway was too short and lengthening took a further month. In order to deceive the enemy, a dummy landing ground was constructed four miles to the east. The station was officially taken over for flying on 17 December and by early 1942, squadrons of many types and nationalities (British, Australian, New Zealander, Greek and South African) were flying in and out of Helwan. Interestingly, two American aircraft arrived there to be overhauled – three weeks before the Japanese attack on Pearl Harbor and the United States' official entry into the war and by mid December, Helwan had become an official staging post for squadrons being posted to the Far East to face the impending Japanese attacks. As a consequence, the airfield again became overcrowded, accommodating 166 officers and 2,000 men over the Christmas period, but as most of the construction work had been completed and the administration was running efficiently, everything seemed to run smoothly. In February 1942, Rees must have had a sense of *deja vu* when a gunnery school was opened on the airfield.

With the station fully operational, and with an ever increasing flow of officers arriving from Britain, the Air Ministry decided that Rees' services were no longer required and, on 27 February, he handed over command to Group Captain GR O'Sullivan. Once again his age was to debar him from serving and he was ordered to take transport back to Britain.

Due to the heavy losses sustained by the RAF and the Royal Navy in the Mediterranean region, it had become customary for transport flights from Egypt to fly overland from Egypt to West Africa and thence to Gibraltar. This was the route home which Rees took and the aircraft in which he flew landed at Takoradi in the Gold Coast after a journey of nearly 4,000 miles from Cairo, broken up by short fuel and rest stops, a total flying time of nineteen hours. When the aircraft had been refuelled and the passengers and crew rested, a head count based upon the manifest revealed that Rees was missing. After what was probably a cursory search, the aircraft left without him. Rees had managed to find himself a job that needed doing and, in his own inimitable way, had simply got on with it without reference to higher authority.

That same month , the Air Ministry had announced the establishment of the Royal Air Force Regiment in order to standardise the defence of RAF establishments and stations both at home and overseas. This applied to the West Africa Command as much as any other, and a number of RAF personnel were distributed to each station with little or no thought being given to their training, duties or command. As one officer recorded in his memoirs.

The trouble had its roots in the official Air Force idea … that the Regiment was merely one of the 'trades' of the Air Force. A station far from civilisation wanted some cooks; very well, send them out half-a-dozen. Let them cook, and the senior administrative officer of the station would look after them. They wanted some RAF Regiment, well, send them eight and a sergeant, and let them get on with it. A section of regular officers with several years of training and discipline behind them, and with an exceptionally good NCO in charge might, if left in peace to their military life by the RAF station commander, have survived like this for a time without losing their cohesion. But these men of the RAF Regiment were, many of them, little above recruit standard in their training, and no higher in their discipline. The men belonged to no unit or sub-unit of the Regiment and their supervision depended upon whether a Regiment officer happened to be considered necessary on the establishment of the station or RAF unit concerned. They were owned by no flight or squadron and, as far as their military side went, were nobody's child.[19]

These units had simply been formed from any personnel engaged in full-time ground defence duties for the RAF. In fact, even in late 1942, some men were unaware that they had changed units and, in some case, changed service from the Army to the RAF.

At Takoradi, there was a small section of the RAF Regiment without a commanding officer. Rees had come across them in the short time he had been on the ground while his aircraft was being re-fuelled. He quickly identified the problem and appointed himself to the position of Station Defence Officer – quite unofficially and without pay. 'Full of enthusiasm and the love of training, he took charge of the squadron … with no other officer to help him, and kept it something more than 'ticking over'.[20]

The problem which he faced was quite a daunting one. The men under his command appeared to lack even the basics of military training and many were deemed unfit for duty. Poor medical examination procedures back in Britain had resulted in men being posted to the Gold Coast who were totally unsuited to the conditions which were testing to even the fittest of servicemen. Rees, who had served in West Africa before the Great War, had a thorough knowledge of the problems which he encountered and, ably assisted by a competent flight sergeant, drew on his experience to try and create a cohesive force out of what could only at best be described as a shambles. Gradually, he managed to establish some semblance of order and, on the arrival of the Command Defence Officer in August, and the appointment of junior officers to each unit, the RAF Regiment detachment at Takoradi began to function as an efficient military unit.

Rees appears to have thoroughly enjoyed himself at Takoradi, no doubt thinking back to his earlier service in the region. As in Egypt, there was always a constant stream of personnel flowing through the station en route to other theatres of operations, and he regularly came across old friends and acquaintances; Lester Brown, to whom he had waved goodbye in Nassau, arrived in 1942, in command of a squadron of Blenheim V light bombers, en route for the Middle East. Delayed by bad weather, Brown wandered into the Officers' Mess, one of the few civilised aspects of life at Takoradi, and was amazed to see Rees standing at the bar, and the two relived earlier, more peaceful days in the Bahamas.

In West Africa, as indeed everywhere, Rees seems to have made a profound impression on those he met. Lieutenant-Colonel Sherbrooke-Walker had very fond memories of him.

Takoradi, with its huge airfield and little army of RAF, was the principal place from our point of view, and our Gold Coast Squadron of some hundred and twenty men was concentrated here under the charge of a remarkable character – one of those men I have known ... who leave one better, but humbler, for having known them.

Rees had been a station commander in the Middle East, but on reaching the allotted span he was retired from the Air Force and sent home. But the authorities were counting without their Rees. Like the good old soldier he was, he refused to 'die', and, dropping off his aircraft at Takoradi ... remained there ... until the slow but remorseless [personnel] machine overtook him. Modest and unassuming to a degree, and with delightfully courteous manners ... it was only by chance that one discovered he owned a string of decorations, headed by the VC.

Rees showed me round everywhere and to keep up with his long and energetic stride I had to put my best foot forward. He knew every tree and bird and always carried a supply of pennies in his pocket for the village children when he went further afield.

It was a sad day when he was allowed to tarry no longer and went on his way home to his coral island – no doubt to take up once more his hobby of sailing the oceans alone in a small boat. O! *Si sic omnes*! if all did thus![21]

The 'remorseless machine' caught up with Rees in November 1942 and he handed over command of his unit to Major JB Moffat and completed his journey back to Britain, retiring from the service on 20 November. Reverting to his old rank of group captain, he headed back to the Bahamas.

Notes

1. Letter from Stanley Toogood to the author, January 1987.
2. 'A Square Deal', LWB Rees, article in *The Nassau Magazine*, January 1938.
3. Ibid.
4. Ibid.
5. Ibid.
6. Letter LWB Rees to Muriel Rees, nd, *c*1937.
7. Percy Frederick Cavill (1875–1940) was a member of a family of noted Australian swimmers. In 1887, he became the first Australian to win a major race abroad when he won both the 440 yards and 5-mile races at the English Amateur Swimming Championships. He moved to the USA in 1900 and in 1902 became the first person to swim 100 yards in under one minute. From there he moved to the Bahamas where he lived the life of a beachcomber.
8. *Out-Island Doctor*, Evans W Cottman (with Wyatt Blassingame), London, 1963. Cottman (1902–76) had arrived in the Bahamas from Indiana in the United States in the late 1930s, with a master's degree in biochemistry. He set himself up as an 'out-island' doctor (an unqualified medical practitioner) on Abaco Island where he practised medicine.
9. Undated letter written by Lester Brown.
10. This is the only reference that suggests that Rees spoke with a Welsh accent and may well be a mistaken identification of an English accent.

11. *Out-Island Doctor*, op cit. It was highly unlikely that Rees would have taken a sterling silver tea service with him on his solo trans-Atlantic crossing, having disposed of so many other far more portable assets such as his decorations and medals. There is no evidence at all that the Rees family ever had any heraldic arms, although this may be a reference to the Brabazon arms passed down to him through his mother.

12. Letter from the Revd JM Hutcheson to the author, 29 July 1985.

13. The 'Truck' or 'Tommy' system, whereby workers were paid in kind or tokens had operated in Britain, particularly during the Industrial Revolution, and was gradually phased out by the passing of various Truck Acts.

14. *Great Inagua*, Margery O Erickson, New York, 1987, p 51.

15. 'The 1937 riot in Inagua, Bahamas', D Saunders, *New West Indian Guide*, 62, 1988, pp 129–45.

16. Letter from Douglas Erickson to the author, 27 August 1990.

17. National Archives, AIR 28/350, Operational Record Book, RAF Helwan, Egypt.

18. Wing-Commander HE Rossiter letters to the author dated 2 & 24 January 1987.

19. *Khaki and Blue*, Colonel Ronald Sherbrooke-Walker, TD, DL, London, 1952, p 81.

20. Ibid, pp 89–90.

21. Ibid.

XIV

ANDROS
(1942–55)

RETURNING TO THE BAHAMAS WITH A WORLD WAR STILL RAGING, Rees would have found the inactivity forced upon him frustrating in the extreme. He was disappointed to discover that there was no role for him at the RAF training bases which had been established at Oakes and Windsor Fields, and he had little choice but to try and pick up the pieces of the life which he had left nearly two years previously. Living on Blue Hill, New Providence, in what can only be described as a wooden cabin, he set about making the *Aline* fit for sailing and, when his friend and landlord Herbert McKinney suggested that he might care to sail to Crooked Island to carry out some survey work, he jumped at the opportunity to resume his nomadic life afloat. Although not a qualified surveyor, his military training had given him more expertise than the average layman, and his descriptions of McKinney's property and the lifestyle of the inhabitants of the island clearly show not only his ability to observe, but also his ever-present sense of humour.

This is the first impression of Crooked Island, & you are getting it because the sun has burnt my lips and back so badly that I am taking a day in the shade.

I reserve the right to alter every statement and any resemblance to places or people is purely coincidental.

First of all the bad. Forsyth was quite right. The place is a desert, & it will take both time & money to do anything with it. The ground has been so burnt over that the country is a cross between the top of Vesuvius & Berlin. Wherever you look smoke is rising from the farms.

The people that I have met are quite the best in the Bahamas & are like the people of Tortola, Virgin Islands. Although very African, they appear to be better educated than most, their huts are cleaner & there is no begging. Wherever I have been I have been invited into the houses & given some orangeade & cakes.[1]

It was during this trip that he appears to have developed his interest in agriculture, something which he had touched lightly upon in the 1930s. He studied how the islanders farmed, or in some cases failed to farm, and formulated his own opinions on how it should be carried out, particularly with regard to the practice, which was common throughout the islands, of burning away the undergrowth, something which he developed an almost evangelical attitude towards trying to stamp out. At Crooked Island, he saw evidence of an alternative method of farming.

The brother of Mr Moss of Mosstown called on me with a present of fresh vegetables and eggs. Another brother of Mr Moss has a beautiful farm. Citrus planted in rows, a patch of bananas whose leaves are green & fresh in spite of the drought. Plenty of sugar cane & onions, beets, tomatoes & cabbage planted in beds. The ground has been levelled off and tons of seaweed have been carried onto the farm. It shows that a farm can be made, but it is probably a very hard job.

The Commissioner showed me a letter he wrote about change of headquarters to Hope Great House, in which he suggested that Long Cay residents be transported to Crooked Island. They all go to church here & it might be pointed out that a man who burns a farm cannot really love God. Therefore God will punish him to the third and fourth generations.

I suggest that every man who is moved from Long Cay to Crooked Island be given his land – and also an equal amount which he must NOT touch till after the third or fourth generation. This means that in 100 years each family will have land with 1 inch of earth on it & a growth of some use. I don't know if a government can take such a long view of such matters.[2]

He concluded his report by informing McKinney,

If this letter has bored you, you cannot get at me to smack me in the eye or anything & I cannot get out of the Sound [Turtle Sound] till next moon with a south wind. I can't guess when that will happen.[3]

His conviction that the burning of the undergrowth was detrimental to good farming seems to have gripped him with an almost crusading zeal and, shortly after his return from Crooked Island, he established himself on a small cay at Andros, the largest island in the Bahamas group, where after seeking advice from the Bahamas Agricultural Board, he set about practising what he had preached. He devoted a great deal of time and an enormous amount of energy to the task, and later reported the results of his endeavours in the *Nassau Guardian*.

I have made my farm for one year and kept it up for one year, working single handed. When I say 'made', I mean it literally. Everything is growing in sand, seaweed, etc, that I myself have carried. The Cay has been so badly burned that there is no humus on it, and it takes a little tree two years to get its roots down into fertile earth.

I am quite independent of rain, as a member of the Board showed me how to bore for water. I have six wells on my little patch, one of which is 30 feet deep, and was dug in two days.

Should I need help, the Trade Winds will pump all the water I require, and I shall farm as they do in Palestine and other parts of the world.

On the Cay, I found a few dying trees, covered with love vine. This year one grapefruit tree gave me 700 fruit, an orange 600, a lime 2,000. All my trees are clean, as the Board told me about ladybirds.

My first corn was planted under instructions I got out of the *Nassau Guardian* and a radio broadcast from ZNS. At the same time a farm was being burned on a cay opposite mine. My corn gave me a 2,000 to 1 return. My opposite number got a few bearing stalks giving about 200 to 1. I thank the Board. My dillies,[4] salved in accordance with information furnished by the Board, gave me the best dillies I have yet seen and are at this moment laden down with young fruit. My peas are the best in the vicinity, and my potatoes, planted as the Board said, are giving excellent results. All sixty of my young trees are doing well, and one seedling planted by me has already borne fruit.

As a matter of interest I might say that I dig my beds with an eight-pound hammer.[5]

His continual reference to the advice which he received from the 'Board' would lead one to think that his farming experiment might even have been sponsored by them as a means of persuading out-islanders to abandon their old traditional methods in favour of a more scientific approach. Whatever influence, or lack of it, he may have had on the islanders, the editor of the *Nassau Guardian* was certainly impressed and extolled his achievements.

It is important to note that … Group Captain Rees chose for his agricultural experiment the most unpromising land, the fields of a 'stoney cay'; that he has challenged the recalcitrant soil of such an islet and has so far broken down its resistance so as to draw from it what, in the circumstances, can only be called more fruitful harvests. All this by the lone efforts of one man, let it be remembered. This amateur farmer – winning fast towards professional status – has further proved that the Bahamian farmer need not be totally dependent upon our erratic rainfall. The example of Group Captain Rees, a modern Cincinnatus cultivating the Bahamian

Rees solo-sailing the
Aline *during the 1950s.*
[Via Evans Cottman]

soil, is an inspiration to all Bahamians and will, we trust, cause many of them to follow the lead he has given.[6]

Strong, if rather poetic words which, because of their style, would probably have fallen upon ears as deaf as the rocky cays were barren. How relevant Rees' experiment was in reality is questionable as his farm was only developed for a limited period and, if so successful, it is strange that the ideas were not universally adopted, if nowhere else then at least on Andros where their value would have been obvious and clearly visible to all.

It is generally accepted that man's desire to cultivate the land is the first step towards the establishment of a more sedentary lifestyle. Arable farming of any description is a long-term process, and the fruits of one year's labour are often not available for harvesting until a lengthy period of time has passed. Certainly, in the case of Rees, the days of wandering around the islands seemed to have come to an end by 1947. The Anglo-Iranian Oil Company, which had been carrying out test drilling for oil at Deep Creek on Andros, had decided to close down operations as the geology of the region made its extraction impractical. The task of winding up the drilling site was given to Rees and it was while he was there that his life underwent a profound change.

Throughout his life Rees does not appear to have had any close relationships with women outside of his immediate family. His sister, Muriel, had certainly played a significant part in his childhood, but since he left home to join the Army, her role had declined, although the two appear to have remained very close throughout their lives. The loss of his mother who had died in Queensland, Australia in 1911, would have certainly had some effect upon him and it would appear that Leonora Rees had been in Australia for some years at the time of her death. It is quite possible that her marriage to Lionel's father had broken down and she had left the family home in Caernarfon to live, initially in Dublin (her will was probated in Dublin in 1912 giving her home address as 11 Connaught Terrace, Rathgar, Co Dublin), and then with her brother Smith William Davids in Cairns, Queensland. Lionel and his sister, however, seem to have remained with their father, who appears to have ceased practising as a solicitor in 1906 and moved out of Caernarfon by 1911. He lived for the next twenty years in south-eastern England, latterly with Muriel in Bromley, Kent.

Perhaps Rees' life had been one that simply did not lend itself to settling down or marrying and his nomadic life-style would have meant uprooting a wife from one military station to another. We can only guess at why he had never married, but by the time he had returned to the Bahamas after the Second World War, he appears to have had enough of the nomadic life and seemed more interested in putting down roots, albeit still in a very isolated location where he was unlikely to meet many people let alone make strong, new relationships.

This all changed in 1947 when he met Sylvia, the eighteen-year old daughter of Alexander and Mary Williams of Pinders, a small settlement near Mangrove Cay. Despite being of pure-blooded West African descent and almost illiterate, she was attracted to this aging Welshman (Rees was now sixty-three) who seemed so wise, well educated and gentle. Officially, she became his housekeeper, looking after the *Aline*, but very soon the two were emotionally involved and neither the wide gulf between their ages, nor even their even wider cultural differences, appeared to matter. In the end, perhaps inevitably, Sylvia discovered that she was pregnant and there appears to have been no question that Rees should do anything but the honourable thing and, consequently, on 12 August 1947, they were married by the Civil Commissioner for Andros.

News of the marriage shocked 'white society' in Nassau. Rees, despite his eccentricities, was seen as a man who could have had his choice of the many eligible ladies in the capital, so why had he chosen a black Androvian? They all reached the same conclusion, Sylvia Williams had laid a trap into which he had fallen. No-one would accept any other explanation; it was unthinkable to them that he could have entered into such a relationship and subsequent marriage of his own free will. He must have felt obliged to marry the girl 'having got her into trouble.' That, they said, was taking 'the manners of an officer and a gentleman too far.' A friend, Walton Smith, who was living in Miami, returned to Nassau for a holiday and found the news of the marriage 'hard to believe, since he [Rees] was extremely shy and even politely hostile to women.' Many believed that the marriage would not last and that Rees would 'very quickly come to his senses.'[7]

Was the opinion of Nassau 'society' correct, or was it simply evidence of the racism which was so prevalent in the 1940s and, indeed is only just below the surface in the Bahamas today?[8] Might Rees not have married Sylvia without coercion, for some other perfectly normal reason. It might simply have been for love. If not for love, then perhaps it was because he was simply delighted at the thought of becoming a father. Throughout his life, he had always displayed a love of children and must have been disappointed that he had none of his own and that he, who had done and seen so much, had no-one to whom he could pass on his experience and knowledge.

Sylvia Rees with their daughter, Aline.
[Cyrus Sharer]

Despite Smith's comment, there is evidence that Rees was far from being averse to female companionship.[9] He certainly did not dislike women as he spent much of his free time until leaving for the Bahamas, with his aunt and female cousin in Scotland, and made a favourable impression on many, such as Lady Joan Portal, during his working career. It may well have been love of his independence and life style which had steered him away from matrimony in the past. Perhaps he yearned for the stability and security of family life. In 1947, Muriel was on the far side of the Atlantic and had no intention of joining him in the Bahamas. Perhaps his ever-dwindling financial resources meant that he could not afford to return to live in Britain. It may simply have been nothing more sinister than the advancing years, or that he had indeed fallen for Sylvia who brought an ageing man a last reminder of youth. We shall never know the true reason as both parties chose to remain silent.

The marriage may have caused scandalous gossip in Nassau, but on Andros it was quite accepted by the community which had an almost naïve but endearing simplicity in its attitude towards life; it was fine for him to have married a girl so many years his junior, so long as he was a gentleman and had plenty of money. One elderly Mangrovian lady went so far as to say, in that bluntly honest style of the Caribbean,' so long as he could do the job, there would be no problems.' Rees had long been accepted by the island community and had acquired a reputation as something of a sage, a man to whom others could resort for advice and assistance. Whenever the Mangrovians had a problem it was to the 'Captain' that they turned, and he assumed the role of an unofficial leader in the community. In the 1980s, his memory was still highly regarded by those who had known him, and he was spoken of with great reverence.

Almost as soon as they were married Rees set about constructing a home for his new wife and eagerly expected child. On the ridge above Mangrove Cay, near Sylvia's family home in Pinders, he built a one-roomed house of very simple design with corrugated iron walls and roof, a drain in the centre of the earth floor and the sleeping accommodation curtained off from the living area. For water, he sank his own well and a small generator supplied electricity, a rare commodity in Mangrove Cay in the 1940s. The basic construction work was carried out by the local population with Rees supervising and personally producing the more technical items such as the blades for his windcharger. By European standards the house was primitive, but on Andros it was regarded as the latest in modern out-island accommodation.

In March 1948, Sylvia gave birth to a son whom they named Ailean Lionel (the first name being a variation on the name of Rees' boat) and, over the next five years, there were two more children, a daughter Aline and a second son, Olvin. As his first son grew, Rees taught him the basics of the few machines and gadgets which the family owned and, when out walking, tried to create in him an awareness of the landscape. Cyrus Sharer, a young American post-graduate student, visited Mangrove Cay in the early 1950s and had fond memories of the Rees family, headed by this highly intelligent elderly man, who seemed to delight in the company of his small son, taking every opportunity to teach him those skills which he regarded as essential.[10] Today, of the three children only Allen (as Ailean has come to be known) has any real recollection of his father and those early days on Mangrove Cay.

My life was carefree and full of days wandering the beaches with my father. He would always talk to me as if I was an adult, I think he wished I was older, so that I could understand much more of the things he was telling me. We talked about his days in North Africa and his life in the RAF. I do remember that he was obsessed with the idea of sailing. It must have been a big disappointment when he finally got ill and could not sail as much as he would have liked.

My father spent many hours studying Greek, and reading classic books. In the evening at

6.00 pm, he would listen to the BBC on the shortwave radio which was powered by storage cells which were charged from a wind generator.

Our house was the first to have electric lights, due to the generator. The plumbing for the house was derived from 55 gallon storage tanks which he had to fill each day. Water had to be pumped manually to a height of approximately twenty feet so that water pressure could be generated in the plumbing. We had a well stocked workshop. Most of the furniture was made by hand in this shop. Before I entered school, I was at least two years ahead of children of my own age and this became somewhat of a problem; kids do not know how to react to others who 'know it all.'[11]

Possibly the last photograph of Lionel Rees, taken on Mangrove Cay, c 1952. Armed with a machete, he is working on his farm. [Cyrus Sharer]

Sadly, this picture of tropical bliss was not to last. Despite being old enough to be his children's grandfather, Rees had hoped to spend many years in their company, but it was not to be. During the early 1950s he became unwell and the illness was diagnosed as leukemia, a cancerous disease which could not be treated locally. Gradually, the debilitating nature of the illness meant that he became less able to do those things, like sailing, which had given him great pleasure. In what must have been very difficult circumstances, he sold *Aline* to a partnership of the Commissioner for Andros and Mr McPhee, who operated her as a ferry between Mangrove Cay and Nassau. In 1953, in a desperate attempt to try and arrest the advance of the disease, Rees returned to Britain where he was admitted to the RAF Hospital at Uxbridge where he received treatment, but the medical staff were unable to delay the inevitable. He realised that he was dying and that his ties were now in the Bahamas and so he made his farewells to his homeland. He had hoped to visit Caernarfon, but when he was discharged from the hospital, he was unable to make the journey and instead wrote to the Mayor and Corporation.

The doctor tells me that I shall soon fade away and that I shall take no further interest in life in a few weeks time. I should therefore (in case the diagnosis is correct) like to make my *adieu* to the Mayor, aldermen, councillors and burgesses of Caernarfon.

In the same way as other people I have had my difficulties. I have met them during the last war, and whilst sailing and just in the ordinary way of life. When things have been really bad I have often said to myself, 'What would a Freeman of Caernarfon do about this?'

The answer has come to me that a Freeman of Caernarfon would just get on with the job. This I have done and the difficulties have disappeared.[12]

This time, however, the difficulties were not going to disappear and the doctor's prognosis was, unfortunately, all too accurate. A few weeks after he had returned to the Bahamas he was back in hospital, being admitted to the Princess Margaret Hospital in Nassau on 20 May 1955. Sylvia, in the tradition of Andros, wanted to remain with him in the hospital and only after considerable difficulty was she persuaded to leave and appear at the official visiting times. His friends in the capital would call, and the members of the Royal Air Force Association arranged for the installation of a radio to help him pass the days of enforced idleness. The matron, Miss Denise Dane, recalled that he was a very sick man, but that his mind and memory were both very good and he spent his days preparing for the inevitable.[13] To Mrs Mallie Lightbourne, chair of the Commonwealth War Graves Commission for the Bahamas (and the daughter of his long-time friend Herbert McKinney), he sent a request that he be buried in the RAF Cemetery but, even with such a sombre request, he was still able to add a touch of humour, commenting that, as he was so much against absentee landlords, he did not intend to leave vacant for very long any land which he might be granted.[14] For his family, he drew up a short and simple will which summed up everything that was important to him.

I leave everything I possess to my wife, Sylvia Rees. I hope that she will keep my books, instruments, tools in good condition, in trust for my children.

I hope that any land which we possess will be kept in proper condition, in trust for my children, that it will not be destroyed by burning and being allowed to erode.[15]

The care of his children he placed in the hands of the church in the hope that both they and their mother would be protected until they were better able to care for themselves. He was obviously aware of the bad feelings which his marriage had aroused and attempted to ensure that his family would not suffer after he had gone. Years later,

The gravestone of Lionel Rees in the RAF Cemetery, Nassau. Originally an upright headstone, it was changed for this flat headstone during the 1970s. [Author]

controversy still existed between the two communities at Mangrove Cay and Nassau, both claiming a different truth. Perhaps Miss Dane summed it up best.

> We had heard of his great career and it distressed most people that he lived in such reduced circumstances on one of the out-islands. We all felt that a hero like Group Captain Rees should have had a happier ending, but he may well have preferred things to be as they were.[16]

Rees declined gradually and died at 10.45 on the morning of Wednesday, 28 September 1955. As was the custom in the tropics, the funeral was arranged for later the same day and a small cortege left the hospital at 16.30. He was buried with full military honours in the RAF Cemetery in Nassau, with members of the RAFA acting as pall bearers and the Royal Bahamas Police providing a Guard of Honour and a Firing Party. The mourners were few and consisted mainly of his immediate family and close friends.

Today, the RAF Cemetery in Nassau is a blaze of colour, the low stone wall which contains an area of bright green crab grass also keeps in check the tropical undergrowth. All around, the Bahamian national tree, the poinciana, provides a dramatic backdrop of brilliant red and the air is filled with the sound of tropical insects. Neat rows of stone with lie on the grass, each bearing the brief details of the young men who died in the service of their country, mostly during the Second World War. Two graves are, however, different and lie next to each other on the left as one enters the cemetery. One is the last resting place of Hilary St George Saunders, noted recorder of RAF history,[17] and the other is that of Lionel Rees, who did more than most to create that history and establish the traditions of which the RAF is justifiably proud.

Let the last words be those of the poet Robert W Service:

> 'May he rest in peace' in the Good Tomorrow
>
> One of those fond and foolish fools
>
> Who, scorning fortune and fame
>
> Turn out with the rallying cry of their schools
>
> Just eager to play the game.

Notes

1. Correspondence between JA McKinney and the author, May 1985.
2. Ibid.
3. Ibid.
4. The dilly tree grows large succulent, fleshy fruit which was once popular throughout the West Indies. It has a different name on each island group e.g. sapadilla, naseberry, mespil and nispero.
5. Letter from LWB Rees to *Nassau Guardian*, 12 January 1947.
6. Newspaper editorial comment on the letter quoted in fn 5.
7. Letter from Mr Walton Smith to the author,
8. When the present author visited the Royal Nassau Yacht Club in the 1980s, when the Bahamas had become an independent, democratic Commonwealth country, with a predominantly black government, he was shocked to see a sign at the entrance barring admission to 'Blacks and Women'.
9. Mrs Margery O Erickson, wife of Jim Erickson of Inagua, wrote in a letter to the author dated 4 July 1990, 'We had heard that Capt Rees was a woman-hater, but this was hard for us to believe because he was without fail the soul of courtesy to myself, Louise, and Diane Pullingen, an unmarried artist-friend of Louise's, in fact Louise and I sometimes wondered if Capt Rees might decide to court Diana. … He had a superb physique and large hands. He was well muscled, but very gentle. We all loved him. His manners were always gentlemanly and he was kindly disposed to everyone on the island. … He was shy, but took part in many discussions, expecially if the talk turned to one of his great interests at that time. His reasoning concerning [the events of the Old Testament] was fascinating.'
10. Conversation with Professor Cyrus Sharer, London, 29 August 1987.
11. Letter from Allan Rees to the author, 30 July 1987.
12. Letter from LWB Rees to the Mayor and Corporation of the Borough of Caernarfon, nd, *c*1953.
13. Letter from Miss Denise Dane to the author, 21 September 1987.
14. Letter from Mrs Mallie Lightbourne to the author, 24 May 1987.
15. Probate Office, Nassau, Bahamas.
16. Letter from Ms Denise Dane to the author, op cit.
17. Hilary Aidan St George Saunders, MC (1898–1951), Welsh Guards. Author of *The Royal Air Force 1939–45*, 2 vols (with Dennis Richards); *The Battle of Britain; Bomber Command; Coastal Command; Per Ardua; The Rise of British Air Power, 1911–39*.

ROYAL FLYING CORPS
SCHOOL OF AERIAL FIGHTING
War Establishment (Provisional) 17.9.17 *

Headquarters	94
Headquarters (Attached)	16
Station Establishment	14
Six Flights	186
Workshop Section	82
Stores Section	19
Aeroplane Repair Section	80

Headquarters

Commandant	1 (graded as Wing Commander)
Chief Instructor	1 (graded as Squadron Commander)
Adjutant	1
Assistant Adjutant	1
Flight Group Commanders	3
Officer i/c Workshops	1
Officer i/c Stores	1
Warrant Officer	1
Clerks (General)	17 (12 female)
Clerks (Pay)	5 (1 female)
Armourers	1
Assistant Armourers	5
Motor Cyclists	8
Drivers Motor Transport	31 (12 female)
Telephonists	2 (female)
Misc. Tailors	4
Misc. Shoemakers	7
Photographers	7

Headquarters (Attached)

Medical Officer	1
RAMC	5
Batmen	10

* A 2 School of Aerial Fighting was proposed on 5 October 1917.

Station Establishment

Quartermaster	1
Quartermaster Sergeant	1
Clerks (General)	1 (female)
Storeman	1
Cooks	10 (female)
Firemen	10

Six Flights each comprising

Flight Commander	1 (Fighting Instructor)
Flying Officers	4 (Assistant Fighting Instructors)
Flight Sergeant	1
Sergeants	3 (2 Riggers, 1 Fitter)
Carpenters	2
Clerks (General)	2
Fitters (Engine)	9
Riggers	9

Workshop Section

Equipment Officer (2nd Class)	1
Flight Sergeant	1
Sergeants	4
Acetylene Welders	3
Blacksmiths	4
Carpenters	8 (including 1 corporal)
Clerks (General)	1
Coppersmiths	2
Coppersmiths' Mates	4
Electricians	4
Fitters (Engine)	14 (including 2 sergeants and 12 corporals)
Fitters (General)	12 (all corporals)
Fitters (Motor Transport)	5 (1 sergeant, 4 corporals)
Fitters (Turners)	4
Sailmakers	9 (including 6 female)
Vulcanisers	2

Stores Section

Equipment Officer (3rd Class)	1
Warrant Officer	1 (Technical)
Flight Sergeant	1
Clerk (General)	1
Clerk (Ledger)	2 (both female)
Clerk (Stores)	4 (including 1 sergeant)
Clerk (Tally Card)	2
Storemen	7 (including 1 sergeant)

Half Aeroplane Repair Section

Equipment Officer (2nd Class)	1
Flight Sergeant	1
Sergeants	1
Carpenters	18 (including 1 corporal)
Clerks (General)	2 (including 1 female)
Clerks (Tally Card)	1 (female)
Draughtsmen	1
Electrician	1
Fitters (Engine)	3
Fitters (General)	1
Fitters (Machinist)	1
Instrument Repairers	2
Miscellaneous Trades	8 (for Salvage purposes)
Photographer Camera Repairer	1
Painters	2
Riggers	19 (including 1 corporal)
Sailmakers	13 (including 3 corporals and 10 females)
Storemen	1
Tinsmith	1
Tinsmith (Sheet Metal Worker)	1

Transport

Heavy Tenders	10
Light Tenders	10
Trailers	5
Touring Cars	1
Motor Cycles	8
Side Cars	8
Ambulances	2

Until such time as Station Workshops are provided, Workshop Lorries will be required

Proportion of Corporals and Air Mechanics:

Corporals	3%
1st Air Mechanics	37%
2nd Air Mechanics	54%
3rd Air Mechanics	6%

The two Firemen are any two men from any Section to be specially trained in Fire Duties.

The establishment of machines will be:

24 Avro Monos
12 Rotary Scouts
12 Stationary Scouts
6 DH4s
6 Bristol Fighters

The six Flights were designated A, B, C, D, E and F, each commanded by a Flight Commander and each pair of Flights commanded by a Flight Group Commander. The Flight Commanders will be graded as Fighting Instructors. There will be four Flying Officers in each Flight graded as Deputy Flying Instructors.

1st Flight Group	A Flight	4 Avros
		6 Rotary Scouts
	B Flight	4 Avros
		6 Rotary Scouts
2nd Flight Group	C Flight	4 Avros
		6 Stationary Scouts
	D Flight	4 Avros
		6 Stationary Scouts
3rd Flight Group	E Flight	4 Avros
		6 DH4s
	F Flight	4 Avros
		6 Bristol Fighters

School will be capable of dealing with 150 pupils per fortnight

[NA AIR 1/122/15/40/137]

Appendix II

ROLL OF HONOUR
RAF TURNBERRY, 1917–18

This list is not definitive

Royal Flying Corps::
Lieut George Guy Barry Downing of Cardiff; 4 September 1917
2 Lieut WHC Buntine, MC; 19 June 1917
2 Lieut CA Cooper; 29 June 1917
2 Lieut EC Hull of Bedford; 17 March 1918
2 Lieut RS MacNair; March 1918
2 Lieut J Stevenson; 1 May 1917
Sgt SC Appleton of Warrington; 19 June 1917
Sgt CWH Bowers; 1 May 1917
2 A/M Edward Ernest Hall, MM, of Cramlington; 25 July 1917
2A/M Harry Towlson of Nottingham; 26 June 1917

Royal Air Force:
Capt James Martin Child, MC, Chevalier Order of Leopold, *Croix de Guerre*, of Leytonstone, London;
    23 August 1918
Capt Ian Henry David Henderson (son of Lieut Gen Sir David Henderson, KCB, KCVO, DSO, RAF)
    of London. Crashed with Lieut Redlar; 21 June 1918
Lieut James Stanley Brown of Nelson, Lancashire; 20 October 1918
2 Lieut CA Fletcher of Hadley; 20 October 1918
2 Lieut J Milligan of Wadsley, Yorkshire; 6 July 1917
Flt Cadet Andrew Anderson Hepburn of Dunfermline; 23 August 1918
Sgt JE Lilley of Sunderland; 28 November 1918
Sgt John Stabb Tuckett of Birkenhead; 26 May 1918
Cpl TA King of Brentwood; 10 December 1918
2 A/M Thomas Inglis of Lanark; 10 March 1919
Lieut Hugh William Elliott of Boxworth, Cambs; drowned after ditching with Lieut Reed, 5 June 1918
Lieut Gerald Arthur Lamburn of Chelsea; 30 September 1918
Lieut Reginald Milburn Makepeace of Liverpool; 28 May 1918
Lieut Harold Bolton Redler, MC, of Cape Town; crashed with Capt Henderson, 21 June 1918
2 Lieut JD Dunbar; 25 July 1918
2 Lieut Charles Henry Albert Godfrey of Kenley, Surrey; 11 December 1918
2 Lieut Charles Alexander Hillock; 8 January 1919
2 Lieut Charles William Janes of Stoke Newington; 11 April 1918
2 Lieut TA McClure of Dun Laoghaire; 28 May 1918

2 Lieut Archibald McFarlan of Castletown, Isle of Man; 23 August 1918

2 Lieut William Arthur Rymal of Toronto; 5 September 1918

Flt Cadet John Hughes of Amlwch, Anglesey; 25 November 1918

Flt Cadet Alexander McLean of Cardonald, Glasgow; 5 September 1918

Australian Flying Corps:

2 Lieut Howard Richmond Henry Butler of Melbourne; 2 June 1918

2 Lieut Raymond Hinton Grove of Adelaide; 19 August 1918

US Aviation Section Signal Corps:

Lieut George Squires of Minnesota; 18 May 1918

Lieut Richard Brumback Reed of Ohio. Drowned after ditching with Lieut Elliott; 5 June 1918

2 Lieut HR Smith; nd

Cadet George Atherton Brader of Pennsylvania; 4 April 1918

Appendix III

Gordon-Shephard Memorial Prize Essay 1929
Second Prize, Group Captain LWB Rees,
VC, OBE, MC, AFC, ADC

Discuss the part which armoured cars and/or armed but unarmoured vehicles should take in the air control of an undeveloped country; their tactical employment; the types of vehicles and equipment which should be developed for this duty; and the training of the unit.

1. Foreword

Before considering the future it is always as well to examine the past so as to make an estimate of the lines along which progress has taken place; and then examine the present to see what the best use is being made of the methods and equipment available. The most easily available literature had to do with Palestine and Transjordan; and as these small countries lend themselves to the 'tip-and-run' tactics of raiders, the hardest kind of tactics to defeat, they will be taken as showing a true type of the problems and their solution.

No consideration is taken of the purely air control of a country except in so far as it lays the basis for car action, but car action will be considered in certain situations that might be dealt with by air alone.

The following legend is adopted throughout the paper:-

Military force	A force of all or any arms used to achieve a result on the ground
The Air	Aircraft acting either in co-operation or independently
Armoured	A wheeled armoured vehicle
Tank	A tracked armoured vehicle
Motin	Motorised infantry
Moticar	The vehicle of the Motin
Tender	The non-fighting vehicle that accompanies the fighting vehicles
Car	General term for all or any of the above vehicles
War	General term for operations, however small

2. Lessons from the past

In Palestine and Transjordan the operations of the Great War were on too large a scale to teach a lesson in minor tactics, except where they emphasise the importance of speed of movement, and difficulty of movement where there are no roads. The Crusades teach little that is not better illustrated by earlier campaigns, except that Posts can not control a Desert country.

The following examples are selected as they are so well known, and yet the lessons have not been learnt. Every rule has been broken during the last few years.

BC 1400. The Israelites could not advance through Transjordan till they had surrounded Edom (Petra), and caught Sihon, on [the site of] Ziza aerodrome, between the two wings of their advance. The ambushed the iron chariots in Gilead, but could not control the country till, on the orders of Joshua, they made roads and felled the trees.

BC 900. David, an unarmed boy, slew Goliath (Conspicuous), the biggest and most heavily armed and armoured of the Philistines.

To meet David's attack, the people of Aman hired chariots (which parked west of Ziza aerodrome) and mercenaries at a cost of some £400,000. It was too late, and the chariots in exceptionally favourable country did not make a proper stand.

BC 150. Antiochus found he could take his elephants along the road to Egypt, but not across the roadless desert to Persia. The elephants, in addition to their crew, always had cavalry and mailed men-at-arms attached to them; and even then, on certain occasions they were surprised and killed by being stabbed from underneath. They would not fight till they were shown the blood of grapes and mulberries.

BC 50. The people of Petra counter-attacked and destroyed the Greek army under Athenaeus that had just successfully raided them. (Alexander's generals failed to make any impression on Petra).

AD 50. The Nabataean Areta IV ruled the country from Medain Saleh to Damascus. Although the Romans constructed Posts, such as Hallabat, Azrak and Rashrashiyeh, they exercised little control in the desert.

3. Modern contravention of the rules

The armoured cars at Ziza (1924) had not made roads and this caused delay. They attacked from one flank and allowed the raiders to escape.

At Sueille (west of Amman) the villagers caught the armoureds and narrowly missed destroying them. At the relief of Sweida, Jebel Druse, the French cars were surprised, turned over and destroyed.

Recently we found that we had not sufficient troops in Palestine to quell the unrest, and it cost us a lot of money.

On account of the absence of roads, many raids have got away untouched by the armoureds. A bomb rolled under an armoured will destroy it. It pays to run fighting vehicles on the best available fuel, or they cannot fight.

The Druses captured the French supply column sent to the relief of Sweida, and thus obtained enough machine guns and ammunition to conduct a two years' war.

About three years ago we lost to the Wahabis the frontier post that was just being built.

4. Resume of lessons

    a. The plan of operations depends on information
    b. Roads are essential
    c. Armoureds must have speed and manoeuvrability
    d. Armoureds must be able to hit. If they cannot do so, mobile unarmoured fire units must be employed
    e. A little extra expense in peace may save a lot in war, and possibly prevent war
    f. The enemy must not be despised
    g. It pays to have a reserve of power in a fighting vehicle, and to supply it with the best fuel available

5. Types of country in which cars work

There are three types of undeveloped country — the desert, the mountainous, and the bush.
Bush country is a specialized form of defile. The desert (grazing areas) is ideal car country. The real sandy desert is impassable to all cars, even a tracked vehicle will not catch a camel in this country.

    The desert may be:–

        Type A — Rolling and covered with stones or light grass. It is suitable for wheeled vehicles, except in patches. After rain the country turns into mud that makes progress difficult.
        Type B — The real sandy desert, which is not suitable for operations by car.
        The mountainous country may be: –

Type C — Mountainous country, sometimes wooded, through which there are roads to towns. Suitable for cars in peace, but in war-time the roads are easily stopped.

Type D — Roadless country. The tracks to villages can be made suitable for cars only with a great deal of expenditure of labour. When the roads are made the country becomes type C.

6. Type of control needed in various types of country

Type A. Tent-dwellers, whose national pastime is raiding, live in the desert. Raids composed of individuals endeavour to loot camels; but the raid may be composed of several thousand and although its primary objective would be loot, if things went well it would endeavour to acquire territory. The raiders are at present mounted on camels (the sheikhs on mares); but there are signs that raids carried in cars will become increasingly frequent.

The speed of these raids on the last day would be anything up to 120 miles in 24 hours, or 8 to 10 mph for a long period. If the raiders are carried in cars the speed would average 30 mph.

The control necessary would be:-

    a. To prevent the raid arriving at its destination.

    b. If it arrived, to recapture loot.

    c. In both events, to arrest the sheikhs.

    d. In certain eventualities, to inflict casualties.

Type B. As for Type A. But a raid over a sandy desert could not be carried in the type of cars available to raiders in an undeveloped country. It would, of necessity, be carried on camels.

Type C. The mountainous country, although undeveloped, is probably settled; and the trouble to be expected would be more of the nature of 'civil unrest' rather than long-distance raiding. A town or group of towns might resist authority, might refuse to pay taxes, might start an internal or external religious strife, or might raid the local markets.

Individuals would move neither far nor fast. They would be mounted on horses, and would therefore be largely dependent on water. They are unlikely to use cars in any numbers. If the trouble spread, it would be by 'waves of unrest' rather than by movement of individuals, and the surrounding towns would become affected.

The control necessary would be:-

    a. To arrest the ring-leaders.

    b. To protect life and property.

    c. In certain eventualities, it might be necessary to destroy crops or even the town itself.

Type D. The control of mountainous country where there are no roads can be by Air alone, or possibly by Air and Cavalry, and is therefore not discussed. If roads are constructed the country becomes Type C.

Bush country can be considered as a defile in any of the above types of country.

7. Composition of the military force

Type A and B

The Wahabi raid on Ziza in 1924 is such an excellent example of how things should, and also should not, be done that it must be described in detail.

The Wahabis crossed the Frontier where it is less than one day's march from Amman, their objective. They were about 3000 strong; and they passed the frontier post of Kaf (80 miles east of Amman) unseen and unreported. The Kaf ration party of ten men was met in the desert and completely destroyed. The raid arrived at Ziza and attacked the nearest villages at [unknown word] The villagers and local Bedouin made some feeble resistance.

At Amman there was an establishment of 4 aeroplanes and 4 armoureds, with a reserve of 8 aeroplanes 45 minutes away. Ziza is 45 minutes by car and 12 minutes by air from Amman.

At first Amman did not believe the rumours, but after a delay of some hours, whilst the raiders burnt, killed and looted, the air and cars came into action. Two difficulties immediately became apparent –

neither the air nor the cars could differentiate between the attackers and the attacked; and the cars, not knowing the short way over the Hejas railway, lost a lot of time.

By pure good judgement on the part of the Political Officer the largest party of the raiders was bombed and shot up. Here the air did excellent work, and it was followed by similar good work by the armoureds. They were brought into action by the air, and they stood off and made casualties without themselves being damaged. The last air reconnaissance of the day flew too low with the result that both pilots were wounded and touch was lost. The cars ran out of ammunition, with no means of refilling.

The military forces made to prisoners and recovered no loot. The raiders moved over 100 miles during the night after the engagement. The ground suited everybody, if anything being in favour of the defence forces.

The casualties are illumination and are (from memory):–

The air obtained by bombs and machine guns 100 casualties, ie 1 casualty per machine on establishment of squadron per hour. They were sufficiently damaged to lose touch.

The local arabs obtained 150 casualties, at what expense is unknown.

The cars obtained 300 casualties – ie 10 per armoured on establishment per hour. They were practically untouched. They would have made more casualties if they had been able to refill.

The lessons are only those already quoted, but they give the requirements, and therefore the composition, of the military force and the air, which is:-

> A. Independent air force.
> B. Air for co-operation.
> C. Armoureds.
> D. Motin.
> E. Tenders.
> F. Commander's car or aeroplane.

8. Role of units of military force
A. Independent Air Force

In peace	To learn the country
	To map
	To photograph
	To keep in touch with movement in the desert
	To carry out routine reconnaissance
In war	To obtain casualties (by bombing and not by machine-gun fire)
	To deny wells and strong points to the enemy till the cars arrive

B. Air for co-operation

In peace	To pick out tracks for armoureds
	To keep car patrols supplied
	To evacuate sick from car patrols
In war	In addition:–
	To photograph
	To bring cars into touch with the enemy
	To supply ammunition, if necessary, during an action

C. Armoureds

In peace	To mark out roads
	To map
	To show themselves to the local inhabitants
In war	To obtain casualties
	To break up formations of the enemy

D. Motin

In peace	To work with the armoureds

In war   To make prisoners
               To arrest sheikhs and head-men
               To recover loot
               To guard camps, etc
               To perform any duties requiring individual attention

E. Tenders

In peace   To carry the necessary stores to keep the cars in the desert

In war   In addition:–
               By long-range fire to help in preventing the enemy from scattering
               To carry the ammunition reserve
               To provide bunks for the wounded in the absence of an ambulance

9. How the duties are performed

A. Independent Air Force

a. The Routine Reconnaissance must collect information about the country and its inhabitants. An Interpreter should always be carried and frequent landings made. The Air should show itself as much as possible so that when it accompanies a Military Force the enemy will not feel disturbed till the Military Force arrives.

b. A Triangulation Network must be constructed, because in undeveloped country there are no maps, and maps are essential for successful operations. The triangulation is made by sighting on distant points with the aldis, using Bomb Sights to get verticality, and reading compass to obtain the required angle. A mean of several bearings gives reasonably accurate results.

c. The Photography required to be done by every Pilot during his monthly training should be organised on a large scale. With good organisation a large number of pin-points and strips will be taken in the ordinary course of duty. Certain photographs are essential for the use of the armoureds.

B. Air for co-operation

Cars can navigate over the desert to within a few miles of a position; but they can be brought in for the last short distance by the Air when time is of importance.

Co-operation machines supply small spares to the cars, many have to supply ammunition; and can carry casualties on the return journeys.

In war the first duty is to keep the cars informed of the location or lay-out of the objective. Dropped photographs are essential for this duty, and can be provided by an adaptation of the 'photo-while-you-wait' camera.

Co-operation aircraft must see all cars through defiles as only they can prevent ambushes. It is only these aircraft that can properly harass an ambush that has been pushed out into the open by the Motin.

C. Armoureds

a. The Routine Reconnaissance must be made sufficiently frequently to ensure that the cars can get anywhere they wish at any time. An interpreter should be carried. The local inhabitants must be imbued with the knowledge that they can be got at whenever it is desired.

b. Speed is essential for cars. At present a four-wheeled car convoy travels over new desert at 8 mph but with Morris six-wheelers the speed goes up to 12 mph (This average is more than counterbalanced by the slow speed – 5 mph – of the Morris six-wheelers over slightly soft ground or up the slightest slope). Under these conditions cars are unlikely to catch a raid which has a start of even 25 miles (see para 6, second sub-para).

c. Roads are the solution to the problem. The cars make road traverses acting on information supplied by the air. Rounds of bearings are taken at every halt. The instruments required are –

compass, milometer, watch and aneroid. If, in addition, sun or star observations are taken with the bubble sextant (with Bygrave slide-rule) surprisingly accurate results are obtained.

d. The Making of Roads is carried out by the leading car which tows old anti-skid chains arranged as shown in Fig A. The armoureds coming behind level the track so made, and the winter rains transform the surface into hard mud; so that in the second year the tracks can be traversed at about 30 mph. At this speed, unless there is a frontier, the cars can give the raiders a start of 100 miles and catch them in time to fight an action on the evening of the second day.

e. The construction of Milestones is an important part of road-making, as only by their means can rendezvous be arranged in the open country. Mounds are constructed on both sides of the road, if possible on a rise, and arms are dug to indicate distance. One arm for 10, two for 20, etc according to a code. Information is dug into the ground. If arrows are constructed the centre should be covered with coal (dust) and raised. The centre should be surrounded with a whitened area bounded by a raised edge. This construction makes the best use of shadows.

In a Moslem country an iron signpost carrying the 'La illahah Allah etc' and the distance to Mecca would survive for some time, if the information required to be conveyed were printed in very small letters.

For the use of air co-operation the cars should make cairns on hill tops and cover then with broken glass to reflect the sun.

f. The Importance of Roads is very great. Not only do they enable cars to get where they are required, but they encourage the local inhabitants to buy cars. A tent-dweller usually has little of value except his animals; but once the sheikhs can be encouraged to buy cars, they immediately possess something of value that could be confiscated when they cause trouble. The confiscation of the cars would also interfere with their activities.

g. Direction Finding W/T is of great use to cars when acting alone. Cross-bearings are a useful check on the other rough methods of triangulation and are accurate to within 2 or 3 degrees. If co-operation aircraft are sent for, D/F brings them to the cars with the least delay.

h. The Making of Casualties, or getting into such a position that the enemy knows that casualties can be made is the most important part of the wartime duties of an armoured. The actual killing power of bombs is very small; and if it is possible for the air to bring the cars into action, the cars should be left to make the casualties. The aircraft are so valuable that they must not be risked for duties that can be better performed by other means. In order to support the 'Moral Effect' it is necessary to teach the inhabitants of an undeveloped country a very sharp lesson about once every generation.

The making of casualties is only a means to an end. The object of car action should be to round up the whole of the enemy. The sheikhs must be arrested and the remainder disarmed. The physical part of these duties must be done by the Motin, but they can only act when under the guns of the armoureds and when they have broken the enemy morale. Although the armoureds must be prepared when necessary to go right in amongst the enemy, this action should not be taken till the enemy morale has been broken, or they are likely to be rushed and captured by weight of numbers.

D. Motin [motorised infantry]

The armoureds have such a small and highly skilled (and trained) crew, that they must never be taken for a duty away from their cars. All individual work must be done by the motin, and for this reason the motin can advantageously be from local recruitments.

The motin should always accompany the armoureds, and they should perform the manual labour of making roads and preparing crossings when the column is in touch with the enemy. They do the actual work of searching tents and houses, and making arrests, under the guns of the armoureds.

The first duty of the motin is fighting an infantry and care must be taken that 'working parties' do not interfere with their training. Large and permanent work should be undertaken as a works service.

The motin should be responsible for the perimeter defence of any camp or leaguer; thus freeing up the armoureds for attack, counter-attack, or for following up a retreat.

When the armoureds go into action, the motin should come behind and round up stragglers, they should hold suitable defiles to delay the enemy for the armoureds, they recapture loot and convey it to the rendezvous. If the ground is favourable they can hold a selected position whilst the armoureds drive the enemy onto it to get caught between two fires.

E. Tenders

The duty of the tenders is to be there when wanted. In suitable country they accompany their fighting vehicles and, standing off at a safe distance, help their fighting vehicles with their long-range fire. They are so very valuable and vulnerable that they must not run into danger.

If the country is at all close the tenders can remain at a rendezvous; but they must allow themselves liberty of movement, and should use their mobility when danger threatens. If they have to move, the air can re-establish communication. The tenders should never 'form leaguer' unless they are with their fighting vehicles.

F. Commander's Car or Aeroplane

It is axiomatic that the best Commander is he who, other things being equal, has the best knowledge of the country and its inhabitants. This knowledge is important, can only be obtained by regular flying and by regularly accompanying car patrols, and should be obtained in peace time.

If the commander could fly in a modernised single-seater pusher, and have available a Radio-Telephone and automatic quick-developing camera, there is not the least doubt but that he should command from the air.

At present none of the essentials are available, so that the Commander must command from the ground. He must rely on his co-operation aircraft for information, and on good doctrine and training once he has launched his attack.

There is little object in putting the Commander into an armoured, as his chief duty after the attack is launched will be to collect information and act as a Reporting Centre. The W/T tender and Commander's car should travel close together.

After the attack is launched, dust will largely prevent any collective signal being made. Even on the 'line of march' it may become necessary to issue orders to individual cars as they pass.

On account (chiefly) of dust and inefficient means of intercommunication Type-Tactics for all occasions must be few and extremely simple.

10. Composition of the Military Force (See also Section 7)

Type C.

As for Types A and B country the requirements will be given in the form of an illustration, which will be the affair at Sueille (near Amman) a few years ago.

Near Sueille trouble was reported, but nobody expected nor wanted war. The reconnaissance aeroplanes failed to clear the situation and cars, unescorted, were sent to investigate.

Without orders Nº 2 Car killed some armed men, and this caused an enemy to open fire on the cars and make an attempt to block the road behind them. The villagers of Sueille came to the aid of the cars who, being unable to distinguish friend from foe, opened an indiscriminate fire on everybody within range. Some of the enemy came so close to the armoureds that the crews had to use their pistols, but they did not press home the attack.

The armoureds were all very badly damaged, one arrived back on its brake-drums as its wheels were shot off. The damage was done whilst the cars were attempting to turn on a road edged with stone walls.

The composition of the military force is as before with the addition of:-

G. Light Tanks (such as Carden-Lloyd).

11. Role of Units of Military Force (See also Section 8)

G. Light Tanks

In peace – there is little useful work these cars can perform in peace time. They should carry out such reconnaissances as are in their endurance.

In war – in enclosed country, to keep the rear of the column free from obstruction immediately in it rear.

In villages, to clear roads and barricades. To form points on which dismounted motin can form.

In both events, where the ground permits, to attack the flank of a position.

12. How the duties are performed (see also Section 9)

G. Light Tanks

Speed is so important, that it may sometimes be better to appear in the place of trouble without waiting for the light tanks. If it is not possible to carry the tanks on a six-wheeled float lorry, they should always accompany the column in enclosed country, or hostile villages.

The clearance of armoureds is so little that two or three large stones will stop a road, and it is the duty of the tanks to cross such a barrier and clear it, or hold a position on the enemy side, whilst the motin clear it.

In defiles or bush country the armoureds will not be able to leave the tracks. Under such conditions, the tanks, where possible, leave the tracks and attack the flank of the enemy.

13. The Tactical Unit

Working as suggested above, the country will be covered with a network of roads radiating from possible advanced bases and interconnecting them. Under these conditions the carrying capacity of a 30-cwt tender fits very well a fighting unit whose endurance is 300 miles or 3 days. That is, normally – a day out, a day's battle, and a day home.

With good intelligence, and especially if there are a few aeroplanes for carrying stores, the bases can efficiently be 200 miles apart. Each base would then control an area equivalent to the S.~E. of England from the line Weymouth–Bristol–Lincoln, supposing that the unit were based on London. In this area armoureds could appear anywhere within 24 hours.

The unit and its tactics will be based on the smallest unit that can work alone. Such a unit can be increased whilst the methods remain the same; but it may not be possible to decrease a larger unit efficiently, and when divided the methods of use may not apply.

Fighting vehicles MUST work in pairs, and it is convenient to allot one tender to each pair, so the smallest tactical unit becomes:–

1. Commander's Car
2. 'A' half-section armoureds – Two cars
3. 'B' half-section armoureds – Two cars
4. 'C' half-section motin – Two cars
5. 'D' half-section motin – Two cars
6. 'a', 'b', 'c' and 'd' tenders (one carrying wireless).
   (Light tanks only in enclosed country and villages).
7. 'E' half-section light tanks – Two cars
8. 'F' half-section light tanks – Two cars

For administrative and repair purposes homogenous squadrons are formed, consisting of a Headquarters and three sections. Allowing for cars under repair and leave of personnel, two sections are always serviceable and ready for action. Squadrons should live and train at their 'war stations'. If it is necessary to find detachments, a proper system of reliefs must be arranged, but a detachment must be a tactical unit permanently ready to move out.

The approximate strength of squadrons would be:–

Armoured Squadron

In fighting vehicles – 5 men per car and 20 to replace casualties	80 men
In tenders	18 men
HQ (say)	25 men
Total armoured squadron	123 men

Motin Squadron

In fighting vehicles 12 men per car and 48 to replace casualties	192 men
In tenders	18 men
HQ (say)	25 men
Total motin squadron	235 men

The motin squadron appears strong because both in peace and war it must protect the base or camp. If the whole number of vehicles went on an expedition, there would remain behind till reserves arrived – 45 men from armoured squadron (including HQ) and 73 men from the motin squadron (including HQ) – a total of 118. But of these 50 would be available for routine camp protective duties.

Light Tank Squadron
The strength of the light tank squadron would be approximate to that of the armoured squadron. If working at maximum distance from the base, the light tanks would also require their tenders.

14. Supplies

When trouble threatens, speed may prevent that trouble [developing]. Therefore some supply vehicles must always be available. The fighting unit (less tanks) contains four tenders, therefore the supply column should consist of eight tenders. These supply tenders can refill the unit every two days, when the unit is two days away from its base. Usually the smallest unit can deal with an emergency, therefore eight supply tenders is the correct proportion for one squadron armoureds and one squadron motin.

In almost every country where fighting vehicles would operate, civilian motorcars are available. These can be impressed if the operations are likely to be protracted.

In open country a civilian transport convoy composed of Nash, Graham or similar chassis shakes itself to pieces in about four months. Ford vans last an even shorter period.

15. Reserves

A base or camp should reckon on the supply of reserves in three days. This would be the time taken to forward trained personnel by air, or to call up the reserve of local recruits.

If an action is fought on the first or second day of operation, the reserve would be required to replace casualties before the fourth. The actual casualties would be replaced by the spare men left, at first, to guard the camp and these men would be replaced by the reserve flown or called up, and which would not at that moment be sufficiently trained to take their place in the firing line.

16. Casualties

Ambulances should accompany the supply convoys, and would therefore evacuate casualties every two days. Lightly wounded men should be accommodated in the tenders till the ambulances arrived. Seriously wounded men must be flown back to the base or to hospital. This duty would be carried out by the co-operation aeroplanes who would leave behind with the fighting unit, if necessary, their observers.

17. Vehicles in reserve

Under ordinary routine two, out of the three, sections of each unit should be immediately available for service. If the emergency is serious, all the vehicles will be required; and therefore a number of vehicles of each type must be kept in the 'Immediate' reserve. This would allow the fighting vehicles to move out complete, and will provide work for the Headquarter mechanics and surplus men left behind at the base.

The correct proportion would be two reserve fighting vehicles per squadron, and five tenders for the twenty tenders that might be in use (i.e. 6 in each squadron and 8 with supplies).

18. Type-Tactics

The majority of troubles in an undeveloped country can be dealt with by the smallest tactical unit. The principles that apply to the smaller unit will apply to the larger forces, but it is not at all necessary that methods suitable for the larger forces will apply to the smaller.

The tactics of the small unit can only be considered, and only the tactics specially applicable to an undeveloped country. The tactics suitable to a great war are already laid down in the manuals.

The situations shown in the diagrams are as though the column had run into an ambush. If a manoeuvre is suitable in an emergency, it is even more suitable when the manoeuvre is employed at leisure in a similar situation.

N° 1 The Line of March
The order of march is:–

> Aeroplanes
> Commander's car
> 'A' half-section armoureds
> 'a' tender (carrying W/T)
> 'C' half-section motin
> 'D' half-section motin
> 'b', 'c' and 'd' tenders
> 'B' half-section armoureds
> Light tanks if employed

The co-operation aircraft fly in front, partly to show the way, and partly to prevent an ambush.

The Commander leads the way. Both his car and 'A1' armoured are keeping a roadbook of the route. If there is room, in this car travel the Political Officer, Interpreter and a Junior Staff Officer.

So long as the Commander has or can have a knowledge of the country, he need not travel by air, but the Auto-gyro has great possibilities as a conveyance for the Commander.

'a' tender is placed well up, partly to keep the W/T near the Commander and partly to keep 'A' half-section as complete as possible.

The motin travel in the centre, although for tactical purposes it would be better for them to be behind the tenders. If too far behind, they get too much dust.

The armoureds are placed behind to protect the rear; and as vehicles in rear close up onto a damaged vehicle, such a vehicle always has protection.

The whole vehicles run at 'dust-distance', which may be 100 yards up to about 400 yards. If a single vehicle is attacked, those in rear can leave the track and take the enemy in the flank.

The column proceeds at the pace of the last vehicle. A 'breakdown' is signalled to the Commander and the vehicles in rear close up. The vehicles in front halt. A signal is made if the tender carrying the fitter and breakdown-kit is required – 'b' and 'c' tenders should each carry a fitter and breakdown-kit.

Nᵒ 2 To attack a party of raiders

The Object of the attack is to round up the whole of the raid. The armoureds leave the 'line of march' and go to the flank and in front of the raiders. Their respective tenders follow them and, keeping at a safe distance, help to keep the enemy from scattering with their long range fire. Armoured and tenders advance by bounds, or their fire is ineffective.

The co-operation aircraft keep the Commander informed by means of wireless, dropped photographs and messages. They may bomb, but should not fly sufficiently low to be damaged by rifle fire from the ground.

The Commander travels near the W/T tender after the attack is launched. These two vehicles form the nucleus of the rendezvous.

It will be practically impossible for the Commander to recall his vehicles once the attack is launched, partly because of the lie of the ground and partly because of dust. Orders for rendezvous should therefore be issued before the engagement. The rendezvous can be the Commander's position, when the scattered vehicles may have to be collected by the ait; or it may be at one of the marks on the roads, a mark well forward being selected.

The motin, complete half-sections, follow the raiders, make prisoners ad recapture loot. In special circumstances they may be sent ahead to hold a defile till the armoureds arrive. Should they be heavily outnumbered and sustain many damaged vehicles they must be prepared to 'form leaguer' and dig themselves in.

Nᵒ 3 To arrest a sheikh in his tent

The Object of the attacking force is to arrest the sheikh without any shooting. They must therefore arrive at the encampment at dawn, having spent the night at such a distance that the dogs in the encampment will not hear them and become restless.

The Commander is supplied with a photograph of the encampment taken the evening previously by the routine reconnaissance, and this is also circulated to all car commanders.

No riflemen must be allowed to leave the tents, CO 'C' half-section motin spread out in rear of the tents with their dismounted machine guns. The armoureds (and tenders) can look after the front of the tents. 'D' half-section motin accompany the Commander and Political Officer to the sheikh's tent and do the physical part of the arresting.

In order to prevent trouble, the attacking force must appear in overwhelming numbers. When this happens not one of the enemy dare even carry a rifle.

Nᵒ 4 To form Leaguer

In an undeveloped country an inefficient encampment invites attack, especially when there is a reasonable chance of stealing rifles.

The Object of the leaguer is to provide an arrangement which will protect the defenders, bring the greatest possible fire-power to bear in each direction, will allow a counter-attack to be launched, and which can be constructed in the minimum time.

Leaguer should be formed each evening; and must be formed when within touch of the enemy should they be in overwhelming numbers, and if several vehicles become damaged. The leaguer shown in the diagram takes about ten minutes to complete.

The Commander halts, and when he orders the leaguer to be formed, the leading half-section armoureds form line and halt in front of him, thus making the two corners of the square. Each armoured supplies a man to stand where the rear half-sect[ion] will halt.

As the other vehicles arrive they drive into the square, tenders to starboard of their No 1 fighting vehicle, and moticars to port of the correspondingly numbered armoured. Finally the rear armoureds back into the two vacant corners. There is no delay. Armoureds face outwards so as to be ready for the counter-attack; whilst unarmoured vehicles face inwards so as to protect their engines.

As soon as the vehicles are in position every unarmoured vehicle dismounts its gun. The pair of guns from the moticars are dug in on each side, whilst each tender digs in its gun between it and the nearest armoured.

The garrison, when lying down, is safe, being protected by the breastworks and the wheels and chassis of the cars.

If waterproof sheets are carried, and slung between vehicles, this leaguer forms a series of arches that give the garrison shelter from the rain and coolth[cools them?] under a hot sun.

Should the leaguer be required to remain in the desert for any length of time, it should be surrounded (except at the corners) by an anti-camel ditch.

When ordered to form line of march, the armoureds move out, and the other cars follow through the gaps left by the armoureds.

If aeroplanes are working actually with the unit, the leaguer can be formed on the aerodrome; and the aeroplanes can be hangared inside the square. A suitable field hangar can quickly be constructed by digging a hole with a ramp running into it, 'T'-shaped in plan. When the undercarriage is sunk so that the lower plane is nearly level with the ground, the tail remains on the ramp. The planes then have negative incidence and the aeroplane will not blow away; and the engine is so low that it can easily be inspected without a ladder.

Nº 5 To negotiate a defile (the outlet of which has been blocked)

The Object of this manoeuvre is to dislodge the enemy riflemen. Whilst on the move all vehicles can use their guns but as soon as an unarmoured vehicle has to halt, its gun must be dismounted and brought into action from the nearest cover.

In a defile the column can run through, and if necessary return to the attack. If the column is unable to reach the turning place, the motin must dismount under cover of the guns of the armoureds. The armoureds and guns from the tenders hold the enemy, whilst the motin execute a flank attack.

If light tanks are with the column they prevent the road being stopped in the rear; and if the terrain is suitable they can leave the road and attack the enemy in flank and rear.

The co-operation aircraft keep the commander informed if possible, and attack the enemy transport, preferably by bombing. They attack the enemy when he has been pushed out into the open.

Nº 6 To deal with an attack in forest country

This is a special case of Nº 5 and the action is the same. The air may not be able to see very much, but they do what they are able to inform the Commander.

The leading armoureds halt in such a position that motin can dismount unmolested.

The armoureds will not see [?] but they act as a pivot of manoeuvre

The dismounted motin work up on each side of the road and if possible surround the enemy. The light tanks follow up the motin, if the terrain is suitable, and protect their flank.

In bush country the Commander might well travel behind the leading armoureds, because attacks are usually made where the road bends, and the leading car bears the brunt.

Nº 7 To enter a hostile village.

There are two methods of dealing with a village (both shown in the same diagram).

If the villagers are in the gardens, the main body of the column halts outside. A strong force advances up the road and keeps pace with the motin who work through the gardens and houses on either side of the armoured vehicles.

If there is a market square in the village, the column can occupy this square. The armoureds control the roads, whilst the motin occupy the houses, as is necessary, working from the inside outwards.

In village fighting the co-operation aircraft have a very important duty in keeping the Commander informed of the movement of the villagers.

Nº 8 To protect a damaged vehicle.

a. Armoured

Every armoured carries a pick and shovel in a quick-release on the starboard side. When one armoured becomes damaged, the other armoured of the pair drives up alongside, starboard to starboard and facing in the opposite direction.

The Lewis gun of each armoured is dug in at its starboard rear. The pair thus form a small fort. The Lewis gunners are protected by the breastwork and the car wheels. The tool box is carried on the starboard side of the engine, so that tools can be got at from under cover. If the damage is on the inside of the formation, it can be repaired under cover.

b. Tender

If the damaged vehicle is a tender, its fighting pair must align themselves alongside, starboard sides towards the tender and facing in opposite directions.

If the fighting pair are armoureds, they dig in their guns at the starboard rear. The tender gunner digs his gun in near his seat in the tender, and the tender driver uses his rifle from the unoccupied gap. The essential is to get the occupants of an unarmoured vehicle under cover, and to bring as great a fire power to bear as possible.

If the fighting pair are moticars, they take corresponding action.

c. Moticar

If a moticar is damaged, the other moticar of the pair drives up alongside as described above. The motin must dismount as soon as possible, and dig themselves in. The four guns available should be dug in between the vehicles and on their outer sides, thus forming a square.

If under fire, the cars cannot be repaired till armoureds arrive and provide the necessary cover.

Nº 9 To choose a camp site

The force may camp on a hill or a rise. If it does so it has a good view by day (but not at night). Its field of fire may be good. A rush will slow up before arriving at the cars. The camp will be visible for great distances, so that the enemy can avoid the camp or investigate as they wish.

The camp may be made, and preferably in a slight hollow following the arab custom.

It is hidden and its field of fire will be better than before. Its view will be limited, except at night, when raiders will be seen against the sky-line.

A camp should not be made actually on a well, because camels at night are noiseless; and if they stumble on a camp their owners may shoot purely on account of fright.

19. Intelligence

No scheme for a military force can be effective unless the intelligence is good. Not only must there be Reporting Centres but there must also be Officers – the SSO– who go and collect the information.

These Officers should be provided with a special body fitted to the standard chassis. It need not be elaborate, but should be in the nature of a caravan body. The Officers must be provided with a place where they can keep their books of reference, instruments, etc, and reasonably good accommodation where they can construct their maps and make out their reports.

The body should include accommodation for the Driver, Servant (both may be local recruitments) and Wireless Operator. Proper protection from the weather keeps a man fit, and therefore is a saving over a period.

20. Reporting Centre

The local informants should be provided with a place where they can report. This should NOT be a small isolated post. Such a post is a positive danger. Anybody wishing to report should do so at some existing village or, in a nomad country, to some sheikh's tent. The routine reconnaissance by air or by cars should collect the information and signal it to Headquarters. It might may to subsidise the Sheikh or Headman who would themselves forward urgent and important information.

21. Posts

In an undeveloped country the military force must have somewhere from which to operate. This should not be a small isolated post which wastes a small garrison, is liable to be rushed without warning, and which an enemy can circumvent. When trouble threatens such a post must be evacuated, and this is the very time the post becomes most important.

The pivot of manoeuvre must be a proper advanced base located, if possible, near a local village where the local recruitments can buy their necessaries and food.

Where the possible enemy has no artillery the post should be constructed on the lines of the old square Roman fort. It had two storeys opening inwards onto a courtyard. The lower rooms housed the cars, animals and stores, whilst the upper rooms housed the men. The upper rooms were loopholed. The Arabs improved the design by building out a small fire post at the top of each corner. There was internal water supply. Only one large gate allowed entrance.

If the possible enemy has artillery, the base should be low bungalow-type houses, which are bullet proof and which line the perimeter. An earthwork and wire defence is constructed round the perimeter. Wireless, power and water are arranged out of sight within the area.

The defence should include efficient fighting outside the wire. Space should be left for aeroplanes inside, or within the defences of the area.

The minimum garrison should be one squadron armoureds, one squadron motin, with the services of one flight aeroplanes. Complete units are necessary to give efficient training.

22. Type of Vehicle

Every Service Journal contains articles on the type of vehicle required in a Great War, and little of interest can be added by one who is not in touch with experiment. The general requirements are well known and are – provision of a continuous track combined with high speed and low engine power, heavy armour combined with small weight per square inch of track bearing surface, and high command for guns to clear obstacles combined with low overall height to enable car to take cover easily – all conflicting.

The following remarks will be confined to immediate requirements, especially where they differ from Army requirements.

Armour should be non-magnetic so that compasses can be used on all cars. Some protection should be given to all drivers and the moticar should have an armoured belt for the protection of the motin.

The Body of an Armoured consists of a turret and an unarmoured portion for carrying stores, kits, etc. The turret should be placed more forward so as to improve visibility; and for balance the engine should be in the middle of the chassis (see also Wheels below).

An armoured may have to remain under fire for some considerable period, so that under armour there should be – First aid outfit, two pints of water for each of crew, one day's iron rations, emergency oil and petrol tanks, at least 2,000 rounds of ammunition for each turret gun.

The Aldis lamp, with back armoured, should permanently replace the searchlight on the turret, and should be operated from inside the turret.

Receptacles should be constructed for all stores, kits, etc.

For the sake of efficiency, quickly released duralumin bunks should be provided (as in an aeroplane) to keep men away from poisons, such as – snakes, scorpions, bugs, mosquitoes, poison vegetables, and also mud.

The Body of all Tenders should be of the same design for easy replacement. Although not necessarily always carried they should be fitted for carrying wireless, petrol and water. The tanks should be approximately 77-gallons capacity, capable of being filled and emptied from outside the body, and carrying a visible contents indicator. The wireless cupboard, its front opening downwards into the front seat of the tender to form a desk for operator is fitted above the tanks and is designed to take the instruments. One mast is fitted to the tender and a second jointed mast is carried.

The cab, weatherproof and permanent, provides accommodation for the driver and gunner by the addition of a shelf (duralumin bunk). The top carries a Lewis gun in a Scarffe mounting, having an all-round arc of fire. The ring is immediately above the gunner's seat and the ammunition is carried above the driver's seat.

Extra personnel are accommodated under the tilt.

The Body of the Moticar should be similar to that already designed by the Morris works, with the addition of a Scarffe ring to carry a light machine gun on a lattice framework in the centre of the body, and giving an all-round arc of fire.

The car should carry, in addition to the driver, ten fighting men (including one signaller) and two guns. As in the armoureds, a frame should be fitted on which the men can sleep.

The Body of the Commander's car, of the type now fitted to the Morris six-wheel tourer, is suitable; but sleeping accommodation under the hood should be arranged.

The Chassis of all vehicles in a column should be of the same design, because a column travels at the speed of the slowest vehicle at every moment. One design eases the provision of spares. The engine MUST BE sufficiently powerful to enable the column to move up a hill on a made road faster than a horse can travel. The Morris six-wheelers climb hills at 5 mph and a single horseman could shoot through their radiators and get away without being caught.

The clearance should be as high as possible, and a streamlined undershield, to prevent dust, should be fitted.

A 30-cwt vehicle is more efficient than a 3-ton lorry. Solid tyres cut up tracks, and a heavy vehicle cannot be man-handled out of a difficult place.

The Dust in a dry country causes great inefficiency. Air intake should be efficiently filtered, and all containers should be dust proof. Crookes spectacles with wire gauze sides should be an issue to the men.

Special Instruments required are the compass, aneroid and mile-measurer. An aeroplane compass is suitable, but an aeroplane compass mounting shakes to pieces when fitted to a car. A surveyor's aneroid may show an error of 500 feet if carried in the driver's seat of a car, so that a proper mounting should be found for it away from the heat of the engine. Existing mile-measurers may indicate a distance travelled across a wadi to be three times as great as the same distance travelled on a made road, on account of wheel-slip.

Jacks are in continual use for changing wheels and for lifting cars on to firm foundations. The points under which a jack is usually applied should be fitted with slides into which the top of the jack could be slipped. The jack would then hang while the foundation was being put in place. The jack should be operated by a drive or pump worked by the engine.

Light Tanks do not lend themselves to use in undeveloped country, except in the villages. If used they should be carried into action on float-tenders. The type most useful is the Carden-Lloyd tank.

Radiator water quickly boils away in a hot country. To prevent this the radiator should be steam proof, with the overflow pipe lead to a condenser (5-gallon drum). The steam condenses in the drum, and almost as soon as the engine is stopped all the water is sucked back into the radiator.

Tools should be carried in a chest of drawers fitted on the outside of the car near the engine. They are then easy to check, and tools do not get left behind in the sand or mud. The tools required for 'immediate action', and corresponding spares, for rectifying such faults as punctures, sticky magneto arms, etc, must be immediately available.

Tracks will be required by every car. In sandy country the present type Morris track takes about half-an-hour to fit. The draw screw that brings the ends of the track together should be worked off a drive from the engine to speed up fitting.

The Turret should be mounted on roller bearings. It should, if possible, contain a wireless telephone. The turret gun must have an efficient ammunition feed that will work even when the car is travelling at speed over rough country.

The Wheels and Drive are the parts of the car that most require immediate development. Pneumatic wheels, to stand up against punctures and shot-holes in action, must be doubled. Yet if double wheels are fitted to the front axles, the car will not steer. The tred should be the broadest part of the tyre, but straight-sided tyres particularly overcome the difficulty. Most wear is caused by tyres scraping against sharp stones. The diameter should be large. The diameter of sand cart wheels in Cairo is over six feet.

A narrow front wheel destroys the track at every corner and breaks the surface. When the front wheel sinks, travelling at speed, excessive stresses are put on the front axle; and as the turret of an armoured tends to set forward the stress will strain and may break the chassis.

The double drive of a six-wheeler should be duplicated in front, turning the vehicle into an 'eight-wheeler'. Each axle should be a driving axle, giving the car an 'eight-wheel' drive, and 'eight-wheel' steering.

Some slip or spring gear should be provided between each pair of driving wheels to take up the stress of slip in soft places.

The springs between each pair of driving wheels should be as long as possible. If short, the pair of wheels bump into the same hole, giving no differential action and causing excessive jolting.

23. Training of Officers

The Junior Officers largely hold Short Service Commissions, so that amongst the Flying Officers and Junior Flight Lieutenants there is little … knowledge of ground tactics and procedures. Service with the cars provides good opportunity to teach the junior officers these subjects, especially the command of men. Every officer should be given command of reconnaissances as often as possible.

The writer should be utilised for in-door work and work on the ranges and manoeuvre ground; whilst the summer, when trouble may be expected, should be employed in practical work in the field.

The special subjects in which a junior officer will need instruction are:–

Camping — including defence of halting places and field cooking and sanitation.

Car tactics — when he is a section commander and when he commands a column.

Driving — so as to appreciate the difficulties of the road, and to check on his men.

Flag signalling — for the purpose of supervising his men.

Ground armament — to appreciate the possibilities of both rifle and machine gun work.

Mapping and field sketching — to record where he has been and to enable reports to be written.

Navigation — so that he may lead his section across unmapped areas.

Practical work — on the road and in the field.

Workshop procedure — to enable him to appreciate the work done by his men.

Store accounting and procedures — to enable him especially to organise an advanced base and get up his spares without delay.

None of these subjects need be gone into deeply, if he is interested he will do that himself; but the junior officer must know something about all of them.

24. Training of the Crew

In order to replace casualties due to service and sickness individuals of the crew, except for specialists, should be interchangable. The specialists, whose trades are – Fitter, Wireless Operator (Mechanic), Cook, Interpreter, Armourer, Medical Airman, should also be able to use a rifle and fire a machine gun.

The special subjects in which the crew will need instruction are:–

Camp — routine and sanitation.

Car tactics — that is, formations and firing.

Care and upkeep of cars and running repairs.

Driving — how to keep exactly to a track and to surmount obstacles, sand stones, etc.

Gunnery — which includes immediate action to clear jambs.

Immediate action — drill to rectify car stoppages, such as punctures, dirty plugs, stopped filters.

Signalling — with flag and lamp and ground strips. On account of dust and mirage, semaphore is of little use.

Car commanders should also receive instruction in map reading.

All ranks should be encouraged to learn the language so as to be able to speak to local inhabitants when on reconnaissance, and to give them an interest for their spare time.

25. Training of the Unit

The year should be divided into the winter or rainy period, during which all indoor and range training should be completed; and the summer or operational period, during which the unit must be ready for service or employed on field training.

At the end of the winter and early in the operational period the whole unit must be exercised as a whole by its Commander, so as to be ready for emergency calls.

During the operational period, small columns under junior officers should be kept continually in the field. All detachments must be recalled to headquarters regularly and frequently for refitting and general 'smartening up', their place being taken by the next unit fit for duty.

Armoureds and motin should train together, and whilst in the field will require their co-operation aircraft.

Every reconnaissance should be made in accordance with some tactical idea, and should include field firing under service conditions. The targets should be recording targets and should be towed.

26. Area of Operation

Areas of operation must be clearly defined, and if possible surrounded by a car road; so that cars from the next post can cut in behind or before an enemy already being chased by a column.

Neutral areas embarrass a commander and are not understood by an undeveloped population.

Illustrative figures

Reproduced from the originals generated by the War Office in 1930 and included with the Gordon-Shephard Memorial Prize entry

LEGEND

Aeroplane.................. ⊬
Moticar.................... ✕
Motin-dismounted.......... ⅢⅢ
Commander's Car........... ⊨
Light Tank................ □
Tent .... ⊠
Line of fire.............. ▬

Armoured................ ⊶
Tender................. ⊹
W/T Tender............. ⊹
Enemy riflemen........ ⅢⅢ
Camels or Horses....... ♂
Dismounted Machine Gun..)—•
Direction of Movement.⟶

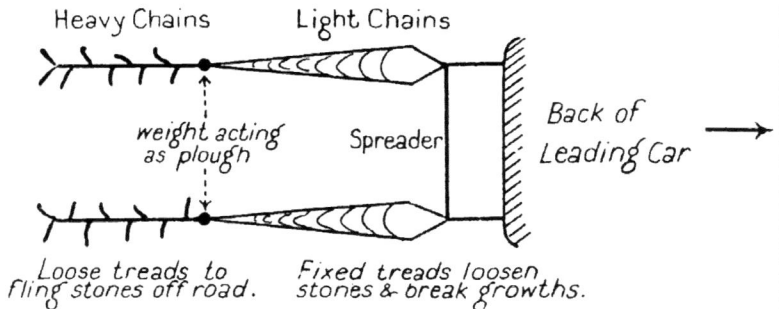

Fig. A.

Heavy Chains   Light Chains

weight acting as plough   Spreader   Back of Leading Car

Loose treads to fling stones off road.   Fixed treads loosen stones & break growths.

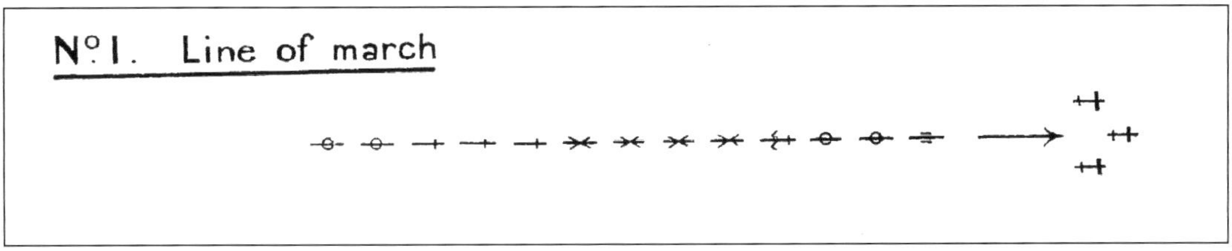

Nº 1. Line of march

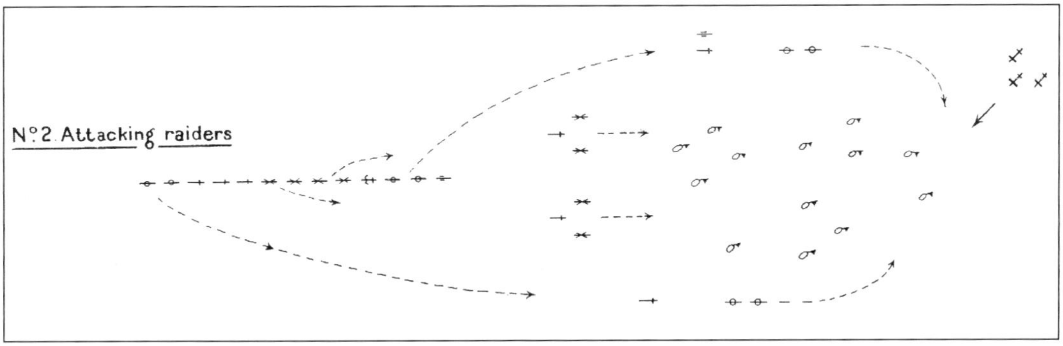

Nº 2. Attacking raiders

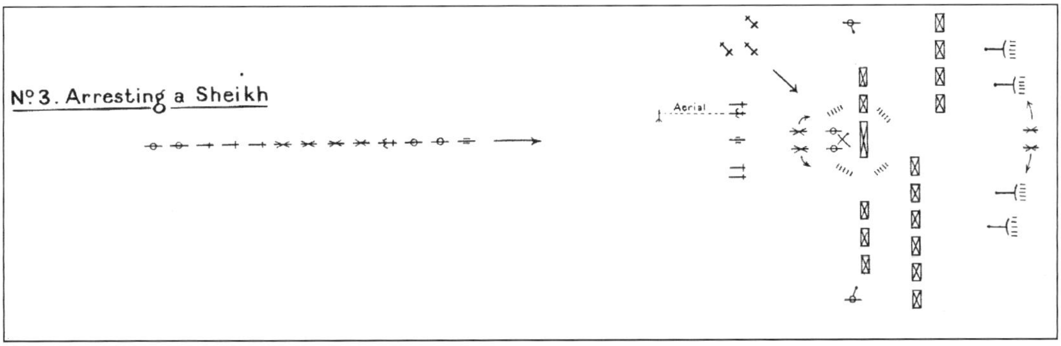

Nº 3. Arresting a Sheikh

Aerial

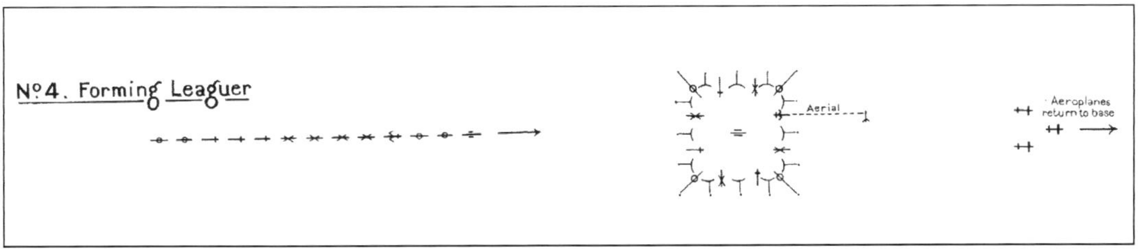

Nº 4. Forming Leaguer

Aerial

Aeroplanes
return to base

No. 5. Negotiating a defile, the outlet of which has been blocked.

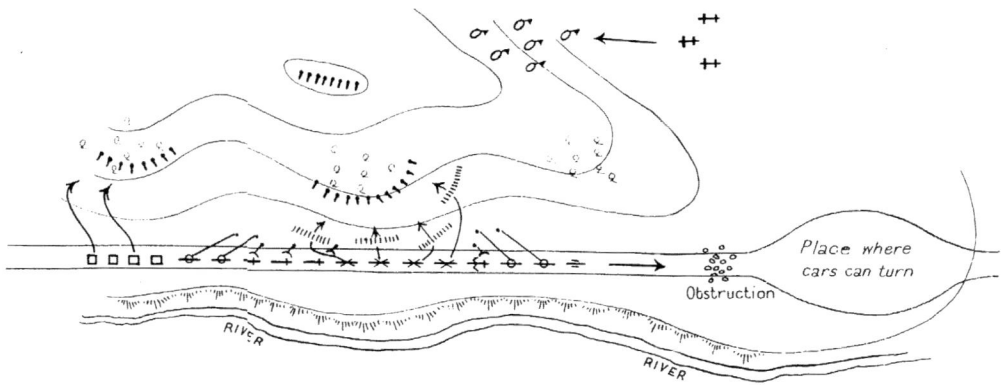

Place where
cars can turn

Obstruction

RIVER

RIVER

No. 6. Dealing with an attack in forest country

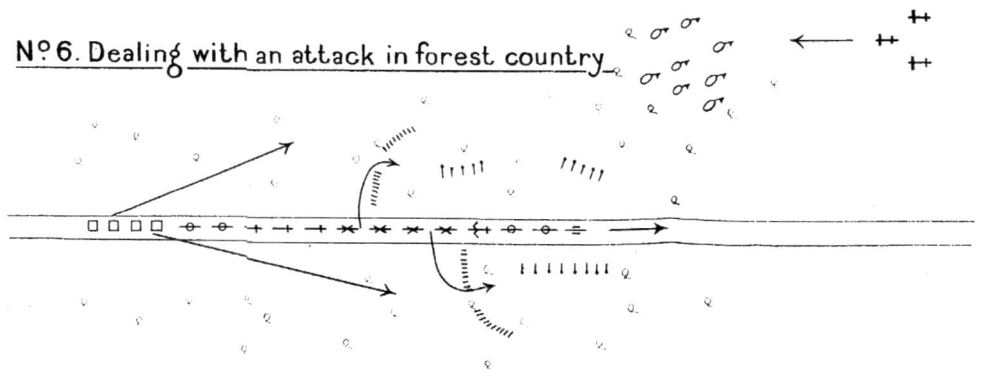

O.R. 492.

War Office 1930.

Nº 7. Entering a hostile village

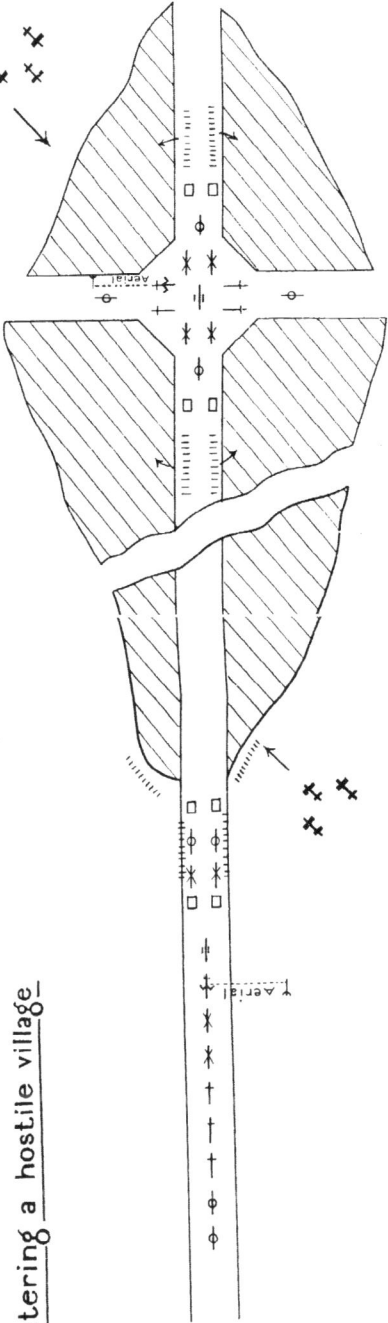

Nº 8. Protecting a damaged vehicle

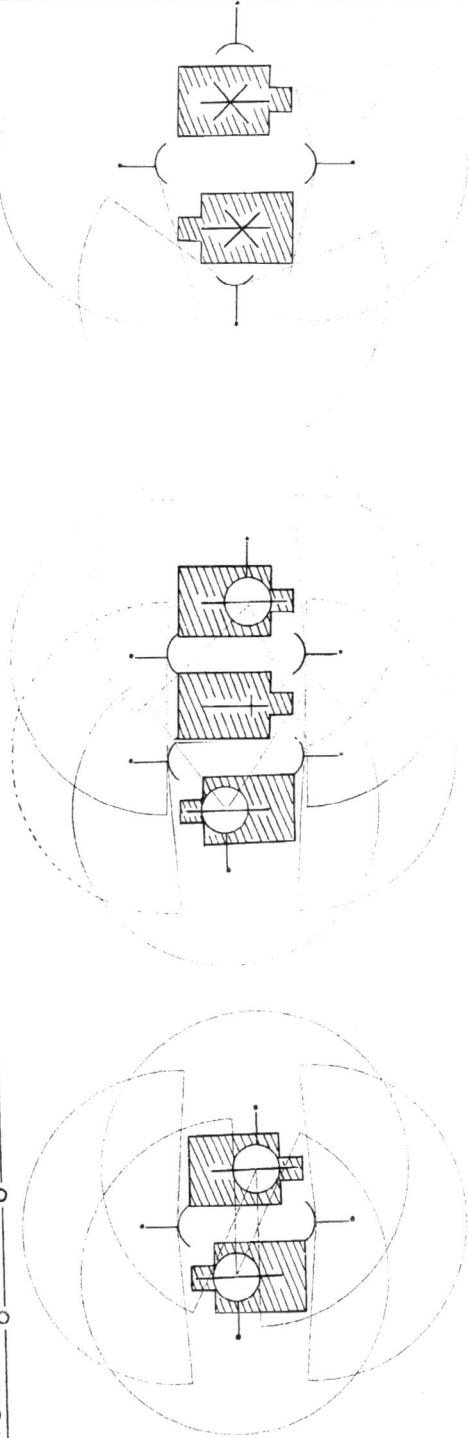

A. ARMOURED

B TENDER

C. MOTICAR

Green shews arcs of fire.

Bibliography

Published books

Arnold, HH, *Global Mission*, New York, 1949.

Bingham, Dr Hiram, *An Explorer in the Air Service*, New Haven, 1920.

Bowyer, Chaz, *For Valour, the Air VCs*, London, 1978.

                History of the RAF, London, 1977.

Brown, Timothy C, *Flying with the Larks, the early aviation pioneers of Lark Hill*, Stroud, 2013.

Bruce, JM, *De Havilland Aircraft of World War One*, London, 1991.

Collier, Basil, *Leader of the Few, the authorised biography of ACM Lord Dowding*, London, 1957.

Cottman, Evans W (with Wyatt Blassingame), *Out-island Doctor*, London, 1963.

Crawford, OGS, *Said and Done: the Foundations of Antiquity*, 1955.

Field, Henry, *North Arabian Desert Archaeological Survey, 1925–50, Papers of the Peabody Museum of Archaeology and Ethnology, Harvard University*, XAVLER, 2, Cambridge, Mass, 1960.

Franks, Norman, *Great War Fighter Aces, 1914–1916*, Barnsley, 2014.

Franks, Norman, Bailey, Frank & Duiven, Rick, *Casualties of the German Air Service, 1914–1920*, London, 1999.

George, David Lloyd, *War Memoirs of David Lloyd George*, 2 vols, London, 1938.

Gribble, Leonard R, *Heroes of the Fighting RAF*, London, 1941.

Hare, Paul R, *Britain's Forgotten Fighters of the First World War*, Stroud, 2014.

Hauser, Kitty, *Bloody Old Britain, OS Crawford and the Archaeology of Modern Life*, Granta, London, 2008.

Henshaw, Trevor, *The Sky Their Battlefield — air fighting and the complete list of Allied air casualties from enemy action in the First War*, London, 1995.

Hilton, Richard, *Nine Lives, the autobiography of an Old Soldier*, London, 1955.

Hudson, James J, *Hostile Skies, a Combat History of the American Air Service in World War I*, Syracuse University Press, 1996.

Insall, AJ, *Observer, memoirs of the RFC 1915–18*, London, 1970.

Jones, Ira T, *Tiger Squadron*, London, 1954.

Joubert, Philip, *The Third Service, the story behind the Royal Air Force*, London, 1955.

Kirkbride, Sir Alex Seath, KCMG, CVO, OBE, MC, *A Crackle of Thorns, Experiences in the Middle East*, John Murray, London, 1956.

Lewis, Wing-Commander Gwilym H, *Wings Over the Somme*, 1916–1918, second edition, Wrexham, 1994.

Lewis, Peter, *The British Fighter Since 1912*, London, 1979.

List of Graduates, the Royal Air Force College, Cranwell, February 5th, 1920 – December 18th, 1962, Cranwell, nd.

Longrigg, Stephen Hemsley, *Syria and Lebanon under French Mandate*, Oxford, 1958.

MacMillan, Norman, *Into the Blue*, London, 1929.

Miller, James F, *DH2 vs Albatros DI/II, Western Front, 1916*, Oxford, 2012.

Norris, Geoffrey, *The Royal Flying Corps a History*, London, 1965.

O'Connor, Mike, *Airfields and Airmen of the Channel Coast*, Barnsley, 2005.

Airfields and Airmen: Somme, Barnsley, 2002.
Omissi, David E, *Air Power and colonial control; the Royal Air Force 1919–1939*, Manchester, 1990.
Pershing, John J, *My Experiences in the World War*, New York, 1931.
Raleigh, W & Jones, HA, *War in the Air*, I–VI, London, 1922–37.
Rees, Lionel WB, *Fighting in the Air*, London, 1916.
Rossano, Geoffrey L (Ed), *Hero of the Angry Sky – the World War 1 diary and letters of David S Ingalls, America's first naval ace*, Ohio, 2013.
   The Price of Honour, the World War One letters of naval aviator Kenneth MacLeish, Annapolis, 1991.
Sherbrooke-Walker, Ronald, *Khaki and Blue*, London, 1952.
Spring, Elliot White, *War Birds – Diary of an Unknown Aviator*, New York, 1926.
Taylor, John WR, *CFS – Birthplace of Air Power*, London, 1987.
Tredrey, FD, *Pioneer Pilot – the great Smith Barry who taught the world how to fly*, London, 1976.
Williams, W Alister, *Against the Odds, the Life of Group Captain LWB Rees, VC*, Wrexham, 1989.
   Heart of a Dragon, the VCs of Wales and the Welsh Regiments, 1914–82, Wrexham, 2008.
Winter, Denis, *The First of the Few, Fighter Pilots of the First World War*, London, 1982.
Wood, Eric, *Thrilling Deeds of British Airmen*, London, 1917.
Wortman, Marc, *Millionaires' Unit – aristocratic flyboys who fought the Great War and invented America's air power*, London, 2006.

Articles/Magazines/Newspapers/Journals
Crawford, OGS, 'Air Photographs of the Middle East,' *Geographical Journal*, v 73, June 1929.
Kennedy, Prof David, 'Pioneers above Jordan', *Antiquity*, 2012.
Insall, Gilbert S, 'The Aeroplane in Archaeology', *Journal of the RAF College*, Cranwell, 1929.
Rees, LWB, Circles etc, in the Basalt Country South-West of Azrak, *Antiquity*, 1929.
   'The Route of the Exodus', *(Palestinian Exploration*, v 80, 1948.
Taylor, SK. *Cross & Cockade International*, v 37, 1, 2006.
The Aeroplane (various issues, 1917).
Air Travel (various issues, USA, 1917).
Georgetown Gazette (various issues, USA, 1917).
Popular Flying (various issues, UK, 1930s).
London Gazette (various issues, UK).
Caernarfon & Denbigh Herald (various issues).
North Wales Guardian (various issues).
New York Times (various issues, USA, 1917).
The World (various issues, USA, 1917).

Television and Radio
Great War Interviews, BBC, 1964 (re-released 2014).
Cavalry of the Air, HTV, 1987.

Internet
Ancestry.co.uk – access to numerous record groups including census returns, military service records, shipping passenger lists and occupational records.

INDEX

People

Adams, Lieut FP — 86
al-Atrash, Sultan
— *199*–200, *199,* 202, 203, 204, 206, 209, 210, 214*f*
al-Atrash, Hayle — 204
Allen, Capt Gerald — 76*f*, 88, *91, 98,* 106, 108, 122*f*
Arnaud, Col (French Army) — 208, 209
Arnold, Lieut-Col Henry 'Hap' — 129, 138, 139*f*, 140*f*, *129*
Aslan, Emir Adil — 203
Atkinson, Capt Edward D — 148, 150, 165*f*, *152, 168*
Atatürk, Kemal — 194
Austin, Sgt Henry (RFC) — 33, 42*f*
Balfour, Rt Hon Arthur (later Earl)
— 139*f*, 194, 128, 130, 133, 135
Balkie, LS — 161
Ball, VC, Capt Albert — 5, 51, 66, 68–9, 75*f*, 77*f*
Barbess, Maurice (Bahamas) — 274
Barratt, Gp Capt (later AVM Sir) Arthur S
— 182, 175*f*, 173*f*
Bath, Lieut Charles L — *93, 98,* 98, 108, 124*f*
Batten, 1A/M ER — 49–51, 120, 124*f*
Beaumont, Cadet (later Flt Lt) Lionel CB — 183, 190*f*
Beazeley, Lt-Col — 218, 237*f*
Becke, Maj John HW — 33, 42*f*
Betts, Dr Alison — 229, 238*f*
Bewsher, Lieut-Col Frederick W (TFF) — 202, 214*f*, *202*
Bingham III, Lieut-Col Hiram (US Army)
— 134, *134, 137, 139f*
Blériot, Louis — 25
Board, Lieut-Col Andrew G — 44, 74*f*, 116, *117*
Boelcke, *Hauptman* Oswald — 75, 77*f*
Boyle, Cadet (later MRAF Sir) Dermot — 7, 179, 191*f*
Brabazon family — 14, 41*f*, 289*f*
Branker, Brig-Gen Sefton — 96, 123*f*
Bridges, Maj-Gen GTM — 130, 139*f*
Brooke-Popham, Major Robert — 29, *29,* 31, 41*f*
Brown, Lester (Bahamas) — 7, 278, 283, 287, 290*f*
Butler, Frank Hodge — 26
Butler, Vera — 26
Carbillet, Gov Maurice V — 198, 214*f*
Cairnes, Maj Thomas — *102*
Cavill, Percy F — 277–9, 288*f*
Chainey, Sqn Ldr George B — 177, 190*f*
Cherry, Maj — 99, 124*f*
Churchill, Rt Hon Winston S — 167, 192, 194, 213*f*

Clarges, Annie T — 14
Clement, Lieut Stephen — 139, 140*f*
Coleman, 2/Lieut Francis H — *90, 92, 98,* 106, 124*f*
Conran, Maj Eric — 88, *88,* 123*f*
Cooper, Lieut HA — 51, 56, 75*f*
Corbett, Lieut R — 98, 125*f*
Corby, 2/Lieut Hugh — *92, 98,* 124*f*
Cottman, Evans W (Bahamas) — 277–8, 288*f*
Crawford, Osbert GS, archaeologist
— 220, 223, 225, 227, 229, 230, 239*f*
Dane, Miss Denise — 7, 298, 299, 300
Darley, Capt Charles — *43, 45,* 74*f*, 75*f*, 77*f*
Davids, Anna Maria — 15
Davids I, Smith William — 15, 14
Davids II, Smith William — 26*f*, 294
Dawes, Maj George WP — 44, 45, 45*f*, 53, 66, 74*f*, 75*f*
Dawson, Cadet (later ACM) Walter L
— 7, 170, 175, 177, 187, 189*f*, 190*f*, 192*f*
de Havilland, Geoffrey, aircraft designer — 42*f*, 44, 80, 82
de Jouvenal, Henri, High Com Syria — 201, 214*f*
Ditchfield, Cpl John (RFC) — 47, 51, 75*f*
Dobson, F/Sgt Eric H — 108, 124*f*, 108*f*
Donald, DCM, 1A/M TH — 65–6, 77*f*
Dourif, Maj (French Army) — 137, 140*f*, 136*f*
Dowding, Capt HCT (later ACM, Lord) — 35*f*, 41*f*, 42*f*
Dunne, Lieut John William, aero engineer — 29, 41*f*, 30
Dussard, René, archaeologist — 227, 238*f*
Duvalier, George — 280
Duvalier, Willis — 280, 281
England, Gordon, flying instructor — *27,* 28–9, 41*f*
England, Sqn Ldr (Cranwell) — *175*
Erickson, Jim (Bahamas) — 280–1, 300*f*
Erikson, Margery O (Bahamas) — 7, 289*f*, 300*f*
Edey, Cpl (Royal Bahamas Police) — 280
Evans, John, Caernarfon publisher — 12, 13
Farman, Henri, aero engineeer — 28
Field, Dr Henry, anthropologist — 217–9, 221–2, 229, 237*f*
Foggin, Maj Cyril — 148, 148*f*, 150, 154, 155–6, *165*
Forsyth, Mr (of Mastic Cay, Bahamas) — 278, 290
Franks, Cadet (later AVM) John G — 7, 183, 187–90, 190*f*
Freebody, Cadet (later AVM) Wilfred L
— 7, 169, 179, 189*f*, 244*f*
French, FM Sir John — 32
Gamelin, General Maurice (French Army) — 199, 214*f*
George, Rt Hon David Lloyd — 127, 139*f*, 167, 199*f*
George V, King — 46, 121, 188, 242, 277

333

Ghaffer Pasha, Abdul 206
Gillmore, Cadet (later AVM) Alan David 190f, 243, 244f
Gilmour, Capt Stanley C
    86, 88, 91, 93, 98, 106, 107, 119, 123f
Godman, Gp Capt Arthur L 175
Gordon, MC, Capt CF 97
Gordon-Kidd, DSO, 2/Lieut Arthur Lionel
    119, 121, 125f
Gracie, Lieut Ralph (US Army) 162, 163f, 168f,
Graham, Cmdr Rober D, (Royal Navy) 255, 258f
Haig, FM Sir (later Earl) Douglas 67, 119
Hargreaves, Flt Sgt James McKinley, DCM
    49, 55, 56, 59, 60, 61–3, 67, 75f, 76f, 79, 171
Harnett, P/O Harry W (RNAS) 151, 153, 166f
Harrison, Eric, flying instructor 27, 28, 29, 41f
Hassan, Mohammed Abdullah (the 'Mad Mullah') 192
Hawker, VC, Maj Lanoe G 42f, 51, 75f, 86–7, 86
Hellyer, Capt Francis
    88, 91, 94, 96, 97, 98, 99, 103, 123f,
Henderson, Lieut-Gen Sir David 33, 41f, 307
Henry, Col (French Army) 209
Henty, Lieut Edric P 91, 97, 98, 108, 124f
Herbert, Lieut-Col Philip 99
Higgins, AVM John 217
House, Colonel Edward M, US diplomat 127, 139
Hubbard, Maj TO 45, 75f, 77f
Hughes-Chamberlain, Lieut 'Robin' 53f, 66, 89, 92, 123f
Hunnisett, 2A/M J, (RFC) 33, 42f
Hunt, Lieut B Philip G 91, 97, 98, 108, 123f, 124f,
Hutcheson, Rev JM, Nassau 7, 279, 289f
Immelmann, Oberleutnant Max 74, 74f, 77f
Ingalls, Lieut David S (US Navy)
    143, 143, 144, 146, 154, 155, 164f, 165f, 166f
Innes-Ker, Maj Lord R 133, 139f
Insall, Lieut Algernon J 'Jack' 50, 50, 56, 74f, 86, 123f
Insall, VC, Lieut (later G/Capt) Gilbert SM
    65–6, 65, 74f, 75f, 77f, 216–7
Joffre, Marshal Joseph (French Army) 57, 130
Jones, 2/AC Rigger Harold 7, 178
Jones, Lieut Ira 'Taffy' Thomas
    69, 77f, 150, 150, 165f, 166f
Jordan, Cadet (later AM Sir) Richard 7, 186, 190f
Jullerot, Henri, flying instructor 27, 28, 29, 41f
Kaddy, Charles 280
Kennedy, Dr David, archaeologist 7, 225, 237f
Kilner, Gp Capt Cecil F 174, 175
Kirkbride, Sir Alec S, diplomat
    209, 214f, 239, 241, 244f
Kölpin, Leutnant Fritz 63
Lane, Lieut CW 54, 55, 75f, 76f
Latta, MC, Capt James D 149, 165f
Latta, Miss Mary 149
Lawrence, Lieut GAK 41f, 35
Lawrence, Thomas E (Lawrence of Arabia) 214f, 220
Le Gallais, Capt Philip EM 152
Leacroft, Capt John 152

Leonhardi, Oberleutnant Ernst 63
Lewis, 2/Lieut (later Wg Cdr) Gwilym H
    6, 71, 77f, 88, 88, 89, 92, 98, 98, 101, 102–3, 105, 118,
    123f, 124f, 125f, 142
Lightbourn, Mrs Mallie (Nassau) 7, 298, 300f
Lloyd-Jones, Maj Griffith (Caernarfon) 17, 246, 250
Londonderry, Lord, Sec State for Air, 217
Longcroft, Air Cdre (later AVM Sir) Charles AH
    74f, 173, 184, 189f, 173, 174, 175
Luke, Sir Harry, diplomat 221–2, 224, 244
McCudden, VC, Maj James B
    5, 66, 81, 122f, 147, 149, 150, 165f, 158
MacDonald, Dr MCA, archaeologist 7, 226, 227, 238f
McDonald, Lieut CY 37, 41f, 42f
McDonnell, Capt HC
McEvoy, Cadet (later ACM Sir) Theodore N
    7, 178, 180, 190f
McKinney, Herbert (Bahamas) 290, 291, 298
MacLeish, Ensign Kenneth (US Navy)
    143, 145, 148, 164f
MacMillan, Capt Norman 153, 154, 166f
McNamara, Lieut 96
McPhee, Mr (Bahamas) 297
'Mad Mullah' (see Mohammed Abdullah Hassan)
Mais, Professor Stuart PB, academic 181, 190f
Maitland, Flt Lt (later AVM) Percy E 228, 229, 238f
Mannock, VC, Maj Edward C 'Mick' 5, 66, 68, 69,
    71, 77f, 150, 165f
Maxwell, Capt Gerald JC 150, 152, 158, 165f
Metford, Lieut LS 35, 41f
Michaud, General Roger (French Army) 199, 214f
Mills, F/Cadet (later ACM Sir) George
    174, 174, 181, 190f
Moffat, Maj JB (RAF) 288
Monroe, John (Bahamas) 280
Moore, Lieut BF 35, 41f
Moore, Mrs Catherine (Auntie Katie) 121, 125f, 159
Moore, Miss Nora 121, 125f
Nathan, Lieut Cush (US Army) 148, 165f
Newton, RA, Capt TC 114
Nicholas, Lieut Charles H 92, 98, 107, 108, 124f
Nixon, 2 Lieut William E 91, 98, 99, 105, 124f
Northcliffe, Lord 133
O'Sullivan, Gp Capt GR 286
Parke, Lieutenant W, RN 28, 42f
Percival, Norman, flying instructor 27, 29, 41f
Perfetti, Maj Raphaelo (Italian Army) 136, 137, 140f
Pershing, Brig-Gen John (US Army)
    128, 129, 134, 139f, 166f
Pike, Capt Robert Maxwell 82, 82, 84, 122f
Pitcher, Brig-Gen Duncan de Greyt
    114–5, 117, 125f
Pizey, Collyns, flying instructor 27, 28, 29, 41f
Playfair, Capt (later AM Sir) Patrick 'Pip' HL
    43, 44, 74f, 75f, 242
Plumer, FM Lord (of Messines) 196

Portal, Sqn Ldr (later MRAF Viscount) Charles 'Peter'
173, 179, 185, 186, 192f, *185*
Portal, Lady Joan 7, 185, 186, 190f, 295
Prickman, Air Cdre Thomas B 7, 244f
Prondzynski, *Ober-sur-zee* Stephan 37, 38, *38*
Raymond, Flt Sgt 64, 77f
Raynaud, Capt Antoine (French Army) 198, 214f
Rees, Aline/Eileen *295*, 296
Rees, Ailean / Alan Lionel 296
Rees, Anne (née Wilmot) 10–11
    Parents 10
    Children 11
    Death 12
Rees, Charles Herbert 12, *14*, 24f, 243, 245,
    Publisher and printer 12, 13
    Qualifies as a solicitor 14
    Carnarvonshire Volunteer Rifles 14
    Freemasonry 14
    Royal Welsh Fusiliers Volunteers 13
    Marriage 14
    Death 243
Rees, Ethel 14
Rees, James
    Birth 14
    Occupation 10, 12
    Children 11, 12, 24f
    Homes 11, *11*, *16*
    Politics 11
    Mayor of Caernarfon 12, *12*
    Death 12–13
Rees, James Wilmot 14, 24f
Rees, Kate 14
Rees, Leonora Maria (née Davids)
13–16, *14*, 293–4
Rees, Lionel Wilmot Brabazon
    Birth 14
    Childhood 14–16
    Education 16–9, *18*
    RMA, Woolwich 19–22
    Royal Garrison Artillery 22–4, 31
    Commission, 2/Lieut *21*, 22
    9 Coy, RGA, Gibraltar 22–3, *22*, *23*
    50 Coy, RGA, Sierra Leone 23
    10 Coy, RGA, Spike Island 23
    Native Local Artillery, Sierra Leone 23
    Flying training, Lark Hill 28–31
    West African Frontier Force 31
    Seconded to the RFC 31
    7 Squadron, RFC 31–3, 37–40
    6 Squadron, Belgium 33–7
    Home defence 37–40
    11 Squadron 43–66, 68–9, 70, 75f
    Military Cross 62, *248*
    Fighting in the Air 67, 70–3, 77f
    Central Flying School 66
    Temporary Major 78, *126*

Notes on De Havilland Fighting Scout (DH2) 84–5
    32 Squadron 86–119
    DSO nomination 114–7, 119
    Victoria Cross 119–21, *248*
    Hospitalisation 119–22
    Balfour Mission, USA 127–33
    1 School of Aerial Fighting 142–56, 163
    1 Fighter School, Turnberry 156–64
    RAF College, Cranwell 173–88
    Air Force Cross 170, *248*
    OBE 170, *248*
    Freedom of the Borough of Caernarfon
170–1, *171*, 173, 189f
    ADC to HM King George V 188, 242
    Gp Capt 188
    OC Palestine and Transjordan 196–242
    Armoured Car / Air co-operation tactics
201–3, 205–6, 212–13, 309–329
    Archaeology 216–237
    Excentricity 239–42
    Final command 242
    May, ketch 245–274, *246*, *251*, *256*, *260*, *270*
    Trans-Atlantic voyage 247–57
    Blue Water Medal 258f, 259
    Caribbean cruise 260–273
    Aline B/Aline, ketch 274–8, *275*, 293
    Employment 277, 280–1, 290, 294
    War service, Egypt 282–6, *284*
    RAF Regiment 286–8
    Farming 291–3, 297
    Marriage and family 294–8
Rees, Muriel Brabazon
15, 119, 121, 125f, 140f, 243, 247, 260, 278, 288f,
293, 294, 295
Rees, Olvin 296
Rees, Sylvia 294–6, *295*, 298
Rhodes, F/Lieut *175*
Rickards, Capt GB 31, 41f
Rogers, Lieut Crook 96
Rolls, Hon Charles 26
Rossiter, Wg Cdr HE 7, 283, 289f
Rowe, Cadet FCT 185, 194f
Salmond, Maj John M (later MRAF Sir)
32, 41f, 194, 213f
Sarrail, Gen Maurice PE (French Army) 200, 214f
Saud, Ibn (later king of Saudi Arabia) 215f
Seguin brothers, aero engineers 47
Sharer, Prof Cyrus, academic 7, 296, 300
Sherbrooke-Walker, Lt-Col Ronald (RAF)
287–8, 289f
Silcox, Flt Lt 218
Simpson, Lieut John C
91, *97*, *99*, *98*, 108–9, *109*, 110, 118, 124f, 171
Simpson, Lieut Sturley P
91, *98*, 101, 104, 105–6, 124f
Sippe, Sydney V 27, 29, 41f

Skeate, Lieut WA   63, 77f
Slade, Lieut RJ   63, 64, 77f
Smith, Lieut HR (US Army)   161,168f
Smith, A/Maj JW (TFF)   205, 207, 214f
Smith, Lieut SW   35, 41f
Smith, Walton (Bahamas)   7, 277, 294–5, 300f
Smith-Barry, Maj Robert
                        141–2, 165f, 166f, 168–9, 214f
Sopwith, Thomas OM 'Tommy', aero engineer   47
Springs, Lieut Elliott W (US Army)   155–6, 165f, 166f
Squires, Lieut George (US Army)
                        160, 161, 162, 166f, 308
Stubbs, Lieut Reginald A   91, 98, 101, 124f
Sykes, AVM Sir Frederick   26, 41f, 167
Taylor, Capt Stanley W   152, 158
Thomas, Lieut Owen V
            92, 98, 101, 103–4, 106–7, 108, 124f
Todd, Lieut Robert Miles (US Army)   156, 157, 166f
Toogood, Stanley (Bahamas)   7, 274, 288f
Trenchard, MRAF Lord Hugh M
        96, 98, 114, 119, 119, 123f, 167, 168, 169, 172,
                        174, 177, 189f, 192
Tute, Sir Richard, judge   247, 255, 258f, 281
Vaughn, Lieut George (US Army)   148, 165f
Villa, Francisco 'Pancho'   128
Vincent, Flt Lt (later AVM) Stanley
                        201, 205, 212, 214f
von Poellnitz, Lieut Herman
            92, 93, 97, 98, 98, 101, 108, 123f
von Richthofen, Freiherr Manfred   71, 75f, 77f
Wadham, Lieutenant Vivian   27, 31, 41f
Ward, Cadet (later A/Cmdr) Ellacott LS   110–11, 191f
Webb-Bowen, AVM Sir Thomas   196, 214f, 242, 244f
Wendler, Leutnant   118
West, VC, Ferdinand 'Freddie' MF   72, 77f
Williams, Alexander, Andros   294
Williams, Mary, Andros   294
Williams, Capt RD, Merchant Marine (Caernarfon)   272
Williams, Lieut Rodney D, (US Army)   147, 149, 164f
Williams/Rees, Sylvia — see Sylvia Rees
Wilson, President Woodrow   127, 128, 139f
Wilson, Mrs Ellen A   130, 139f
Windsor, Duke of   282
Worthington, Cadet (later AVM Sir) Geoffrey L
                        7, 178, 190f
Wright, Orville, aero engineer   134
Zimmermann, Leutnant Erich   109, 118, 119, 124f, 125f

General

Aden   194
Ain Ankiyeh, Transjordan   207, 208
Ain Beda, Transjordan   208
Airco DH2, aeroplane
        67, 80–96, 80, 81, 84, 85, 87, 95, 98, 99–101, 100,
            102, 103, 105, 107, 108, 109, 110, 113, 122f
Aircraft Manufacturing Company (Airco)   80
Allen, Son & Co, Bedford, engine manufacturers   47
Amari Wells, Transjordan   210–11
Amman, Transjordan   196, 200, 202, 203, 206,
        208, 211, 217, 218, 219, 221, 222, 223, 227, 236,
                        239, 241, 242, 243, 311
Anglo-Iranian Oil Company   293
Avonmouth, Gloucestershire   97
Azores   250–4, 258
Baghdad, Iraq   124f, 194, 221, 222
Bahamas
    Andros Island   263, 264, 290–9
    Berry Islands   257
    Bimini Harbour   256
    Bimini Islands   257
    Blue Hill   290
    Cape Verde   264
    Castle Island   265
    Conception Island   276
    Crooked Island   290, 291
    Crossing Hills Cave   279
    Deep Creek, Andros   293
    Eluthera Island   276, 279
    Exuma Cays   276
    Fleur-de-Lys Cay   263, 264
    Fortune Island   265
    Great Inagua Island   265, 280, 282
    Great Isaac lighthouse   257
    Gregory Town, Eluthera   279
    Gun Cay, Bimini   256
    Harbour Island   276
    Hatchet Bay   276
    Hogsty Reef   265
    Johnson's Yard, Nassau   274
    Mangrove Cay, Andros   294, 296, 297, 297, 299
    Mastic Cay   278
    Matthew Town   265
    Mosstown   291
    Nassau   254–6, 259–60, 262, 269, 274, 276–8,
            279–82, 287, 294–5, 297, 298, 299, 2999
    New Providence Island   254, 256, 262, 263, 290
    Oakes Field   290
    Pinders, Andros   294, 296
    Prince George's Wharf, Nassau
    Princess Margaret Hospital, Nassau   298
    Providence Channel
    RAF Cemetery, Nassau   299, 299
    Royal Bahamas Police   299
    San Salvador Island   255
    Symonette's Shipyard, Nassau   257–8, 262
    Tongue of the Ocean   257, 263
    Turtle Sound   291
    Windsor Field   290
Bangor Normal College   12
Basalt (Harra or Barra), Transjordan

206–7, 210, 217, 219, 220, *220*, 225, 227, 229, 230
Bayir Wells/Wadi Bayir, Transjordan   218, 222, *222*
Beaulieu river, Hampshire   247, 249
Bene Sakhr tribe   202
Boulogne, France   33, 36, *75f*
Bring Down Your Hun   74
Bristol & Colonial Aeroplane Company   29, *30*
   Bristol Flying School   *29*
British & Empire Army units and formations
   2 Canadian Clearing Hospital   119
   3 (V) Battalion, Royal Welsh Fusiliers   13
   22 (Anti-Aircraft) Battery, RA   117
   Sierra Leone Company, Native Local Artillery   23
British Virgin Islands
   St Kitts   273
   St Lucia   273
   St Vincent   272
   Saba   272
   Tortola   272, 290
Bromley, Kent   24f, 243, 294
Buckingham Palace   121, 172, 242, 244f
Caernarfon
   Borough Council   13, 170–1, *171*, 180f
   Caernarfon Borough Court   12
   Caernarfon Castle   9, *10, 11*, 15, 216, 246
   Caernarfon County Court   12
   Carnarvon Harbour Trust   12, 13
   Carnarvon Horticultural Society   13
   Carnarvon Rowing Club   14
   Carnarvon Sailing Club   172
   Carnarvon Volunteer Rifles   13
   Castle Street   5, 11, *11*, 12, 13, 14, 15, *16*
   Freedom of the Borough   170–1, *171*, 173, 189f
   High Street   11
   Porth-yr-Aur   5, 245, *248, 258f*, 272
   Promenade   15, *17*, 23, 245
   Royal Naval Artillery Volunteers   21
   Royal Welsh Yacht Club
      7, 13, 15, 16, *17, 172*, 245, *259f*, 267, *270*
   Segontium Masonic Lodge   13
   Segontium Permanent Building Society   13
   Slate Quay   *10*, 15
Cairo, Egypt   194, 283, 286, 324f
Cape Ortegal, Spain   249
Carnarvon & Denbigh Herald/Carnarvon Herald
      10, 11, 24f
Cliffe, Kent   38
Corunna, Spain   249
Countess of Pembroke's Private Hospital for Officers
      120, 121
Cuba   254, 280–1
Curaçao   273
Damascus, Syria   198, 199, 200, 214f, 217, 222, 310
Dartford, Kent   38, 43f
Dominican Republic
   Alta Vela   268, 272

Aux Cayes   267, 268
Beata Island   268
Cadiera Bay   269
Cape Rojo   268
Gravios Point   267
Santo Domingo   267–70, 272
Dover, Kent   25, 33, 37
Druze tribesmen
   197–212, 214f, 216, 217, 218, 220, 221, 225, 230, 236
Dunkirk, France   34, 36
Eastbourne College   7, 16–19, *18*, 184, 190f, *248, 258f*
   Officer Training Corps   17, *18*
Edgware, London   244, 247
Egypt   194, 198, 230, 231, 232, 235, 242,
      282, 283, *284*, 286, 287, 310
Elms Preparatory School, Colwall   16
Erith, Kent   38
Falmouth, Devon   249, 252, 257, *258f*
Feld-Flieger Abteilung 23   63, *76f*
Feld-Flieger Abteilung 32   *76f*
Field Museum, Chicago   217, 220, 223, *223*, 237f
Fighting in the Air   67, *70–3*,77f
First Yale Unit   142, 164f
Folkestone, Kent   33, 34, 47, 97, *97*
Gibraltar   22–3, *22, 23*, 286
Gordon-Shephard Memorial Prize Essay
      215f, 236, 238f, 309–29
Grain, Kent   38
Gravesend, Kent   38
Greenhall, Blantyre, Lanarkshire   125f, *122*, 140f
Haiti
   Cape Dame Marie   267
   Mole St Nicholas   266, 267
   Port au Prince   267
Horta, Azores   252, 253, 255
Jaffa, Palestine   194, 212
Jamaica
   Careening Island   271
   Galleon Harbour   271
   Goat Island   271
   Kingston   271
   Ocho Rios   271
   Port Antonio   271
   Port Morant   271
   Port Royal   271
   Portland Bight   271
Jebel el-Druze, Syria   198, 199, 200, 209, 212, 214f
Jebel Hassan, Transjordan   207
Jerusalem, Palestine   194, 214f, 229, 232, 252f
Kafr, Syria   199
Kampfgeschwader 3 OHL (Kagol 3)   109
Lark Hill, Salisbury Plain   25, 28, *29, 30*, 41f
Le Havre, France   99
Llanbeblig Church, Caernarfon   13
Longford Castle Military Hospital, Wiltshire   121, 125f
Miami, Florida   165f, 256, 257, 294

Menai Strait, Wales	9, 15, 216, 246
Monosaupape rotary engine	
	80–1, *81*, 84, 87, 89, 109, 180
Mount Sinai, Egypt	231–2, 234–5, 236
Nairn Overland Transport Co	218
Notes on De Havilland Fighting Scout (DH2)	84–5
Penybryn Quarry, Nantlle	15
Petra, Transjordan	227, 309, 310
Pirbright, Surrey	185
Plas Llanwnda, Caernarfon	11, *11*, 12, 14, *16*
Plas Maesincla, Caernarfon	15
Poperinghe, Belgium	36
Provisional Syrian Government	199
Qasr Amr, Transjordan	228
Qasr al-Azrak, Transjordan	
	202, 204, 205, 206, 209, 211, 220
Qasr Tuba, Transjordan	222, *222*
Ras Teida, Transjordan	221
Red Sea (Israelites crossing of)	233–4
RM Preece & Co (printers)	13
Robertson & Sons, Alexander, boatbuilders	245
Royal Aero Club (RAeC)	26, *27, 30*, 88
Royal Air Force (RAF) & Royal Flying Corps (RFC)	
units & establishments	
Aerodromes	
Ayr, Ayrshire	
	142–56, 159, 163, 165*f*, 166*f*, 171
Bertangles, France	64, 66, 91
Brooklands, Surrey	38, 41*f*
Eastchurch, Kent	26, 38, 169–70, 175, 187
El Adem, Egypt	283
Heliopolis, Egypt	283
Helwan, Egypt	283–6, *284*
Hendon, London	82, 88, 96, 267
Hounslow, London	37, 42*f*, 86
Joyce Green, Kent	37, 39, 40, 42*f*
Leysdown, Kent	27
Netheravon, Wiltshire	
	29, *37, 41, 43, 47, 51, 52*, 71, 86, 88, 96,
	97, 97, 98, 99, 141, 154
Ostend, Belgium	35–7, 164*f*
Ramleh, Palestine	196, 241, *241*
St Omer (RFC HQ), France	
	39, 47, 49, *95*, 98, 99, 103, 107
South Farnborough, Hampshire	25, 37, 38
Takoradi, Gold Coast	286–8
Treizennes, France	99, *105, 106*
Turnberry, Ayrshire	
	143–5, *152*, 157–63, *159, 164*, 166*f*, 167,
	171, 173, 189*f*, 307–8
Vert Galant/Galand, France	
	47, 49, 51, 53, 55, 56, 59, 75*f*, *101, 102*
Villers Bretonneux, France	58, 59, *59*, 63, 64
Squadrons	
1 (R) Squadron	141
2 Squadron	108
3 Squadron	32
4 Squadron	32, 36 49, 50, 53, 184
5 Squadron	32, 82, 84
6 Squadron	33–8, *37*, 42*f*
7 Squadron	31, 37, 39, 40
11 Squadron	43–74, 75*f*, *50, 51, 54, 58, 59*, 120
14 Squadron	197, *195*, 201, 202
19 Squadron	119
19 (R) Squadron	97
23 Squadron	86
24 Squadron	87, 89, 91, 94
24 (R) Squadron	96
25 Squadron	99, 103, 107, 108
27 Squadron	99
29 Squadron	*85*, 86, 94, 99, 123*f*, 150
32 Squadron	71, 78, 86–119, 142
74 Squadron	150, 165*f*
Training units	
1 Fighter School, Turnberry	156–64, 167
2 Fighter School, SE Area	165, 171
2 Auxiliary School of Aerial Gunnery	143
1 School of Aerial Fighting	142–56, 163
21 (Training) Group, West Drayton	242
24 (Training) Wing, Grantham	173
Air Gunnery and Bombing School,	
Eastchurch	170
Central Flying School, Upavon	66
North Western Area Flying Instructors'	
School	159, 166*f*
RAF College, Cranwell	173–88
1 Aircraft Depot (RFC)	*95*
1 Brigade (RFC)	107, 114, 125*f*
10 (Army) Wing (RFC)	74*f*, 114
2 Armoured Car Company (RAF)	197, 218
RAF Benevolent Fund	244, 247
RAF, creation of	149
RAF Hospital, Uxbridge	297
RAF Inland Area Depot, Uxbridge	242
RAF Middle East Command	194, 196, 242, 282
RAF Regiment	286–7
RAF West Africa Command	286
RFC, creation of	25
Royal Antediluvian Order of Buffaloes, Amman	241
Royal Artillery (RA)	
School of Gunnery, Shoeburyness	23, 31
Tombs Memorial Prize	20, 24*f*
Royal Engineers, Air Battalion	25
Royal Field Artillery (RFA)	20–1
Royal Garrison Artillery (RGA)	
9 Company	22, *22*
50 Company	23
Royal Horse Artillery (RHA)	20–1
Royal Military Academy (RMA), Woolwich	19–22
Royal Military Tournament	20
Royal Naval Air Service (RNAS)	171
Rualla tribe	206, 208

Salkhad, Syria   199
Sao Jorge Island, Azores   252
Sarafand, Syria   197
Sargasso Sea   253
Segontium (Roman fort)   9
Seiont river, Caernarfonshire   9, *10*
Sheerness, Kent   39
Sierra Leone   23, 26
Somaliland   194, 282
Suwayda (Sweida), Syria   199, 212
Terceira Island, Azores   253
Tilbury, Essex   38
Transjordan Frontier Force (TFF)
    196, 197, *197*, 198, 201, 202, *202*, 203, 205, 208, 214f
Trinidad   262, 266, 272, 273

Umm el-Jimal, Syria   206, 209, 228
Unknown Soldier, funeral of   172
Ushant Island, France   249
Vickers FB5, aeroplane
    31, *40*, *44*, 46, 47, 62, 64, 68, 79, 86, 88, 93, 97
Wahabi tribe   213, 215f, 310, 311
Wilderness of Zin   234
William Potter & Co (printers)   11
Wilton House, Wiltshire   120, *120*
Y Herald Gymraeg   12
Zeebrugge, Belgium   38
Zeppelin airships   39, 41f, 46
Zerqa, Tranjordan   206
Zionism   197